Sport Pedagogy

Sport Pedagogy

An Introduction for Teaching and Coaching

Edited by
Kathleen Armour

University of Birmingham

Routledge
Taylor & Francis Group

LONDON AND NEW YORK

First published 2011 by Pearson Education Limited

Published 2013 by Routledge
2 Park Square, Milton Park, Abingdon, Oxon OX14 4RN
711 Third Avenue, New York, NY 10017, USA

Routledge is an imprint of the Taylor & Francis Group, an informa business

ISBN: 978-0-273-73258-7 (pbk)

British Library Cataloguing-in-Publication Data
A catalogue record for this book is available from the British Library.

Library of Congress Cataloging-in-Publication Data
A catalog record for this book is available from the library of Congress.

Typeset in 10/13 pt Minion by 73

Printed and bound by CPI Group (UK) Ltd, Croydon, CR0 4YY

Dedication
For Charlie, Georgie and Jamie

And to the memory of Michael and Margaret

Brief contents

Contents

Acknowledgements

I would like to thank all my colleagues from the UK and Ireland who have authored chapters for this collection. I am particularly grateful for the time and effort that you took to ensure the chapters are accessible, interesting and also challenging at this introductory level. Aspiring physical education teachers and coaches can learn much from your wise words and, as a result, more children and young people should have better learning experiences in sport.

I would also like to record my thanks to Pearson for your support for the project from inception to publication. You have made the task of editing this collection as smooth as possible and I have enjoyed working with you.

Publisher's acknowledgements

The publisher would like to thank the following for their kind permission to reproduce copyright material:

(Key: b-bottom; c-centre; l-left; r-right; t-top)

Photos
Author's own: 34b, 134cl, 134cr, 135bl, 135br; Dorling Kindersley: 45; Getty: 43b; Pearson Education Ltd: 48tr; Rick Diesslin: 42t; The Association for Physical Education: 34t; University of Bedfordshire Archive: 28c, 31t

Text
Extract on page 39 from Digital Natives, Digital Immigrants, *On the Horizon*, Vol 9, No. 5 (Prensky, M. 2001), NCB University Press; Extract on pages 71–72 from *Education, Disordered Eating and Obesity Discourse*, Routledge (Evans, J., Rich, E., Davies, B and Allwood, R. 2008), From: Education, Disordered Eating and Obesity Discourse, J. Evans, E. Rich, B. Davies and R. Allwood, © 2008, Routledge. Reproduced by permission of Taylor & Francis Books UK; Extract on page 105 from *Freaks, Geeks & Asperger Syndrome: A User Guide to Adolescence*, Jessica Kingley Publishers (Jackson, L. 2002) p130; Extract on page 153 from *Freaks, Geeks & Asperger Syndrome: A User Guide to Adolescence*, Jessica Kingsley Publishers (Jackson, L. 2002) pp128–130

In some instances we have been unable to trace the owners of copyright material, and we would appreciate any information that would enable us to do so.

Introduction

Sport is an area of human activity that greatly interests citizens of the European Union and has enormous potential for bringing them together, reaching out to all, regardless of age or social origin . . . In addition to improving the health of European citizens, sport has an educational dimension and plays a social, cultural and recreational role.

(European Commission, 2007, section 1)

Through its role in formal and non-formal education, sport reinforces Europe's human capital. The values conveyed through sport help develop knowledge, motivation, skills and readiness for personal effort. Time spent in sport activities at school and at university produces *health and education benefits which need to be enhanced.* [ibid., section 2.3, emphasis added]

Studying sport

If you are reading this book, it can be assumed that you have a practical and/or theoretical interest in one or more aspects of sport. It is also possible that you have gained much of personal value from your engagement in sport and sport-related activities, and with the broad institution of sport. As such, you could be in agreement with the European Commission's (EC) sentiments expressed above, i.e. that 'sport has an educational dimension'. You probably encountered sport in school as part of physical education, through youth sport in the community, at local sports clubs, or as a leisure activity enjoyed with family and friends. A few of you will have found great success in sport; for others, your experiences may have been rather more varied, not all of which were positive. Nonetheless, you have elected to study sport, so it is reasonable to assume that whatever your pathways through life to this point, sport, in one form or another, has captured your interest and enthusiasm. One consequence of these experiences is that you might have a strong belief that others should be able to access the rewards that engagement in sport can offer, and some of you will be committed to helping children and young people to gain as much from sport as you did – or more. The EC claims that engagement in sport 'produces health and education benefits *which need to be enhanced*'. That's where this book comes in.

Sport as a 'good' thing?

This book does not begin from the starting point that engagement in sport is *inevitably* a 'good thing' for all children and young people. Instead, the contributors recognise that sport has the *potential* to be a force for good in young lives, especially if it is taught and coached by knowledgeable adults who have the ability to harness its power effectively. If you have had very positive personal experiences, it might come as something of a surprise to find that this book does not pay uncritical homage to sport. Yet a moment's reflection on the experiences of some of your peers at school, and on the sometimes dubious practices of professional sport, should remind you that sport has both positive and negative dimensions. As the EC (2007) puts it: 'sport is also confronted with new threats and challenges which have emerged in European society, such as commercial pressure, exploitation of young players, doping, racism, violence, corruption and money laundering'. Indeed, for some children and young people, early experiences in sport are so negative that it takes years to recover and to re-engage. Sometimes these negative experiences are simply the result of poor teaching or coaching. For those of us who care about sport, and about the good things it can offer, this must be a concern.

Children's rights: your responsibilities

While not supporting claims that sport is some kind of panacea for all society's ills, this book *is* based on the belief that children and young people, whatever their abilities, have much to gain from participation in high-quality sport and sport-related activities. Put more strongly, the book rests on the premise that:

- all children and young people have a *right* to sport provision that goes some way towards meeting their individual and complex needs;
- the adults teaching or coaching young people have a *responsibility* to meet those needs wherever feasible.

This premise has important consequences because it means that physical education teachers and youth sport coaches need to be expert in more than the technical and scientific aspects of sport. To do their work successfully, teachers and coaches also need to be experts in *pedagogy* which is, essentially, about learning. This book is not, therefore, a step-by-step 'How to coach' manual to be used in planning sessions for coaching an individual sport. Such manuals are readily available for most sports and are invaluable tools in the pedagogical process. Instead, this book provides you with some of the prior knowledge you need to make best use of coaching manuals and other resources. In so doing, you, as a teacher or coach, will be well placed to offer an effective and professional learning service to your clients: children and young people in sport.

What is sport pedagogy?

The aim of this book is to provide a comprehensive introduction to sport pedagogy for those who aspire to offer children and young people high-quality learning experiences in and through sport. 'Sport pedagogy' is a complex term and is explored in greater detail in Chapter 1. In summary, 'pedagogy' is about learning in practice. It refers both to the ways in which individuals learn, and to the pedagogical knowledge and skills that teachers and coaches need to support them to learn effectively. 'Sport' is conceptualised broadly to include all forms of recognised sport or sport-related physical activity; in other words, if you believe an activity fits the category of 'sport', then the chapters in this book can be applied to that activity. Moreover sport, within the concept of sport pedagogy, is understood simultaneously as sport-specific content knowledge (learning *about* and *in* sport) and as a 'vehicle' for learning wider knowledge, skills or attributes (learning *through* sport). 'Sport pedagogy', therefore, is the study of that complex and crowded place where sport and education come together in practice. Although this book focuses on children and young people, sport pedagogy is also the foundation of adult learning in sport.

The definition of sport pedagogy used in this book seeks to embrace all these complexities. 'Sport pedagogy' is defined as a sub-discipline of sport sciences (and related areas of study) that has three complex dimensions that are made more complex as they interact to form *each pedagogical encounter*:

1 **Knowledge in context**: views on the nature of valued or appropriate knowledge to be taught, coached or learnt change because they are contingent upon a range of historical, social and political contextual factors. An understanding of context helps professional teachers and coaches to take a critical and informed stance towards existing and new knowledge.

2 **Learners and learning**: children and young people are diverse learners. At the core of sport pedagogy is expertise in complex learning theories, and a deep understanding of diversity and its many impacts on the ways in which young learners can learn.

3 **Teachers/teaching and coaches/coaching**: in any pedagogical encounter between teacher/coach and learner, all three dimensions of pedagogy are present and are interacting. Effective (professional) teachers and coaches are lifelong learners who can harness the power of sport.

As was noted earlier, children and young people have a *right* to sport experiences that acknowledge their individual needs, and teachers and coaches have a *responsibility* to meet those needs wherever feasible. Gaining knowledge and understanding of the three-dimensional concept of sport pedagogy is the first step towards ensuring that the rights of large numbers of children and young people to effective learning experiences in and through sport are not denied.

Teachers and coaches . . . the same but different

Although this book is addressed to aspiring and practising teachers and coaches, there is no suggestion that these two occupational groups are the same, or that schools are the same as sports clubs or community sports contexts. Physical education is a subject that is located firmly in the school context. Specialist physical education teachers are highly trained members of a recognised profession who are responsible for the educational needs of pupils. In this context, sport forms one part of the wider subject matter of physical education. Sport coaching is not yet a profession in the traditional sense although it aspires to professional status. Youth sport coaches vary from those with substantial training and experience to those with little or none. Yet, for children and young people when they engage in a sport, these differences may count for little. They encounter sports or sport-related activities in different contexts, but in each one they are learners with the potential to gain much of value from the experience; or, indeed, very little. This book, therefore, takes the young learner in sport as its focal point, rather than dwelling on the somewhat artificial boundaries between physical education and sport; i.e. a child learning to play hockey is the same child, learning the same sport, whether they are learning in or out of school. In taking this stance the book acknowledges difference, but focuses on the commonalities between teaching and coaching, and between physical education and youth sport.

Remember, you were once a young learner in sport

Finally, it is important to recognise that you have a vast reservoir of experience upon which to draw in this study of sport pedagogy. You have been a young learner in sport at some point in your life, either in physical education, youth sport, community sport, family sport, or possibly all four. At the end of each chapter you will be asked to reflect critically and constructively upon your experiences and those of your peers. Whether positive, negative or mixed, your prior experiences will exert a strong influence on what and how you learn now. *Crucially, however, those personal experiences also influence your beliefs about what and how all children and young people can and should learn*; what Bruner (1999) labelled 'folk theories'. Such theories, based only on you and your experiences, tend to govern what you feel is 'good' or 'best' for all the young learners you encounter, and this may – or may not – be appropriate. Critical interrogation of your folk theories, therefore, provides a robust platform upon which to base current and future learning about yourself and young learners. If you opt to become a fully fledged professional in physical education and/or youth sport, such critical reflection on your needs as a learner, and on the needs of children and young people as learners, must form the core foundation of your professional career.

How this book is organised

It has already been noted that sport pedagogy is a complex area of study in which all the component parts are intertwined in practice. Separating the components into sections and chapters is, therefore, always likely to be somewhat arbitrary. The three sections that follow can be read in any order, and chapters can be selected and combined in ways that support your learning as a practitioner at any specific time.

The sections and chapters address many different aspects of the three dimensions of pedagogy, although it must be recognised that no single text could cover everything. The chapters also address sport pedagogy from different disciplinary perspectives including history, sociology, social policy, psychology and education theory.

Each chapter takes a similar format including extracts from research, 'comments' to summarise key points, individual and group learning tasks, a suggested resource for further reading and a reference list to enable you to follow up points of interest. Many of the authors have written directly to you, the reader, to encourage you to link the material presented to your particular learning needs and interests.

Overview of Section 1

Pedagogy in physical education and youth sport

This section focuses on some key theoretical and contextual issues in sport pedagogy. In Chapter 1, *Kathleen Armour* addresses the question: 'What is sport pedagogy and why study it?'. The importance of recognising the shifting nature of knowledge, meeting the needs of diverse learners, and being 'professional' as teachers and coaches is emphasised. *David Kirk*, in Chapter 2, traces the historical development of physical education, illustrating vividly that what is considered to be valid and valuable knowledge for children to learn changes over time. In Chapter 3, *Fiona Chambers* provides an overview of key learning theories, making clear how each theory leads to a different view of learning and teaching/coaching.

Chapters 4 and 5 focus on the highly topical issue of health through physical education and sport. In Chapter 4, *Lorraine Cale* and *Jo Harris* analyse the presumed links between physical education, sport and health. They argue that although there is strong evidence to suggest that engagement in physical education, physical activity and sport can lead to health benefits, there is much more to be done to ensure that health pedagogies lead to effective learning in those contexts for more children. *John Evans, Emma Rich* and *Brian Davies*, in Chapter 5, take an even more critical stance towards the ways in which health messages are delivered. These authors illustrate the damage that can be done to children and young people where health, obesity and physical activity messages are promoted in un-critical and oversimplified ways.

The final two chapters in this section have an international focus. In Chapter 6, *Iain Lindsey* and *Ruth Jeanes* consider youth sport policy in three different national contexts: England, Australia and Zambia. A comparison between the three countries illustrates some common features including the need for evidence to support policy, and the proliferation of organisations involved in youth sport. In Chapter 7, *Dikaia Chatziefstathiou* takes us to Greece and other parts of the world as she explores the development of 'Olympism' as an educational philosophy and considers its potential to inspire young learners in physical education and youth sport.

Overview of Section 2

Children and young people: diverse learners in physical education and youth sport

This is the longest section in the book and perhaps that is fitting given its core focus on young learners. In Chapter 8, *Ann MacPhail* foregrounds young people's voices in physi-cal education and youth sport. She points out that when we listen to young people – and take the trouble to hear what they have to say – we might learn some things that are un-comfortable. In other words, if we are to take youth voice seriously, we might have to change our practices. *Chris Spray*, in Chapter 9, draws on psychology to explain why and how young people can be motivated to learn. He concludes that we need much more re-search focused on motivation issues in specific physical education and youth sport set-tings if we are to understand how to inspire greater numbers of young people to engage in lifelong physical activity.

The next eight chapters focus on specific groups of learners. It is important to recognise that these are not homogeneous groups, and many young people fit into several groups at once. However, in each case, the authors highlight some key issues and ask us to consider ways in which teaching and coaching practices might be more effective. For example, in Chapter 10, *Laura Azzarito* draws on a current research project to illustrate ways in which young people's identities are shaped by media representations of 'ideal' and sporting bodies. In Chapter 11, *Frances Murphy* and *Dierdre Ní Chroinín* remind us that the youngest learners in physical education, those up to the age of about seven, require very specific pedagogical approaches to meet their needs. In Chapter 12, *Hayley Fitzgerald* points out that for many young disabled learners, current practices in physical education and sport are *disabling* for them. What these young people need is to be taught and coached in ways that afford them the same right to be physically active as any other young person.

In Chapter 13, *Rachel Sandford* and *Rebecca Duncombe* highlight the role of sport in re-engaging disaffected or disengaged young people in education. They use the concept of positive youth development (PYD) and report some research that shows the impact of two sport-based interventions. *Symeon Dagkas*, in Chapter 14, considers the role of social class as a barrier to learning, illustrating the role of family background in gaining access to sport. He concludes that social class does, indeed, still matter. *Louisa Webb*, in Chapter 15, raises a range of ethnicity issues that practitioners need to consider if they are to respect and value diversity in their practices, and *Anne Flintoff*, in Chapter 16, reminds us that as teachers or coaches, we are in a position to either challenge or reproduce the gender inequities young people encounter in and through physical education and sport. Finally, in Chapter 17, *Kathleen Armour, Rachel Sandford* and *Rebecca Duncombe* consider the needs of 'looked-after children'. They point out that these children face a number of major barriers to participation in physical activity and sport. Unless teachers and coaches are aware of the issues facing looked-after children, it is likely that their effective exclusion will endure.

Overview of Section 3

Being a professional teacher or coach in physical education and youth sport

The theme of professionalism runs throughout this book. It is argued that if teachers and coaches are to meet the complex needs of diverse young learners, they must be effective and committed learners themselves. Initial training, or a one-off certificate, will never be sufficient. In this section, some of the issues to be considered in developing professional practitioners are highlighted. In Chapter 18, *Kathleen Armour* argues that effective career-long professional development is one of the cornerstones of sport pedagogy. Without it, practitioners are likely to become stale and outdated in their practices, thereby short-changing children and young people. In Chapter 19, *Kyriaki Makopoulou* considers the concept of 'personalised learning' and suggests that it has much to offer teachers and coaches who wish to ensure that their practices are evolving in ways that lead to inclusive achievement.

In the next three chapters, some of the practical and philosophical steps to be considered in becoming a teacher or coach are outlined. *Frank Herold*, in Chapter 20, draws on research and his experience as a teacher educator to offer advice on becoming a secondary school physical education teacher. *Mike Jess*, in Chapter 21, considers two different approaches to being a primary school physical education teacher. The first views PE as 'easy', resulting in little pupil learning. The second approach recognises the complexity of learning in primary classrooms and adopts pedagogies to match, resulting in high levels of learning. In Chapter 22, *Julia Walsh* details steps towards becoming an effective coach. She argues that prospective coaches must be ready to invest in their learning in a wide range of settings including formal coach education, at training, during competition, in conversation with athletes, mentors, and with other coaches, through professional development, from observation, by reading books and accessing electronic media.

The last three chapters focus on different learning strategies to support professional development. In Chapter 23, *Mark Griffiths* explores the value of mentoring as a professional learning strategy. He draws on research in coaching to illustrate potential pitfalls where mentoring is not organised in ways that meet practitioners' needs. In Chapter 24, *Deborah Tannehill* provides an overview of the theory and practice of developing communities of practice. Drawing on her experience of working with teachers, Deborah points out that communities of practice require support and structure to ensure they are effective in supporting professional learning. Finally, in Chapter 25, *Toni O'Donovan* introduces 'models-based practice' as an alternative to traditional practices that prioritise the learning of an activity or sport. In models-based practice, teachers and coaches can plan specifically to deliver learning in the activity, but also some of the broader pupil learning outcomes that are often claimed but rarely delivered in organised ways.

References

Bruner, J. (1999) Folk pedagogies. In: J. Leach and B. Moon (eds) *Learners and Pedagogy*, London: Paul Chapman, 4–20.

European Commission (2007) White Paper on Sport, http://ec.europa.eu/sport/white-paper/index_en.htm, accessed on 22 March 2010.

Pedagogy in physical education and youth sport

1

What is 'sport pedagogy' and why study it?

Kathleen Armour, University of Birmingham

. . . the aim of education should be to develop to the full the potentialities of every child.

(Board of Education, 1937, p. 12)

You've got to recognise that those 20 people in front of you will have different ways of learning. Some can take it straight away just by listening to what you say. However, just because I believe in a certain thing and I have pictures in my mind of how it's going to happen doesn't mean that all the players do . . . they all have different learning rates and preferences.

(Elite football coach, Jones, Armour and Potrac, 2004, p. 26)

High-quality PE and sport always: enable all young people, whatever their circumstances or ability, to take part in and enjoy PE and sport; promote young people's health, safety and well-being; enable all young people to improve and achieve in line with their age and potential.

(Government document on high-quality physical education and sport, DfES, 2004, p. 1)

Personalised learning, tailoring teaching and learning to individual need, is essential in helping children to achieve the best possible progress and outcomes. It is critical in raising standards and narrowing the attainment gaps that exist between different groups of pupils.

(DCSF, 2010, Personalised Learning website, accessed March 2010)

 ## Why sport pedagogy?

Children in schools often ask why they have to study a subject or topic if its relevance to them and their lives is not immediately obvious. It is a reasonable question for any learner to ask. This chapter, therefore, begins with a rationale for sport pedagogy as an area of study in further and higher education, moves on to definitions and analysis of its core terms, and then delves into the wider literature to explore some of the issues and challenges inherent in the terms 'pedagogy' and 'sport pedagogy'. Some of the arguments in this chapter are relatively easy to follow while others might be more challenging; nonetheless, as you delve further into the book, some of the complex issues will become clearer.

The study of 'sport pedagogy' is relevant to those adults who have a personal interest in sport, and also a strong interest in helping children and young people to develop their 'potentialities' through sport. Essentially, pedagogy is about children as learners and about education (although not necessarily about schools) so 'sport pedagogy' is about children learning both *in* and *through* (in addition to *about*) sport. It is worth noting that pedagogy is used in the context of adult learning too, and although the term 'androgogy' would be more accurate, it is rarely used.

Sport pedagogy is interested in the ways in which children and young people can be supported to learn sport-specific skills *and*, importantly, how that learning can be structured and managed to ensure they also gain wider personal, social and health benefits from their participation. The wider benefits to be gained from participation in sport are not insignificant. Consider, for example, growing evidence of the importance of regular physical activity for health. Engagement in sport is one important and enjoyable way in which large numbers of children and young people can become (and remain) physically active. Yet, if learning experiences are poor, young people tend to avoid sport, or drop out as soon as they have the choice. The term *sport pedagogy* is appropriate, therefore, because this book is about children and young people, their complex and individual needs as learners in sport (wherever they may find sport) and the ways in which teachers and coaches can fulfil their obligations to meet those needs.

In order to understand the scope of sport pedagogy, it is important from the outset to disaggregate learning and education from schools – children can and do learn in many different places. On the other hand, teaching, coaching and learning do occur in schools which are easily recognised as educational contexts. Physical education is compulsory for many children and young people and, amongst other things, physical education teaches children about, in and through a range of sports. In addition, sport is a major part of extracurricular activities and the extended curriculum in schools. The use of the term sport pedagogy in this book, however, stretches beyond school boundaries in a deliberate attempt to foreground children learning in sport *wherever that may occur.*

Historically, there have been debates about the conceptual and practical distinctions between 'sport' and 'physical education' and between teaching and coaching. In focusing on sport pedagogy as its organising concept, this book is not trivialising the very real differences between the physical education and sport workforces, nor the historical battles fought by the physical education profession to gain recognition in schools. Indeed, both of these issues are addressed in some of the chapters that follow. Nonetheless, the position taken in this book is that in addition to the differences, there is much common ground between physical education and youth sport, and between teaching and coaching. Indeed, as was noted in the Introduction, any distinctions can appear relatively meaningless to young sports participants. An attempt is made, therefore, to (partially) neutralise some of the historical tensions between physical education and youth sport in an attempt to prioritise the needs of young learners in sport wherever they happen to be learning.

> **Comment**
> *Sport pedagogy is the foundation of effective teaching and coaching in physical education and youth sport.*

So, what is sport pedagogy?

Sport pedagogy can be conceptualised as a sub-discipline of the academic field of sport sciences. For the purposes of this book, sport sciences is used as an umbrella term that covers a range of related programmes of study including sport(s) science(s); sports studies, coaching science/studies, kinesiology (USA), *éducation physique et sportive* (France) and human movement studies (Australia). As with most terms, there is some debate about the precise definition of the term 'sport pedagogy' and about its value as a sub-discipline. Both 'pedagogy' and 'sport' are contested terms, so perhaps this should come as no surprise. Moreover, sport sciences is a relatively young area of study that has struggled – and continues to struggle – to gain full academic acceptance within the academy and at degree level. As part of that struggle, sport sciences has sought to align itself with traditional fields of study, hence the popularity of sub-disciplines such as exercise physiology and sport psychology. Yet, at some point, all disciplines collide in the real world; in this case in the practice that is sport. If children (*all* children) are to get the best from sport, someone has to bring individual disciplines together in meaningful and helpful ways in order to support young learners. This is no easy task, yet it is the task facing teachers, coaches and other adults who attempt to teach, coach and support diverse children and young people as learners in and through sport.

In the introduction to this book, 'sport pedagogy' was defined as a sub-discipline of sport sciences (and related areas of study) that has three complex dimensions that are made even more complex as they interact to form *each pedagogical encounter*:

1 **Knowledge in context**: what is viewed as valued or appropriate knowledge to be taught, coached or learnt is contingent upon a range of contextual factors. Schools, for example, may have to follow a national curriculum which changes over time, usually as a result of a range of political, social, economic and cultural factors. Similarly, historical analysis of the links between physical education, sport and health illustrates shifting priorities that are influenced by the broader social concerns about health issues. The key point to be made about the 'knowledge in context' dimension of pedagogy is that the selection of any knowledge to be taught, coached or learnt is always a context-bound decision that reflects, reinforces, reproduces (and sometimes challenges) what powerful individuals or groups believe is valuable at any given time.

2 **Learners and learning**: this dimension of pedagogy foregrounds children and young people as diverse learners and the ways in which they can be supported to learn effectively in and through sport. It is obvious that young learners vary in their needs and interests. It is important, however, to consider that statement in at least two ways: very young children have different needs from those of adolescents, yet *within* those two broad categories the range of diversity will also be vast. This range is likely to include ability, disability, gender, race, class, interest, health status, obesity level, disaffection and more, all of which can impact upon learning. At the core of sport pedagogy, therefore,

is expertise in learning theories, and in understanding children and young people as diverse learners.

3   **Teachers/teaching and coaches/coaching:** the key point to grasp about any pedagogical encounter between teacher/coach and young learner is that all three dimensions of pedagogy are present and are interacting, which explains why teaching and coaching are challenging (and exciting) activities. Effective teachers and coaches are lifelong learners themselves who continuously and critically reflect upon their personal capacities to meet the needs of young learners. To be considered as true 'professionals', teachers and coaches must commit to 'growing' their expertise continuously in the sport-related knowledge available to be taught or coached and in the range of pedagogical tools and models from which to draw in order to harness the power of sport. In this way, teachers and coaches model lifelong learning for children and young people.

Perhaps most important of all, however, is the requirement to grasp that as a sub-discipline of the field of sport sciences, sport pedagogy is in the unique position of being characterised by its function of assimilating all the other relevant sub-disciplines into practitioner knowledge.

> **Comment**
> *Sport pedagogy is a multidimensional, multilayered term that represents the complex learning process in physical education and youth sport.*

The multilayered, multidimensional definition of sport pedagogy presented above borrows from and adapts numerous earlier definitions of both pedagogy and sport pedagogy, and some of these are explored in the next two sections of this chapter. In particular, the work of Kirk, Macdonald and O'Sullivan (2006), Rovegno (2003), Grossman (1989), and Shulman (1987) must be acknowledged because all define and explain pedagogy as a complex multifaceted concept. As was noted earlier, understanding sport pedagogy in this way is important in order to establish it as that conceptual and practical space where knowledge from all the other sub-disciplines of sport sciences programmes comes together in the interests of children, young people and their learning.

The key theoretical roots of sport pedagogy are in educational theory, sociology, psychology, history, philosophy and social policy. In addition, an effective teacher or coach will need to draw upon knowledge and skills learnt in physiology, biomechanics, practical sport, perhaps some arts subjects – indeed, from almost anywhere that connects to sport. This explains why undergraduates find sport pedagogy to be practically and conceptually challenging; like all multidisciplinary endeavours it lacks the comforting (albeit illusory) certainty of a single discipline boundary. Yet, without expertise in this multidimensional and unifying (interdisciplinary) sub-discipline, it is difficult to imagine how teachers and coaches can design or deliver effective programmes of activity in sport that can attempt to meet the diverse needs of children and young people. In other words, being a great physiologist or psychologist will not, on its own, make you a great teacher or coach.

> **Comment**
> *Sport pedagogy is that place where you will bring together your knowledge from all the other sub-disciplines of sport sciences.*

Gardner and Boix-Mansilla (1999) argued that 'any individual who not only applies more than one discipline but actually strives to combine or synthesise these stances is engaged in that rare but precious practice called interdisciplinary work' (p. 87). Teachers and coaches in youth sport routinely draw on a range of disciplines within and beyond sport sciences which are then synthesised in practice. This means that teachers and coaches are *always* engaged in 'interdisciplinary work', suggesting that sport pedagogy, with its focus on synthesis, is an academic challenge entirely appropriate to critical study in further and higher education. Further to this, sport pedagogy cannot be categorised as a wholly sport-led model of learning, nor is it wholly child-centred. Instead sport is valued both for itself and for what it can offer each child and young person. The study of sport pedagogy, therefore, contributes to the development of skilful, professional teachers and coaches (and other adults), enabling them to bring sport and young people together in meaningful pedagogical encounters.

In addition to sport pedagogy being a sub-discipline that informs the development of effective teachers and coaches, it is important to remember that it is also a discrete area of research. For those interested in the role of sport in learning, there are opportunities to conduct research at degree level, higher degree level and beyond in a range of areas including, for example:

- youth disaffection and re-engagement through sport;
- health education in and through sport;
- inclusion and youth sport;
- the rights of the child in sport;
- effective professional development for teachers and youth sport coaches.

Indeed, research questions in sport pedagogy seek to address some of the most pressing social problems in contemporary societies.

As befits any complex area of study, it is important to have a critical understanding of key terms and their historical foundations. Although sport pedagogy is explained and illustrated from different perspectives through each chapter in this book, it is helpful to begin this learning journey with a preliminary critical analysis of the terms 'pedagogy' and 'sport pedagogy'. It was noted in the Introduction that 'sport' is understood in its broadest terms throughout this book. There are academic debates around the margins and boundaries of sport/not sport, and some of these issues surface in the following chapters, but these are not addressed in detail here.

> **Comment**
> *There are many areas of sport pedagogy that would benefit from additional research.*

Pedagogy revealed . . . and confounded

The extracts that opened this chapter are from the fields of education, physical education and sport. They span a period of over 70 years, yet they all express similar sentiments and these are at the core of any understanding of pedagogy. The first extract is from the *Handbook of Suggestions for Teachers* issued by the Board of Education in England in 1937, and its focus is on *every child*. The second is a quote from Graham Taylor, an elite-level football coach in England, who speaks of learners having *different learning rates and preferences*. The third is from a recent government document on physical education and sport which suggests that high-quality provision will *enable all young people to improve and achieve in line with their age and potential*. The fourth extract is from a current and major focus of education policy in England, personalised learning, that emphasises the importance of *tailoring teaching and learning to individual need*. Taken together, these extracts highlight two important points: first, similar concerns are apparent from education, sport and physical education perspectives and, second, historical insights serve as a powerful reminder of the enduring challenges to be faced in designing effective learning structures and processes.

Historically, the term 'pedagogy' derives from ancient Greece where a 'pedagogue' was not a teacher but a well-educated servant in a wealthy household who took responsibility for a child's social and moral development (Savatar, 1997). The pedagogue, therefore, was responsible for the overall development of the child. Although the term pedagogy has evolved over time, its etymological roots are significant because it is clear it would be inappropriate to reduce the concept of pedagogy to 'merely' instruction or to a transmission definition of learning; something more is going on. Watkins and Mortimore (1999) reviewed a range of definitions of pedagogy and concluded that 'learning' is at its core. They commented, however, that pedagogy is poorly understood, and that there has been a neglect of:

> this most important of topics – affecting the way hundreds and thousands of learners of different ages and stages are taught . . . Instead of systematic collections of evidence, teachers have had to rely on ideological positions, folk wisdom and the mantras of enthusiasts for particular approaches.
>
> (Preface)

Stone (2000) made a similar case for clarification, arguing that the term pedagogy had become so flexible that it had become amoeba-like, and its study had become 'as rigorous as a jellyfish' (p. 94).

Perhaps the easiest way to begin an analysis of the term 'pedagogy' is to Google 'definitions of pedagogy'. A quick analysis of the results reveals key words that recur: instruction, education, the art and/or science of teaching, profession of teaching, etc. The main territory covered by the concept of pedagogy becomes immediately apparent. Leach and Moon (1999), however, suggested that although at its simplest pedagogy can be viewed as teaching and learning, a more complex understanding recognises the relationship between four key elements of any educational encounter: teachers, learners, the learning task and the learning environment. Importantly, these authors argued that 'at the heart of this dynamic process is a personal view of the purposes of education, what constitutes good teaching, and a belief in the purposes of the subject' (p. 274). More recently, Alexander (2008) argued that 'pedagogy is still very much a work in progress'; nonetheless, he echoed Leach and Moon's complex view of pedagogy when he defined pedagogy as 'the act of teaching together with the ideas, values and beliefs by which that act is informed, sustained and justified' (p. 4). Alexander further commented that although teaching is at the heart of pedagogy, there is more to it. In particular, Alexander pointed to the 'extraordinary richness of pedagogy as a field of intellectual exploration and empirical enquiry' (p. 183) and, in echoes of Leach and Moon's argument:

> for the sake of the students whose interests we claim to serve we have an obligation to make explicit and debate those ideas, values, beliefs and theories that may be hidden even from ourselves yet powerfully shape what both teachers and students do. (p. 183)

In similar vein, Ireson, Mortimore and Hallam (1999) claimed that one of the main problems with understanding pedagogy was that there had been insufficient focus on the goals of education up to that time; they argued that the question 'What are we teaching for?' (p. 213) had not been posed often enough – and was rarely answered. This issue is revisited later in this chapter.

> ### Comment
> The term pedagogy has its roots in ancient Greece where it referred to the holistic development of children.

Alexander (2008) draws the threads of this conceptual discussion together in his claim that 'Pedagogy has a purpose. It mediates learning, knowledge, culture and identity' (p. 183). The work of John Holt provides a practical illustration of this key point. In 1964, in a damning critique of schools and approaches to learning, Holt argued that children were failing to learn effectively because of the prevailing educational practices. In 1968, Holt wrote a second book entitled *How Children Learn* in order to offer more positive insights into young learners and their learning. His purpose was to 'describe children – in a few cases adults – using their minds well, learning boldly and effectively' (Foreword). Holt believed that 'only a few children in school ever become good at learning', claiming that 'most of them get humiliated, frightened and discouraged' (ibid.). Holt felt it was important, therefore, to observe and describe children (especially young children) engaged in effective learning, in order that adults might better understand the learning process. In the extract below, Holt recounts his analysis of children being taught to swim by their parents, and draws on his critical observations of teaching his own child. In particular, Holt noticed that 'The courage of little children (and not them alone) rises and falls, like the tide – only the cycles are in minutes, or even seconds' (p. 117). This insight led Holt to observe:

> At one time or another I have watched a number of parents trying to teach their very little children to swim. On the whole they don't get very far because they are so insensitive to this rise and fall of courage in the child. Is it because they don't notice? Or because they don't care? Perhaps they feel that the child's feelings are unimportant, to be easily overridden by exhortation and encouragement, or anger and threats . . . In any case such would-be-teachers, even when they are not wholly unsuccessful, lose a great deal, since a child who is allowed to return to babyhood for a while when he feels the need of it, to fill up his tank of courage when he feels the need of it, when he feels it run dry, will move ahead into the unknown far faster than we adults could push him. (p. 118)

Holt added:

> If we continually try to force a child to do what he is afraid to do, he will become more timid, and will use his brains and energy to avoid the pressures we put on him. If, however, we are careful not to push a child beyond the limits of his courage, he is almost sure to get braver. (p. 119)

Holt's observation is fascinating because it raises so many questions that are central to pedagogy. Formulating answers to these questions can illustrate the complex ways in which the different aspects of pedagogy interact in the pedagogical encounter of teaching/coaching, and each is also applicable to the sport context; for example:

- What are we teaching or coaching?
- Why are we teaching and coaching this activity/sport in this way at this time?
- How are we teaching or coaching and why this way?
- How do we know this is the best sport or the best approach for this child at this time?
- What has led us to hold these beliefs?
- What pressures are there on us (implicit and explicit) to 'make' this child succeed?
- Does it matter if the child fails in this activity – and to whom?
- Is this the best setting in which this child can learn?
- Do I know enough about children, learning, education and this (sport) activity to create a positive learning experience for this child?
- Is my stock of knowledge relevant, current and growing?

At the very least, therefore, it could be argued that Holt forces us to confront pedagogy in the kind of complexity advocated by both Leach and Moon (1999) and Alexander (2008). Moreover, in his use of swimming as an example, Holt's observations also nudge us towards critical analysis of the concept of sport pedagogy.

> **Comment**
> *An understanding of pedagogy reveals the complexity inherent in planning effective teaching and coaching sessions.*

 ## Sport pedagogy revealed . . . and confounded

Tinning (2008) has undertaken a comprehensive review of the concept of sport pedagogy within sport sciences (although he mainly uses the US term 'kinesiology'). His paper has been identified as one of the additional resources to accompany this chapter, so although a summary of the key points is included here, reading the paper in full will be beneficial. Tinning analyses the concept of pedagogy and points out that the term has subdivided into numerous 'types' of pedagogy ranging from critical pedagogy to feminist pedagogy. (Here again, Googling the term 'pedagogy' is revealing as something of the range of contexts in which the term is used becomes apparent.) Tinning also highlights some of the complexity and overlap between the core terms denoting pedagogy, and he reinforces the key point made earlier: 'the ways in which people think about pedagogy are underpinned or in-formed by particular knowledge paradigms and ways of seeing the world' (p. 409). In particular, Tinning is keen to avoid narrow conceptualisations of pedagogy, believing that a broader notion is of more value for the field. On the other hand, Tinning is also critical of the way in which scholars from different theoretical perspectives have appropriated the term 'pedagogy', making it difficult to find common ground.

Recognising that the term sport pedagogy is 'amorphous', Tinning (2008) states that it is 'generally accepted that sport pedagogy is a subdiscipline of the field of kinesiology' (p. 412).

He cites the view of Haag (1989) that 'sport pedagogy has a central position within sport science, in every teaching and learning process in physical activity' and that it resides 'between sport science and the science of education' (p. 413). Interestingly, however, as Tinning traced the use of the term 'sport pedagogy' through various lectures, conferences and publications in the broad field and from around the world, it became clear that the term has been used only intermittently and with little clarity. This is unhelpful for students and scholars who may be attempting to enter the field. Tinning, however, proposed a way forward, arguing that pedagogy is fundamentally about 'the processes of knowledge (re)production' and that it is the 'consequence of pedagogical intentions' (p. 416). Thus, for Tinning, *pedagogical work* within kinesiology is:

> that effect or influence on ways of thinking, beliefs, practices, dispositions and identities regarding physical activity performance and participation, bodily practices and understand- ings and self-awareness related to health and well-being that is produced by an individ- ual's encounter with certain prescribed pedagogical practices and devices.   (p. 417)

This description is complex and can appear difficult to unpick, but Tinning then goes on to consider sport pedagogy as a 'foundational subdiscipline' of kinesiology, and this makes his view clearer. Importantly, kinesiology (like sport sciences) is often a very broad field of study covering 'human movement' across domains and well beyond sport. Thus, Tinning argues, we need to understand pedagogical work related to 'physical activity, bodies, and health' wherever it takes place. He also argues that we need to understand the pedagogical work undertaken by other 'cultural players' in the field, such as those working in obesity/health.

Comment
Definitions of sport pedagogy are contested but it has clear links to pedagogies in health and personal/social development.

It is apparent that the three-dimensional definition of sport pedagogy that is used in this book shares some common ground with Tinning's (2008) view, but also that it has a slightly different starting point. Whereas there is agreement that an understanding of sport pedagogy should enable scholars and practitioners to draw upon and connect knowledge from different orientations, it is suggested in this book that the pivotal focus of sport peda- gogy should be the needs and interests of children and young people learning in and through sport. What this means is that the ability of teachers and coaches to '*diagnose*' learners' needs in sport, and their own abilities to teach/coach effectively to meet those needs, become the core focus of sport pedagogy. So, whereas 'sport pedagogy' is not the same as 'health pedagogy', there are clear links because if a young learner encounters effec- tive, appropriate and uplifting learning experiences in sport they are more likely to retain an interest in engagement which may, in turn, lead to health benefits for some.

In a major text in the field of physical education, Kirk, Macdonald and O'Sullivan (2006) defined pedagogy 'by its three key elements of learning, teaching and curriculum' and stated that they 'understand these three elements to be interdependent' (p. xi). The context of the book is mainly (although not exclusively) school-based physical education, and the chapters tend to focus on one or other of the different elements of pedagogy. Nonetheless, this text draws together the work of respected scholars from around the world, and there are several chapters that offer useful insights for this discussion on sport pedagogy. For example, De Martelaer and Theeboom explored the relationship between physical education and youth sport, identifying their commonalities and the roots of their pedagogical differences. Tsangaridou undertook a detailed analysis of teachers' knowledge, drawing upon the work of key educational theorists such as Shulman (1987). Trudel and Gilbert undertook an extensive analysis of coaching and coach education, concluding that 'Sport coaches, and those who train them, must be "perpetual students" who constantly seek new information' (p. 532). Thus, this handbook, and those chapters specifically, are identified as additional resources to support this chapter.

Finally, as was noted in the Introduction of this book, it is important to remember that the study of sport pedagogy is not founded on an uncritical understanding of sport; there is also a 'flip side' to consider. Sport practices can be harmful for young learners, including inflicting physical, social and emotional harm. Indeed, a historical analysis reveals that this potential for harm has long been recognised. In 1927, the Board of Education in England produced a guide on *The Education of the Adolescent*. In a section entitled 'Physical Training and Games' it noted:

> It is generally admitted that games have an educational as well as a recreative use. They encourage and develop self-reliance, teamwork, loyalty, self restraint, and resourcefulness. The weak point in games is that they often benefit most the strongest and healthiest pupils, who require them least. (Board of Education, 1927, p. 245)

Furthermore, although the European Commission White Paper on Sport (2007) proclaimed the 'educational dimension' and the 'social, cultural and recreational role' of sport, there were also some (albeit limited) expressions of caution. It is interesting in this context to consider Myerson's (2005) story. She wrote in some detail about her personal experiences as a child learning in sport. In a book entitled *Not a Games Person*, Myerson's recollections of the way sport was taught suggest that the Board of Education's (1927) claim was prophetic in her case, and that John Holt's observations about children becoming frightened, discouraged and humiliated were not overstated. For Myerson, 'Sports Day' was the worst day in the entire school year:

> I hate this day and I hate being in this sack, but I have no choice . . . Because school is character-building, my mum always says, it's where they make you Be A Sport and Join In and although they make you do that several times a week, once a year they make you do it with equipment and organised lines and the awfulness of an audience: Sports day. I hate it and dread it so I must need to have my character built. (p. 21)

What can be taken from all this is that whereas it is unrealistic to expect all sports to appeal to all children and young people all of the time, it is also worth questioning the wisdom of putting children and young people into and through sports activities and experiences where they are, in essence, learning how to fail and to become discouraged. Belief in the value of sport and its potential as a broad educational tool would suggest it is incumbent upon teachers and coaches, and any other adults involved in youth sport, to use sport effectively to meet the needs of children, rather than assuming that simply pushing children through sports experiences will, in some magical way, result in positive outcomes for all of them. As Myerson illustrates above (and Holt pointed out earlier), using sport uncritically as some form of 'character-building' process for children is naive at best, and damaging at worst.

> **Comment**
> *Sport pedagogy is founded on the recognition that it is essential to 'diagnose' learners'
> needs as a key step in designing practice. This is important in order to counteract some
> of the potential harm done to young learners when they are engaged in inappropriate
> learning activities.*

Conclusion

It might be helpful to conclude this analysis of the concept of sport pedagogy with questions about *purpose.* In an earlier section, it was noted that questions about the 'purpose' of education are rarely asked or answered, and this is interesting in the context of 'sport pedagogy'. Clearly 'sport' is a key feature of sport pedagogy, yet, as was noted earlier, in the sub-discipline of sport pedagogy, the needs and interests of the young learners in sport are paramount. This means that traditional, adult or elite forms of sport must always be subjugated to the educational needs of children and young people, and it challenges directly the notion that youth sport should be viewed primarily as a training ground for adult sport or, indeed, lifelong participation in sport. On the contrary, youth sport, from a pedagogical perspective, has to serve the needs of children and young people *at the time in which they engage.* What this means, in practice, is that in order to be effective, teachers and coaches need to recognise (diagnose) individual learners' needs and interests, consult young people about them, reflect on their personal and professional capacities as teachers or coaches to meet those learning requirements, update personal knowledge as required (driven by their analysis of learning need) and then design and deliver appropriate pedagogical encounters in sport in the form of programmes, lessons, sessions or activities.

Undoubtedly, 'needs and interests' is a loaded phrase: a child's conception of 'need' might be very different from an adult's or what can be provided in reality, and it is unrealistic to expect that all children and young people can have all of their interests supported all of the time. In the three-dimensional definition of pedagogy presented earlier, it was made clear that knowledge and context are interlinked, and that beliefs about what is considered to be valuable or valued knowledge shift over time and in response to social contextual factors. Nonetheless, if there is an underpinning belief that engagement in appropriate sport activities can be a 'good' thing for children and young people, offering a range of sport-specific and personal, educational, social and health benefits, then the principle of understanding and addressing individual need, where possible, is non-negotiable. This reinforces earlier points made about the importance of critically interrogating the source of all personal knowledge and beliefs, what Bruner (1999) called folk theories, about what is 'good' or 'best' for children and young people in sport. Such beliefs always reflect personal history, and wider structural beliefs about children, education and sport (and much else besides). Whether folk theories are acknowledged or not, they influence what is taught or coached, and what children and young people may be prepared to learn.

The premise underpinning this book was identified as a belief in children's rights in sport, and adults' responsibilities. Knowledge and understanding of sport pedagogy are the first steps towards ensuring that the rights of large numbers of children and young people to effective learning in and through sport are not denied.

Learning tasks

Individual task: memories of teachers and coaches past

1 Think back to your experiences as a young learner in physical education and youth sport. Identify the two best and the two worst teachers/coaches that you can remember, then write a 200-word narrative on each, explaining how they helped or hindered your learning.

2 Undertake a critical review of your four narratives. Can you draw any tentative conclusions about effective teaching and coaching?

3 Critically review your conclusions. These are likely to form the basis of any 'folk pedagogies' that you hold about what is 'good' for other young learners. Can you identify any of your conclusions that might – and might not – be applicable to different kinds of learners in physical education and youth sport?

Group task: the bigger picture

This activity can be done in pairs or larger groups.

1 Share the key outcomes from the individual learning task and create a group (draft) poster that maps clearly your findings about effective and ineffective teachers/coaches.

2 Conduct a literature search to find at least four publications (books or journal articles) on effective teachers and/or coaches. The publications could come from the physical education and youth sport literature, or the wider education literature.

3 Compare the findings from the literature search with the findings from your analysis of your personal narratives, identifying any similarities, differences and additional information.

4 Finalise your poster so that it becomes an accurate representation of your group's analysis of the key features of effective and ineffective teachers/coaches.

Further reading

Tinning, R. (2006) Pedagogy, sport pedagogy, and the field of kinesiology, *Quest*, 60, 405–24.

Tinning, R. (2010) *Pedagogy and Human Movement*, London: Routledge.

Kirk, D., Macdonald, D. and O'Sullivan, M. (eds) (2006) *The Handbook of Physical Education*, London: Sage. Several of these chapters are relevant, including:

- 4.8 'Teachers' knowledge' by Niki Tsangaridou
- 4.9 'Coaching and coach education' by Pierre Trudel and Wade Gilbert
- 5.6 'Physical education and youth sport' by Kristine De Martelaer and Marc Theeboom.

References

Alexander, R. (2008) *Essays on Pedagogy*, London: Routledge.

Board of Education (1927) *The Education of the Adolescent*, London: HMSO.

Board of Education (1937) *Handbook of Suggestions for Teachers*, London: HMSO.

Bruner, J. (1999) Folk pedagogies. In: J. Leach and B. Moon (eds) *Learners and Pedagogy*, London: Paul Chapman.

DCSF (2008) *Personalised Learning: a Practical Guide*, Nottingham: DCSF Publications.

DCSF (2010) *Personalised Learning*, http://nationalstrategies.standards.dcsf.gov.uk/search/inclusion/results/nav:46354, accessed 22 March 2010.

De Martelaer, K. and Theeboom, M. (2006) Physical education and youth sport. In: D. Kirk, D. Macdonald and M. O'Sullivan (eds) *Handbook of Physical Education*, London: Sage, 652–64.

DfES (2004) *High Quality PE and Sport For Young People*, Nottingham: DfES Publications.

European Commission (2007) White Paper on Sport, http://ec.europa.eu/sport/white-paper/index_en.htm, accessed on 22 March 2010.

Gardner, H. and Boix-Mansilla, V. (1999) Teaching for understanding in the disciplines – and beyond. In: J. Leach and B. Moon (eds) *Learners and Pedagogy*, London: Paul Chapman, 78–88.

Grossman, P.L. (1989) A study in contrast: sources of pedagogical content knowledge for secondary English, *Journal of Teacher Education*, 40, 24–31.

Haag, H. (1989) Research in 'sport pedagogy': One field of theoretical study in the science of sport, *International Review of Education*, 35, 1, 5–16.

Holt, J. (1964) *How Children Fail*, London: Pitman.

Holt, J. (1968) *How Children Learn*, London: Pitman.

Ireson, J., Mortimore, P. and Hallam, S. (1999) The common strands of pedagogy and their implications. In: P. Mortimore (ed.) *Understanding Pedagogy and its Implications*, London: Paul Chapman, 212–32.

Jones, R., Armour, K.M. and Potrac, P. (2004) *Sports Coaching Cultures*, London: Routledge.

Kirk, D., Macdonald, D. and O'Sullivan, M. (2006) (eds) *The Handbook of Physical Education*, London: Sage.

Leach, J. and Moon, B. (1999) (eds) *Learners and Pedagogy*, London: Paul Chapman.

Myerson, J. (2005) *Not a Games Person*, London: Yellow Jersey Press.

Rovegno, I. (2003) Teachers' knowledge construction. In: S. Silverman and C. Ennis (eds) *Student Learning in Physical Education: Applying Research to Enhance Instruction*, Champaign, IL: Human Kinetics, 295–310.

Savatar, F. (1997) *El Valor de Educar*, Barcelona: Ariel.

Shulman, L. (1987) Knowledge and teaching: foundation of a new reform, *Harvard Review*, 57, 1–22.

Stone, E. (2000) Iconoclastes: poor pedagogy, *Journal of Teaching for Education*, 26, 1, 93–5.

Tinning, R. (2008) Pedagogy, sport pedagogy, and the field of kinesiology, *Quest*, 60, 405–24.

Trudel, P. and Gilbert, W. (2006) Coaching and coach education. In: D. Kirk, D. Macdonald and M. O'Sullivan (eds) *Handbook of Physical Education*, London: Sage, 516–39.

Tsangaridou, N. (2006) Teachers' knowledge. In: D. Kirk, D. Macdonald and M. O'Sullivan (eds) *Handbook of Physical Education*, London: Sage, 652–64.

Watkins, C. and Mortimore, P. (1999) Pedagogy: what do we know? In: P. Mortimore (ed.) *Understanding Pedagogy and its Implications*, London: Paul Chapman, 1–19.

Children learning in physical education: a historical overview

David Kirk, University of Bedfordshire

The term 'physical education' has been in general use for a few years; before that the term was 'physical training', which in turn was preceded by an activity known as 'drill'. A further, and very descriptive term – 'physical jerks' – is familiar to many, and recalls the quality of movement that used to be regarded as an effective means of setting up physique and ensuring discipline . . . The use of these different phrases is interesting because they reflect the gradual development of certain ideas. The 'physical education' of the present day not only embraces a much wider scope of activities than the 'drill' lesson of the beginning of the century; it also reflects a different relationship between the teacher and the class, and a different conception of discipline. Drill was inherited from military manoeuvres; physical education has emerged from the observation and study of the needs of growing children.

(Ministry of Education, 1952, pp. 83–4)

The curriculum in the Colleges of PE is ever-widening. This is something that I rejoice to be able to report, and my only comment is 'high time, too!'. We are British people – for which I can find no cause for apology – and we are a games-playing nation. It has always puzzled me, for instance, that gymnastics should be regarded as being synonymous with Physical Education. Gymnastics is a part – a very valuable part – of a vast subject, and in some countries it may have been looked on as being the main fraction of the whole. No longer is that so here. However good a system may be, the folly of adopting it in its entirety and foisting it upon people, unadapted to peculiar needs, is at last recognised. What may delight the Germans or the Danes, and what suits their national characteristics, does not necessarily make a similar appeal here. Now we are recognising this!

(Hugh Brown, Director, the Scottish School of Physical Education, reported in
Physical Education, 1959, 50, p. 92)

Introduction

As was pointed out in Chapter 1, it is important to understand the historical foundations of the field of sport pedagogy. This importance does not derive from mere curiosity about the past. Most historians understand that history's real value lies in assisting us to better understand the present and the future. It could be argued that the current generation of workers in the field of physical education and sport, exercise and leisure – the field's teachers, coaches, administrators and scientists – know little about the history of their profession or their field of study. This means that they are not as well equipped as they might be to respond constructively to contemporary challenges. Historians argue that to choose to be ignorant about history is, effectively, to choose to take no active, informed part in constructing our collective future. If we choose not to understand the history of our field, it should come as no surprise to learn that many of today's 'innovations' are yesterday's recycled failures.

This chapter asks you to consider the changing nature of children's experiences of learning in physical education over the past century, a period that constitutes the subject's modern history in schools and colleges. You will see seven photographs (plus two cartoons) dating from 1906 to 2006 that, along with an accompanying narrative, tell a story about these changing experiences. In addition to providing brief descriptions of the contents of each photograph, the narrative will seek to explain what lies behind the descriptions. The focus is on understanding the nature of physical education at the time the photo was taken and the relationships of that particular form of physical education to other forms.

The narrative thread surrounding this sequence of photographs might look to you like a story of progress and enlightenment; as someone once remarked, it could read like a 'victory narrative', telling of the progressive liberation of children's schooled bodies. So you will read about shifts from drilling and exercising to learning sports skills by numbers, from Swedish gymnastics to educational gymnastics, from gymnastics-based forms of physical education to sport-based forms, from gender-segregated to co-educational programmes, and from a relatively narrow to an ever-widening range of activities in school programmes.

While this summary of the narrative is at one level entirely correct, the telling of this story around images is intended to encourage you to make up your own mind about what you see in each photograph. In particular, you will be invited to imagine what each image suggests about how it might have felt to learn physical education in each of the settings or forms the pictures represent. Part of this imagining involves looking beyond the surface of the photograph, to consider the bodily sensations of living each form of physical education. And while in conventional historical fashion we begin in the past and work progressively towards the present, do not be seduced by this approach into believing that time unfolds uniformly everywhere in a straight line. If it did, the future would be easy to predict. Clearly, it is not. As you consider each of the photographs and put yourself inside each frame, think about the kinds of pasts the children of the time might have remembered and of the futures they might have hoped for.

Physical education as drilling and exercising, 1906

Massed drill in the yard of an Elementary School, 1906

Source: McIntosh, P.C. (1968) *PE in England since 1800,* 2nd edn, London: G. Bell and Sons Ltd. Reading University Archive.

In this photograph, taken in 1906, we can see rows of children in exactly the same position, feet apart, arms outstretched, chests out and heads thrown back. All appear to be dressed in their everyday school clothes with white collars, dark jackets, knee-length breeches, tall socks and boots or shoes. There are ten lines in all, with around 18 to 20 pupils in each line. All appear to be boys. There is a male teacher standing in front of the pupils, and another six or so at the back of the ranks. The brick school building rises up in the background, at least two storeys high, and we can see a row of houses in the street beyond the school wall. This is, in all probability, a large state school in an urban area. Typical of such schools, the playground is relatively small and cramped for such a large number of boys. It would not be suited to physical activities that involved a lot of movement in space, such as football or rugby; not, at least, for this number of pupils.

What is going on here is one of the earliest forms of physical education in government schools, which we might describe as 'drilling and exercising'. The photo clearly shows the drilling part of this couplet. The rank-and-file arrangement of the boys reflects a military influence, typical of the arrangement of troops in the parade ground. Indeed, in this school setting, inspection was an important part of the drilling process. This arrangement meant that each pupil could be seen easily by at least one of the teachers at all times. In other words, the pupils were under surveillance (Kirk, 1998).

Why was surveillance of pupils so important? By 1906, the year this photo was taken, compulsory mass schooling was only 20 or so years old. The school as an institution was still in the process of taking shape, which included the imposition of its authority on the unruly bodies of working-class children who, until around the 1880s, had not been required to attend school (McIntosh, 1968). The government-funded elementary schools catered for children from a wide range of social backgrounds, as modern-day primary schools do now, and was concerned mainly with the 'three Rs' of reading, writing and arithmetic. These schools were for children aged six to 13 years. By age 13, children were expected to leave school to find work. Only the 'brightest' had an option in the early 1900s of staying on to receive a secondary education. These elementary schools contrasted markedly with the private secondary schools and their preparatory schools catering for a minority of social elites, which offered a broad curriculum, including sport and academic subjects. Discipline and corporal punishment were commonplace in both types of school. For the socially elite pupils, however, learning to obey was mixed with learning to lead and command. For elementary school pupils, in contrast, learning to be obedient and to respond to the commands of leaders was of greater importance given their future lives as workers.

The exercises themselves played a significant part in this training process in elementary schools. The camera has captured these boys performing movements that formed part of the Swedish or Ling system of gymnastics (Smith, 1974). The Swedish system was developed in the early nineteenth century by Per Henrik Ling in Stockholm. By the middle of the 1800s it had been adopted by the British navy as an alternative form of discipline to corporal punishment (most typically, flogging). The Swedish system was based on freestanding exercises that sought to exercise all of the body's major joints and muscle groups through intricate and detailed flexions and extensions. The various British government syllabuses of physical training published between 1909 and 1933 show that lessons were set out in tables. Each table was carefully graded by experience of the class, each progressing in difficulty from introductory to advanced levels (Board of Education, 1909, 1933).

Swedish gymnastics was, in short, a complete system of exercises that sought to have an impact on the entire range of gross muscular movement of the body (Kirk, 1998). It was based entirely on correctness of performance, and allowed no opportunity for individual interpretation or creativity. This is why all of the boys are attempting to perform exactly the same movement at the same time and in the same ways, limited only by their individual body shapes, sizes and physical capabilities.

> **Comment**
> *Drill and rigid forms of systematic exercise dominated this period. They were based on a particular understanding of what working-class children needed to learn.*

Outside the school, in specialist physical training colleges for teachers, in the armed services, and in gymnastics clubs, this requirement for absolute precision of movement of the group was rigidly enforced. Gymnastics at this time was also strongly segregated by sex, and different approaches to the Swedish and other systems began to emerge for women and men. As we noted in Chapter 1, to be properly understood, pedagogical knowledge needs to be located in the context in which it is created. In terms of Swedish gymnastics, its variations sought to reflect the commonly accepted qualities of femininity and masculinity that prevailed at particular times. For example, the women gymnasts began to add musical accompaniment and rhythm to their exercises (Fletcher, 1984), while the men developed daring feats of vaulting and agility (McIntosh, 1968).

In schools, though, while the disciplinary features of drilling and exercising were emphasised, generalist classroom teachers would rarely have had the training required to teach such precise movement effectively. Then, as now in primary schools, generalist teachers struggled to teach all aspects of the curriculum to high levels. Furthermore, although in this photo we see only boys, it was not uncommon in smaller schools to find boys and girls being drilled and exercised together, in contrast to the preferred segregated practice among specialist adult gymnasts and in private schools for the social elites.

> **Comment**
> *The roots of issues affecting the ways in which primary school children can learn physical education and sport today can be found in historical accounts from the early 1900s.*

 ## Anyone for tennis (by numbers)? 1920s

Tennis by numbers, 1920s

Source: Flectcher, S. (1984) *Women First: the female tradition in English Physical education 1880–1980,* London: Althone. University of Bedfordshire Archive.

The drilling and exercising form of physical education persisted for another 40 years, into the middle of the twentieth century (McIntosh, 1968). Nonetheless, the 'command' style of pedagogy and the concern for specific movement techniques have remained powerful residual aspects of the practice of physical education in schools. An early example of the application of this teacher-centred approach to organising learning experiences can be seen in the photograph of female student teachers learning tennis 'by numbers'. This photo, shot at Bedford Physical Training College in the 1920s, differs from the elementary school drilling and exercising example in a number of ways, not only because these students are older and are female, but also because they are from a relatively wealthy social background. They are also learning to play a game rather than to perform gymnastics.

There are also some unmistakable similarities between this photo and the first; for example, the rank-and-file arrangement of the players is similar, so that each individual is clearly within the visual range of the teacher. The focus on the technique of movement is another, though perhaps less obvious, similarity. Although they are learning to serve in tennis, the Bedford students are learning (by numbers) the component parts of the skill of serving. A 'by numbers' approach means that each part of the skill was deconstructed and learned in isolation and out of the context of the actual game of tennis, before being reassembled into one complete skill. That, at least, was the aspiration of this approach to learning to play games. We will see later in this chapter that it is more or less still with us today.

> **Comment**
> *Skill learning by numbers remains a popular contemporary pedagogical approach used by physical education teachers and youth sport coaches.*

Freeing the body through educational gymnastics, 1951

Physical education at Upton County Primary School, Kent, 1951

Source: McIntosh, P.C. (1968) *PE in England since 1800,* 2nd edn, London: G. Bell and Sons Ltd. Reading University Archive.

This photograph of a school physical education lesson, taken in a primary school in Kent in 1951, offers as radical a contrast to the 1906 image as we might imagine possible. Here boys and girls, taught together, are all engaged in making shapes in the air with their bodies.

They are outdoors, on a grassy playing field in what is clearly warm weather, since the children are wearing only gym knickers. They are all jumping to make shapes in the air, but in contrast to their 1906 counterparts, they are encouraged here to interpret the task and create their own unique shapes. The outcome for the children is a tremendous range of possibilities, even though there are only seven children in shot. The effect of this photo even today is dramatic, as it was intended to be at the time, suggestive of childish freedom and exuberance; children who are barefoot and bare-chested, seemingly in touch with nature.

The developments that lay behind this form of physical education, informed by what was known variously as educational gymnastics, basic movement and movement education, had also been dramatic. It is worth recalling that at this time and until the 1980s, the training of physical education teachers was strictly segregated by sex. From as early as the 1920s, the female specialist teachers, who between the 1880s and the 1940s were by far the dominant group in physical education, had begun to challenge the artificiality and rigidity (as they saw it) of Swedish gymnastics (Fletcher, 1984). By the 1940s, a pedagogical 'war' had erupted in Britain between the 'old school' who wanted to retain Swedish gymnastics and the 'new school' of educational gymnasts. The new school had been influenced by Rudlof Laban (in particular) who was the originator of modern dance. His teachings made their way to England via his pupils and colleagues in advance of his own arrival from Nazi Germany in 1938. Laban's approach was not written down and published formally until the late 1940s (Laban, 1948). This meant that much of his work was communicated through short professional development courses for teachers and through personal contacts, leading to a certain allure and mystique. Nevertheless, so rapid was the uptake of this new approach in women's physical education that many of Laban's ideas, and their development by English physical educators, had become official government policy by the early 1950s. His work can be seen in two key Ministry of Education (MoE) publications, *Moving and Growing* (MoE, 1952) and *Planning the Programme* (MoE, 1953).

The drilling and exercising form of physical education that had dominated practice previously was teacher-dominated, using the appropriately named 'command' style of instruction. Educational gymnastics, on the other hand, was avowedly student-centred, with much emphasis placed on the child's interpretation of tasks set by the teacher, and on creative solving of movement problems (Fletcher, 1984). A typical task would have been one where the pupil was asked to travel along the gymnastics mat transferring weight from feet to hands and back to feet. Possible solutions to this task included a forwards or backwards roll, a cartwheel or a hand spring, as well as many variations on these more standard gymnastics skills.

Comment

Educational gymnastics was sometimes associated with creative movement, in which children were challenged to combine movement with creativity, imagination and individual solutions to problems.

The next photo dating from around the 1960s shows female students at Bedford College providing creative responses to precisely the gymnastics task outlined above. It involved transference of weight, in two cases using a bench as apparatus, thus increasing the difficulty of the challenge, and in the third involving a twisting roll. It was in primary school physical education and in women's gymnastics that the Laban-inspired approach was to

The Movement–Anti-Movement controversy. Transference of weight

Source: Fletcher, S. (1984) *Women First: the female tradition in English physical education 1880–1980*, London: Althone. University of Bedfordshire Archive.

have the greatest impact, persisting well into the 1970s. On the other hand, educational gymnastics had only a very limited influence on physical education as it was practised by male specialists, perhaps in part due to its radical departure from forms of physical education influenced by drilling and exercising. Men began to enter the field in large numbers in the late 1940s to staff the new government secondary schools, and by the end of the 1950s they outnumbered the women specialists (Fletcher, 1984).

The masculinisation of physical education as gymnastics, Carnegie, 1950s

It was suggested in Chapter 1 that physical education has been, historically, a veritable battleground for competing ideas. Educational gymnastics was to be just one of several bones of contention during a period of increasing male dominance in physical education and the waning influence of females. While the women were wholeheartedly engaged in their debates over Swedish versus educational gymnastics during the 1940s and 1950s, the men were busily taking forward an explicitly teacher-centred style of physical education similar to Swedish gymnasts (Kirk, 1992). In the early period of this development, the first male specialist colleges of physical education such as Carnegie and Loughborough appeared in the early 1930s (some 40 years after the first women's colleges). In these colleges the men developed new forms of gymnastics that made use of apparatus and brought together exercises from various systems. They were, however, increasingly influenced by the German

Turnen, which was witnessed for the first time by many male physical educators as a competitive sport at the London Olympics of 1948 (McIntosh, 1968).

Early gymnasium, City of Leeds Training College, c. 1920s
Source: The Carnegie Archive, Leeds Metropolitan University Library, Headingley Campus

This photo shows one of the gymnasia at Carnegie, built originally in the 1920s for the City of Leeds teacher training college, which the men's specialist college later shared. We can see the kind of facility that was to become the mainstay of secondary school physical education following the introduction of mass secondary schooling in the late 1940s. The dimensions of the gym were uniformly 60 feet by 30 feet, complete with sprung wooden floor, wall bars, climbing ropes, balance beams, benches and floor mats. We can see, in the foreground, a 'pommel' on one of the beams, simulating the pommel horse. In the middle of the shot is a 'buck', used for vaulting, and at the very back of the gym a full pommel horse.

This facility was the specialist physical education teacher's domain. While in England, even as late as the 1970s, it was commonplace to find mathematics or history teachers supervising and sometimes teaching outdoors games lessons, only qualified physical education specialists could operate this indoor facility with its many possibilities for human movement. When the curriculum shifted away from gymnastic forms of physical education towards games and sports-based forms during the 1950s, physical education teachers had to make do with the 60 feet by 30 feet gym facility in which to play basketball, volleyball, netball, badminton and so on (Munrow, 1963; Whitehead and Hendry, 1976). This situation had an unfortunate and unanticipated influence on the practice of games and sport-based physical education that persists to the present day. The limitations of the facility led to a focus on teaching and learning sports techniques rather than on playing and performing the activity in full, an approach not unlike learning the tennis serve by numbers as described earlier.

In the 1950s, however, a form of gymnastics based on the German system and practised as a competitive Olympic sport was being fully developed by male physical educators. In the photograph of the new gymnasium at Carnegie College of Physical Education, shot in the early 1960s, we can see how well this form of gymnastics was accommodated within this kind of facility. Here we can see a familiar range of gymnastic activities being practised, including pommel horse, high bar, parallel bars, vaulting and trampoline.

Gymnasium at Carnegie College of Physical Education, 1960s
Source: The Carnegie Archive, Leeds Metropolitan University Library, Headingley Campus

Comment
The design and kitting out of the 60 feet by 30 feet gymnasium was based on a particular concept of physical education and implied learning of specific activities, in a particular way, requiring a very specific physique and physical capabilities.

It was this contrast between 'Olympic' gymnastics and educational gymnastics that formed the basis of a decade and a half of conflict between the women and the men physical educators, dating from the 1950s through to the 1970s. The men argued for the development of specific gymnastics skills that required the application of new knowledge from physiology and biomechanics to develop strength and technique, and for competition. The women argued for creativity, for flexibility over strength, for cooperation rather than competition, and for the importance of the aesthetic dimensions of movement. The exchanges, both in print and face-to-face, were often heated, each camp accusing the other of exaggeration and hyperbole and both claiming to have the interests of children and their learning at heart. This dispute also spilled over to affect wider philosophies of physical education and its place and value in the school curriculum. The two cartoons of Sacred Cow and Sacred Bull were printed in *The Leaflet*, the magazine of the professional physical education association in December 1968 and January 1969. They caricature both sides of the argument.

Sacred cow and sacred bull cartoons in *The Leaflet*

Source: The Association for Physical Education, University of Worcester, *The Leaflet*, 1968 and 1969

Discontinuity and continuity: the silences of and echoes from the past?

Floorball in a primary school, sport education season, 2006

The final photo we will consider in this chapter was taken in 2006. It features boys and girls playing a game called 'floorball' – a cross between ice hockey and field hockey – in a primary school playground. Apart from the white T-shirts and coloured bibs, there is very little uniformity in the children's dress. We can see one set of goals and an orange-coloured ball close to a player with a yellow stick, who is probably a defender. At least two of the players facing the ball, probably attackers, seem poised for action, with their weight on the front foot. With the bibs and T-shirts to demarcate the teams, and with the players prepared for action, it would appear that this game is being played as a sport and so is keenly contested. Given the portable nature of the goals and the confusion of lines on the tarmac playing surface, we might also conclude that this is a general rather than a specialised playing space, which would be typical of many state primary schools in the UK and elsewhere.

Discontinuities: the silences

We can contrast this image with the photograph taken around 100 years earlier to pose questions about the ways in which physical education, for state school pupils at least, has changed. What, in historical terms, are the discontinuities with the past? At first glance there would appear to be quite dramatic differences, even improvements and progress, over this century of physical education.

On more detailed analysis, the images do indeed reveal several discontinuities between the past and the present. To begin with, it is interesting to note the activities in which the children are engaged. In 1906, it was drilling and exercising; in 2006, a team game played as a sport. The shift in physical education from gymnastic-based content to sport-based content was already in place in Britain's privileged private schools by 1906, but did not become part of the regular curriculum in the schools that served the vast majority of the population until much later, beginning in the late 1940s. Even so, sport-based physical education was for another 20 to 30 years confined to secondary schools, with primary school physical education strongly influenced by educational gymnastics (our photograph from 1951), and forms of children's chasing games such as 'Fox and Geese' that were quite unlike the sport-based games exemplified by floorball.

The subject matter of physical education in 2006 also illustrates another discontinuity with the past. When sport-based physical education first appeared in government secondary schools in the late 1940s and early 1950s, the sports on offer were very self-consciously described by physical educators as 'national sports'. These sports were shaped by the season and by cherished notions of gender-appropriateness. For boys, the 'winter games' were football and rugby. For girls in winter, hockey and lacrosse were standard, with netball often played as an indoor game. Cross-country running was a staple winter activity for both sexes, particularly when playing fields were wet. In summer, boys played cricket and girls netball and rounders, while both sexes participated in athletics and tennis. Swimming and gymnastics were also offered throughout the year to boys and girls in schools that had access to appropriate facilities, along with various forms of dancing. While this curriculum grew steadily through the 1960s and 1970s, adding 'new' games such as volleyball, badminton, squash and basketball, the sports available were relatively fixed (Whitehead and Hendry, 1976). Floorball, in contrast, is a game that we have already noted is an amalgam of ice hockey and field hockey, and has no specific gender connotations. It is just one example of the increasing willingness of teachers, particularly in primary schools, to use modified and non-traditional games and sports in physical education to enhance children's learning in physical education, an innovation that first became noticeable in the 1990s.

We can note a further discontinuity with the past in the 2006 image, which involves boys and girls playing together. As was discussed earlier in this chapter, physical education has been for most of its modern history a subject strictly divided by sex. There is, moreover, particularly in contrast to the 1906 image, a relative lack of uniformity in the children's dress. Nor is there a suggestion in the later image of a concern for the control over and disciplining of children's bodies that was so evident in the 1906 version of physical education. In addition, while we might assume that the teacher in the 2006 image is perhaps refereeing the match and so continuing to exert some direct influence over the class, the referee in this particular case was in fact another pupil, highlighting an additional discontinuity with the teacher-directed past.

Continuities: echoes from the past?

The analysis of discontinuities, of the silences between the past and the present, is however only one part of the story of physical education's history. There are also important continuities between the past and the present; echoes from the past that continue to exert an influence on practice in the present. So, for example, while the 2006 photo does signal a profound shift from gymnastics-based to sport-based physical education, it would be misleading to assume that playing sport is a common feature of sport-based physical education. That might sound like an odd statement. However, while playing a game as a sport may be typical in some contemporary physical education programmes, it is far from universal. Instead, children's common experience is practising the techniques of sports, typically of sports such as rugby, football, hockey, netball, basketball and athletics, along with non-competitive versions of swimming, gymnastics and dance. In other words, it is commonplace for physical education to take the form of practising techniques *in preparation for* playing games rather than playing the games themselves (Kirk, 2010). And while teachers rarely if ever now teach techniques such as the tennis serve 'by numbers', it is arguably only the numbers that are missing. Otherwise, it could be suggested that many practices are almost identical, particularly in the organisation of children into lines, the extensive use of command or direct teaching styles, and the resulting surveillance and control of pupils' behaviour.

When pupils do play games as sports in physical education, i.e. as a competitive contest, it is quite usual for a player to be in a different team each lesson; that is, teams are formed of different pupils each time a class meets. In the 2006 photo, and although we can not tell from the photo, these pupils are, unusually, playing in the same team for the duration of the floorball unit because they are involved in a form of physical education known as sport education (Siedentop, 1994). The child in the foreground of the photo has his number and an abbreviation of his team name on his back. This incorporation of some of the authentic elements of sport into regular physical education lessons was innovative in 2006 and remains so, even though sport-based physical education has formed the main subject matter of physical education since the 1950s in secondary schools and the 1990s in primary schools.

The 2006 photo shows boys and girls playing together. Increasingly this is the norm in primary schools and in many secondary school programmes. But co-educational physical education is far from universal in Britain. In some schools boys and girls continue to be taught in single-sex classes and to experience 'traditional', gender-differentiated programmes of activities. The move towards co-educational physical education was the general trend from the 1980s in secondary schools. Britain has nevertheless lagged behind many other economically advanced countries in this development. The comparative pedagogical value of single-sex/co-educational physical education remains a highly contested matter in the research literature (see e.g. Flintoff, 2008 and Chapter 16 in this book).

A final continuity is worth noting. The fact that both the 1906 and 2006 physical education classes are taking place on general-purpose tarmac playgrounds is highly significant. There were many more playing fields and specialised facilities available to government schools in 2006 compared with 1906. Many secondary schools, in particular, now have playing fields, indoor facilities and in some cases swimming pools on site, reflecting the shift in subject matter from gymnastics to sport. Nevertheless, some secondary schools continue to use as their main indoor facility the 60 feet by 30 feet gymnasium which, as we learned earlier in this chapter, was built and equipped with a quite different view of physical education in mind. And even though primary schools attempt to run physical education programmes that offer children a wide range of physical activities, many have to bus children off site for some core activities. They also continue to use general rather than specialised spaces for physical education, with the main indoor facility doubling as the dining and assembly halls and all-weather hard surface playgrounds for outdoor activities.

Conclusion

The seven photographs presented in this chapter provide a brief historical overview of physical education as it has been practised over the past century. The images suggest that there has been considerable change in the forms that physical education has taken during this time period. Looking at and analysing these photographs, you might conclude that they represent a century of progress, moving from possibly unpleasant and even repressive activities such as drilling and exercising to more enlightened and empowering forms of activities such as educational gymnastics and games and sports.

This is indeed one narrative that this selection of photos could support, a kind of 'victory narrative'. But, by itself, this does not tell the whole story. Just as there are discontinuities between the past and the present, so too there are strong echoes from the past. To understand how physical education in the present came to be the way it is, you need to be able to recognise these echoes, to know something about their sources, and about the intentions for physical education and children's learning contained in them. Armed with this understanding, you are more likely to be able to tell the difference between genuine innovations and yesterday's recycled failures.

Learning tasks

Individual task

Consider and write about any personal experiences of physical education that resonate with one or more aspects of this historical account. Or, alternatively, if there is nothing in this chapter that resembles your own experience, consider and write about why that might be the case.

(continued)

Group task

As a group, select one of the major forms of physical education (e.g. drilling and exercising, Swedish gymnastics, learning skills by numbers, educational gymnastics) summarised in this historical account and research it in some depth. Then develop a lesson based on that form of physical education. Teach the lesson to another group. Reflect critically on the process and analyse the learners' responses to the lesson.

Further reading

Kirk, D. (1992) *Defining Physical Education: the social construction of a school subject in postwar Britain*, London: Falmer.

References

Board of Education (1909) *Syllabus of Physical Exercises for Schools*, London: HMSO.

Board of Education (1933) *Syllabus of Physical Training for Schools*, London: HMSO.

Fletcher, S. (1984) *Women First: the female tradition in English physical education 1880–1980*, London: Althone.

Flintoff, A. (2008) Targeting Mr Average: participation, gender equity, and school sport partnerships, *Sport, Education and Society*, 13(4), 393–411.

Kirk, D. (1992) *Defining Physical Education: the social construction of a school subject in postwar Britain*, London: Falmer.

Kirk, D. (1998) *Schooling Bodies: School practice and public discourse 1880–1950*, London: Leicester University Press.

Kirk, D. (2010) *Physical Education Futures*, London: Routledge.

Laban, R. (1948) *Modern Educational Dance*, London: Macdonald and Evans.

McIntosh, P.C. (1968) *PE in England since 1800*, 2nd edn, London: Bell.

Ministry of Education (1952) *Moving and Growing*, London: HMSO.

Ministry of Education (1953) *Planning the Programme*, London: HMSO.

Munrow, A.D. (1963) *Pure and Applied Gymnastics*, 2nd edn, London: Bell.

Siedentop, D. (ed) (1994) *Sport Education: quality PE through positive sport experiences*, Champaign, IL: Human Kinetics.

Smith, W.D. (1974) *Stretching their Bodies: the history of physical education*, London: David and Charles.

Whitehead, N. and Hendry, L.B. (1976) *Teaching Physical Education in England*, London: Lepus.

Learning theory for effective learning in practice

Fiona Chambers, University College, Cork

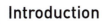

Introduction

Arnold (1979) believed that physical education is education about movement, through movement and in movement. As outlined in the opening chapter, central to sport pedagogy is the idea of how children learn. This chapter will explore 'learning' in order to investigate the ways in which our understanding of this complex topic has evolved in the past 160 years. To begin, we will consider learning a contemporary skill that will be familiar to many of us . . .

> ### Should you give your four-year-old an iPhone?
>
> When I recently upgraded my iPhone 3G to the 3Gs (after almost one year, so I got the discount) I had to decide what to do with the old one. My four-year-old son was clamoring for it, and I said OK. But then I thought about it. It's a pretty expensive, complex, breakable, adult device. Should a four-year-old really have an iPhone?
>
> My answer, after only a couple of months is – absolutely – with only a few caveats. The first is that I bought him a nice bright red safety case, so that he could find the iPhone easily, differentiate it from mine, and hopefully not break it if he dropped it (although as far as I know, that hasn't actually happened). Second, I disabled the phone function, so he can't make or receive calls. What has he used his iPhone for (almost entirely without my guidance)? His favorite thing is voice recording. He sings,

(continued)

he makes up conversations; he runs his imaginary taxi business. He records in a couple of ways. At other times he uses the recorder built into his 'Wheels on the Bus' app. iPod? He uses it often. His favorite song is Michael Jackson's 'ABC', which, somehow, he again found without me. Camera? He uses it all the time . . . Internet? He's explored, but the absence of Flash is so far the biggest disappointment, as he can't play Curious George and his other favorite games. Writing? He does lots of it, using the on-screen keyboard. And while it looks like gibberish to me, he knows exactly what it says and to whom it is addressed. Reading? We've begun to read simple words and stories together. Reading on the iPhone is great!

(Prensky, 2001, p. 1)

Questions to consider

1 How did this four-year-old learn this technology?

2 When did you learn to use a mobile phone (cell phone)?

3 Can you describe the experience?

4 Who taught you?

5 How did they teach you?

Metaphors to explain learning

Vakkayil (2008) provides a helpful overview of some of the myriad ways in which learning has been explained. As you consider each explanation, try to make links with the mobile phone example above: which one works best to explain the child's learning?

- Learning as *transfer*. Knowledge is portable stuff that can be passed around and the learner is a container.

- Learning as *corrective change*. Observable behaviours can be changed and the instructor needs to have objectives in terms of the desired end behaviours from the learner.

- Learning as *computing*. The mind is a computer that processes large quantities of data and the learning is a process of reprogramming mental structures, scripts and algorithms.

- Learning as *building connections*. The human brain is like a neural network where learning is the strengthening or weakening of pathways of neurons.

- Learning as *self-organisation*. Humans are self-organising adaptive systems that continuously produce their own components and organisation in the context of being embodied, and embedded, in a culture and history. Learning is the emergence of new knowledge based on all these contextual factors.

- Learning as *propagation*. Cultural ideas ('memes') are transmitted through humans who act as hosts and transmitters of these ideas. Humans are robots under the evolutionary influence of both genes and memes.

- Learning as *coordination*. Knowledge is distributed and doesn't reside within any individual. It is partially held by each learner, and is found in collective artefacts made through collaboration.

● Learning as *participation*. Learning is also distributed, but is found in the social interaction among individual learners. Learning is always associated with a community, and it happens through joint action.

> **Comment**
> *Learning is a complex concept. Our view of what it is influences how we believe children can (or should) learn.*

The explanations of learning listed above are rooted in learning theories, i.e. theories that help us to make sense of the learning process as it happens. Four key explanations (or theories) of learning have been influential between the late 1800s and the present day: behaviourism, cognitivism, constructivism and social theories of learning. This chapter considers these theories by looking at each under four headings:

● General overview

● How is learning theorised?

● Implications for teachers and coaches

● Key points to remember.

> **Comment**
> *Understanding the range of learning theories makes it more likely that you will understand children's learning in physical education and youth sport. Learning theories are complex and what is presented below is a simplified overview to help you to consider their implications for teaching and coaching.*

Behaviourism

General overview

The dominant theory of learning in the first half of the twentieth century was behaviourism (Harris, 2000). Behaviourism is a world view that operates on a principle of stimulus–response, i.e. the environment provides a stimulus to which the person learns to respond. In this view, all behaviour can be explained without the need to consider what is happening in a child's brain during learning. Watson (1919), the first proponent of this theory, developed the stimulus–response model. Other theorists, such as Ivan Pavlov, extended this work by studying animals' responses to conditioning. His most renowned experiment, using a dog, demonstrated this concept of conditioning.

Pavlov's dog cartoon
Source: Rich Diesslin, 2011

Unconditioned stimulus (food) = unconditioned response (salivation)

Unconditioned stimulus (food) + conditioned stimulus (bell)
= unconditioned response (salivation)

Conditioned stimulus (bell) = conditioned response (salivation)

Pavlov believed that humans could be conditioned to react to stimuli in the same way as dogs by using a reflex response (Cheetham and Chivers, 2001; Atherton, 2003a). In this way, learning was deemed to be a product or a result of the conditioning:

> Learning is defined as a change in behavior. In other words, learning is approached as an outcome – the end product of some process. It can be recognised or seen. This approach has the virtue of highlighting a crucial aspect of learning – change. Its apparent clarity may also make some sense when conducting experiments. However, it is rather a blunt instrument.
> (Smith, 1999, p. 1)

In spite of the fact that behaviourism originated in the field of psychology, it has had a much wider application. Its concepts are used in education, forming the basis of the behaviourist theory of learning.

Experiments by behaviourists identify *conditioning* as a universal learning process. There are two different types of conditioning:

- *classical*;
- behavioural or *operant* conditioning.

Each results in a different behavioural pattern. Classical conditioning occurs when a natural reflex responds to a stimulus, e.g. Pavlov's dog experiment. Essentially, in this view, animals and people are biologically designed so that a certain stimulus will produce a specific response (Cheetham and Chivers, 2001). Building on the work of Pavlov, Skinner developed the notion of behavioural or operant conditioning. This occurs when a response to a stimulus is reinforced, so operant conditioning is a simple feedback system. If a reward or reinforcement follows the response to a stimulus, then the response becomes more probable in the future (Atherton, 2003a).

How is learning theorised?

It is clear that behaviourism is a theory that centres on behaviour modification through stimulus–response and selective reinforcement. This is called 'connectionism'. Behaviourists define learning as the acquisition of new behaviour and this means that successful learning is measured in terms of changes in behaviour. This might be described as an 'outside-in' view of learning because behaviourist learning theorists focus on the role of the external environment, meaning that the behaviour of the learner person is adapted without intention – but merely in response to a stimulus. From this viewpoint, it is not necessary to consider what happens in the mind of the learner because learning is viewed as a specific behavioural outcome. As Harris (2000) notes, this view means that the mind is viewed as an impenetrable 'black box', implying that, for behaviourists, learning is mainly a passive act.

Implications for teachers and coaches

From a behaviourist perspective, it is important to build teaching and coaching around clear behavioural learning objectives; for example: 'By the end of this session, participants will be able to. . .'. This approach is linked to a concern with competencies and product approaches to the curriculum. The teacher or coach is viewed as a transmitter of important knowledge and the learner is, therefore, a relatively passive receiver of that knowledge. In this case, the teacher or coach controls the external environment (stimuli) of the classroom to reinforce desired changes in behaviour (or learning) in his or her pupils. Examples of typical pedagogical strategies linked to behaviourism include teaching in instructional steps, rote learning, learning drills, and trial and error learning towards a fixed outcome.

> ### Key points to remember about behavioural learning theories
>
> - *Activity is important.* Learning is better when the learner is engaged in activity to achieve specified outcomes ('learning by doing').
> - *Repetition, generalisation and discrimination.* Frequent practice and practice in varied contexts are necessary for learning to take place.
> - *Reinforcement is the cardinal motivator.* Positive reinforcers such as rewards and successes are preferable to negative events like punishments and failures.
> - *Learning is helped when session learning objectives are clear.* This pedagogical approach views learning as gaining a series of competencies and specified curriculum outcomes. (Hartley, 1998)

Cognitivism

Source: Getty

General overview

In 1912, Gestalt theories emerged in opposition to behaviourism. *Gestalt* is the German word for 'pattern', 'figure', 'shape' or 'form' (Atherton, 2003b). Kohler criticised behaviourism as follows:

> The stimulus – response formula . . . ignores the fact that between the stimuli *there occurs a pattern of organisation*, particularly the formation of group-units in which parts acquire new characteristics.   (Kohler, 1947, p. 164, emphasis added)

In contrast to the work of the behaviourists, cognitivists such as Piaget, Bruner, Gagne and Lewin attempted to see into the 'black box' of the human mind: 'The black box can be opened and it can become a "glass box"' (Lave and Wenger, 1991, p. 102). The founders of this Gestalt theory believed that learning was a more complex process than behaviourism suggested. They believed that it was important to take into account cognitive processing. So, whereas behaviourists focused mainly on the products of learning (the behaviour or outcome), cognitivists concentrated their theories on the processes by which people learn. So, in contrast to behaviourists who focused on the response to a stimulus, the cognitive perspective centres on 'what happens between stimulus and response' (Atkins, 1993, p. 257) and seeks to understand processes such as 'memorising, concept formation and the use of symbols and language' (Cheetham and Chivers, 2001, p. 251). Cognitivists argue that while the environment, for example, is an important input, learning is more than simply a collection of inputs leading to the production of outputs. Instead, and importantly, cognitivists recognise that the mind has the ability to synthesise, analyse, formulate and extract received information and stimuli. In other words, stimulus A may not lead to response A. Instead, something happens inside the learner's mind that can change stimulus A to something else resulting in a whole range of responses. This means that learning cannot be attributed directly to the inputs given; in other words, there is more to it.

How is learning theorised?

For cognitivists:

> The individual learner gains environmental data via the senses (sensory input). These data are processed and organised (thinking). Thereafter, the learner can act on the world (the output of thinking – activity).   (Harris, 2000, p. 2)

From a cognitive perspective, therefore, learning is largely detached from the environment or context and, instead 'is essentially learning "within the head" of the individual' (Klix, 1982, p. 388). Learning is, thus, viewed as processing and the transmission of information through communication, explanation, recombination, contrast, inference and problem solving (Wenger, 1998). In addition, learning is understood mainly as an asocial activity, which means there is little pedagogical value attached to group work (Harris, 2000). Much emphasis is placed on linking prior knowledge to new knowledge and learning at both 'surface' and 'deep' levels. Surface learning is often viewed as short-term memorising. Deep learning is more long-term learning and comes from understanding and internalising a concept. Deep learning is more 'real' in that it is connected to the person's life experiences and, as such, is less likely to be forgotten.

Implications for teachers and coaches

The cognitivist view of learning argues that the 'black box' of the mind should be opened and understood. The learner is viewed as an information processor (similar to a computer). In cognitivism, tasks are first analysed and then broken down into steps. These chunks of information are organised and then taught/coached from the most simple to the most complex, depending on the learner's prior schema or knowledge. The role of the teacher or coach is to prepare information and transmit it to learners; the learners' role is to receive, store and act upon this information (Tishman *et al.*, 1993). From this perspective, the teacher is the manager of the information-input process (as in a behaviourist approach) but the learner is understood as a more active participant in the learning process. Teaching and coaching are not, therefore, activities 'done' to learners, but instead they involve the learner by empowering their internal mental processes. Cognitivism has contributed the following ideas to education: attention theories, memory techniques (short and long term), mental imagery, language acquisition, problem solving and decision making.

> ### Key points to remember about cognitive learning theories
>
> - *Metacognition*. The mind is like a computer or information processor. Learners receive, store and act on information.
> - *Transmission model*. Teacher/coach are seen as expert and pupil/athlete are viewed as novice.
> - *Context of learning* is largely irrelevant to the learning process as learning happens within the individual.
> - *Thinking and learning are viewed as skills*, the effectiveness of which is determined by individuals' innate cognitive structures.
> - *Learning is seen as asocial.*
> - Learning is viewed as involving the development of *links between short-term and long-term memory.*

Constructivism

General overview

Constructivism describes a range of theories about learning which emphasise a person's active involvement in learning. These theories are based on the belief that learning is most effective when it is active, interactive and authentic (Newmann, 1994). Within the umbrella term, constructivism,

Source: Dorling Kindersley

there are two main branches of constructivist theory: cognitive constructivism and social constructivism.

Cognitive constructivism emerged from the work of Swiss biologist and psychologist Jean Piaget who argued that learners understand things in terms of developmental stages and learning styles. Initially, Piaget worked extensively with water snails and then moved on to studying children and how they learn! Interestingly, rather than merely observing children, Piaget engaged actively with them to discover how their minds work and mature over time, thus enabling them to develop a growing understanding of the world around them. Piaget proposed that children's thinking progresses through four developmental stages:

- sensori-motor;
- preoperational;
- concrete operations;
- formal operations.

However, the transition between each stage is not a smooth process. Instead, Piaget's theory was based on the understanding that each child has key maturation spurts where learning 'takes off' and moves into completely new areas and capabilities (Atherton, 2003b). In this way, Piaget placed an emphasis on the active role of the individual in learning. Drawing on some of the cognitive ideologies, Piaget also believed that children's minds were much more than empty vessels to be 'filled' with knowledge. Instead he argued that children actively processed the material presented to them through accommodation and assimilation (ibid.) Furthermore, he emphasised that prior knowledge played a crucial role in learning (Duncombe and Armour, 2004). Piaget summarised his approach as follows:

> Education for most people means trying to lead the child to resemble the typical adult of his society [whereas] for me education means making creators. (Palmer, 2001, p. 38)

Social constructivism, founded on the work of Vygotsky, puts emphasis on the ways in which meanings and understandings grow out of social encounters, particularly when young learners are in contact with adults or more experienced learners (Atherton, 2003b). Vygotsky developed a *social cognition* learning model. This model is built on the understanding that culture is the prime determinant of individual development (Doolittle, 1997). Culture impacts on intellectual development by teaching an individual both what to think (knowledge) and how to think (tools of intellectual adaptation). Thus, learning occurs through engaging in shared problem-solving experiences with an adult educator or peers, and responsibility for learning gradually shifts to the learner.

The mechanism for learning in social constructivism is the language of the culture (Vygotsky, 1962). Essentially, through what Vygotsky (1962) called 'dialogues', we interact and communicate with others to learn the cultural values of our society. Importantly, a difference exists between what a learner can do on his/her own and what the learner can do with help. Vygotskians call this difference the 'zone of proximal development' (ZPD). The theory of ZPD formed the foundation of social constructivist theory because Vygotsky discovered that in order to advance pupil learning, an adult or expert needed to challenge learners. Thus the ZPD is:

> The distance between the actual developmental level as determined by independent problem solving and the level of potential development as determined through problem solving under adult guidance or in collaboration with more capable peers. (Vygotsky, 1978, p. 86)

How is learning theorised?

Constructivist theory refers to the learner's ability to construct knowledge through active engagement with their environment:

> Meaningful learning relies on active engagement in planning, problem solving, communicating, and creating, rather than rote memorisation and repetition. Learning is a process by which people make sense of their environment and personal history. The acquisition of new knowledge is affected and shaped by prior knowledge, interaction with others, experience, and inherited predispositions. Our ability to learn is also influenced by logic, emotion, intuition, and motivation.
>
> (Malone, 2003, p. 61)

Constructivists contend that students actively build their own knowledge and that through this endeavour they develop critical thinking skills and problem-solving abilities (Sewell, 2002). What this means is that as the processes of thinking, perceiving and remembering (cognition) are better understood, there is a drive for curriculum delivery that embraces active learning. In essence, from a constructivist perspective, learning is most effective when characteristics such as active engagement, participation in groups, frequent interaction and feedback, and connections to real-world contexts are present (Roschelle *et al.*, 2000; Foreman *et al.*, 2004).

Implications for teachers and coaches

Constructivists actively encourage learners to construct new understandings and meanings drawing upon their prior learning and experiences. This is in contrast to other learning theories where the emphasis is on the learner passively receiving the external, 'objective' reality from an authority, i.e. a teacher or a book (Duncombe and Armour, 2004; Atherton, 2003b). What this means is that teachers and coaches must begin the learning process by understanding a learner's prior learning such that new learning can be built upon it (constructed) through active learning. In short, the teacher/coach has a responsibility for 'facilitating the development of learner agency in the process of meaning construction' (Harris, 2000, p. 5). Thus, the pedagogical focus is 'task-oriented . . . hands-on, self-directed activities oriented towards design and discovery' (Wenger, 1998) and the learning environment is likely to be active, energetic and noisy (Holt-Reynolds, 2000).

Key points to remember about constructivist learning theories

Through social learning and group work, young learners engage in:

- *Cooperative problem solving* where teacher/coach and pupil/athlete or peers work together to address a problem. Teacher/coach may employ *guided discovery* techniques to facilitate meaningful pupil/athlete learning.
- *Peer tutoring* within small groups to allow co-construction of learning.
- *Group work* where learning is both shared and negotiated by group members.
- *Situated learning* allows *experiential learning* involving active learning or 'hands-on' experience which is both contextualised and applied.
- Both teacher/coach and pupil/athlete engage in *reflective practice* which encourages *self-directed learning*.

Social theories of learning

General overview

All the theories of learning reviewed so far have, to a greater or lesser extent, emphasised the role of the individual in learning. It has been argued that such theories are based on the assumption that learning 'has a beginning and an end; that it is best separated from the rest of our activities; and that it is the result of teaching' (Wenger 1998, p. 3). Jean Lave and Etienne Wenger proposed an alternative view, i.e. that learning is social and evolves largely from our experience of participating in daily life. Their model of *situated learning* is based on the theory that learning is a process of engagement in a 'community of practice'.

Source: Pearson Education Ltd/Photodisc

Communities of practice, according to Wenger (1998) are everywhere and we are generally involved in a number of them whether at university, school, home or work; in other words, they are an integral part of our daily lives. Wenger (2006) describes how:

> Communities of practice are formed by people who engage in a process of collective learning in a shared domain of human endeavour: a tribe learning to survive, a band of artists seeking new forms of expression, a group of engineers working on similar problems, a clique of pupils defining their identity in the school, a network of surgeons exploring novel techniques, a gathering of first-time managers helping each other cope. In a nutshell: Communities of practice are groups of people who share a concern or a passion for something they do and learn how to do it better as they interact regularly.   (p. 1)

How is learning theorised?

In a community of practice, learning is a highly interactive process. Newcomers, i.e. those who have just come into the community of practice, remain initially on the fringe or periphery until they learn the practice of the community from old timers (long-term members of the community of practice). Lave and Wenger (1991) use the term *legitimate peripheral participation* to describe the position of the newcomer in these early stages; an example would be a teacher who has just qualified and then joins a school as a newly qualified member of staff. Through their initial access to the community, newcomers learn to perform new tasks and develop new understandings. It is through this process of 'enculturation', or belonging, that learning occurs. Thus, becoming knowledgeable results in the 'production of new meanings' and also the 'construction of identities'; processes which are intertwined (Lave and Wenger, 1991, p. 5).

As the newcomer learns the social practices of the community, he/she moves toward the core of the community of practice to full participation (Lave and Wenger, 1991, p. 37). Learning is also understood as a multidirectional social process with newcomers and old timers learning from each other (Lave and Wenger, 1991; Hanks, 1991). Lave and Wenger refer to the constant turnover of community of practice members as 'reproduction cycles' (Lave and Wenger, 1991, p. 98). This term describes the process whereby old timers leave and newcomers enter.

Implications for teachers and coaches

According to Etienne Wenger (2006, p. 1), three elements are crucial in distinguishing a community of practice from other groups and communities:

The domain. A community of practice is something more than a club of friends or a network of connections between people. 'It has an identity defined by a shared domain of interest. Membership therefore implies a commitment to the domain of interest, e.g. basketball coaching, and therefore a shared competence that distinguishes members from other people.'

The community. 'In pursuing their interest in their domain, members engage in joint activities and discussions, help each other, and share information. They build relationships that enable them to learn from each other.' This means that the community members share expertise.

The practice. 'Members of a community of practice are practitioners. They develop a shared repertoire of resources: experiences, stories, tools, ways of addressing recurring problems – in short a shared practice. This takes time and sustained interaction.' Therefore, the practice is developed over a long period of time during which community members interact on a continuous basis.

Taking these three elements into account suggests that teachers and coaches need to work towards developing their learning settings into communities of practice where new learners can develop shared practice with all participants; hence the notion of a 'social' theory of learning.

Key points to remember about social theories of learning

- *Socialisation.* In order to become a member of the community of practice, participants are encouraged to engage in shared norms, customs, values, traditions, social roles, symbols and languages associated with the community of practice.
- *Social roles.* The community of practice consists of experts (old timers) at the core. Novices (newcomers) are socialised by experts into the practice of the community and move toward the core as they learn the practice of the community.
- *Multidirectional learning.* This reminds us that old timers and newcomers learn from each other. Collaborative learning is, therefore, central to this theory.
- *Mentoring (apprenticeship).* Old timers (mentors) guide newcomers (mentees) in a spirit of trust and friendship.
- *Group work and teamwork.* The members of the community work together to perpetuate the language, meaning and values of the community.
- *Informal learning.* This comprises daily interactions and shared relationships among members of the community.

Table 3.1 Mapping learning theories

Paradigms	Behaviourism	Cognitivism	Constructivism	Social theories of learning
Learning theorists	Pavlov Skinner Thorndike Watson Tolman	Ausubel Bruner Gagne Koffka Lewin (Piaget)	Dewey (Piaget) Rogoff (Vygotsky)	Bandura Engestrom Eraut Lave and Wenger Salomon (Vygotsky) (Piaget)
How is learning theorised?	Change in behaviour due to environmental stimulus	Internal mental processes (mind like a computer)	Construction of subjective meaning of objective reality	Interaction with and observation of others in a social context; situated learning
Centre of learning	Stimuli in external environment Learner is passive	Internal cognitive structuring	Internal construction of reality by individual	Interaction of person's behaviour and environment
Purpose of education	Produce behavioural change in a desired direction	Develop reason, intuition and perception	Construct knowledge New knowledge linked to prior knowledge	Model new roles and behaviour

Conclusion

In 1916, Dewey argued that education should be an empowering *process* focusing on originality, independence and initiative. Nearly 100 years on, that statement still has currency. Children and young people need knowledge, skills and understandings that will enable them to function in contemporary society and, at the same time, build future (as yet largely unknowable) societies. In order to prepare young learners to learn effectively in physical education and sport, teachers and coaches need to be *learning experts*.

Learning experts are cognizant of all the available learning theories and how they might apply to – and be adapted for – different learners in different activities at different times. Learning theories are complex and overlapping, and they form the foundation of all teaching and coaching models and practitioner theories that might follow. Learning about learning is not, therefore, optional for teachers and coaches. Knowing about learning is an essential part of the professional toolkit that will help to ensure that children and young people have the best possible learning experiences in physical education and sport.

Learning tasks

Individual task

A PE teacher/coach is teaching basketball. Give an example of how the game might be taught through each of the following theoretical frameworks. Use 'journalistic'

(continued)

questions 'who, what, when, where, why and how (W, W, W, W, W and H)' to help you in each case:

(a) Behaviourism

(b) Cognitivism

(c) Constructivism

(d) Social theories of learning

Group task

In groups of three, research and develop a 10-minute PowerPoint presentation entitled: 'The history of learning in physical education and youth sport: from Aristotle to . . .'

Further reading

The website http://www.infed.org is an interesting resource which will give you a deeper understanding of this chapter and will lead you to further reading in the area.

References

Arnold, P. (1979) *Meaning in Movement, Sport and Physical Education,* London: Heinemann.

Atherton, J.S. (2003a) *Learning and Teaching: Behaviourism,* http://www.dmu.ac.uk/~jamesa/learning/behaviour.htm, accessed March 2007.

Atherton, J.S. (2003b) *Learning and Teaching: Constructivism,* http://www.dmu.ac.uk/~jamesa/learning/constructivism.htm, accessed March 2007.

Atkins, M. (1993) Rejoinder: theories of learning and multimedia applications: an overview, *Research Paper in Education: Policy and Practice,* 8, 251–71.

Cheetham, G. and Chivers, G. (2001) How professionals learn in practice: an investigation of informal learning amongst people working in professions, *Journal of European Industrial Education,* 25, 248–92.

Dewey, J. (1916) *Democracy and Education. An introduction to the philosophy of education* (1966 edn), New York: Free Press.

Doolittle, P.E. (1997) Vygotsky's zone of proximal development as a theoretical foundation for cooperation learning, *Journal on Excellence in College Teaching,* 8, 83–103.

Duncombe, R. and Armour, K.M. (2004) Collaborative professional development learning: from theory to practice, *Journal of In-service Education,* 30, 141–66.

Foreman, J., Gee, J.P., Herz, J.C., Hinrichs, R., Prensky, M. and Sawyer, B. (2004) Game-based learning: how to delight and instruct in the 21st century, *EDUCAUSE Review,* 39, 50–66.

Hanks, W.F. (1991) Foreword. In: J. Lave and E. Wenger (eds) *Situated Learning: legitimate peripheral participation,* Cambridge: Cambridge University Press.

Harris, J. (2000) Re-visioning the boundaries of learning theory in the assessment of prior experiential learning (APEL), SCRUTEA 30th annual conference, University of Nottingham.

Hartley, J. (1998) *Learning and Studying. A research perspective,* London: Routledge.

Holt-Reynolds, D. (2000) What does the teacher do? Constructivist pedagogies and prospective teachers' beliefs about the role of a teacher, *Teaching and Teacher Education,* 16, 21–32.

Klix, F. (1982) Are learning processes evolutionary invariant? An unproved assumption in psychology of learning revisited, *Zeitschrift für Psychologie,* 190, 381–91.

Kohler, W. (1947) *Gestalt Psychology: An introduction to new concepts in modern psychology*, New York: Liveright Pub. Corp.

Lave, J. and Wenger, E. (1991) *Situated Learning and Legitimate Peripheral Participation*, Cambridge: Cambridge University Press.

Malone, S.A. (2003) *Learning about Learning: An A–Z of training and development tools and techniques*, London: The Cromwell Press.

Newmann, F.M. (1994) School-wide professional community, *Issues in Restructuring Schools*, Madison, WI, Center on Organization and Restructuring of Schools, University of Wisconsin.

Palmer, J. (2001) *Fifty Modern Thinkers on Education: From Piaget to the present*, London: Routledge.

Prensky, M. (2001) Digital natives, digital immigrants, *On the Horizon (NCB University Press)*, 9.

Roschelle, J., Pea, P., Hoadley, C., Gordin, D. and Means, B. (2000) Changing how and what children learn in school with computer-based technologies, *The Future of Children*, 10(2), 76–101.

Sewell, A. (2002) Constructivism and student misconceptions: why every teacher needs to know about them, *Australian Science Teachers' Journal*, vol. 48, no. 4, 24–8.

Smith, M.K. (1999) Robert Putnam, http://www.infed.org/thinkers/putnam.htm, accessed March 2007.

Tishman, S., Jay, E. and Perkins, D. (1993) Teaching thinking dispositions: From transmission to enculturation, *Theory into Practice*, 32, 147–53.

Vakkayil, J. (2008) Learning and organizations: towards cross-metaphor conversations, *Learning Inquiry* 2, 13–27.

Vygotsky, L.S. (1962) *Thought and Language*, Cambridge, MA: MIT Press. (original work published 1934).

Vygotsky, L.S. (1978) *Mind in Society: The development of higher psychological processes*, Cambridge, MA: Harvard University Press.

Watson, J.B. (1919) *Psychology from the Standpoint of a Behaviorist*, Philadelphia: J.B. Lippincott.

Wenger, E. (1998) *Communities of Practice: Learning, meaning and identity*, Cambridge: Cambridge University Press.

Wenger, E. (2006). *Communities of Practice: A brief introduction*, http://www.ewenger.com/theory/, accessed 30 January 2010.

Learning about health through physical education and youth sport

Lorraine Cale and Jo Harris, Loughborough University

Learning about health is crucial for the youth of today. If we can believe what we hear and read in the media, then most youngsters these days are unhealthy, inactive, overweight, and certainly less healthy, active and much fatter now than when we were young. They must be storing up a whole host of health problems. The thing is there are so many more opportunities for young people growing up today to be unhealthy and sedentary, what with the internet, computer games, fast food and all that. It's only right that we take the issues seriously and educate young people about health and healthy, active lifestyles. Besides, the National Curriculum requires us to.

(Head of Physical Education in a secondary school)

 ## Introduction

The concerns and views expressed by the head of department above are typical of those of many physical education (PE) teachers today and they offer a convincing argument for teaching young people about health through PE and youth sport. At the same time, it is important to recognise that much of what is reported in the media about young people's health, activity and obesity levels is inaccurate, exaggerated and, therefore, misleading. This point is well made in the following chapter on 'Critical health pedagogy' and highlights the need to adopt a critical and cautious attitude towards contemporary health issues and messages. This is not to argue, though, that the very real health issues facing some young people can be ignored.

The contribution that PE and sport can make to the health and well-being of children and young people has attracted increased interest in recent years. With respect to PE, Shephard and Trudeau (2000) consider the key goal of the subject to be the promotion of active, healthy lifestyles, and Green (2002, p. 95) refers to the 'taken-for-granted role of PE in health promotion'. Furthermore, a number of government policies and initiatives in England over recent years have identified PE and sport as instrumental in providing opportunities for young people to improve their health. A few notable examples include *Game Plan* (Department for Culture, Media and Sport, 2002), *Every Child Matters* (Department for Education and Skills, 2004) and *Healthy Weight, Healthy Lives* (Department of Health and Department for Children, Schools and Families, 2008).

This chapter focuses on learning about health through PE and youth sport. The role that PE and youth sport play in promoting learning about health is initially explored, including consideration of the place of health within the PE curriculum in England. The latter part of the chapter then highlights some important issues relating to learning about health within both the PE and wider youth sport contexts.

First though, it is important to clarify the terms PE and youth sport. PE takes place in schools during curriculum time, is statutory for all young people, and is delivered by trained PE teachers (or other appropriately qualified school staff). Youth sport, on the other hand, is characterised by voluntary participation by young people, can take place in a variety of contexts and be delivered by a range of individuals. For example, youth sport may be delivered in schools, clubs, sports/leisure centres or youth centres by coaches, volunteers, parents, youth workers or others. Thus, whilst there is a clear distinction between PE and youth sport, as is acknowledged in Chapter 1 and will become even more evident later on, there is much common ground between the two. Both represent key contexts for young people's learning about health through physical activity and sport and share similar issues with respect to this area of learning.

The role of physical education and youth sport in promoting learning about health

The obvious contribution that PE and youth sport make to health is engagement in physical activity. Put simply, both provide opportunities for young people to be, and to acquire and develop the skills to be, physically active. It is commonly accepted that PE has the goal of educating about and through physical activity and sport, given its dual focus on 'learning to move' and 'moving to learn'. In this way, PE sets the foundation for lifelong participation in physical activity and sport (Association for Physical Education (afPE), 2008). A similar case could be made for the educational value of youth sport where coaches are interested in the holistic development of young people through sport. This educational function is important given mounting evidence of the health benefits to be gained from engagement in physical activity. Physical activity has been found to have a role in the prevention and management of overweight and obesity in young people, and there is good evidence of an association between physical activity levels and risk of type 2 diabetes and cardiovascular disease, and physical activity and bone health in children and adolescents (Stensel *et al.*, 2008). Physical activity can also enhance self-esteem and cognitive function and reduce symptoms of depression and anxiety in young people (National Institute for

Health and Clinical Excellence (NICE), 2007a; Stensel *et al.*, 2008). The above is relevant given that a sizeable proportion of young people are known to be inactive and to lead relatively sedentary lifestyles (Cale and Harris, 2005; McElroy, 2008).

There is also specific evidence to suggest that PE and youth sport can successfully contribute to the promotion of healthy lifestyles and learning about health. For example, school-based physical activity interventions, particularly those including some focus on PE, have been reported to have a positive influence on young people's health, activity and fitness levels, as well as on their knowledge, understanding and attitudes towards physical activity (Cale and Harris, 2006; Salmon *et al.*, 2007). In addition, participation in structured and community youth sport has been found to have beneficial effects on the physical activity behaviours, lifestyles and psychological well-being of young people (Brustad *et al.*, 2008; Pate *et al.*, 2000; Dzewaltowski, 2008). A further point to note regarding the contribution of PE in England is that, under the 2002 Education Act and the requirements of the National Curriculum, schools and PE have a statutory responsibility to promote learning about health to all young people. Details of the place of health within the National Curriculum in England are outlined in the following section.

Despite what has been said so far, and the sheer weight of evidence about the value of physical activity, it is also important to be realistic about what PE and youth sport can achieve in health given that they have a range of objectives and account for only a small proportion of young people's time. PE represents less than 2 per cent of a young person's waking time (Fox and Harris, 2003), at least half of which can justifiably involve only light or physically passive activity (Stratton *et al.*, 2008) and, as already noted, youth sport is voluntary and it is neither available nor inclusive to all (Brustad *et al.*, 2008; Dzewaltowski, 2008). The latest PE and Sport Survey in England revealed that an average of just 30 per cent of youngsters participate in community sports, dance and multi-skill clubs (Quick *et al.*, 2009). The need for youth sport programmes to reach more youth, become more inclusive (Brustad *et al.*, 2008), and to build skills and assets for lifelong physical activity has been acknowledged (Dzewaltowski, 2008). Given these and other reasons which are explored later, the contribution of youth sport to learning about health is inevitably more limited than PE and more variable in quality.

> ### Comment
> *PE and youth sport have an important role to play in promoting learning about health, but it is equally important to be realistic about what they can achieve.*

Finally, it is important to be realistic about the numerous factors within and beyond the school and sport settings which influence children's health and physical activity levels, and to appreciate the complexities involved in changing health behaviours (NICE, 2007b). Tinning (2010) notes that it is unrealistic to expect individuals to change their lifestyles and behaviours simply because they acquire some new knowledge, and to expect that 'knowing' will translate into 'doing' is naive (p. 181). Thus, whilst it is generally accepted that PE and youth sport, and particularly the former, have an important role to play in young people's learning about health, they clearly cannot (by themselves) meet all health and physical activity needs, nor be held responsible for improving the health and activity status of all children and young people. In short, improving health is a far more complex aspiration.

Learning about health within the PE curriculum

The association between health and PE is not new. Concerns about children's health and physical condition were instrumental in the introduction of PE into the education system in England, albeit in the form of prescribed exercises (Harris, 2010). However, by the end of the Second World War, a range of additional objectives for PE came to the fore. It was not until the 1980s that there was a return to health as a key objective of PE, as 'a solution to the problem of improving the healthy lifestyles of children' (Tinning, 2010, p. 177). In the UK, this renewed interest was expressed as 'health-related fitness' or 'health-related exercise', although other terms have also been adopted for this work. According to Harris (2010), these approaches attempted to broaden the traditional, competitive team-sport orientated programme in place at the time to include education about lifetime physical activity (i.e. activity that can readily be carried over into adulthood) and to introduce lifetime physical activities including fitness-related activities such as aerobics and circuit training.

Since the 1980s, the emphasis on and interest in health within PE have continued to flourish. The first National Curriculum for PE (NCPE) in England (1992) incorporated 'health' as a statutory component, but only as a theme to be embedded implicitly across a range of activity areas (e.g. athletics, games). This themed approach, however, was criticised for marginalising health. Within subsequent revisions of the NCPE, the health-related focus of the subject has arguably been strengthened (Fox and Harris, 2003; Cale and Harris, 2005; QCA, 2007). In terms of the coverage of health-related issues within the current secondary NCPE in England, for instance, 'healthy, active lifestyles' is a key concept and 'making informed choices about healthy, active lifestyles' and 'developing physical and mental capacity' are key processes. Furthermore, 'exercising safely and effectively to improve health and wellbeing, as in fitness and health activities' represents one of the six areas within the 'range and content' from which teachers should draw when teaching the key concepts and processes.

> *Comment*
> *The place of health within PE has been strengthened over the years. Most would consider this to be good news but do you foresee any potential challenges with this?*

Issues

The contribution that PE and youth sport can (and in the case of PE must) make to learning about health has been outlined. In theory, this may seem quite straightforward and achievable; however, in practice, there are a number of issues which make the reality quite different. A few of these have already been alluded to, but these and some other issues are now highlighted.

Time and status

Many countries around the world have witnessed a decrease in the time made available for PE in schools (Hardman and Marshall, 2005) although, exceptionally, time for the subject in England has increased in recent years (OFSTED, 2005). But, more time does not necessarily equate to increased attention to health and it would seem that this has been a problem in England. Indeed, Ofsted reports in recent years (e.g. OFSTED, 2005, 2009) have consistently criticised the PE profession for marginalising and paying insufficient attention to health, noting that this has led to weaknesses and confusion in many pupils' knowledge and understanding of the area.

In terms of the status of health, whilst PE teachers purport to value health and see this as an important objective of PE (Cale, 2000; Ward, 2009), there is evidence to suggest that their practice does not always reflect this. According to Green (2009), despite many teachers' philosophies incorporating several ideas or ideologies regarding the nature and purpose of PE, including health, the most prominent theme is that of sport, with many viewing the subject as predominantly skill-centred and games-focused. Moreover, even when teachers make claims about the importance of health, sport is still seen as the main vehicle for achieving health goals (Green, 2009).

With respect to youth sport, it seems that the health philosophy issue is exacerbated. Dzewaltowski (2008) notes that the promotion of physical activity is not a primary goal of many organised sport community settings. Rather, and according to Brustad *et al.* (2008), youth sport tends to be very much bound by tradition, focusing more on skill development and competitive strategies and outcomes, and making it less responsive to current social trends and needs such as the need to promote a physically active lifestyle.

> **Comment**
> *It is worth considering whether health should be prioritised as an objective of PE and youth sport . . . should both teachers and coaches be 'required' to contribute to learning about health?*

Focus and content

It could be regarded as a major concern that although PE and youth sport represent ideal opportunities to educate children and young people about physical activity and health, contradictory philosophies concerning their role in health promotion hinder the development of effective health policy and practice. Indeed, a study of health-related exercise policy and practice in secondary schools in England and Wales found minimal change in the expression of health in PE over an eight-year period (Leggett, 2008). This reinforces earlier research findings suggesting that whilst many PE teachers articulate and value a 'fitness for life' philosophy, their delivery is usually oriented towards 'fitness for sports performance'. Further, this is linked to sport- and fitness-related contexts that are often dominated by training and testing concepts (Harris, 1997; Leggett, 2008; Ward, 2009). Similarly, Green and Thurston (2002) have noted how an ideology of sport has penetrated deeply into the core assumptions of both PE teachers and government in relation to the promotion of health through PE.

At one level, the link between sport ideologies and health could be regarded as unproblematic, even 'natural'; the concern, however, is that a sport focus which is based on competitive sports and team games has limited appeal for many children and young people (Green, 2002; Fox and Harris, 2003). An overemphasis on 'traditional (sport-based) PE' (Fox and Harris, 2003) also results in a rather narrow curriculum with limited provision of a range of more recreational and individual lifetime activities; this may alienate some young people from the subject and possibly from physical activity participation beyond school and later in life (Stratton *et al.*, 2008).

Similarly, whilst it could be argued that a fitness orientation with an emphasis on fitness activities and fitness testing is an acceptable part of learning about physical activity for health, this approach can be narrow, limited, and unappealing for many children (Cale and Harris, 2009). For instance, such a focus may lead to undesirable practices such as forced fitness regimes, directed activity with minimal learning, or dull, uninspiring drills, which are likely to be counterproductive to the promotion of healthy, active lifestyles in young people (Cale and Harris, 2005).

The same argument has been levelled at youth sport with calls for youth and community sport to design and provide sport experiences that are effective and attractive to participants (Dzewaltowski, 2008). It is suggested that, despite adults involved in youth sport having good intentions, they do not necessarily provide an experience for children and young people that will facilitate their continued physical activity involvement. Consequently, Brustad *et al.*, (2008, p. 371) recommend that influential adults such as coaches and parents must help to establish a climate in youth sport in which lifelong health goals are valued. This would, of course, entail a corresponding de-emphasis on traditional competitive goals.

> *Comment*
> *Many activities offered, traditionally, through PE and youth sport fail to capture the interest of young people and do little to encourage their participation.*

What can be concluded at this point is that establishing a solid foundation for continued engagement in physical activity is contingent upon young people learning about health in appropriate and supportive PE and youth sport environments. This, in turn, relies on practical, caring and inclusive teaching and/or coaching strategies which recognise and place young people's diverse learning needs and interests at the core. This point is made and firmly reinforced by Kathy Armour in Chapter 1.

Perspectives on learning about health

The way in which learning about health is presented to young people is clearly critical to their experiences in and understanding of the area, and there is some debate about the most suitable approach(es) to delivering health within the school curriculum. Traditionally, learning about health has had primarily medico-scientific, biophysical and psychological foundations and has been dominated by the ideology of healthism. This ideology is grounded in the belief that individuals have control over and should be responsible for their own health, leading to a pedagogy directed towards the transmission of prescriptive 'truths' or 'facts' about how we, as individuals, should live our lives (Tinning and Glasby, 2002). From this perspective, 'not exercising' is viewed simply as a lack of motivation or just plain laziness on the part of the individual: a classic form of 'victim blaming'. It assumes individuals have the freedom to choose one set of lifestyle practices over another, and it underplays the social, cultural, emotional, economic or other factors that influence people's actions (Tinning, 2010).

More recently, and in response to critiques of the more traditional scientific and individualistic approaches, the sociocultural perspective on the delivery of health has emerged and is gaining increasing popularity. Cliff *et al.* (2009, p. 167) define this perspective as:

> a way of examining health and physical activity issues that highlights social (power relations, political and economic factors, and dominant subordinate groups) and cultural (shared ways of thinking and acting such as ideas, beliefs, values and behaviours) aspects and influences.

The sociocultural perspective, therefore, moves beyond viewing health purely as personal responsibility. Drawing on knowledge from sociology and cultural studies, this approach takes into account the social and cultural environments and circumstances in which individuals live. Working from this perspective, a teacher would ask questions about the place of physical activity in people's lives, highlighting the sociocultural circumstances (e.g. location, cost, cultural background) which could influence engagement in physical activity.

At a deeper level, the sociocultural perspective is generally understood as part of a broader student-centred, inquiry-based approach to education and learning that also encompasses problem solving and critical enquiry (Wright, 2004). This approach requires teachers to be facilitators rather than traditional 'experts', given that much of the knowledge around health can be regarded as 'grey' (Macdonald and Hunter, 2005) and is constantly shifting. For many PE teachers, however, with a predominantly scientific background and tendency to rely on 'facts', adopting such an approach can be something of a challenge. Yet health is a complex issue requiring a broad approach that draws on knowledge in a wide range of domains; essentially, there are no easy solutions to health concerns and issues linked to physical activity.

Other approaches to health education in schools that have attracted increasing interest in England in recent years are whole-school approaches such as Healthy Schools and the Active School (see, for example, Cale and Harris, 2005; Fox and Harris, 2003). Whole-school approaches consider the role of the broader school environment in promoting learning about health, thereby making it a collective responsibility for teachers, students, parents, coaches and youth leaders (Stratton *et al.*, 2008). These approaches can likewise overcome the limitations of traditional approaches, acknowledging the need to move beyond a 'restrictive, one-dimensional focus on traditional curricular physical education and sport' (Fox *et al.*, 2004, p. 344). In particular, they recognise the multiple influences within and beyond the school environment which impact on young people's physical activity; for example, the influence of peers, family, and the 'hidden curriculum' in the form of policies and other practices (Cale and Harris, 2005).

> **Comment**
> *Due to the limitations of more traditional approaches to learning about health, the sociocultural perspective and whole-school approaches are gaining support.*

Health-related knowledge and professional development

In Chapter 1, Kathy Armour introduced the three-dimensional definition of pedagogy, identifying 'teachers/teaching and coaches/coaching' as the third dimension, alongside 'knowledge in context' and 'learners and learning'. This dimension foregrounds how, to be effective, teachers and coaches need to be lifelong learners, taking responsibility for 'growing' their expertise and knowledge. It is, thus, interesting to consider the expertise of those adults in PE and youth sport who are expected to deliver health and physical activity learning outcomes. Given that schools and PE also have a statutory responsibility to deliver learning about health, it might be assumed that PE teachers at least have the knowledge, expertise and commitment to their own learning to do so effectively . . . but evidence suggests that this is not the case. A recent national survey of secondary school teachers in England revealed that health-related exercise had not been formally addressed within half of all teachers' initial teacher training, and over two-thirds of teachers had not participated in any relevant continuing professional development (CPD) in the previous three years (Ward, 2009). Similarly, evaluation of a recent national PE professional development programme found that the 'health-related modules' on offer were not selected by a high percentage of teachers (Armour and Harris, 2008).

If such findings are representative, this leads to questions concerning whether and where PE teachers are acquiring the knowledge they need to enable them to effectively deliver learning about health. The answer seems to be that, at least for the majority, they are not. Research suggests that many PE teachers have a profound lack of knowledge in this area (Miller and Housner, 1998; Castelli and Williams, 2007). Castelli and Williams (2007), for example, conducted a study which involved teachers taking a cognitive health-related fitness test (designed for 9th-grade students) and a self-efficacy questionnaire. Whilst the teachers were found to be 'over'confident about their health knowledge, with most thinking that they would pass the test, only just over a third actually did so.

This, as with other issues raised in this chapter, is of even greater concern in the context of youth sport. A much broader range of individuals contribute to the delivery of youth sport and their training is much more variable in depth and quality than that within the PE profession. Furthermore, given there is no comparable statutory 'requirement' to deliver learning about health through youth sport, it is likely that practice is often inadequate. Indeed, Brustad et al. (2008, p. 354) note that 'coaches are typically hired because of their experience with the skills, techniques and competitive strategies of the sport and not for their knowledge about or interest in promoting physical activity for youth through sport'.

> **Comment**
> *Evidence suggests there are limitations in the knowledge and professional development of those responsible for delivering learning about health through PE and youth sport.*

What is clear is that in both PE and youth sport, those charged with supporting young people to learn about physical activity and health need adequate initial and continuing professional development. It is a major concern that whereas this need has been identified with respect to PE teachers in the past (Cale, 2000; Cardon and De Bourdeaudhuij, 2002), PE teachers tend not to recognise this need for themselves. Harris (2010) has argued that this may be due to predominantly sport science backgrounds, leading PE teachers to believe that they already know enough about health. Tinning (2010) has made a similar point, suggesting that university and college courses which prepare PE teachers have tended to be dominated by a traditional scientific perspective. Yet such backgrounds offer a poor preparation for physical education and youth sport practitioners who need to be flexible, student-centred, continually updating knowledge, and able to draw confidently upon a range of health perspectives including a sociocultural perspective.

Conclusion

It is clear that PE and youth sport have an important role to play in promoting learning about health and there is undoubtedly a growing interest and sound rationale for both to do so. That said, a number of issues are constraining the potential of PE and youth sport to effectively deliver in this area, and there are concerns and/or confusion regarding teachers' philosophies/ideologies, and the focus, content and delivery of health. There are additional concerns about the limited health-related knowledge of, and professional development available to, those responsible for delivering learning about health. In Chapter 1, Kathy Armour argued that pedagogy is complex and three-dimensional, with 'knowledge in context', 'learners and learning' and 'teachers/teaching and coaches/coaching' all being key considerations in any learning context or episode. If PE teachers, coaches and others working within PE and youth sport could be encouraged and supported to focus on all three of these dimensions when promoting learning about health, they would be more likely to be successful in engaging more young people in a healthy, active lifestyle both now and in the future.

Learning tasks

Individual task

1 To date, what is your experience of learning about health through PE and youth sport? Can you recall ways in which teachers and coaches attempted to deliver health messages? Were they effective?

2 Draw upon your personal experiences, views and what you have just read to write a short narrative on 'How children and young people learn about health through PE and youth sport'. In doing so, consider the following questions:

   • What role can, should and do PE and youth sport play in promoting learning about health? Should the role be the same for both?

   • What are some of the key issues associated with learning about health through PE and youth sport, and why? Are there any other actual or potential issues?

3 Read the following article which focuses on the promotion of healthy, active lifestyles through PE in the United States: McKenzie, T. L. and Lounsbery, M. A. F. (2009) School physical education: The pill not taken, *American Journal of Lifestyle Medicine*, 3(3), 219–25. Then:

   • Compare and contrast the profile of PE (including the issues raised) presented within this article with the one in this chapter. What are the main similarities and differences?

   • Critique the authors' main arguments, views and recommendations.

(continued)

Group task

As a group of teachers, governors, coaches or parents concerned about the coverage of health within a PE or youth sport context of your choice, prepare:

- a case;

- an action plan

for further strengthening the focus on learning about health within either of these contexts. Consider the issue by focusing on all three dimensions of pedagogy.

Guidance:

- From the perspective of one of the above groups, and for either PE or youth sport, argue the case (outlining why learning about health should be strengthened) and draw up a clear action plan (indicating how it will be strengthened).

- Try to anticipate any opposition to your case and plan, from whom this might come (e.g. which groups/parties), and prepare suitable responses. The next chapter on 'Critical health pedagogy' may provide some further ideas in this respect.

- The case and plan might be presented as a written report, newspaper article, poster or oral presentation.

Further reading

A key resource providing further information on this topic is: **Cale, L. and Harris J.** (eds) (2005) *Exercise and Young People: Issues, implications and initiatives*, Hampshire: Palgrave.

References

Armour, K. M. and Harris, J. (2008) Great Expectations . . . and Much Ado About Nothing? Physical education and its role in public health in England, paper presented at the American Educational Research Association (AERA) annual conference, New York, March 2009.

Association for Physical Education (afPE) (2008) *Health Position Paper*. www.afpe.org.uk/public/downloads/Health_Paper Sept08.pdf

Brustad, R. J., Vilhjalmsson, R. and Fonseca, A. M. (2008) Organized sport and physical activity promotion. In: A. L. Smith and S. J. H. Biddle (eds) *Youth Physical Activity and Sedentary Behaviour. Challenges and Solutions*, Leeds: Human Kinetics, 351–75.

Cale, L. (2000) Physical activity promotion in schools – PE teachers' views, *European Journal of Physical Education*, 5, 158–68.

Cale, L. and Harris, J. (2005) (eds) *Exercise and Young People: Issues, implications and initiatives*, Hampshire: Palgrave.

Cale, L. and Harris, J. (2006) School-based physical activity interventions – effectiveness, trends, issues, implications and recommendations for practice, *Sport, Education and Society*, 11(4), 401–20.

Cale, L. and Harris, J. (2009) Fitness testing in physical education – a misdirected effort in promoting healthy lifestyles and physical activity?, *Physical Education and Sport Pedagogy*, 14(1), 89–108.

Cardon, G. and De Bourdeaudhuij, I. (2002) Physical education and physical activity in elementary schools in Flanders, *European Journal of Physical Education*, 7(1), 5–18.

Castelli, D. and Williams, L. (2007) Health-related fitness and physical education teachers' content knowledge, *Journal of Teaching in Physical Education*, 26(1), 3–19.

Cliff, K., Wright, J. and Clarker, D. (2009) What does a 'sociocultural perspective' mean in health and physical education? In: M. DinanThompson (ed.) *Health and Physical Education: Issues for curriculum in Australia and New Zealand*, Victoria: Oxford University Press, 165–82.

Department for Culture, Media and Sport. (2002) *Game Plan: A strategy for delivering government's sport and physical activity objectives*, London: DCMS Strategy Unit.

Department for Education and Skills. (2004) *Every Child Matters*, London: HMSO.

Department of Health and Department for Children, Schools and Families. (2008) *Healthy Weight, Healthy Lives: A cross-government strategy for England*, London: HMSO.

Dzewaltowski, D. A. (2008) Community out-of-school physical activity promotion. In: A. L. Smith and S. J. H. Biddle (eds) *Youth Physical Activity and Sedentary Behaviour: Challenges and solutions*, Leeds: Human Kinetics, 377–401.

Fox, K. and Harris, J. (2003) Promoting physical activity through schools. In: J. McKenna and C. Riddoch (eds) *Perspectives on Health and Exercise*, Basingstoke: Palgrave Macmillan, 181–201.

Fox, K., Cooper, A. and McKenna, J. (2004) The school and promotion of children's health-enhancing physical activity: perspectives from the United Kingdom, *Journal of Teaching in Physical Education*, 23, 336–55.

Green, K. (2002) Physical education, lifelong participation and the work of Ken Roberts, *Sport, Education and Society*, 7(2), 167–82.

Green, K. (2009) Exploring the everyday 'philosophies' of physical education teachers from a sociological perspective. In: R. Bailey and D. Kirk (eds) *The Routledge physical education reader*, London: Routledge Taylor & Francis, 183–206.

Green, K. and Thurston, M. (2002) Physical education and health promotion: a qualitative study of teachers' perceptions, *Health Education*, 102(3), 113–23.

Hardman, K. and Marshall, J. (2005) Physical Education in schools in European context: charter principles, promises and implementation realities. In: K. Green and K. Hardman (eds) *Physical Education: Essential issues*, London: Sage Publications, 39–64.

Harris, J. (1997) Physical education: a picture of health? The implementation of health-related exercise in the National Curriculum in secondary schools in England, unpublished Doctoral thesis, Loughborough University.

Harris, J. (2010) Health-related physical education. In: R. Bailey (ed.) *Physical Education for Learning: A guide for secondary schools*, London: Continuum.

Leggett, G. (2008) A changing picture of health: health-related exercise policy and practice in physical education curricula in secondary schools in England and Wales, unpublished Doctoral thesis, Loughborough University.

Macdonald, D. and Hunter, L. (2005) Lessons learned . . . about curriculum: five years on and half a world away, *Journal of Teaching in Physical Education*, 24, 111–26.

McElroy, M. (2008) A sociohistorical analysis of US youth physical activity and sedentary behaviour. In: A. L. Smith and S. J. H. Biddle (2008) (eds) *Youth Physical Activity and Sedentary Behaviour: Challenges and solutions*, Leeds: Human Kinetics, 59–78.

McKenzie, T. L. and Lounsbery, M. A. F. (2009). School physical education: The pill not taken, *American Journal of Lifestyle Medicine*, 3(3), 219–25.

Miller, M. G. and Housner, L. (1998) A survey of health-related physical fitness knowledge among pre-service and in-service physical educators, *Physical Educator*, 55(4), 176–86.

National Institute for Health and Clinical Excellence (NICE) (2007a) *Physical Activity and Children. Review 1: Descriptive Epidemiology*, NICE Public Health Collaborating Centre: www.nice.org.uk

National Institute for Health and Clinical Excellence (NICE) (2007b) *Physical Activity and Children. Review 3: The Views of Children on the Barriers and Facilitators to Participation in Physical Activity: A Review of Qualitative Studies*, NICE Public Health Collaborating Centre: www.nice.org.uk

OFSTED (2005) *Physical Education in Secondary Schools*, London: OFSTED.

OFSTED (2009) *Physical Education in Schools 2005/08: Working towards 2012 and beyond*, London: OFSTED.

Pate, R. R., Trost, S. G., Levin, S. and Dowda, M. (2000) Sports participation and health-related behaviours among US youth, *Archives of Pediatric and Adolescent Medicine*, 154, 904–11.

Qualifications and Curriculum Authority (QCA) (2007) *Physical Education. Programmes of Study. Key Stage 3. Key Stage 4*, www.qcda.org.uk/curriculum

Quick, S., Dalziel, D., Thornton, A. and Simon, A. (2009) *PE and Sport Survey 2008/2009; Research Report No DCSF-RR168*, London: Department for Children, Schools and Families.

Salmon, J., Booth, M. L., Phongsavan, P., Murphy, N. and Timperlo, A. (2007) Promoting physical activity participation among children and adolescents, *Epidemiological Reviews*, 29, 144–59.

Shephard, R. J. and Trudeau, F. (2000) The legacy of physical education: Influences on adult lifestyle, *Pediatric Exercise Science*, 12, 34–50.

Stensel, D., Gorely, T. and Biddle, S. (2008) Youth health outcomes. In: A. L. Smith and S. J. H Biddle (eds) *Youth Physical Activity and Sedentary Behavior: Challenges and solutions*, Leeds: Human Kinetics, 31–57.

Stratton, G., Fairclough, S. and Ridgers, N. (2008) Physical activity levels during the school day. In: A. L. Smith and S. J. H. Biddle (eds) *Youth Physical Activity and Sedentary Behaviour: Challenges and solutions*, Leeds: Human Kinetics, 321–50.

Tinning, R. (2010) Pedagogy and health-oriented physical education (HOPE). In: R. Tinning. *Pedagogy and Human Movement*, Oxon: Routledge, 169–83.

Tinning, R. and Glasby, T. (2002) Pedagogical work and the 'cult of the body'. Considering the role of HPE in the context of the 'new public health', *Sport, Education and Society*, 7(2), 109–19.

Ward, L. (2009) Physical education teachers' engagement with 'health-related exercise' and health-related continuing professional development: a healthy profile?, unpublished Doctoral thesis, Loughborough University.

Wright, J. (2004) 'Being healthy'. Critical inquiry and problem solving in physical education. In: Wright, J., Macdonald, D. and Burrows, L. (eds) *Critical Inquiry and Problem Solving in Physical Education*, London: Routledge.

Critical health pedagogy: whose body is it anyway?

John Evans and Emma Rich, Loughborough University
Brian Davies, Cardiff University

They're always going on about obese kids at school . . . the government needs to stop stressing.
(Ruth, secondary school pupil)

 ## Introduction

Do physical education and school sport contribute to 'good health'? Or, as the above pupil comment indicates, do they contribute to pressures that leave some children feeling overly anxious and upset about trying to be the right shape and weight? Certainly, physical education (PE) claims to offer health benefits and is even entitled Physical Education and Health (PEH) in some countries. Even when not so distinctively labelled (e.g. in the UK), health issues comprise core elements of PE curriculum, a match made in heaven (some might say): curriculum variants of peaches and cream. 'Health' has long been associated with the PE curriculum but in recent years has not only achieved a prominent position, but defines the very ways in which we think about and speak of teaching PE and sport in schools. However, the starting point for this chapter is to suggest that such a relationship is profoundly problematic.

Unusually, maybe unpalatably for some readers, we question the contemporary PE/health orthodoxy and ask: Are the current configurations of health in the PE curriculum and related sport initiatives good for children's well-being and health? We encourage you to think about which definitions and understandings of 'health' are being justified within PE and school sport, and why. It is worth remembering as you read that definitions of health within society are constantly shifting across time, culture and context. This fact leaves teachers and coaches with the professional responsibility to critically evaluate fads and fashions in health in the interests of the children and young people they serve.

Arblaster (1974, p. 20) argued that no matter where or how we position ourselves in education, there is one general obligation which falls upon us all:

> It is [our] business to be critical. For [us] to do no more than pass on certain skills and methods and bodies of knowledge as if these constituted some kind of sacred and unquestionable gospel, is a fundamental betrayal of the primary duty [of education] to society . . . Education serves society, not through subservience, not through propping up its dogmas, but by subjecting them to questioning and debate.

We invite you to take a critical attitude toward some of the 'gospels' that feature in contemporary discourses around 'health' by examining essential 'tropes' and instructional 'facts' that may be uncritically mediated through the *body pedagogies* of teachers, in and outside school.

> 'Body pedagogies' refer to any conscious activity taken by persons, organisations or the state designed to enhance individuals' understandings of their own and others' corporeality. Occurring over multiple sites of practice, they define the significance, value and potential of the body in time, place and space. In obesity discourse, for example, individuals' character and value and sense of self come to be judged essentially in terms of 'weight', size or shape.
> (Evans, Rich, Davies and Allwood, 2008, p. 17)

This view of pedagogy echoes that of Kathy Armour, outlined in Chapter 1 of this book. She alludes to Robin Alexander's (2008) injunction that pedagogy always 'has a purpose. It mediates learning, knowledge, culture and identity' (Alexander, 2008, p. 183). Body pedagogy is no different in this respect; it seeks to influence the value, status and worth we place on our own and others' bodies.

> **Comment**
> The concept of 'body pedagogies' not only presses us to consider who has influenced us most in thinking about our body's value, status and worth, but also where such influences originate and occur in our daily lives.

Why has 'health' become such an important topic?

Fat kills!

Across Western and Westernised countries, there are constant claims that populations are 'too fat', 'overweight' or 'obese' and that remedial measures ought to be taken. Countless stories have appeared in the popular and 'quality' press and TV and film (see Evans, Rich, Davies and Allwood, 2008; Rich and Miah, 2009) whose intent seems to be to inform, scare and evoke private and public action.

> Campaign to tackle the perils of obesity . . . Weighty Britain . . . It's a national epidemic and we have to do something about it before it's too late   (*Daily Mirror*, 29 August 2006)

> Obesity is deadlier than smoking and can knock 13 years off your life
> (*Daily Mail*, 17 October 2007)

14 st. size 18 . . . aged 9   (*Sun*, 28 February 2006)

War on Obesity. Docs Fight New Black Death   (*Daily Mirror*, 2004)

The 'New Black Death' heralded a 'terrifying increase in the number of children with type 2 diabetes', 'early death, heart disease, breast cancer, diabetes, colorectal cancer' (the list goes on) in language as certain as it is loaded with emotion. 'The whole environment is conspiring against people. One high-profile obesity report (Foresight, 2007) claimed "we are putting on weight even when we don't want to, because the forces ranged against us being slim are so powerful" (*Guardian Unlimited*, 2007: 2).

Even though such claims are later shown to be widely exaggerated (http://news.bbc.co.uk/cbbcnews/hi/newsid_8330000/newsid_8339300/8339390.stm) they tend to enter popular discourse as matters of fact. Furthermore, schools, teachers and youth sport coaches are claimed to be ideally positioned to redress them through improved catering and increased time spent on health education, fitness testing, exercise and sport. While such messages, repeated uncritically in the media, are prevalent worldwide, their subtexts in the UK that 'fat equals working class failure, thin equals virtue and middle class success' (see Evans, Davies and Rich, 2008) are particularly insidious and blatant. The message seems clear and indisputable. In the grip of a global 'obesity epidemic' (World Health Organization, 1998), it is supposed that we face serious health problems and certain decline unless measures are taken officially, institutionally and, most critically, individually. Thus we are exhorted to choose to eat less and better, and exercise more to lose weight, instead of choosing to get fat, become ill and die young. New health curricula, fitness regimes and mechanisms to monitor the weight and health of children (see Rich *et al.*, 2010; Evans and Colls, 2010) have been introduced in abundance in schools in the hope of ensuring that pupils learn the benefits of healthy lifestyles, take enough exercise, eat better food and work harder at losing weight and becoming thin. It is difficult to argue against these 'truths' which appear to have become largely self-evident . . . Or is it?

Look at the facts – the evidence base

Statistics based on body mass index (BMI) measurements of height and weight may well be indicative of important changes where increasing longevity is taken as its measure. But such measures are often overgeneralised, indiscriminate and potentially misleading. Account is rarely taken of confounding factors or problems associated with the use of BMI as a measure (see Evans, 2003; Gard and Wright, 2005; Campos *et al.*, 2006). Notwithstanding such fault lines, BMI (see table below) has become a central tool in defining ourselves and others as corporeally inadequate or potentially ill. Note how this BMI chart medicalises 'weight', advocating 'treatment' for all but 'normal' weight conditions.

BMI (classification)		
18.5 or less	Underweight	Treatment
18.5 to 24.99	Normal weight	No treatment
25 to 29.99	Overweight	Treatment
30 to 34.99	Obesity (Class 1)	Treatment
35 to 39.99	Obesity (Class 2)	Treatment
40 or greater	Morbid obesity	Treatment

Source: http://www.bmi-calculator.net/ (accessed 27/1/2010)

The spectre of obesity has, as a consequence, become the source of a global, multibillion-pound industry of published diets, fat clubs, exercise centres, gyms, TV programmes, health foods/vitamins and slimming magazines (see Monaghan, 2007). A cynic might argue that Western economies would be poorer indeed if diet or exercise plans were discovered that actually made and kept populations thin. Aphramor (2005) goes so far as to question whether it is even ethical to focus on weight loss given the staggering failure rates of such programmes.

Should those engaged in teaching and coaching reject, accept or indeed base teaching, coaching and health initiatives upon received wisdom about obesity? Hardman and Stensel (2009) provide an excellent critical overview of obesity literature and many others have critically scrutinised the adequacy and 'certainties' of research knowledge concerning 'weight' (Aphramor, 2005; Campos, 2004; Campos *et al.*, 2006; Gaesser, 2002; Gard and Wright, 2005; Monaghan, 2005; Warin *et al.*, 2007). Gard and Wright (2005, p. 1), for example, claim that contemporary obesity science and popular commentary are:

> a complex mix of highly uncertain knowledge, familiar moral agendas and ideological assumptions, and that it is both unhelpful and unwise to talk about 'modern Western lifestyles' as if everyone had lived in the same way.

These authors challenge the claims that physical activity levels are declining, food consumption is rising and television and computers are making children fat. Indeed, Gard (2010) argues convincingly that contrary to received wisdom, a global health crisis has not materialised and evidence now suggests that obesity rates are levelling off in Western societies while life expectancy continues to rise in many non-Western ones. Good science rarely makes claims to certainties, and Gard reminds us that the science concerning 'obesity is inevitably, and will remain, uncertain' and that uncertain knowledge is not necessarily 'bad knowledge'. Even when teachers are asked to make their practices 'evidence based', it is important to remember that philosophical and political contingencies inevitably come into play. Thus, 'obesity facts' may serve purposes other than nurturing 'health', including helping teachers and sports coaches, as it has done historically, to secure valuable resources in the face of competing claims in schools.

Why are fat facts potentially so dangerous?

Even disputed fat facts are important when we consider how their expression in health policy and school curricula can impact young people's body images and developing sense of self. Like Beckett (2004), Burrows and Wright (2004), Halse *et al.* (2008) and Wright and Harwood (2009), our research suggests that there is a need to examine how 'fat facts' in contemporary health discourse are 'recontextualised' (de-located, relocated and refocused) in schools as 'body-centred talk', and how they then impact upon the health and embodied subjectivities of young people. How do particular narratives around health and obesity come to be recognised as 'truths' or conventional wisdom that can influence the ways in which children and young people perceive themselves and are perceived by others, both in and out of school?

Fat orthodoxy

Incessant health messages relating to obesity contribute to what some theorists have described as the '*medicalisation*' of our daily lives. As part of this process, 'normal anxieties' in relation to food, relationships, exercise and work are reinterpreted as medical ones. What this means is that human experience invariably comes with a health warning and a medical explanation; 'being potentially unwell' is 'the default state we live in today' (Furedi, 2007, p. 2). Illness has, therefore, become part of our identity, so much so that it is now 'as normal as health (and wellness)', and 'if we don't buy into this discourse then we revert to "being ill"' (ibid.). Not wanting to achieve or engage with a range of inherently 'good things', like being thin and regularly partaking of sanctioned exercise, leads to the risk of being labelled aberrant, deviant or subversive. For some, this leads to the charge of being irresponsible citizens who let us all down at great cost to personal and public health. Hardly surprising to find then, in the research that we and others have conducted (e.g. Evans, Rich, Davies and Allwood, 2008; Wright and Harwood, 2009; Evans, Davies, Rich and De-Pian, in press) that children seemed to live in fear of the possibility of being defined as 'overweight' or 'fat' by their peers or teachers at school.

Fat reductions

The use of BMI as a measurement tool reduces 'health' to indices of measurable size and weight with numerical value (a BMI score; see table above) (see Evans and Colls, 2010; Rich *et al.*, 2010). Weight and height are thus to be acknowledged by teachers, coaches, pupils and parents as primary indices of the 'health' of young persons, thus becoming the grammar and syntax of health and PE in schools. Other, more holistic, views of health are removed to the margins of popular discourse. The result is an education system that endorses behaviours such as weighing children, putting them in fat camps and persuading them to adhere to strict diet regimes. These behaviours amount to a sanctioning of excessive exercise and weight loss which is potentially deeply damaging to some young people's health. As one of the girls in our study (see Evans *et al.*, 2008, p. 75) commented:

> We used to have to get weighed in the class and that was terrible . . . because then everyone knew your weight and then . . . a lot of the lads actually used to go . . . and . . . you know . . . shouting out your weight in the class . . . things like that . . . that was terrible . . . really terrible. (Rebekah)

For those of us who would claim to have an interest in the welfare of children and young people, the questions to be considered here, then, are not 'What's wrong with obesity discourse?' but 'How did behaviour that is potentially so dangerous come to be considered so morally, politically and educationally correct?' and 'Should physical education and youth sport be aligned with such practices?'

Allocating blame: good food, bad food – good citizens, bad citizens!

The discursive tendencies outlined thus far are a concern because official and popular reports around obesity, such as *Super Size Me* (see Rich and Miah, 2009) reveal implicit *moral* as well as *medical* overtones concerning the 'right' amount of exercise, the 'right' diet and the 'correct' body shape. It is unsurprising, then, to find that alongside the obesity discourse, levels of 'body disaffection' and eating disorders, such as anorexia nervosa and bulimia, especially among women and young girls, are higher than ever, and not just in the UK (Grogan, 1999; http://www.disordered-eating.co.uk/eating-disorders-statistics/eating-disorders-statistics.html). Increasingly, boys are also falling foul of disordered eating.

In the prevailing blame-the-victim culture, the terms *obesity* and *overweight* have become 'the biomedical gloss for the moral failings of gluttony and sloth' (Ritenbaugh, 1982, p. 352). In this view, fat is interpreted as an outward sign of neglect of one's corporeal self; a shameful, dirty or irresponsibly ill condition, in effect reproducing and institutionalising moral beliefs about the body and citizens. Fear, anxiety, guilt, and regulation underpin obesity panics, resulting in obsessive attention to 'self-control' through diet, exercise and even more extreme measures to achieve contemporary, slim ideals (Gordon, 2000, 2001). The uncertainties and contradictions generated can be deeply unsettling. Importantly, these uncertainties can have a profound effect on the identities of children and young people with damaging affective and emotional consequences for some as they attempt to live the experience of unattainable, corporeal ideals. Here again the question to be asked is: to what extent should physical education and youth sport practitioners wish to align themselves with such discourses?

Voices: don't blame the victim

Clearly the issues raised in this chapter should matter for teachers, coaches and health workers because young people increasingly construct their corporealities (see Evans, Rich, Davies and Allwood, 2008) and health/illness through the language of dominant health discourses. They get to know about their bodies and health not only through the language of official 'experts', such as health educators and teachers in schools, but also from 'unofficial' media 'experts' (e.g. the popular TV chef, Jamie Oliver) and informal interaction with peers and friends. Young people in our research in a variety of schools have tended to speak with a single voice about the ways in which their schools transmit 'body perfection codes' (see Evans and Davies, 2005). Such codes define 'acceptable' body size, shape and demeanour and generate widespread body disaffection and dissatisfaction. For example, some young women commented that they had lost weight in order to receive greater recognition from their PE teachers. It was suggested that these teachers equated 'thin' not just with being 'healthy' but as an indication of commitment both to the subject of PE and the aim of losing weight:

> In PE they used to tell us not to be lazy and call people lazy if they thought they weren't trying hard enough at what we were doing.
>
> (Claire, interview; Evans, Rich, Davies and Allwood, 2008, p. 85)

Similarly, another young woman, Mia, was encouraged by her swimming coach to lose weight so that she 'would move faster through the water'. She reported that problems over meeting competition requirements had led her to change schools and that she was among the best swimmers in her new team. This achievement coincided with reaching her lowest body weight, so she had been able to meet simultaneously the symbiotic expectations of 'academic performance' and body perfection codes.

During focus group discussions, interviews and in diary and poster presentations, several other young women reported pressure not only in curriculum subjects such as PE, health and personal and social education, but a wider surveillance of their corporeal propriety through social relationships in corridors, at play times, during lunch breaks and interactions with peers in and out of school. Their experiences were 'totally pedagogised' (Bernstein, 2001), i.e. health messages were inescapable and everywhere:

Tracy: The pressure to look perfect took over your study work . . . everyone used to look at you . . . you wouldn't go to school if you had a spot.

Vicky: Yeah, but some girls when I was like at my lowest weight . . . one girl said to me 'You look really good'.

Kate: All my friends said to me 'Oh God, you've lost so much weight, you look well good!' and 'You look fantastic'. . . and I was like 'Yeah, thanks . . . I know!' . . . cos I thought I looked good . . .

Lara: You get a lot of like 'Oh, you've lost weight' and then you feel like you can't put it back on cos they'll like notice it . . . d'ya know what I mean?

(focus group; Evans et al., 2008, op. cit., pp. 86–7)

Lunchtimes were particularly virulent environments, with girls assiduously surveying their own and others' behaviour. As Tracy explained:

Everyone at school's got like food issues . . . all the girls are always looking for like what's got the least fat and that . . . and people will comment on each other like if someone has two chocolate bars someone will say like 'Oh, haven't you had one already? and stuff

Others concurred with Tracy's view during focus group discussion:

Ra (researcher): Anything at school that you felt influenced you?

Anne: Yeah . . . people not really eating properly, which made me think 'Hold on . . . what am I doing . . . I'm eating so much more than them.'

Vicky: I was like that too! [Most people in the group agree.] . . . Yeah . . . some other people weren't eating anything . . .

Kate: Yeah.

Vicky: Not many people were eating like a proper lunch so there was no way I was going to. [. . .]

Kate: At my school . . . all the girls have like a tiny, tiny little bread roll when there's like a big variety of stuff and they just go and get one tiny little bread roll . . . it's like that big (indicating with her hand) . . . little bread roll and that's it . . . or nothing.

Ra: Did many people feel like that then . . . that people weren't eating a proper lunch?

Lara: I did but . . .

Vicky: My friends didn't eat their lunch at school, though . . .

Lara: I started like not eating and then like everyone else did too . . . well, not like everyone else but a lot of people did and that made me feel like I couldn't start eating it again . . . cos like . . . when I was like trying to get better and that . . . no one else ate it then . . . so I didn't wanna be the only one starting eating it again.

These young women drew on the 'moral' authority of governmental and health agency expertise, advice and information referring to 'healthy eating' in order to rationalise and guide their own 'radical' actions toward food that were ultimately to make them ill. Soon, for some of these young people, the only diet worth following was to have no diet at all.

Peer pressure

While not all young people are as disturbed by health messages prevailing in schools, none can avoid them and these young people were engaged not just in pursuit of 'health' but also status and value in the eyes of peers, teachers and friends. They seemed to know that achieving the correct size and shape took time but could provide markers of distinction as to how disciplined and 'good' they had become. For many of the girls and boys in our research, magazines, TV and, sometimes, family life provided further endorsement of their health knowledge and behaviour. Well-intentioned parents reconstituted 'appropriate' public discourse concerning the 'right' attitudes toward weight, diet and food, sometimes with dire health consequences, as related by Kate, Vicky and Claire:

Kate: OK . . . well . . . before . . . when I was happy with how I looked . . . I wasn't over-weight or anything . . . I was like happy . . . and then like my dad said to like . . . he was gonna take me, my brother and my two sisters on holiday and he said . . . he told us to all lose weight for the holiday so we'd look good in our swimwear . . . so me and my little sister we made a diet thing . . . we had to stick to that we had to eat . . . like it was no chocolate or anything . . . and then I just took it too far cos like . . . my dad said . . . 'You could do with losing a bit of weight' . . . and then like . . . when I went to school like . . . and I'm used to things like . . . when I went before all my friends were like skinny and I'm not . . . I never used to think that at all.

Vicky: Neither did I . . .

Kate: And then I just started thinking that and looking . . . and then I wouldn't be able to walk past a window or a mirror without looking in it and thinking 'Oh, my God' . . . so that's really all my dad's fault.

Claire: Ermmm . . . well . . . my mum used to go to Weight Watchers and then like she always said what was healthy and I used to read loads of magazines and on the telly it was like 'Eat lots of fruit and vegetables, eat five portions a day.'

Ra: Yeah

Claire: . . . and then . . . I knew that like chips and burgers were fatty and crisps and chocolate and so anything . . . I think anything that you like is like . . . bad and things that are like boring are good. (Evans *et al.*, 2008)

For these girls, their changing bodies were inescapably subjected both to their own and others' evaluative gaze: at home, at leisure and amid the pressures of totally pedagogised schools.

When I started secondary school I'd like . . . I'd started sort of . . . puberty quite early I'd say cos ermmmmm . . . I started getting acne and stuff . . . Nobody had really mentioned anything about it before at primary school but when I went to secondary school . . . a couple of the lads started picking on me. (Amanda)

I had started to develop much quicker than everyone else and I was interested in lads. All the girls turned against me and started calling me a slag and I felt like I had to live up to it. (Lara)

Avoiding being 'othered' can be a permanent battle during adolescence, i.e. avoiding being made to feel different, less worthy and excluded. For some young people, not eating or engaging in excessive physical activity in order to achieve the distinction of being 'thin' can become a perfectly rational, morally acceptable goal.

It is of course important to remember that many people are dissatisfied with their bodies and most do not become ill as a result, just as not everyone who is dangerously thin has become so because of the influence of popular media's affection for slender body ideals. Corporeal dissatisfaction is a normative condition in all societies and at all times and places, and so must be distinguished from disorder that may damage people's health. However, the voices of the young people in our research lament being/feeling 'invisible', 'ignored' and powerless in a performative school culture. They seem to feel impotent to change their circumstances and they talk of being constantly on display, monitored, assessed, compared, judged and overwhelmed by constant pressures to be successful in meeting the expectations of parents and schools. Sadly, their accounts reveal impoverished relationships with their bodies. Nowhere in these accounts is there evidence of the pleasure of food, or the joy of movement and expression which, historically, was one of the goals of physical education and youth sport.

Conclusion

A critical view of health raises questions about whether the contemporary expression of health in physical education and youth sport is appropriate for children and young people. Is it possible to achieve a form of pedagogy 'with a central focus on redefining success away from the current focus on weight loss, and towards promoting a healthy lifestyle, long-term amelioration of medical problems and improved quality of life' (O'Dea, 2005, p. 263)? In this chapter we have sought to highlight the potential implications for the curriculum, pedagogies, identities and well-being of children when we support uncritical attitudes towards the 'modern' discourse of ill health. It could be argued that teachers and coaches have a professional responsibility to recognise the uncertainties and contradictions that abound in the primary research databases that inform health discourses (Gard, 2004). In our view, the culture of risk and fear being nurtured in society by obesity reports and attendant policies and pedagogies have created new 'hierarchies of the body' that potentially damage the identities of children and young people in society, in schools and in sport.

Learning tasks

Individual task: my body, my self

1 Think back to your experiences as a young learner in physical education and youth sport. Were physical education/school sport justified with reference to 'health' issues? Can you recall ways in which your teachers or coaches have influenced the way in which you think about your own and others' bodies, especially their value and potential for involvement in physical activity and sport? Write a 500-word narrative explaining how teachers or coaches have negatively and/or positively influenced your thinking about your body.

2 Undertake a critical review of your narrative. Can you draw any tentative conclusions about 'effective' teaching and coaching – i.e. pedagogies that are least likely to damage children's health?

(continued)

3 What would a health-promoting pedagogy in physical education and school sport look like?

Group task: the bigger picture

This activity can be done in pairs or larger groups. Share the key outcomes from the individual learning task and create a group (draft) poster that maps clearly your findings about effective and ineffective teachers/coaches in the context of health. In this case 'effective' means pedagogies that leave children feeling good, positive and confident about their bodies.

1 Conduct a literature search to find at least two policy documents dealing with (or alluding to) 'the obesity crisis' (e.g. in the UK, go to websites on *Every Child Matters* or *Healthy Schools*).

2 Compare the statements in the literature search with the findings from your analysis of your personal narratives. Is policy for physical education and school sport sensitive to the issues raised in this chapter and in your personal narratives?

3 Finalise your poster so that it becomes an accurate representation of your views on this subject

Further reading

- To see how other countries are dealing with some of the issues raised in this paper, dip into any of the chapters in: **Dinan Thomson, M.** (2009) *Health and Physical Education. Issues for curriculum in Australia and New Zealand*, Oxford: Oxford University Press.

- For a reminder that race and ethnicity, as well as social class and gender, matter in any discussion of weight, 'fat', physical education and school sport, read: **Azzarito, L.** (2009) The rise of the corporate curriculum: fitness, fatness and whiteness. In: **J. Wright and V. Harwood** (eds) *Biopolitics and the 'Obesity Epidemic'*, London: Routledge, 183–99.

- Consider how (or if at all) issues of ethnicity are reflected in the teaching of physical education and school sport in relation to weight and health concerns.

References

Aphramor, L. (2005) Is a weight-centred health framework salutogenic? Some thoughts on unhinging certain dietary ideologies, *Social Theory and Health*, 3:315–40.

Arblaster, A. (1974) *Academic Freedom*, Harmondsworth: Penguin Books.

Ball, S. (2004) Performativities and fabrications in the education economy: towards the performative society. In: S.J. Ball (ed.) *The RoutledgeFalmer Reader in Sociology of Education*, London: RoutledgeFalmer.

Ball, S. (2006) *Education Policy, CeCEPS Launch Education Policy*, Institute of Education, London, 1 March 2006.

Beckett, L. (2004) Special issue: health, the body, and identity work in health and physical education, *Sport, Education and Society*, 9, (2): 171–5.

Bernstein, B. (2001) From pedagogies to knowledge. In: A. Morias, I. Neves, B. Davies and H. Daniels (eds) *Towards Sociology of Pedagogy: The contributions of Basil Bernstein to research*, New York: Peter Lang.

Bourdieu, P. (1986) The forms of capital. In: J. Richardson (ed.) *Handbook of Theory and Research for the Sociology of Education*, New York: Greenwood Press.

Burrows, L. and Wright, J. (2004) The discursive production of childhood, identity and health. In: J. Evans, B. Davies and J. Wright (eds) *Body Knowledge and Control*, London: Routledge.

Campos, P. (2004) *The Obesity Myth*, New York: Gotham Books.

Campos, P., Saguy, A., Ernberger, P., Oliver, E. and Gaesser, G. (2006) The epidemiology of overweight and obesity: public health crisis or moral panic?, *International Journal of Epidemiology*, 35 (1): 55–60.

Cogan, J. (1999) Re-evaluating the weight-centred approach toward health: The need for a paradigm shift. In: J. Sobal and D. Maurer (eds) *Interpreting Weight: The social management of fatness and thinness*, New York: Aldine De Gruyter.

Department of Health (2005) *National Healthy School Status*, London: DH Publications Orderline.

Evans, B. (2006) 'Gluttony or Sloth?': critical geographies of bodies and morality in (anti)obesity policy', *Area*, vol 38, 3, pp. 259–67.

Evans, B. and Colls, R. (2010) Doing more good than harm? The absent presence of children's bodies in (anti)obesity policy. In: Rich, E., Monaghan, L. and Aphramor, L. (eds) *Debating Obesity: Critical perspectives*, Basingstoke, UK: Palgrave Macmillan.

Evans, J. (2003) Physical education and health: a polemic, or, let them eat cake!, *European Physical Education Review*, 9: 87–103.

Evans, J. and Davies, B. (2005) Endnote: The embodiment of consciousness. In: Evans, J., Davies, B. and Wright, J. (eds) *Body Knowledge and Control. Studies in the sociology of physical education and health*, London: Routledge.

Evans, J., Davies, B. and Rich, E. (2008) The class and cultural functions of obesity discourse: our latter-day child-saving movement, *International Studies in Sociology of Education*, 182, 117–33.

Evans, J, Davies, B., Rich, E. and De-Pian, L. (in press) Health imperatives, policy and the corporeal device: schools, subjectivity and children's health, in special edition 'Contemporary school health policies, practices and pedagogies', *Policy Futures in Education*.

Evans, J., Rich, E. and Allwood, R. (2005) Disordered eating and disordered schooling: what schools do to middle class girls, *British Journal of Sociology of Education*, 22, 2, 123–43.

Evans, J., Rich, E., Davies, B. and Allwood, R. (2008) *Education, Disordered Eating and Obesity Discourse*, London: Routledge.

Fitz, J., Davies, B. and Evans, J. (2006) *Educational Policy and Social Reproduction*, London: Routledge.

Foresight (2007) *Tackling Obesities: Future Choices Project Report*, London: Government Office for Science.

Furedi, F. (2007) *Our unhealthy obsession with sickness*, http://www.spiked-online.com/Articles/0000000CA958.htm, accessed 19 March 2007.

Gaesser, G. A. (2002) *Big Fat Lies*, Stanford: Gurz Books.

Gard, M. (2004) Desperately seeking certainty: Statistics, physical activity and critical enquiry. In: J. Wright, D. Macdonald and L. Burrows (eds) *Critical Inquiry and Problem Solving in Physical Education*, London: Routledge.

Gard, M. (2010) *The End of the Obesity Epidemic*, London: Routledge (forthcoming).

Gard, M. and Wright, J. (2005) *The Obesity Epidemic: Science morality and ideology*, London: Routledge.

Gordon, R. A. (2000) *Eating Disorders: Anatomy of an epidemic*, Oxford: Blackwell.

Gordon, R. A. (2001) Eating disorders East and West: a culture-bound syndrome unbound. In: A. Nasser, M. N. Katzman and R. A. Gordon (eds) *Eating Disorders and Culture in Transition*, East Sussex: Brunner-Routledge.

Grogan, S. (1999) *Body Image: Understanding body dissatisfaction in men, women and children*, London: Routledge.

Guardian Unlimited (2007) Obesity crisis to cost £45bn a year, http://observer.guardian.co.uk/uk_news/stoty/0,,2190844,00.html, accessed 17 October 2007.

Halse, C., Honey, A. and Boughtwood, D. (2008) *Inside Anorexia: The experience of girls and their families,* London: Jessica Kingsley Publishers.

Hardman, A. E. and Stensel, D. J. (2009) *Physical Activity and Health: The evidence explained* (2nd edn), London: Routledge Taylor and Francis Group.

Independent Inquiry into Inequalities in Health Report http://www.archive.official-documents.co.uk/documents/doh/ih/part/ih/part1b.htm, accessed 2 February 2006.

Johns, D. P. (2005) Recontextualising and delivering the biomedical model as a physical education curriculum, *Sport, Education and Society*, 11, 1: 69–84.

Miah, A. and Rich, E. (2008) *The Medicalization of Cyberspace*, London and New York: Routledge.

Monaghan, L. F. (2005) Discussion piece: a critical take on the obesity debate, *Social Theory & Health* 3 (4): 302–14.

Monaghan, L. (2007) McDonaldizing men's bodies? Slimming, associated (ir)rationalities and resistances, *Body & Society*, 13(2): 67–93.

O'Dea, J. A. (2005) School-based health education strategies for the improvement of body image and prevention of eating problems: an overview of safe and effective interventions, *Health Education*, 105 (1): 11–33.

Oliver, J. E. (2006) *Fat Politics. The real story behind America's obesity epidemic*, Oxford: Oxford University Press.

Orbach, S (2006) *Fat is a Feminist Issue*, London: Hamlyn.

Rich, E. and Evans, J. (2009) Now I am NO-body, see me for who I am: The paradox of performativity, *Gender and Education*, 21(1), 1–16.

Rich, E. and Miah, A. (2009) Prosthetic surveillance: the medical governance of healthy bodies in cyberspace, *Surveillance and Society*, 20, February.

Rich, E., Evans, J. and De-Pian, L. (2010) Surveillance and the obesity crisis. In: Rich, E., Monaghan, L. and Aphramor, L. (eds) *Debating Obesity: Critical perspectives*, Basingstoke, UK: Palgrave Macmillan.

Ritenbaugh, C. (1982) Obesity as a culture-bound syndrome, *Culture, Medicine and Psychiatry*, 6: 348–61.

Shilling, C. (2005) Body pedagogics. A programme and paradigm for research, paper presented to the School of Sport and Exercise Sciences, University of Loughborough.

Shilling, C. (2007) *Embodying Sociology: Retrospect, progress and prospects*, London: Blackwell.

Teachernet (2006) National Healthy Schools Standard (NHSS) http://www.teachernet.gov.uk/management/atoz/n/nhss/index.cfm?code+main, accessed 16 May 2006.

The Sunday Times (2003) Fit or fat: The new class war, 8 June.

Warin, M., Turner, K., Moore, V. and Davies, M. (2007) Bodies, mothers and identities: rethinking obesity and the BMI, *Sociology of Health & Illness*, 30, (1), 37–111.

World Health Organization (1998) *Obesity: Preventing and managing the global epidemic*, Report of a WHO consultation on obesity, Geneva: WHO.

Wright, J. and Harwood, V. (eds) (2009) *Biopolitics and the 'Obesity Epidemic'*, London: Routledge.

Youth sport policy: an international perspective

Iain Lindsey, Edge Hill University and Ruth Jeanes, Monash University

The practice of sport is vital to the holistic development of young people, fostering their physical and emotional health and building valuable social connections. It offers opportunities for play and self-expression, beneficial especially for those young people with few other opportunities in their lives. Sport also provides healthy alternatives to harmful actions, such as drug abuse and involvement in crime. Within schools, physical education is an essential component of quality education. Not only do physical education programmes promote physical activity; there is evidence that such programmes correlate to improved academic performance.

(United Nations, 2003, p. v)

 ## Introduction

The quote above, from the United Nations report on sport for development and peace, highlights both the aspirations commonly associated with youth sport policies and also some of the more problematic issues associated with such policies. Across the world, youth sport has become an increasingly important policy priority not only because of its supposed benefits but also due to heightened concern about issues that affect young people. However, the extent to which the ambitious aspirations expressed in youth sport policies are realistic and can be universally delivered is open to question.

This chapter begins to explore some of these issues. Through case studies of three different countries, England, Australia and Zambia, the chapter will offer a comparative perspective on issues surrounding the development and delivery of youth sport policy. A comparative analysis is helpful in illuminating key contextual features of youth sport policies as well as highlighting shared challenges for those individuals and organisations expected to enact them. Looking beyond familiar contexts can help teachers and coaches to see old problems in new ways, so as you read this chapter it will be helpful to draw comparisons with your personal experiences of physical education and youth sport.

In order to be coherent, a comparative analysis of youth sport policy requires the adoption of a common conceptual framework. The conceptual framework that structures each of the following case studies is adapted from the political system model proposed by David Easton (1965) (see Figure 6.1). Thus each of the following case studies will consider:

- the *environment* and *inputs* which influence youth sport policies;
- the *content* and *delivery* of youth sport policies;
- the *outputs* and *outcomes* that result from youth sport policies.

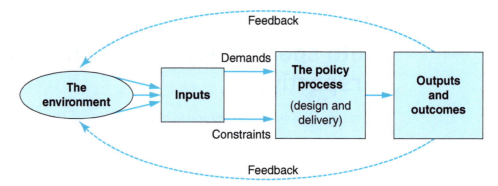

Figure 6.1 Conceptual framework
Source: Adapted from Easton (1965)

> *Comment*
> *Conceptually based comparisons of youth sport policies in other locations can help develop understanding of similar policies in local contexts.*

 ## Youth sport policy in England

Environment and imputs

The context of youth sport policy in England is one in which there have been high levels of public and political concern about children and young people. The government has argued that 'too many children and young people suffer unhappy childhoods because of disadvantage or problems that are not addressed, or tackled too late' (DCSF, 2007, p. 5). More specifically, for some time there has been a growing concern regarding levels of obesity and inactivity amongst young people (Flintoff, 2003). Despite some evidence to the contrary (Bloyce and Smith, 2009), issues regarding young people's health have been linked to a perceived decline in PE and school sport.

Youth sport policy in England is made in a complex environment where a wide range of national organisations and agencies have influence. In terms of government departments, the Department for Culture, Media and Sport has increasingly taken a strong interest in physical education and sport in schools alongside the government department responsible for education. Since its formation in 1994, the Youth Sport Trust (a charity) has also become increasingly prominent in the development and delivery of youth sport policy (Houlihan and Green, 2006).

> **Comment**
> *National agencies have different motivations for their involvement in youth sport policy.*

Content and delivery

The installation of John Major as Conservative prime minister in 1990 was a turning point for youth sport which became an increasingly important policy issue for government. In *Sport: Raising the Game,* the first substantial government sport policy document for over 20 years, the prominence of youth sport was highlighted in the statement that 'sport in schools is the single most important element in the sporting continuum' (DNH, 1995, p. 6). Under subsequent Labour governments, youth sport has continued to be a substantial component of government policy documents such as *A Sporting Future for All* (DCMS, 2000) and *Game Plan* (DCMS/Strategy Unit, 2002).

Despite changes in government, there has been a high degree of consistency over the period since 1990 with regard to one of the key historical debates identified by Kathy Armour in Chapter 1. Sport, rather than physical education or physical activity, has continued to dominate policies (Flintoff, 2008) although the focus has expanded beyond John Major's very specific focus on traditional competitive team games such as football and cricket. There has also been a growing emphasis on the role of youth sport in delivering wider social benefits. While there has been a clear interest in the health benefits of sport participation, policies have also emphasised the role of youth sport in improving educational attainment, and reducing crime and drug use amongst young people (Houlihan and Green, 2006; Flintoff, 2008).

> **Comment**
> *Youth sport has become an increasingly important policy focus based on beliefs about its potential to deliver wider social benefits.*

Perhaps the biggest change seen under the Labour government that took office in 1997 was in the resources and structures put in place to deliver youth sport policy aspirations. John Major's Conservative government allocated few additional resources to youth sport and sought to achieve its policy goals through persuasion and coercion, for example by increasing the monitoring of PE and school sport by OFSTED (Houlihan, 2000). The setting and monitoring of targets, the main one being that all pupils should receive two hours of high-quality PE and school sport per week, were also pursued enthusiastically by the Labour government in order to achieve its policy goals. Under that government, however, such targets were accompanied by a substantial increase in funding for PE and, particularly, school sport. Over the period from 2003 to 2008, £1.5 billion was invested in the PE, School Sport and Club Links (PESSCL) strategy. Investment was continued through the subsequent PE and sport strategy for young people and together these two strategies represented the core element of the Labour government's plan to achieve its youth sport goals.

Two of the programmes that made up the PESSCL strategy, namely School Sport Partnerships (SSPs) and Specialist Sport Colleges, represented major reforms to the structure through which youth sport policy goals have been delivered. Rolled out across all maintained schools in England over six years from 2000, SSPs comprised families of secondary and primary schools each with additional staff employed to develop all aspects of school sport. This was, arguably, the most fundamental change to the structures of physical education and youth sport seen in England in over 60 years.

> *Comment*
> *Youth sport policy goals have been pursued through allocation of additional funding, developing new organisational structures and setting targets.*

Outputs and outcomes

A nationwide picture of the impact of youth sport policy and programmes will be presented in this section, drawing mainly on national evaluations commissioned by government. However, it is worth noting that there remain significant variations in the impact of these policies in different schools and contexts across England (Flintoff, 2003). Nevertheless, by the government's primary output measure, there has been a significant improvement in participation in PE and school sport. The percentage of young people participating in two hours of high-quality PE and school sport each week increased from an estimated 25 per cent in 2002, through 62 per cent when first measured officially in 2003–4, to 90 per cent in 2007–8 (TNS, 2008). The SSP programme has contributed, in particular, to improvements in PE and school sport in primary schools (up to age 11), although there is less evidence of impact in the later secondary school age groups (OFSTED, 2006; TNS, 2008). Furthermore, reflecting the diversity amongst young people recognised throughout this book, concerns have been raised about the impact of the programme amongst those traditionally underrepresented in sport including girls, young people with a disability and those from ethnic minority backgrounds (Loughborough Partnership, 2007; Flintoff, 2008).

Linking to the policy discourse described earlier, while traditional sports continue to dominate in schools, there has been a broadening of the types of sports and physical activities available to pupils (Loughborough Partnership, 2007; TNS, 2008). Moreover, while the overall picture of participation in PE and school sport has improved, evidence of any resultant impact on aspects such as educational attainment, pupil behaviour and attendance in schools remains mainly anecdotal rather than systematic (Loughborough Partnership, 2008a, 2008b, 2008c). To date, there is a lack of any evidence that the increased focus on youth sport has had a significant impact on the health of young people.

> *Comment*
> *There is evidence that some youth sport policy goals have been met but this may not be universal across locations or groups of young people.*

Youth sport policy in Australia

Environment and inputs

Sport success is highly valued by Australians, something that has been reflected in their sport policies (Stewart *et al.*, 2004). The prominence of elite sport development in Australia is significant for understanding the influences on and contexts in which youth sport policy has been developed. Over 90 per cent of government funding for sport has been used for high-performance programmes (Stewart *et al.*, 2004). Despite a lack of evidence (Hogan and Norton, 2000), youth sport policies have been justified on the premise that success at elite level creates a 'trickle-down' effect that inspires young people to take part in sport. Mass-participation initiatives, including youth policies, have been considered a low priority and relatively poorly funded as a result (Brown *et al.*, 1999).

Whilst the funding of successive sports policies has been focused on elite targets, the rhetoric has claimed a commitment to developing community participation as a way to improve the health of the nation and, more recently, to assist with the development of social capital in communities (Stewart *et al.*, 2004). Similarly to the UK, the Australian government has voiced concerns regarding the growing levels of obesity and inactivity of both children and adults (Department of Health and Ageing, 2008) and this has influenced the content of community sport policy and, in turn, youth sport policy.

Delivery of sport in Australia involves three levels of government: national, state and local. Traditionally community sport and mass participation, including youth sport, have been funded at both state and local level and, as a result, policies vary considerably in different locations. There is no single agency with a responsibility for designing and implementing youth sport policy. At a national level, the Australian Sports Commission provides national frameworks but alongside this, National Sports Organisations (NSOs) have each developed and implemented their own youth sport policies specific to their particular sport. Clubs and schools are the key delivery agents for youth sport policy but there is a dislocation between broader sports structures and education-orientated organisations and many junior clubs exist that are not affiliated to their NSO (Independent Sport Panel, 2009).

> **Comment**
> *Elite success has been the key priority in political terms. Youth sport policy varies considerably across states in Australia.*

Content and delivery

The first national youth sport initiative was developed by a Labour government in the 1980s. With the increasing belief that a broad youth participation base was essential for the development of elite athletes, the government instigated their 'Aussie Sport' programme in 1986. The aim of this programme was to 'contribute to the enrichment of sporting experiences and opportunities by influencing the practice of key agencies in the development and delivery of junior sport' (Stewart *et al.*, 2004, p. 60). A key component of this initiative was to support the customising of sports for junior participants. The perceived value of this approach was evident in the 1994 *National Junior Sports Policy: a framework for developing junior sport in Australia* (ASC, 1994). This reinforced the emphasis on tailoring sports opportunities to meet the specific needs of children and young people.

In 1996, the newly elected Liberal government presented their sports policy: *Encouraging Players, Developing Champions* (ASC, 1996). Although again focusing mainly on the development of elite performers, the policy did recognise the need to increase the physical activity levels of Australians and the 'Active Australia' programme was derived as a result. This programme aimed to encourage all Australians, and young people in particular, to be actively involved in sport, recreation and physical activity with an assumption this would lead to a happier and healthier nation (Liberal Party, 1996).

The Liberal government's revamped 2001 sports policy, *Backing Australia's Sporting Ability: A More Active Australia* (BASA), contained a significant switch to community participation from the philosophy underpinning the Active Australia campaign. The community element focused explicitly on encouraging Australians to participate in sport through formal structured sports clubs (Stewart *et al.*, 2004). The BASA policy contained an explicit commitment to increasing participation in youth sport and this was underpinned by funding allocated to NSOs to assist with the development of junior sports clubs. Similarly to previous policies, however, the funding available for community sport objectives, including youth, was fractional when compared with the elite budget (Stewart *et al.*, 2004).

In 2005, in response to the increasing criticism of the government's focus on elite sport (Green, 2007; Independent Sport Panel, 2009) and its lack of attention to wider health issues created by a lack of physical activity (Australia had been classified as the second most obese nation in the world: Stewart *et al.*, 2004) funding was made available for a national initiative that used sport to improve the health of young people. The Active After-School Community programme (AASC), developed by the Australian Sports Commission, was designed to raise the physical activity levels of primary school children and create links with community provision to encourage lifelong participation.

> **Comment**
> *The development of junior sport structures and systems has been a key priority but this has been undertaken through NSOs and clubs. The focus on curriculum-based PE has reduced in recent years.*

Outputs and outcomes

Australia's elite sport success would suggest that youth sports policy has been effective in providing player pathways for young people to develop to elite level (Green, 2007). There is also some evidence to suggest that youth sport policy has been effective in engaging young people more generally in sport. Survey data indicate that 63 per cent of children aged between five and 14 years participate in sport outside school hours, which could be regarded as an impressively high figure (Australian Bureau of Statistics, 2006). The evaluation of the Active After-School Community programme indicates that it has also been successful in raising activity levels. On average, participating children in the AASC programme almost doubled their structured physical activity hours per week (ASC, 2008).

There has been limited evidence that this initiative and other youth sport policies have led to an increase in participation in organised club sport, which has been one key focus of sport policy since 1996 (Independent Sport Panel, 2009). Similarly to the UK, however, there is a lack of evidence on whether the increases in participation and activity levels have had a positive impact on young people's health and well-being. On the other hand, and in contrast to policy in England, it has been argued that the lack of PE within youth sport policy since the 1980s has resulted in the subject being in serious decline (Olds *et al.*, 2004). In some schools, PE time has been significantly reduced in response to pressure to increase time for other priority 'academic' subjects (Brown *et al.*, 1999; Independent Sport Panel, 2009).

> **Comment**
> *Participation rates for young people have been high but there is little connection between school and community junior sport provision and a significant decline in PE and school sport.*

Youth sport policy in Zambia

Environment and inputs

Zambia is a landlocked country in sub-Saharan Africa with a population of approximately 11.7 million. Recent statistics show Zambia to be one of the least developed countries in the world, coming 164th out of the 182 countries on the UN Human Development Index (UNDP, 2009). As with many other African countries, Zambia has been significantly affected by the HIV/AIDS pandemic with approximately one in six of the population infected with the HIV virus. It is estimated that 600,000 children have been orphaned by the pandemic and nearly half of Zambia's population is under 15 years of age (UNAIDS, 2008).

In this context, it is unsurprising that sport has not been a significant priority for government. National funding for sport has been minimal and has, in fact, been outstripped by that provided for specific sport programmes by international agencies (Banda, 2010). Although sport is the responsibility of the Ministry of Youth, Sport and Child Development, Banda (2010) recognises that the government and national sporting agencies have traditionally been focused on organising performance-level sport and competitions.

At a local level, a diverse mix of organisations is involved in the provision of sporting opportunities for young people. Each of the three types of schools (government, community and private) follows a national curriculum, of which physical education is a formal component. While most schools lack anything more than basic sporting grounds and equipment, this problem is particularly acute in community schools whose income, from government or through pupil fees, is very limited. In addition to schools, recently there has been a significant expansion in the number and capacity of so-called 'sport for development' non-government organisations (NGOs) working with young people. Youth sport clubs are another provider of sporting opportunities, primarily football, although such clubs often operate on a very informal basis.

> **Comment**
> *In a context such as that found in Zambia, improving youth sport is a significant challenge.*

Content and delivery

Zambia launched a new national sports policy in 2009 in which youth participation in sport was a significant focus. As was noted in Chapter 1, young people can learn both during and through sports participation, and this learning can be maximised where teachers and coaches have a deep understanding of sport pedagogy. Zambian youth sports policy has focused heavily on developing young people through sport and, in particular, using sport 'as a tool to create awareness for mitigating the impact of HIV/AIDS infections among the youth' (Chipungu, 2009). Whilst national funding has been used at adult level to develop elite performance, youth sport policy in Zambia has tended to concentrate on using sport as a social development tool for young people rather than developing sporting opportunities and performance pathways. Funding from the Ministry of Youth, Sport and Child Development for youth sport has been devolved mainly to NGOs in order to deliver sport for development programmes in local communities. As well as the national sports policy, some NSOs do have youth sport policies. The Football Association of Zambia devised a youth development strategy in 2007 which focused on developing player pathways for young people. Generally NSOs have struggled with delivering youth sport policy and have tended to invest their limited finances into elite development (Banda, 2010).

PE tends to be taught as a stand-alone subject in the mainly private and government schools in Zambia that have access to playing fields and equipment. There is a shortage of trained PE teachers and those that are trained usually have to focus on delivering more 'academic' subjects. However, despite the clear constraints, there is a reasonably well-structured school sport system with competitive sport acting as a substitute for PE, particularly within community schools in Zambia (Carmody, 2004 and authors' own research). School sport tournaments at provincial level serve as a talent-identification forum for sports federations, and international junior teams are largely selected from young people who participate in such tournaments. There are, therefore, some functional links between various youth sport providers in Zambia. In general, however, agencies delivering youth sport policy in Zambia operate in isolation.

Within their broader remit of using sport as a social development tool, NGOs have been responsible for developing youth sport provision in communities in Zambia, particularly those suffering from acute poverty. From NGO activities, many of these communities have developed junior sports clubs that participate in local leagues and tournaments. There is, however, limited dialogue between NGOs and national sports federations which, to date, has led to much of this provision being outside the formal sports structures in Zambia (Magee and Jeanes, 2009). Youth sport policy and delivery in Zambia, therefore, have been fairly fragmented, with some evidence of effective provision. Whilst there is considerable enthusiasm for sport amongst young people, provision differs greatly across different communities and for different sports.

> **Comment**
> *Youth sport policy has focused heavily on achieving wider social development aims.*

Outputs and outcomes

There is little information available on the outcomes of youth sport policy in Zambia. Participation data are not collected and there has been limited analysis at governmental level on the impact of national sports policies. As part of broader research examining the use of sport as a developmental tool within communities, the authors collected some interview data from young people who participated in sport in either a school context or within their communities. These interviews illustrate the enthusiasm and enjoyment young people have for sport in Zambia, particularly football. The following quotes are illustrative:

> I love football, for me it is life. I never thought girls would be able to play football but there are now four teams in my community. I love playing, it makes me feel strong. So many girls here now want to play, we cannot organise enough teams for them all.
>
> (15-year-old female coach and football player)

> The young people in my community love sport. It is everything to them, it gives young people something to do but it also provides a family for us. I will try any sport, any team that is formed here I want to be part of.
>
> (18-year-old boy)

With regard to policies aiming to use sport to deliver wider social outcomes, the challenges faced in collecting robust data in any context are well known (Coalter, 2007). Within Zambia there is limited information indicating whether sports programmes are successfully addressing wider social and health issues such as HIV/AIDS infection rates. The authors' data does suggest, however, that sport is viewed as an effective pedagogical tool for health education programmes and it can engage young people who are not enthused by more traditional education methods (Kay *et al.*, 2007). In addition, the authors' research stressed the importance of participating in sport, both formally and informally, for developing young people's social networks and support structures.

What can we learn from this comparative analysis?

Despite the differences between the three countries considered in this chapter, a number of common themes emerge from comparing their youth sport policies. This final section will consider these common themes, identify differences, and suggest what we might learn from the comparison.

In all three countries, there has been increasing awareness of generic social issues affecting young people, and youth sport policies to address these issues have become more prominent. However, it is also the case that youth sport policies have been shaped significantly by commonly held beliefs that may not stand up to the kind of evidence-based, critical examination that is called for throughout this book. Beliefs about the supposed decline in PE and school sport in England and the contribution of youth sport to elite success in Australia are notable examples of this trend. It could also be argued that, in all three countries, youth sport remains either a secondary focus within broader sport policies or is valued primarily for the broader objectives that it can deliver. Increasingly in Australia and especially in England and Zambia, policy has been based on the contribution that youth sport can make to the broader development of young people, in particular to their physical health. Moreover, and in contradiction to the suggestions made in the opening chapter of this book, elite sport has been a clear policy priority in Australia and Zambia, arguably to the detriment of the development of participation in youth sport. The continuing dominance of elite sport policy provides one explanation for the dominance of competitive youth sport over physical education or physical activity more broadly in all three countries. It is interesting to consider the effects of this policy trend on children and young people, most of whom will not be seeking a future in elite sport.

A further common issue identified in all three countries, and which has been addressed to differing extents in policies, is the large number of organisations involved with youth sport. Typically, it has been sport-orientated government departments or organisations that have had a stronger influence on youth sport policy than their education-orientated counterparts. In terms of the organisations that have been allocated the main role in delivering youth sport policy, it is interesting to note the differences between the three countries. In England, recent youth sport policy has been focused on school-based delivery. Alternatively, sports governing bodies and non-governmental organisations have been more prominent in Australia and Zambia respectively. It has also been recognised that there is a need to provide a continuous pathway for young people between organisations that facilitate initial participation, such as schools, and those that support progress to higher levels of performance or continued participation. Although there has been some policy focus on this issue in England and Australia, effective integration between delivery organisations remains an elusive goal.

In terms of the outputs and outcomes of contemporary youth sport policies, any summary must balance positive aspects with concerns. In England and Australia, evidence shows the positive impact of particular youth sport programmes in delivering stated participation objectives. Key to achieving such impact has been the financial resources that have accompanied programmes. Conversely, in Zambia especially, youth sport policies have often made little headway due to the limited funding accompanying them. Furthermore, even where there is evidence of overall positive impact, national programmes have often had very different levels of impact across different geographical areas and across different groups of young people, such as girls and young people with a disability.

A final important point, which has been identified in all three countries, is the limitations of the evidence regarding any impact of youth sport policies on broader social objectives such as health. Given that such objectives are commonly a key focus of youth sport policies, this lack of systematic evidence may be a significant problem for advocates of youth sport policy.

 ## Conclusion

Although teachers and coaches may certainly be advocates for youth sport, it is understandable that, in their own coaching or teaching context, they may feel a certain dislocation from the broader debates of youth sport policy. The relative lack of priority given to training of teachers and coaches within youth sport policies may only add to this feeling of dislocation. However, 'knowledge in context' is identified in this book as one of the cornerstones of sport pedagogy, and youth sport policies certainly have a key role in shaping the contexts in which teachers and coaches work. From a pedagogical perspective, therefore, teachers and coaches should be prepared to take a critical stance towards youth sport policies in order to understand how they both facilitate and constrain practice. Certainly, the youth sport policies considered in this chapter prioritise certain objectives and, in some cases, particular groups of young people. Teachers and coaches must, therefore, engage with and sometimes resist youth sport policies in order to achieve the pedagogical purpose of engaging all young people in a positive sporting experience.

Learning tasks

Individual task

Critically reflect on your experience of participating in sport as a young person. Can you identify any ways in which national physical education and/or youth sport policies acted as either an enabler or a barrier? Search for information on any education/youth sport policies that were in operation at the time you recall, and critically analyse them to see whether their impact on you was intentional and anticipated – or unanticipated.

Group task

In groups of four. Each member of the group takes one of the following four roles in order to design national youth sport policy: sports minister, education minister, health minister, community development minister. Debate the relative merits of taking different approaches to youth sport policy and try to agree a set of core goals.

Further reading

- For more information on PE and school sport policies, programmes and impacts, access the teachernet website http://www.teachernet.gov.uk/teachingandlearning/subjects/pe/.
- **Houlihan and Green** (2006) offer a critical consideration of ongoing changes in youth sport policy in England.

References

Australian Bureau of Statistics (2006) *Participation in Sport and Physical Activity*, Catalogue No 41770, Canberra: ABS.

Australian Sports Commission (ASC) (1994) *National Junior Sports Policy: a framework for developing junior sport in Australia*, Canberra: ASC.

Australian Sports Commission (ASC) (1996) *Encouraging Players, Developing Champions*, Canberra: ASC.

Australian Sports Commission (ASC) (2001) *Backing Australia's Sporting Ability – A More Active Australia*, Canberra: ASC.

Australian Sports Commission (ASC) (2008) *An Interim Report of the Evaluation of the Australian Sports Commission's Active After-school Communities Programme 2005–2007*, Canberra: ASC.

Banda, D. (2010) Sport policy development in Zambia, *International Journal of Sport Policy*, 2(2), 237–52.

Bloyce, D. and Smith, A. (2009) *Sport Policy and Development: An introduction*, Abingdon: Routledge.

Brown, R., Lewis, F., Murtagh, M., Thorpe, S. and Collins, R. (1999) *100 Minutes Projects: researching PE and sport in DETE schools*, Adelaide: Flinders University of South Australia.

Carmody, B. (2004) *The Evolution of Education in Zambia*, Ndola: Mission Press.

Chipungu, K. (2009) Zambia: New sports policy launched, quoted in *the Lusaka Times*, 7 May 2009, http://www.lusakatimes.com/?p=12104, accessed 25 August 2010.

Coalter, F. (2007) A *Wider Social Role for Sport: Who's keeping the score?*, London: Routledge.

Department for Children, Schools and Families (DCSF) (2007) *The Children's Plan: Building brighter futures*. Norwich: The Stationery Office.

Department for Culture, Media and Sport (DCMS) (2000) *A Sporting Future for All*, London: DCMS.

Department for Culture, Media and Sport/Strategy Unit (2002) *Game Plan: a strategy for delivering the government's sport and physical activity objectives*, London: DCMS.

Department of Health and Ageing (2008) *Healthy Weight 2008 – Australia's Future – A National Action Agenda for Young People and their Families*, Canberra: Department of Health and Ageing.

Department of National Heritage (DNH) (1995) *Sport: Raising the game*, London: DNH.

Easton, D. (1965) *A Framework for Political Analysis*, Englewood Cliffs: Prentice-Hall.

Flintoff, A. (2003) The school sport co-ordinator programme: changing the role of the physical education teacher? *Sport, Education and Society*, 8:2, 231–50.

Flintoff, A. (2008) Targeting Mr average: participation, gender equity and school sport partnerships, *Sport, Education and Society*, 13:4, 393–411.

Green, M. (2007) Olympic glory or grassroots development? Sport policy priorities in Australia, Canada and the United Kingdom, 1960–2006. In: *The International Journal of History in Sport*, Vol 24 (7), 921–53.

Hogan, K. and Norton, K. (2000) The 'price' of Olympic gold, *Journal of Science and Medicine in Sport*, 3 (2), 203–18.

Houlihan, B. (2000) Sporting excellence, schools and sports development: the politics of crowded policy spaces, *European Physical Education Review*, 6 (2), 171–93.

Houlihan, B. and Green, M. (2006) The changing status of school sport and physical education: explaining policy change, *Sport, Education and Society*, 11:1, 73–92.

Independent Sport Panel (2009) *The Future of Sport in Australia*, Canberra: ASC.

Kay, T., Jeanes, R., Lindsey, I., Fimusamni, J., Collins, S. and Bancroft, J. (2007) *Young People, Sports Development and the HIV-AIDS Challenge: Research in Lusaka, Zambia, 2006*, Loughborough: Institute of Youth Sport.

Liberal Party (1996) *Encouraging Players, Developing Champions*, Election policy statement on sport, Canberra.

Loughborough Partnership (2007) *School Sport Partnerships: Annual Monitoring and Evaluation report for 2006*, Loughborough: Institute of Youth Sport.

Loughborough Partnership (2008a) *The Impact of School Sport Partnerships on Pupil Attainment*, Loughborough: Institute of Youth Sport.

Loughborough Partnership (2008b) *The Impact of School Sport Partnerships on Pupil Attendance*, Loughborough: Institute of Youth Sport.

Loughborough Partnership (2008c) *The Impact of School Sport Partnerships on Pupil Behaviour*, Loughborough: Institute of Youth Sport.

Magee, J and Jeanes, R. (2009) *Developing Women's and Girls' Football in Zambia: A scoping study conducted for the Football Association Zambia*, Uclan publication.

Office for Standards in Education (OFSTED) (2006) *School Sport Partnerships: A survey of good practice*, London: HMSO.

Olds, T., Dollman, J., Ridley, K., Boshoff, K., Hartshorne, S. and Kennaugh, S. (2004) *Children and Sport*, Canberra: ASC.

Stewart, B. Nicholson, M., Smith, A. and Westerbeek, H. (2004) *Australian Sport: Better by design? The evolution of Australian sport policy*, Oxon: Routledge.

TNS (2008) *School Sport Survey 2007–8*. London: TNS.

UNAIDS (2008) *Epidemiological Fact Sheet on HIV and AIDS: Zambia*, Geneva: UNAIDS.

United Nations Development Program (2009) *Human Development Report 2009 Zambia*, http://hdrstats.undp.org/en/countries/country_fact_sheets/cty_fs_ZMB.html, accessed 5 January 2009.

United Nations Inter-Agency Task Force on Sport for Development and Peace (2003) *Sport for Development and Peace: Towards achieving the millennium development goals*, Geneva: United Nations.

Olympism: a learning philosophy for physical education and youth sport

Dikaia Chatziefstathiou, Canterbury Christ Church University

Gentlemen, this is the order of ideas from which I intend to draw the elements of moral strength that must guide and protect the renaissance of athletics. Healthy democracy and wise and peaceful internationalism will make their way into the new stadium. There they will glorify the honour and selflessness that will enable athletics to carry out its task of moral betterment and social peace, as well as physical development. That is why every four years the restored Olympic Games must provide a happy and fraternal meeting place for the youth of the world, a place where, gradually, the ignorance of each other in which people live will disappear. This ignorance perpetuates ancient hatreds, increases misunderstandings, and precipitates such barbaric events as fights to the finish.

(Coubertin 1894: lines 336–50)

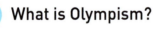 ## What is Olympism?

The term 'Olympism' was first coined by the founder of the modern Olympic Games, the French aristocrat Baron Pierre de Coubertin (Segrave and Chu, 1981). Coubertin understood, towards the end of the nineteenth century, that sport would become a central point of popular culture and was working towards the definition of a universal philosophy that would have sport and physical activity at its core (Parry, 1994). In his *Olympic Memoirs* (1931) Coubertin interpreted Olympism as a 'school of nobility and of moral purity as well as of endurance and physical energy – but only if . . . honesty and sportsmanlike unselfishness are as highly developed as the strength of muscles' (p. 208). Thus, Olympism, for Coubertin, aimed at the harmonious development of the intellectual, moral and physical aspects of a human being through athletic competition (Segrave and

Chu, 1981). In this respect, it can be argued that the concept of Olympism is tightly linked with 'sport pedagogy' as defined by Armour in Chapter 1 of this book. Therefore, Olympism is also relevant to those adults who have a personal interest in sport, and also a strong interest in helping children and young people to develop their 'potentialities' through sport.

The concept of Olympism and the content of the Olympic philosophy have always been strongly linked with education. In the 1880s, Coubertin was working towards an educational reform in collaboration with the French government. While he travelled in England, Germany, America and Canada visiting educational institutions, he was inspired by sport education in England and the intercollegiate competitions in America and Canada (Müller, 2000). His biographers (Weber, 1970; Eyquem, 1981; MacAloon, 1981) suggest that Coubertin, after years of study and field research, developed his project for the Olympic Games as a response to political and social crises in his country. He was deeply concerned with the rapid industrialisation and urbanisation which resulted in poverty and conflict (Kidd, 1996). Thus, although Olympism was the product of many different influences and trends, it was related to Coubertin's concern for the reform of French education (Kidd, 1996; Müller, 2000). Coubertin viewed education as 'the key to human happiness' and he was convinced that education was the best response 'to the accelerated pace of change in the world' (Müller, 2000, p. 25).

> ### Comment
> *Olympism is a philosophy conceived by the French aristocrat Baron Pierre de Coubertin, founder of the modern Olympic Games. It was always linked strongly with education and aimed at the harmonious development of the intellectual, moral and physical aspects of a human being through athletic competition.*

The fundamental principles of Olympism are stated in the Olympic Charter, of which the first version is estimated to have been published around 1898. Since then, the Olympic Charter has been the official 'rule book' of the International Olympic Committee (Loland, 1994). As is stated in the Charter itself (Olympic Charter, 2007), it constitutes 'the codification of the Fundamental Principles, Rules and Bye-Laws adopted by the International Olympic Committee (IOC). It governs the organisation, action and operation of the Olympic movement and sets forth the conditions for the celebration of the Olympic Games' (p. 9). The Olympic movement consists of the IOC, the Organising Committees for the Olympic Games (OCOGs), the National Olympic Committees (NOCs), the international federations (IFs), the national associations, clubs and, of course, the athletes (IOC official website). The Olympic Charter (2007) provides the following information in relation to Olympism:

Modern Olympism was conceived by Pierre de Coubertin, on whose initiative the International Athletic Congress of Paris was held in June 1894. The International Olympic Committee (IOC) constituted itself on 23rd of June 1894. In August 1994, the XII Congress, Centennial Olympic Congress, which was entitled the 'Congress of Unity', was held in Paris. (p. 11)

> Olympism is a philosophy of life, exalting and combining in a balanced whole the qualities of body, will and mind. Blending sport with culture and education, Olympism seeks to create a way of life based on the joy of effort, the educational value of good example and respect for universal fundamental ethical principles.   (Fundamental Principle 1; p. 12)

> The goal of Olympism is to place sport at the service of the harmonious development of man, with a view to promoting a peaceful society concerned with the preservation of human dignity.   (Fundamental Principle 2; p. 12)

The links between Olympism and 'sport pedagogy' are very clear. Both are interested in the ways in which individuals (and especially children and young people) learn *in* and *through* sport. Their common focus is supporting young people to learn sport-specific skills *and*, importantly, as part of the learning process, to gain wider benefits such as personal, social and health benefits. Loland (1994) has argued that Olympism, from the perspective of the history of ideas, has four main goals: to educate and cultivate the individual through sport; to cultivate the relations of men (*sic*) in society; to promote international understanding and peace; and to worship human greatness and possibility (pp. 36–8). However, the definitions of Olympism have been many and various (Arnold, 1996). For example, Olympism has been referred to as a social philosophy that emphasises the role of sport in world development, peaceful coexistence, international understanding and social and moral education (Parry, 1994). It has also been defined as 'sport in the service of man *sic* everywhere' (Lekarska, 1988, p. 73); 'the pursuit of excellence in a chivalrous manner' (Clarke 1988, p. 99); and 'a nebula of speeches, a sea of myths, ideologies and prejudices' (Caillat and Brohm, 1984; cited in Landry, 1985, p. 143).

Comment

Olympism and its values underpin the modern Olympic movement and have been included in the Olympic Charter, the official rulebook of the movement since 1898. There are strong links between Olympism and sport pedagogy.

Hoberman (1995) views Olympism in the context of other 'idealistic internationalisms' which appeared in three periods that are roughly separated by the First and Second World Wars. The establishment of the Olympic movement in 1894 coincided with the growth of international organisations sharing humanistic and universal values such as the Red Cross, Esperanto and Scouting. These organizations were products of late nineteenth-century liberalism, which emphasised values of equality, fairness, justice, respect for persons, rationality, international understanding, peace, autonomy and excellence (Hoberman, 1995; Parry, 1994). Coubertin's contribution was to locate these values in the milieu of sport and he emphasised that Olympism shares the values of liberal humanism or perhaps simply humanism. Boulogne (1999) similarly emphasised the point that 'Coubertinian neo-Olympism asserted itself as a humanism' (p. 37). Anthony (1994) agrees that Olympism and humanism share the same ideals, and Olympic leaders and dominant Olympic institutions have claimed that 'Olympism is Humanism' (MacAloon, 1996, p. 69). As it is shown later in this chapter, however, such suggestions are the subject of considerable debate. Nevertheless, despite the paradoxes and discrepancies in this ideology, Olympism can be utilised by teachers and coaches who are concerned to harness the potential of sport for children and young people through an emphasis on values such as equality, fairness and respect.

> **Comment**
> *The International Olympic Committee (IOC) was founded in a period when other international humanistic movements also emerged. The Olympic movement linked the humanistic values of peace, fraternity and goodwill with the practice of sport.*

The critiques of Olympism

Despite its grand ideals as detailed in the Olympic Charter, Olympism has been the subject of major criticisms (Hoberman, 1986; Simson and Jennings, 1991; Hill, 1992). These include:

- the rise of nationalisms that are emphasised in the competitions;
- the involvement of politics in sport and the advent of successive Olympic boycotts;
- accelerating commercialisation;
- the professionalisation of athletes;
- evidence of discrimination in the areas of race, gender and ethnicity in the Olympic arena;
- the Eurocentric and Western character of the Olympic movement;
- the scandals concerning bribery of the IOC members.

Moreover, the Olympic leaders and their moral values have been questioned as a result of incidents occurring at the Winter Olympic Games of 2002 in Salt Lake City. Before 1995, the city had attempted several times to secure the games, but had failed each time. In 1995, Salt Lake City was announced as the host city, but in 1998 the members of the International Olympic Committee (IOC) were accused of taking bribes from the Salt Lake Organizing Committee (SLOC). This is, perhaps, the most vivid example of the gap that exists between organisational ideals and organisational conduct within the Olympic movement (Segrave, 2000). Indeed, Simson and Jennings (1991) have accused the Olympic leaders of bribery, hypocrisy and other serious shortcomings, though it has also been argued that these authors undermine their arguments by the use of 'overblown rhetoric' (Houlihan, 1994, p. 109). Seppanen (1984), without resorting to the extremes of Simson and Jennings, has also criticised the Olympic movement for its inability to promote the Olympic ideals that should be at its core. In similar vein, for others, the Games have become a global business and the values embedded in the Olympic Charter have almost been forgotten (Milton-Smith, 2002). On the other hand, Chatziefstathiou (2010) has provided extensive evidence that Olympism has in fact been plagued by inherent paradoxes throughout the history of the modern Olympic movement. However, to conclude that Olympism has now become merely an apologetic myth to counterbalance the materialistic and excessive nature of the Olympic Games would be a simplistic and unidirectional assumption.

> **Comment**
> *It has been argued that there is a gap between the ideals of the Olympic movement and some of its practices.*

Olympism as a learning philosophy

It could be argued that Olympism is a stand-alone philosophy that is not dependent upon the Olympic Games (and also Paralympic Games that were later added), and that it would be more honest if the Olympic and Paralympic Games continued without pretensions to Olympism (Wamsley, 2004). Nonetheless, the Olympic movement (the IOC, OCOGs, NOCs, IFs, national associations, clubs and athletes) has developed a global network through which the values of Olympism are disseminated not only through the conduct of the Olympic Games, but also by the organisation of Olympic education programmes. Specifically, the International Olympic Committee, through the 'Five Steps' programme and the subcommittees for Culture and Olympic Education (founded in 2000) and Olympic Solidarity (founded in 1972), promotes global cultural and sports development programmes including the Olympic Youth Camps and the training of athletes and coaches particularly in Africa, Asia, Oceania and South America. The Olympic Study Centre and the Olympic Museum in Lausanne are also key initiatives of the IOC which aim to disseminate Olympic ideals and the development of research on the Olympic movement.

> *Comment*
> *Olympism and the Olympic values are not only linked with the event of the Olympic Games but are also disseminated through the organisation of Olympic education programmes.*

There is also a range of Olympic education programmes delivered in the International Olympic Academy (founded in 1961 in Olympia, Greece), which functions as an International Academic Centre for Olympic studies, education and research and is in close collaboration with the National Olympic Academies around the world. In addition, Olympic education is delivered through several institutions and Olympic Study Centres located in different countries (such as the UK and Spain) that have an interest in focusing on Olympic research in higher education or specifically in Olympic pedagogy. Moreover, Olympic education, or some parts of it, have been incorporated into various national PE curricula.

Naul (2008) provides a very good overview of the dissemination of Olympic education as a part of physical and sport education at school. Naul claims that it is difficult to clearly map out how and whether national PE curricula have included elements of Olympic education because education ministries tend to refer only to 'curriculum frameworks' which are then developed into regional curricula in a way which is rather flexible and vague for local schools. Thus, what happens in most European countries is that although the term 'Olympic' may not be mentioned in the national curriculum, or even the regional ones, individual schools have been reported to have used the subject of Olympics in theoretical and practical strands of their curricula (Telama *et al.*, 2002; cited in Naul, 2008, p. 93). This lack of clarity in disseminating Olympic education in national curricula for PE also reflects a vagueness in defining Olympic education or Olympic pedagogy. The term has sometimes been used interchangeably with sport education, sport pedagogy or physical education, mainly because the ideals of fair play, friendship, respect, excellence, etc. are shared between them.

Pühse and Gerber (2005; cited in Naul, 2008, p. 94) conducted a secondary analysis of the Swiss project 'International Comparison of Physical Education' that included 35 national reviews from all over the world and found that although PE was often associated with the attainment of values and norms, only five of these studies (Germany, Greece, Lithuania, New Zealand and Poland) linked those values with anything Olympic; the rest mostly associated them with the social learning processes of sport. Such ambiguities have led to debates about what really constitutes Olympic education and the nature of its pedagogical concepts. Naul (2008) argues that five major Olympic pedagogical approaches, which undoubtedly do borrow ideas from each other, can be identified throughout the history of the modern Olympic movement and around the world:

- Pierre de Coubertin's Olympic pedagogy;
- Olympic education as sport education;
- Olympic education as physical education;
- Olympic education as a focus on values education;
- Olympic education as lifelong learning.

Pierre de Coubertin's Olympic pedagogy

Pierre de Coubertin (1863–1937) saw himself first and foremost as an educator. As was noted earlier, his primary aim was to reform French education in a period after the defeat of France in the Franco-Prussian War in 1870 which had damaged the image of the country and led to calls for a reinvigoration of French youth. Initially, his plans were centred on France and he aimed to make modern sport, as he experienced it in England and America, a necessary ingredient of the French school curriculum. Coubertin never used the term 'Olympic education', but he referred to the concept of 'sporting education' which was also the title of his book, *Pedagogie Sportive*, published in 1922.

There are very real links here with the concept of sport pedagogy as presented in the chapters in this text. Norbert Müller, a historian and scholar of Olympic education from Germany, has been a key researcher of Coubertin's pedagogical teachings and understandings. Müller has always highlighted Coubertin's interpretation of Olympism as an educational subject (quoting among many other texts Coubertin's essay entitled '*L'Olympisme à l'école. Il faut l'encourager!*'). In his most recent work (2008), Müller emphasised the relevance of Coubertin's 'Olympic education' for schools at the beginning of the twenty-first century. He focused on five features:

1 the concept of the harmonious development of the whole human being;

2 the idea of striving for human perfection through high performance, in which scientific and artistic achievement have equal value to sporting performance;

3 sporting activity voluntarily linked to ethical principles such as fair play and equality of opportunity, and the determination to fulfil those obligations, including the ideal of amateurism, which has been almost totally abandoned in international sport today;

4 the concept of peace and goodwill between nations, reflected by respect and tolerance in relations between individuals;

5 the promotion of moves towards emancipation in and through sport.

> **Comment**
> *Coubertin's 'Olympic education' was related to a sport pedagogy which he called 'pedagogie sportive' and this has links with some of the sport pedagogy concepts that are described in this book.*

Olympic education as pedagogy through sport and culture

The pedagogical philosophy that underpins Olympism is heavily influenced by Coubertin's '*pedagogie sportive*' but it also draws on Carl Diem's and other German scholars' interpretation of Olympism (Chatziefstathiou, 2005; Naul, 2008). Carl Diem was the chief organiser and general secretary of the Berlin Games in 1936, initiating many new ideas in their realisation. For the first time, the notion of the Olympic village was conceived, bringing most facilities together. A theatre (*Waldbühne*) was also added to emphasise the cultural character of the Games, and a bell tower with a bell calling the youth of the world (*Ich rufer die Jugend der Welt*) was built (Haag, 1982). Carl Diem also invited 30 students of physical education from every participating country to a youth camp during the Games, and they performed gymnastic displays (Haag, 1982). However, Carl Diem's biggest innovation at the Berlin Games was to add to the modern Olympic ceremony–a highly symbolic connection between the modern Olympic event site and the ancient site of Olympia in Greece – by organising a torch relay from Olympia.

Due to his close collaboration with Coubertin, Diem undertook and brought into fruition several Olympic projects such as the publication of the *Olympic Review* (which Diem continued publishing during the years of the Second World War), and the establishment of a Centre for Olympic Studies. Diem had long proposed the establishment of a pedagogical centre of Olympism, where young people from around the world would be taught the Olympic values. On a national level, he had been involved with the establishment of the *Haus des Deutschen Sports* in Germany, a major centre for research in physical education and recreation equipped with swimming pools, gymnasia and classrooms. Moreover, in response to Coubertin's longing for the foundation of a Centre for Olympic Studies, he proposed and successfully established, with the cooperation of the Third Reich of Germany, the International Olympic Institute in Berlin. However, one of his most ambitious plans involved the continuation of the archaeological excavations in the ancient sport sites of Olympia in Greece and the establishment of the International Olympic Academy near this site.

> **Comment**
> *In today's context, the pedagogical concept of Olympic education based on sport and culture is closely linked with the activities that are planned as part of the Cultural Olympiads, embracing the Olympics as a world festival rather than solely a sporting event.*

Olympic education as physical education

Jim Parry, a philosopher, pedagogue and scholar of Olympic studies, has long claimed that the philosophical anthropology of Olympism, with its focus on ethics and an idealised conception of what it is to be human, can be beneficial if used for pedagogical purposes. He perceived that PE had a low status in schools, leading him to suggest there was a need to:

> seek to develop an account of culture and human experience which gives due weight to those forms of athletic, outdoor, sporting, aesthetic activities which focus on bodily performance, and which are generally grouped under the heading of physical education. Such an account, combining claims about human capacities and excellences with claims about the importance of a range of cultural forms, would seek to develop arguments which could justify the place of PE on the curriculum. (1988, p. 117)

He has since argued in addition that Olympism can produce a valuable framework for ethical applications within the *practices* of PE. Parry's suggestion was that 'PE activities should be seen as "practices" which act as a context for the development of human excellences and "virtues", and the cultivation of those qualities of character which dispose one to act virtuously' (1998, p. 164). It could be argued that this resonates with elements of the concept of sport pedagogy, as defined in Chapter 1, particularly where it refers to learning both *in* and *through* sport. Parry particularly emphasised the importance of education through the physical and argued for PE as Olympic education in the form of moral education (mainly through an emphasis on the values of equality, justice and fairness to all).

Comment
Physical education and youth sport could use Olympism as a valuable pedagogical tool.

Olympic education as a focus on values education

Where Olympism is focused on values, i.e. as a 'philosophy of life', there is a strong emphasis on the ways in which teachers and coaches can contribute to the development and reinforcement of positive values and behaviours in young people. Deanna Binder, an international expert from Canada on Olympic education, has developed her own interpretation of Olympic education. She focuses on values education, which does not refer merely to schools or physical education but to an integration of the Olympic idea in everyday life. As was noted by Armour in the first chapter of this book, in order to understand the scope of sport pedagogy, it is important from the outset to disaggregate learning and education from schools alone. Similarly, Olympism can 'happen' in schools during PE lessons or through a set range of sport activities but it can also extend *beyond school boundaries, encompassing children learning in sport wherever that may occur.*

Binder's approach formed the five 'basic objectives' which constituted the pedagogical foundation for an international teacher's handbook on the values of Olympism: *Be a Champion in Life*, produced by the Foundation for Olympic and Sport Education (Binder,

2000). According to the statement of objectives, Olympic education programmes should include activities which will:

- enrich the human personality through physical activity and sport, blended with culture and understood as lifelong experience;
- develop a sense of human solidarity, tolerance and mutual respect associated with fair play;
- encourage peace, mutual understanding, respect for different cultures, protection of the environment, basic human values and concerns, according to regional and national requirements;
- encourage excellence and achievement in accordance with fundamental Olympic ideals;
- develop a sense of the continuity of human civilization as explored through ancient and modern Olympic history.

This approach that frames Olympic education as values education has also been embraced by the IOC and their 'Olympic Value Education Project' (OVEP). Led by Binder, the project aims to promote global education based on Olympic values and five shorter concepts: the joy found in physical effort; fair play; respect for others; achieving peak performance; balance between body, mind and spirit (Naul, 2008, p. 112).

Olympic education as interdisciplinary learning

Up to this point, Olympic education has been conceptualized as a form of sport pedagogy, physical education, a cluster of cultural activities and values education. This last pedagogical approach extends the contexts where Olympic education can be applied. These can include contexts within the curriculum (in the form of the different disciplines and knowledge subjects) and outside school (under the notion that education must extend beyond the school itself). The former is evident in the London 2012 educational initiative, 'Get Set', which aims to involve children and young people in the excitement of the Olympic and Paralympic Games. The web-based programme includes interactive quizzes, sounds, fact files and other activities based on the Olympic and Paralympic values across the curriculum for ages from three to 19 (Get Set, 2010).

Undoubtedly, in the run up to an Olympic games, any 'Olympic' initiative or issue is deemed newsworthy, particularly in the host country, gaining extensive coverage in the media including the social network media such as YouTube, Facebook and Twitter. This includes both the positive attributes of the Games and the negative sides (such as doping). In both cases there are increasing numbers of young people who are exposed to information about Olympic issues and practices. As Naul (2008) argues, therefore, it is important for educators to consider the learning potential of all the places where young people encounter sport, including school, sports clubs and community/family sport. Specifically Naul emphasises that:

> Olympic education's terms of reference in schools must take into account these formal and informal learning processes for Olympic learning in the various social settings where children live and where sports and physical activities are alive. All such influences and constraints must be included when planning and conducting lessons, investigations and projects address [sic] learning in the direction of Olympic values.   (p. 115)

Conclusion

In the same way that Olympism has been open to several interpretations throughout the history of the modern Olympic movement (Chatziefstathiou 2005, 2010), Olympic education or Olympic pedagogy has also been defined and delivered in different ways. If Olympism as a concept is 'unpacked' it becomes clear that the so-called 'Olympic ideals' are embedded in programmes of physical education, sport education and youth development. It can be argued that the terms 'Olympic education' and 'Olympic pedagogy' refer to a series of different activities which are all based on the same fundamental principles of the Olympic Charter and are associated with the Olympic ideals and the multifaceted ideology of Olympism. One could also argue that, as Olympism is sprinkled with the so-called 'magic dust' of the Olympics, there is also a sense of the 'magic dust' of Olympism in education. Hence, an 'Olympism' focus could enhance the values, norms and virtues that teachers and coaches are already trying to teach in physical education and youth sport and, indeed, in wider educational contexts.

Clearly Olympism, or Olympic pedagogy, can be critiqued for being rather vague but, at the same time, it could be argued that this is the very essence of this pedagogical approach. It is a flexible tool to be used by educators in conjunction with the mega event of the Olympic and Paralympic Games. The Olympic and Paralympic Games can act as the 'Trojan horse' ($\Delta o\acute{u}\rho\epsilon\iota o\varsigma$ '$\iota\pi\pi o\varsigma$) wherein several messages can be offered to the youth of the world in many different ways: inside or outside the school curriculum, through PE or any other knowledge subject, through cultural activities or lifelong learning, as well as through social media or international sport development programmes (e.g. Olympic Solidarity and the International Inspiration Project).

Certainly it should be remembered that Olympic pedagogy is not a single approach. Five key approaches can be identified but *they do borrow* concepts and ideas from each other:

- Pierre de Coubertin's idea of *pedagogie sportive*;
- Olympic education as pedagogy through sport and culture;
- Olympic education as physical education;
- Olympic education as a focus on values education;
- Olympic education as interdisciplinary learning.

Learning tasks

Individual task

Write a 500-word narrative summarising the core features of Olympism and the Olympic values and their links to education.

Group task

Prepare a poster illustrating how Olympism can be used as a specific learning tool within the PE context with students of a specified age/stage of learning.

(continued)

Further reading

Read the introductory chapter in 'Post-Olympism? Questioning sport in the twenty-first century' by **J. Bale and M.K. Christensen** (Eds) (2004), Berg: Oxford. Answer the following questions:

- What are the differences between Olympism and Post-Olympism?
- If post-Olympism creates new opportunities and further challenges, how could this concept be developed into a valuable pedagogical tool for students' learning?

References

Anthony, D. (1994) The humanistic mission of the Olympic movement and the role of Olympic solidarity in the developing countries, *34th session of young participants in the International Olympic Academy*, 18 July–2 August 1994, International Olympic Academy.

Arnold, P. J. (1996) Olympism, sport and education, *Quest*, 48, 93–101.

Binder, D. (2000) *Be a Champion in Life! A book of activities for young people based on the joy of participation and on the important messages of the Olympic idea. An international teachers' resource book for schools*, Athens: FOSE.

Boulogne, Y. P. (1999) *Pierre de Coubertin. Humanism et Pédagogie: Dix Leçons sur L'Olympisme*, Lausanne: International Olympic Committee.

Chatziefstathiou, D. (2005) The changing nature of the ideology of Olympism in the modern Olympic era, unpublished doctoral dissertation, Loughborough University, UK.

Chatziefstathiou, D. (2010) Paradoxes and contestations of Olympism in the history of the modern Olympic movement, *Sport in Society*, forthcoming.

Clarke, K. (1988) Olympism at the beginning and at the end of the twentieth century – immutable values and outdated factors, *International Olympic Academy: 28th Young Participants Session*, 1988, International Olympic Academy, 99–104.

Coubertin, P. (1894) The Neo-Olympism. Appeal to the people of Athens (16 November 1894). Lecture given to the Parnassus Literary Society at Athens. In: N. Müller (ed.) *Pierre de Coubertin 1863–1937 – Olympism: Selected Writings*, Lausanne: International Olympic Committee, 533–41.

Coubertin, P. (1931) *Olympic Memoirs*, Lausanne: International Olympic Committee.

Eyquem, M. T. (1981) *Pierre de Coubertin: L'Époque Olympique*, Paris: Calman-Levy.

Get Set (2010) http://getset.london2012.com/en/home, accessed 1 June 2010.

Haag, H. (1982) Life and work of Carl Diem, the father of modern physical education in Germany, *International Journal of Physical Education*, 19(2), 24–30.

Hill, C. (1992) *Olympic Politics*, Manchester: Manchester University Press.

Hoberman, J. (1986) *The Olympic Crisis: Sport, politics and the moral order*, New Rochelle, NY: Caratzas Publishing.

Hoberman, J. (1995) Toward a theory of Olympic internationalism, *Journal of Sport History*, 22(1), 1–37.

Houlihan, B. (1994) *Sport and International Politics*, London: Harvester-Wheatsheaf.

Kidd, B. (1996) Taking the rhetoric seriously: proposals for Olympic education, *Quest*, 48, 82–92.

Landry, F. (1985) Olympic education and international understanding: educational challenge or cultural hegemony?, *International Olympic Academy: 25th Young Participants Session*, International Olympic Academy, 139–49.

Lekarska, N. (1988) Olympism – immutable values and outdated factors, *International Olympic Academy: 28th Young Participants Session*, International Olympic Academy, 73–80.

Loland, S. (1994) Pierre de Coubertin's ideology of Olympism from the perspective of the history of ideas, *Second International Symposium for Olympic Research*, 1994.

Macaloon, J. (1981) *This Great Symbol: Pierre de Coubertin and the origins of the modern Olympic Games*, Chicago: University of Chicago Press.

MacAloon, J. J. (1996) Humanism as political necessity? Reflections on the pathos of anthropological science in Olympic contexts, *Quest*, 48, 67–81.

Milton-Smith, J. (2002) Ethics, the Olympics and the search for global values, *Journal of Business Ethics*, 35, 131–42.

Müller, N. (2000) *Pierre de Coubertin 1863–1937: Olympism, Selected Writings*, Lausanne: International Olympic Committee.

Müller, N. (2008) Olympic education. In: Ren, H., DaCosta, L. P., Miragaya, A. and Jings, N. (eds) *Olympic Studies Reader. A multidisciplinary and multicultural research guide* (Vol. 1), Beijing Sport University Press, 345–62.

Naul, R. (2008) *Olympic Education*, Oxford: Meyer & Meyer.

Olympic Charter (2007) available: www.olympic.org, accessed 28 February 2010.

Parry, J. (1988) Olympism at the beginning and end of the twentieth century – immutable values and principles and outdated factors, *International Olympic Academy: 28th Young Participants Session*, International Olympic Academy, 81–94.

Parry, J. (1994) The moral and cultural dimensions of Olympism and their educational application, *International Olympic Academy: 34th Session Young Participants*, International Olympic Academy, 181–97.

Parry, J. (1998) Physical education as Olympic education, *European Physical Education Review*, 4(2), 153–67.

Segrave, J. O. (2000) The (Neo) Modern Olympic Games, *International Review for the Sociology of Sport*, 35(3), 268–81.

Segrave, J. and Chu, D. (1981) *Olympism*, Champaign, IL: Human Kinetics.

Seppanen, P. (1984) The Olympics: a sociological perspective, *International Review for the Sociology of Sport*, 19(2), 113–27.

Simson, Y. and Jennings, A. (1991) *The Lords of the Rings: Power, money and drugs in the modern Olympics*, London: Simon and Schuster.

Wamsley, K. B. (2004) Laying Olympism to rest. In: J. Bale and M. K. Christensen (eds) *Post-Olympism? Questioning Sport in the Twenty-first Century*, Oxford: Berg, 231–42.

Weber, W. (1970) Pierre de Coubertin and the introduction of organised sport in France, *Journal of Contemporary History*, 5, 3–26.

Section
2

Children and young people: diverse learners in physical education and youth sport

Youth voices in physical education and sport: what are they telling us and what do they say they need?

Ann MacPhail, University of Limerick

Chasing a ball around a pitch seems pretty futile to me. In basketball or a sport like that, someone jumps up for a ball and, even if they don't catch it, everyone cheers. All very strange! It's at these times that I really do feel as if I come from another planet and, to be quite honest, I like mine better. Beam me up, Scotty! . . . Now I am in secondary school, this sports issue is even worse. I am in a private school and here it seems we are now expected to love talking about rugby or golf. Well, whoopee doo . . . I would rather watch paint dry. Quite literally. The thought of doing games really makes me feel ill. I can't even think about sleeping at night when I have games the next day. I can't concentrate on the lessons before as my worst nightmare is slowly approaching. When it is time for the lesson, I genuinely do feel sick and have a headache from all the worrying. Of course I am told that I will be able to run it off or just ignored completely. It is my worst time at school and I have done all I can to avoid it.

(Jackson, 2002, p. 130)

 ## Introduction

The opening extract is from Luke Jackson, a 13-year-old boy who has Asperger's Syndrome, which results in heightened sensitivity to particular physical activity environments. Although it is a negative view, and clearly there are many young people who feel differently, the extract does encourage us as teachers or coaches to critically review our awareness of the views and attitudes held by children and young people in physical education and sport. Young people's attraction to and engagement with physical education and sport are complex, varying from those who embrace being physically active whenever the opportunity arises to those who are negative about both. Moreover, youth voice in physical education and sport is compounded by young people's construction of what these activities entail, and also the current positioning of each young person in the context of their family and friends, community and popular culture (MacPhail, Collier and O'Sullivan, 2009).

By listening to and reporting what young people tell us about their experiences of learning in physical education and sport, this chapter seeks to acknowledge young people as diverse and complex learners with a multiplicity of needs and interests. In Chapter 1, Armour argued that in order to be effective, teachers and coaches need to recognise – or diagnose – learners' needs and also consult young people about them. The ability to 'hear' youth voices is, therefore, a key pedagogical skill.

> **Comment**
> *A young person's multifaceted relationship with physical education and sport can be lost when young people are only considered as a group.*

Youth voices in physical education and sport

There are many different approaches that can be used to hear youth voice in physical education and sport (O'Sullivan and MacPhail, 2010). It is argued in this chapter that by listening to youth voice, there is the potential to understand the reality of physical education and sport experiences for young people. Such listening has consequences, however, and may lead teachers and coaches to question cherished aspects of their provision and practice. In other words, if a decision is taken to find out about young people's views, it is important to decide what will happen if those views suggest that pedagogical changes are required. It is also important to note that finding an authentic youth voice on physical education and youth sport is a complex process (Long and Carless, 2010).

Information on student consultation in physical education, including how to consult students and about what, is documented in some detail elsewhere (MacPhail, 2010). The focus of this chapter is to explore what young people are telling us about physical education and, as a result, what they seem to need from the subject in schools and elsewhere. Youth conceptions of sport vary based on different experiences, ranging from self-organised and informal sport to adult-organised, education-located and community-based sport. In addition, for many young people, media representations of sport are likely to have influenced their knowledge and understandings (Lines, 2007). Added to this, characteristics such as gender, physical skill ability, (dis)ability, socioeconomic status and ethnicity may influence young people's interaction, participation and performance in both physical education and sport. So, while the next two sections report what young people say about their experiences, it is important to recognise that: some findings may be more prevalent in some social groups; no findings apply in the same way to all members of such groups; and the issues discussed are not an exhaustive list of young people's views. In other words, the picture that emerges when we listen to young people is often very complex. This chapter is organised into three sections: young people's voice in physical education, young people's voice in youth sport, and the relationship between effective learning environments in physical education and youth sport.

> **Comment**
> *Listening to – and hearing – youth voice can result in complex pedagogical challenges for teachers and coaches.*

What young people tell us about their experiences of physical education

The physical education curriculum

The physical education curriculum is one of the most important influences on young people's participation in physical activity. There is evidence to suggest that positive attitudes, once established, remain consistent across the transition from primary to secondary school (Dismore and Bailey, 2010). Young people report liking physical education when the curriculum has relevance to their lives, has variety and choice, encourages social interaction through team sports, and provides opportunities for fun and enjoyment (Dismore and Bailey, 2010; Smith and Parr, 2007). Some young people report choosing to participate in physical education to improve and maintain health:

Susie: It [physical education] keeps you fit and active.

Jenna: It's, like, exercise isn't it? Well, it's exercise and every other lesson you're not really doing much . . . it's active, so it will keep you healthy and stuff.

[Group laughs]

Rebecca: Well yeah, if you didn't do any exercise, then you would just be fat, wouldn't you?

Susie: Yeah, I think it's for obesity and trying to combat it.

(15–16-year-old girls, Smith and Parr, 2007, p. 45)

Enjoyment of physical education is, at times, linked to the change of learning environment and context that physical education offers in comparison with a classroom subject. Young people report that they enjoy getting out of the classroom and moving about (Cothran and Ennis, 1998; Smith and Parr, 2007);

Natalie: It's [physical education] fun.

Sarah: It's a break from academic lessons that you have to use your head for.

Jessica: It's different . . . you just have a bit of fun.

Natalie: You're getting something out of it as well . . . it's just an hour of something that's not sat down at a desk.

Jane: Yeah, you're not sat down just copying at a board.

Kim: You can talk with people as well as do your sport in lessons; in other lessons you're not allowed to talk and you can hardly move . . . but in PE you can run around.

(15–16-year-old girls, Smith and Parr, 2007, p. 44)

On the other hand, having to change and shower within a shared space with peers can act as a barrier to participation in physical education even where the curriculum is offering interesting activities. In addition, some young people report a strong aversion to sweating and having to go to the next class feeling 'sweaty', particularly when sufficient time is not allocated to changing and showering (Rees *et al.*, 2006). Young people also report, unsurprisingly perhaps, that they dislike physical education when the curriculum repeats the same activities every year, does not relate to their needs, is boring and is too competitive:

> We do the same thing [in physical education] every week, over and over exactly like there's no difference . . . first of all he [teacher] gets us warmed up and so we go like that [rotates arms] to warm up and then makes you run like ten laps like up and down, up and down and you're not allowed to stop.
>
> (Amy, 5th grade primary school student, McMahon, 2007)

There is evidence to suggest that young people appreciate having opportunities to co-construct the physical education curriculum with peers and teachers, such that their opinions inform curriculum development (Oliver, Hamzeh and McCaughtry, 2009). The opportunity to share their physical activity preferences, inform the focus of learning, influence the pace at which they work and have their preference for working with particular peers respected is also appreciated. However, Smith and Parr (2007) warn that it is not necessarily the curriculum that is of most concern to students, but rather the range and ways in which those activities are provided. The importance of an effective and appropriate teacher or coach should not, therefore, be underestimated.

Comment
Young people have much to say about their learning experiences and they value opportunities to contribute to the development of physical education programmes.

Attributes of a physical education teacher

Physical education teachers play a key role in determining young people's attitudes and feelings towards physical education. Young people identify a number of teacher attributes that encourage positive learning experiences: for example, being thoughtful and considerate about students' needs, having patience and possessing an 'appropriate' sense of humour (Mulvihill, Rivers and Aggleton, 2000). Young people perceive that some physical education teachers lack a pedagogical interest in less able pupils, preferring to focus on those who are more proficient and may play in school teams:

> Well, we're not the best and we aren't in the important school teams. If you're in one, then . . . You know it's like Mr Evans does the football team and he spends the lesson with the good players and he's not bothered about us.
>
> (Andy, young physically disabled boy, Fitzgerald, 2005, p. 47)

Young women, in particular, record very definite and often negative opinions about physical education teachers, suggesting they tend to spend more time with and give more attention to boys, allow no choice in the activities, convey a lack of sensitivity and respect, are insensitive to the need for privacy when changing, and can 'pick on' less physically able students (Mulvihill, Rivers and Aggleton, 2000):

> Sometimes they [PE teachers] are really horrible to people that can't do things. They don't realise that they just can't do things. They don't believe and then they embarrass them on purpose.
>
> (Female, 15 years old, white, Mulvihill, Rivers and Aggleton, 2000, p. 193)

Comment

Physical education teachers are perceived by some young people to be insensitive to the needs of low-ability pupils.

Body image

Young people going through puberty are particularly conscious of body image and can be sensitive both about wearing required physical education kit and sharing changing facilities with their peers (Laws and Fisher, 1999). Research has found that most teenage girls, when asked, describe their physical education kit as uncomfortable and embarrassing (Sport England, 2005). Evidence from adolescent boys suggests that their body esteem grows as they progress through each school year, whereas for girls the reverse is the case, resulting in young people with body-image concerns who avoid participation in physical education due to embarrassment or weight-related teasing (Duncan *et al.*, 2004). However, while girls consistently report greater body dissatisfaction and lower body self-esteem compared with boys, overweight boys also face challenges in taking part in physical education:

> PE didn't make me good at anything. It just made me realise how slow I was and how fat I am. Yeah, I always dreaded PE classes. I really dreaded it because I could never do a push-up [or] a curl-up.   (Lucas, young adolescent boy, Trout and Graber, 2009, p. 277)

Comment

Due to the practical, physical and shared environment of a physical education lesson, young people's awareness of issues related to body image is heightened.

Perceived physical competence and social competence

Research suggests that males tend to have a higher level of physical self-perception than females, and this may be partially explained by the fact that the girls are generally less physically active than boys (Fairclough and Stratton, 2005). There is a tendency for girls to focus more on social competence, with the desire to be popular, socially accepted and to have high social status. Peer interaction and friendship are extremely important to girls (Garrett, 2004). Flintoff and Scraton (2001) present data from 15-year-old young women that convey the heightened awareness they experience when confronted with mixed-sex physical education lessons:

> [Mixed PE] depends on what we are doing. Gym and aerobics are not good mixed 'cause it is like the boys are there, they are watching you and if you are on your own you can do what you want to . . . you just feel just small around them . . . on your own you can do things without making people look small and that. You can be yourself. When the boys

are there you change, you are quieter than you usually are – you don't say owt, they just take over. You know that they are immature and you know that they will say something to make you feel embarrassed.   (Karen, School 1, Flintoff and Scraton, 2001, p. 15)

There is no easy answer to the question of whether mixed or single-sex PE classes are 'better'; some research suggests that a combination of single-sex and mixed classes is desirable from the perspective of young people (Rees *et al.*, 2006). Furthermore, while males tend to have a higher level of physical self-perception than females, it is important for teachers and coaches to be conscious of the feeling of vulnerability that young boys can experience in physical education contexts that foster hyper-masculinity:

They pretty quickly realised I was hopeless and one kid, who was really good at it, seemed to get a kick out of watching me fumble, drop and miss most of what came my way. He started to deliberately give me difficult passes and then bag me when I stuffed it up. Other kids joined in with him. I remember just wanting to get the hell out of there but I couldn't.   (Mark, 12 years old, Hickey, 2008, p. 153)

> **Comment**
> *Young people may experience physical education classes in very different ways from each other and from the ways intended by the teacher.*

What young people tell us about their experiences of youth sport

Attraction and barriers to sport

The most prominent reasons young people give for participating in sport are making friends and meeting people, developing physical competence, feeling included, gaining encouragement from positive feedback and reinforcement, and enjoyment. Success in competition and a desire to perform better than others seem less important to many young people (Sit and Lindner, 2005). Indeed, key barriers to young people's involvement in sport include an overemphasis on elite performance, competition for time with other activities, appearing incompetent and (especially among girls) a general feeling of inertia linked to feeling embarrassed and self-conscious about the body (Rees *et al.*, 2006).

A range of structural and financial barriers to young people's participation in sport includes poor access to quality coaching and facilities, transport difficulties and limited resources and support services (MacPhail, Kirk and Eley, 2003). In addition, socio-economic status has been demonstrated to be a factor in levels of participation, and middle-class children are often found to be over-represented in sport clubs (Kirk, 2004). There is also concern that culturally appropriate sporting opportunities for black and minority ethnic communities are limited (Sporting Equals and Sports Councils, 2009).

> **Comment**
> *Young people both access and experience sport in different ways as a result of their diverse social and cultural backgrounds.*

Pervasiveness of sport

The pervasiveness of sport in young people's lives appears to be stronger for younger learners, i.e. up to approximately age 11. For example, in written narratives, primary school students reported the frequency of their participation in sport and the variety of sports in which they engage:

> I have lots of hobbies: they are skipping, football, basketball, baseball, volleyball, swimming, and chicken limbo. My favourite hobbie [*sic*] is swimming. We go swimming during school time.   (Girl aged between 10 and 12, Collier, MacPhail and O'Sullivan, 2007, p. 199)

As young people move through the school years, sport competes with a growing range of other interests (MacPhail, Collier and O'Sullivan, 2009). Young males, however, tend to remain familiar with sporting role models, become consumers of as well as participants in sport, specialise in a smaller range of sports, and privilege sport over other activities. As one boy wrote:

> Sport plays an important part in my life. I like nearly every sport but there is one sport in the world that is my favourite and that sport is soccer. I love everything about soccer. I even love hearing about the transfer gossip on the papers and on t.v. I would watch every match that would be on the tele but I would not watch it if Rangers, Man. Utd were playing because I dispise them two teams, the only team I would watch with attention would be Liverpool. The reason why I support Liverpool is because they are a good team with lots of potential they are being held back by Man. Utd and Arsenal. Every Liverpool fan is a true fan unlike the so called Man. United fans who start supporting them after they won the premiership. The sport's that I participate in are soccer with [name of village], Gealic Football with [name of town], and I also coach handball with the young people of my estate which is very enjoyable. This goes to show that sport has a huge influence on my life.
> (Written narrative from a 15/16-year-old boy (coded BCS45) contributing to the Write Now (1999) project that asked school students to write a page describing themselves and the Ireland that they inhabit)

There is a wealth of research to suggest that young females tend not to name sporting role models, limit their involvement in sport participation and report a wider range of leisure-time options (see MacPhail, Collier and O'Sullivan, 2009). It is not necessarily that girls are disinterested in being involved in sport or physical activity, but rather that they are disengaged from the particular structure and opportunities available to them (Sandford and Rich, 2006).

Gendered socialisation

The decision to participate in sport can be linked to the ways in which young people perceive their feminine/masculine role in society. For young women, appearing overly masculine can be a barrier to participation in sport:

> I think it is fashionable to be good at sports . . . The majority, well, em . . . or most girls think it is . . . Girly girls wouldn't want anyone to know that they were good at sports and they would hide it.   (Teenage girl, O'Donovan and Kirk, 2008, p. 79)

As was noted earlier, it is particularly evident that adolescent girls participate in lower levels of physical activity compared with adolescent boys, and that they take part in a wider range of social and cultural activities:

> My friends and I go out every weekend. We go to each others houses, to the cinema, to the arcade and bowling alley, to discos & to partys . . . I love to sail, play sports

but I'm not a sports fanatic and I absolutely love to go to the beach or out with my friends.

(Written narrative from a 15/16-year-old girl (coded GSS52) contributing to the Write Now (1999) project that asked school students to write a page describing themselves and the Ireland that they inhabit).

If girls do participate in sport, research suggests that many prefer non-competitive and individual sporting activities (Williams, Bedward and Woodhouse, 2000). Boys, on the other hand, are reported to prefer team sport participation and are keen to focus on their skilfulness and sporting accomplishments. Boys also tend to be involved in physical activity pastimes, either as active participants or as invested supporters, and are followers of particular sports, teams or sports personalities, as was illustrated in the boy's written narrative presented earlier. However, while there are more opportunities for boys to be involved in sporting activities, there is also evidence that there may be less diversity in the sporting/leisure choices available to young men compared with those available to young women. In addition, compared with girls, there are fewer competing options for boys' leisure time (Wright, Macdonald and Groom, 2003). Similarly to physical education, concerns about body shape have been reported as the main reasons for the non-participation of young girls in sport (Sport England, 2005).

> *Comment*
> *Gender socialisation in sport is a two-way relationship between the sporting opportunities that are available and the positioning of the young person.*

Support structures

Relations with family, community and school affect the critical support structures needed for young people's involvement in sport (Wright, MacDonald and Groom, 2003). Leisure-time sports participation among adolescents has a tendency to be socially stratified, and is related to the sports participation of family members:

> My favourite sport is boxing and I have been boxing for a year. My brother has been boxing for fifteen years . . . He trained me for a few years and then I joined a club and I spar him most of the time.
>
> (Written narrative from a 15/16-year-old boy (coded BCS45) contributing to the Write Now (1999) project that asked school students to write a page describing themselves and the Ireland that they inhabit)

What seems apparent from the evidence presented so far is that young people are complex and diverse learners and that when asked, they tell us much from which we can learn in planning physical education or sport learning experiences. There is also a clear overlap between young people's experiences in physical education and sport.

> *Comment*
> *There is a close connection between what young people identify as encouraging learning experiences in both physical education and youth sport environments.*

Conclusion

If we acknowledge that young people are complex learners with a multiplicity of needs, then it seems clear that programmes and interventions designed to encourage higher levels of participation in physical education and sport should be multilevelled and differentiated (Mulvihill, Rivers and Aggleton, 2000). Taking into account young people's views about positive experiences in physical education and sport can be used to inform the development of meaningful, relevant and worthwhile opportunities. For example, helpful strategies might include:

- combining physical activity engagement with opportunities for socialising;
- being sensitive to the needs of less confident and lower-ability young people;
- modifying the organisation and provision of physical education classes;
- improving access to a diverse range of opportunities for physical activity;
- involving young people in the development of curriculum.

In a survey of 600 volunteer sport leaders, aged 14–18, responses to the question 'What can be done to help young people participate in sport?' suggested that making links between school and sport club provision was particularly important (MacPhail, Kirk and Eley, 2003). Thus, if school-based physical education is to support young people to develop an appreciation of physical activity and a healthy lifestyle, it should also help young people to find ways of being active after school. It could be argued, therefore, that the remit of the physical education teacher should extend beyond the school gates to wider sports communities. This approach might also suggest that the physical education teacher needs to establish a curriculum, in consultation with young people, that will complement the physical activity opportunities that are available to them outside school. Suggestions have also been made that physical education should be integrated into school-wide positive youth development programmes (Wright and Li, 2009), encouraging the physical education teacher to take a wider view of young people as learners in their school environment.

In England, the *PE and Sport Strategy for Young People* encourages those involved in promoting physical education and community sport to work together to offer all young people aged five to 16 the opportunity to participate in five hours a week of physical education and sport. The *Guide to Delivering the Five Hour Offer* (Sport England, YST and PE and Sport for Young People, 2009) outlines a vision for the strategy and the five-hour offer in particular, providing case-study examples illustrating how the school and community can interact to provide the five hours of physical education and sport. There is an acknowledgement that the roles and responsibilities of the providers need to be shared, and that providers should make physical education and sport more accessible, attractive, affordable and appropriate to the needs of young people. Certainly it can be argued that the realities of young people's lives should inform evidence-based initiatives and policy making whether it be at a curriculum, school, club or national level.

> *Comment*
> *Establishing links between school-based physical education and sport opportunities outside school is important in order to encourage young people's lifelong engagement in physical activity.*

Learning tasks

Individual task

Young people advise us that one aspect of creating a positive learning environment in physical education and sport is fostering a sense of value of the body in order to enhance body image. Thinking back to your own experiences as a young learner in physical education and/or youth sport, consider the extent to which you were conscious of your own body image and the body images of others. Based on your experiences, what proposals can you make to address adolescents' body-image concerns in physical education/sport? Is there a difference between the proposals you would make for young females and young males?

Group task

Young people suggest that for physical education to be most effective for them, it needs to be able to reflect changing times and also the unique interests of young people. How might a physical education teacher take these views into account when planning a curriculum to optimise student participation?

Further reading

O'Sullivan, M. and MacPhail, A. (eds) (2010) *Young People's Voices in Physical Education and Sport*, London: Routledge.

References

Armour, K. (2011) What is 'sport pedagogy' and why study it? In: K. Armour (ed.) (this volume).

Collier, C., MacPhail, A. and O'Sullivan, M. (2007) Student discourse on physical activity and sport among Irish young people, *Irish Educational Studies*, 26(2), 195–210.

Cothran, D. and Ennis, C. (1998) Curricula of mutual worth: comparisons of students' and teachers' curricular goals, *Journal of Teaching in Physical Education*, 17, 307–26.

Dismore, H. and Bailey, R. (2010) 'It's been a bit of a rocky start': attitudes toward physical education following transition, *Physical Education and Sport Pedagogy*, iFirst Article, 1–17.

Duncan, M. J., Al-Nakeed, Y., Nevill, A. and Jones, M. V. (2004) Body image and physical activity in British secondary school children, *European Physical Education Review*, 10(3), 243–60.

Fairclough, S. and Stratton, G. (2005) 'Physical education makes you fit and healthy.' Physical education's contribution to young people's physical activity levels, *Health Education Research*, 20(1), 14–23.

Fitzgerald, H. (2005) Still feeling like a spare piece of luggage? Embodied experiences of (dis)ability in physical education and school sport, *Physical Education and Sport Pedagogy*, 10(1), 41–59.

Flintoff, A. and Scraton, S. (2001) Stepping into active leisure? Young women's perceptions of active lifestyles and their experiences of school physical education, *Sport, Education and Society*, 6(1), 5–22.

Garrett, R. (2004) Negotiating a physical identity: girls, bodies and physical education, *Sport, Education and Society*, 9(2), 223–37.

Hickey, C. (2008) Physical education, sport and hyper-masculinity in schools, *Sport, Education and Society*, 13(2), 147–61.

Jackson, L. (2002) *Freaks, Geeks & Asperger Syndrome: A user guide to adolescence*, London: JKP.

Kirk, D. (2004) Sport and early learning experiences. In: *Driving up Participation: The challenge for sport*, London: Sport England, 69–78.

Laws, C. and Fisher, R. (1999) Pupils' interpretations of physical education. In: C. A. Hardy and M. Mawer (eds) *Learning and Teaching in Physical Education*, London: Falmer Press, 23–37.

Lines, G. (2007) The impact of media sport events on the active participation of young people and some implications for PE pedagogy, *Sport, Education and Society*, 12(4), 349–66.

Long, J. and Carless, D. (2010) Hearing, listening and acting. In: O'Sullivan, M. and MacPhail, A. (eds) *Young People's Voices in Physical Education and Sport*, London: Routledge, 213–25.

MacPhail, A. (2010) Listening to pupils' voices. In: R. Bailey (ed.) *Physical Education For Learning: A guide for secondary schools*, London: Routledge, 228–38.

MacPhail, A., Collier, C. and O'Sullivan, M. (2009) Lifestyles and gendered patterns of leisure and sporting interests among Irish adolescents, *Sport, Education and Society*, 14(3), 281–99.

MacPhail, A., Kirk, D. and Eley, D. (2003) Listening to young people's voices: youth sports leaders' advice on facilitating participation in sport, *European Physical Education Review*, 9(1), 57–73.

McMahon, E. (2007) 'You don't feel like ants and giants': student involvement in negotiating the physical education curriculum, Master's thesis, University of Limerick, Ireland.

Mulvihill, C., Rivers, K. and Aggleton, P. (2000) Views of young people towards physical activity: determinants and barriers to involvement, *Health Education*, 100(5), 190–99.

O'Donovan, T. and Kirk, D. (2008) Reconceptualizing student motivation in physical education: An examination of what resources are valued by pre-adolescent girls in contemporary society, *European Physical Education Review*, 14(1), 71–91.

Oliver, K. L., Hamzeh, M. and McCaughtry, N. (2009) 'Girly girls *can* play games's / '*Las niñas pueden jugar tambien*': Co-creating a curriculum of possibilities with 5th grade girls', *Journal of Teaching in Physical Education*, 28(1), 90–110.

O'Sullivan, M. and MacPhail, A. (eds) (2010) *Young People's Voices in Physical Education and Sport*, London: Routledge.

Rees, R., Kavanagh, J., Harden, A., Shepherd, J., Brunton, G., Oliver, S. and Oakley, A. (2006) Young people and physical activity: a systematic review matching their views to effective interventions, *Health Education Research*, 21(6), 806–25.

Sandford, R. and Rich, E. (2006) Learners and popular culture. In: D. Kirk, D. Macdonald and M. O'Sullivan (eds) *The Handbook of Physical Education*, London: SAGE, 275–91.

Sit, C. H. P. and Lindner, K. J. (2005) Motivational orientations in youth sport participation: using achievement goal theory and reversal theory, *Personality and Individual Differences*, 38, 605–18.

Smith, A. and Parr, M. (2007) Young people's views on the nature and purposes of physical education: a sociological analysis, *Sport, Education and Society*, 12(1), 37–58.

Sport England (2005) *Understanding Participation in Sport: A systematic review*, London: Sport England.

Sport England, YST and PE and Sport for Young People (2009) *The PE and Sport Strategy for Young People. Guide to delivering the five hour offer*, London: Sport England.

Sporting Equals and Sports Councils (2009) *A Systematic Review of the Literature on Black and Minority Ethnic Communities in Sport and Physical Recreation*, Birmingham: Sporting Equals.

Trout, J. and Graber, K. C. (2009) Perceptions of overweight students concerning their experiences in physical education, *Journal of Teaching in Physical Education*, 28(3), 272–92.

Williams, A., Bedward, J. and Woodhouse, J. (2000) An inclusive National Curriculum? The experience of adolescent girls, *European Journal of Physical Education*, 5, 4–18.

Wright, J., Macdonald, D. and Groom, L. (2003) Physical activity and young people: beyond participation, *Sport, Education and Society*, 8(1), 17–33.

Wright, P. M. and Li, W. (2009) Exploring the relevance of positive youth development in urban physical education, *Physical Education and Sport Pedagogy*, 14(3), 241–51.

Write Now (1999) *Information for schools*, Dublin Millennium Committee, Guidelines for Teachers.

Understanding young people's motivation in physical education and youth sport

Christopher M. Spray, Loughborough University

Case study: Jayne

At primary school Jayne really enjoyed physical education (PE) and looked forward to lessons each week. She was keen to improve in everything she attempted and also to show that she was better than her classmates. She tried hard in lessons, particularly when she was confident of outperforming her peers. In short, she felt competent and 'chose freely' to do PE and organised sport outside school. However, when Jayne transferred to secondary school her motivation changed. She no longer enjoyed a physical advantage over many of her new peers and she did not feel one of the most able in class; she had become a 'smaller fish in a bigger pond'. Consequently, Jayne began to feel less confident about, and satisfied with, her physical abilities. She started to believe that ability in PE was something that was impossible to improve. She noticed that she did not enjoy PE as much as she did in primary school and was quite anxious about performing more poorly than others in her class. Her effort levels in lessons declined significantly. She only took part in lessons because she felt she should and because she did not want to be punished for missing class. Eventually, Jayne saw no point to PE at all, started to skip lessons and frequently brought in notes that claimed she was unwell. Her involvement in leisure-time sport beyond school also declined dramatically.

What does motivation look like?

Jayne's story illustrates some of the behaviours that can be observed in a typical PE lesson, and that may lead teachers and pupils to infer a particular individual's motivation. Such behaviours include the choice of personally challenging skills and activities when tasks of varying levels of difficulty are provided, the willingness to devote physical effort to attempting such tasks, and persistence when progress is not as good as one would hope or expect. Choice, effort and persistence are all behavioural indicators of motivation (Roberts, 2001). However, researchers are also interested in 'how' children and adolescents experience the PE class, examining such variables as enjoyment, sense of autonomy, anxiety, concentration, attributions for success and failure, and intentions to be physically active beyond the compulsory school curriculum into leisure-time physical activity. In other words, as well as behaviour, it is important to know about affect (emotions) and cognitions (thoughts) experienced in PE classes and other settings where children and young people encounter sport.

Behaviours, cognitions and emotions can be seen as the outcomes of a chain or sequence of motivational processes. Often in the psychological literature, reference is made to 'adaptive' and 'maladaptive' motivation. Adaptive motivation refers to a positive profile of outcomes (from a pedagogic viewpoint). For example, some young people demonstrate high levels of effort and persistence, choose to become involved in sports, enjoy the activities, concentrate on the task at hand, experience feelings of pride and satisfaction, show willingness to ask for help when required, and possess strong intentions to continue with physical activity. In contrast, others exhibit maladaptive motivation including low levels of effort and persistence, feelings of anxiety, boredom, shame and embarrassment, and intentions to avoid or quit participation in PE, sport and other physical activities.

The concepts that researchers utilise to 'explain' adaptive and maladaptive outcomes will vary depending on the theoretical perspective(s) they adopt. Contemporary theories of motivation focus on individual difference variables and environmental factors that help to account for behavioural and emotional engagement in achievement settings such as PE and youth sport. *Individual differences* refer to personal, disposition-like variables that are seen as relatively stable, such as the way a young person tends to think of or define 'success' in PE and sport activities. *Environmental factors* refer to what goes on in PE lessons or coaching sessions, such as how the teacher groups pupils for particular activities, how a coach structures sessions, and the type of feedback given in response to effort.

This chapter will introduce readers to contemporary theories of motivation, outline relevant research and its implications for teaching/coaching practices, and suggest future research needs where appropriate. Rather than adopt a narrow theoretical focus, a number of interrelated psychological factors will be discussed. These include factors that have received sustained attention in research into PE and sport and that have the potential to further illuminate young people's motivational processes in these domains. These factors are:

- personal and situational achievement goals;
- beliefs about ability;
- physical self-concept;
- self-determination;
- social comparison processes.

Personal and situational goals: 'What am I aiming to achieve?'

Personal goals

In PE and sport, some young people define success in self-referenced terms, thus seeking to improve and master physical skills. These individuals are concerned with acquiring abilities, and their notions of competence are linked to the task itself, not the achievements of others. On the other hand, some other young people will define their own success in terms of what their classmates can do, thus seeking to demonstrate their own superior ability (Nicholls, 1989). Goals that are concerned with self-improvement and task mastery are typically given the label 'mastery' or 'task' goals, whereas goals that are concerned with showing superiority over others are typically given the label 'performance' or 'ego' goals.* A large body of research, mainly focusing on affective and cognitive responses to PE and sport, has shown that more adaptive responses are associated with the adoption of task goals (see Biddle, Wang, Chatzisarantis and Spray, 2003).

More recently, research attention has turned to understanding goals that direct individuals' concerns toward incompetence and failure, in addition to those goals outlined above that aim to develop or demonstrate competence and success. In the swimming pool, for example, pupils may be concerned about doing poorly compared with others in their class (finishing last in a race), and/or they may be concerned about failing on a task (inability to tread water for two minutes). The first type of concern is other-referenced, whereas the second type of concern is task-referenced. In both cases, however, pupils strive to avoid the adverse prospect of demonstrating incompetence. These types of ego and task goals that focus on negative possibilities are termed avoidance goals. Goals that focus on the positive prospect of showing or developing competence are known as approach goals (Elliot, 2005).

Research in PE and youth sport that includes both approach and avoidance forms of achievement goals is in its infancy and it is difficult to say with confidence at this point whether the approach–avoidance distinction gives better insight into pupils' motivational processes and outcomes than the study of approach goals alone. However, it appears potentially fruitful to examine both approach and avoidance goals in PE and youth sport settings because teachers and coaches should become more aware of the scope of individuals' aims and their consequences. For example, two studies by Warburton and Spray (2008, 2009) found that pupils in Year 6 (age 10–11) and in Key Stage 3 (age 11–14) endorsed task-avoidance goals in school PE lessons. These longitudinal investigations also revealed that task-approach goals declined over time, a potentially worrisome finding given the positive motivational outcomes associated with such goals. Moreover, differences in goal adoption were evident between boys and girls at the end of primary school, with boys more strongly endorsing task-approach goals and both types of ego goals. These gender differences

---

*Throughout this chapter the terms task and ego refer to self/task- and normatively referenced goals respectively.

persisted into the first year of secondary school. Further work is necessary to determine the motivational consequences associated with these changes in goal emphasis.

> **Comment**
> *Young people can adopt four goals: task- and ego-approach goals and task- and ego-avoidance goals. These goals differ in terms of whether they are self/task- or other-referenced and in terms of whether they focus on success or failure.*

Situational goals

In addition to individual tendencies to adopt particular goals, perceptions of the environmental or situational goals that have been created by the teacher or coach are held to be an important determinant of motivation (see Ames, 1992). A great deal of research activity has targeted two types of environment or 'motivational climate' which parallel the personal task and ego goals discussed earlier. First, a task-involving climate prevails when teachers/coaches are perceived to encourage learners' decision making, emphasise the value of effort and improvement over ability and competitive outcomes, and provide private self-referenced feedback to individuals. Second, an ego-involving climate prevails when coaches/teachers are perceived to be authoritarian and directive, and when they publicly praise the superior performers for successful competitive outcomes or better performance on particular skills. Reviews of motivational climate research in PE and sport point toward the adaptive consequences of young people perceiving a task-involving atmosphere (see Harwood *et al.*, 2008). There is, however, a need for further research that examines the impact of specific pedagogic practices. An example would be identifying when it is more advantageous, from a motivational standpoint, for teachers and coaches to arrange homogeneous (individuals of similar ability working together) versus heterogeneous (individuals of different ability working together) groupings when in the gymnasium, swimming pool or on the games field. Moreover, the interactive (combined) effects of perceived climate with dispositional goals have not received extensive examination. The impact of teaching and coaching behaviours on the approach or avoidance nature of goal strivings also deserves greater systematic inquiry (Keegan *et al.*, 2009).

> **Comment**
> *Teachers and coaches matter because their practices will influence the achievement goals held to be important by young learners in PE and sport.*

Beliefs about ability: 'Is it possible to improve?'

Researchers in sport and PE have begun to examine young people's beliefs about ability and the links between these beliefs and motivation. Beliefs about the nature of ability (or 'implicit theories') centre on an individual's view of whether such ability is fixed, stable and a given gift, or whether ability is malleable and increasable through learning. The former view has been termed an entity theory, whereas the latter view has been labelled an incremental theory. It is argued that individuals holding an entity perspective will be more likely to adopt ego goals in order to demonstrate their 'gift', whereas those espousing incremental views will tend to adopt task goals in order to develop their learning and skills (see Dweck, 1999). Investigations in sport and PE have largely confirmed these proposed relationships, showing that children tend to endorse the incremental theory more than the entity theory, at least when beliefs are assessed at the level of sport/PE in general rather than in relation to specific activities. Research findings also link the incremental perspective with task goals and enjoyment, whereas the entity perspective has been linked with ego goals and amotivation (Biddle, Wang, Kavussanu and Spray, 2003; Warburton and Spray, 2008, 2009).

Evidence suggests, therefore, that coaches and teachers should facilitate an incremental view whilst attempting to downplay the entity perspective. Encouraging an incremental theory will most likely be achieved through task setting that is appropriate to an individual's needs. Differentiation in task setting can help to offset outcome comparisons and allow for a focus on the self. Moreover, consistent exhortation of the importance of effort, understanding, strategy, ideas, learning and practice may help to challenge notions of ability being stable, uncontrollable and a gift that one is either given or not. Although more research is needed, beliefs about the fixed nature of physical ability are likely to be cultivated by setting tasks and activities that are simply too difficult for some children as well as alluding to the natural, innate talent of particular individuals via praise and feedback. Research is also needed to examine young people's views about more specific aspects of PE and sport (i.e. beliefs about gymnastics versus games, for example, or beliefs about particular skills involved in one sport). Such work would provide more comprehensive information about the views held by young people and thus help teachers and coaches to challenge potentially maladaptive beliefs.

> **Comment**
> *Entity and incremental beliefs about ability have been linked with important motivational outcomes in PE and sport.*

Physical self-concept: 'How do I feel about myself physically?'

Physical self-concept (PSC) refers to how satisfied individuals are with their physical self. Possessing a positive self-concept in any of life's key domains would seem to be a desirable outcome in its own right as well as serving to underlie other positive outcomes such as achievement (Marsh and Craven, 2006). PSC is likely to lead to greater effort, meaningful choices and persistence in youth sport and PE which will facilitate achievement over time. Consequently, the development of a positive sense of the physical self in young people is a valued aim. Most research to date has focused on the development and validation of measures that have elucidated the multidimensional structure of PSC. For example, work by Marsh and colleagues in developing the Physical Self-Description Questionnaire identifies nine factors that underpin PSC, which in turn forms a part of global self-esteem. These factors are ratings of appearance, health, strength, sports competence, body fat, coordination, physical activity, flexibility and endurance (Marsh *et al.*, 1994).

In an attempt to examine the antecedents of young people's PSC, Spray and Warburton (2010) examined change in both overall and specific elements of PSC in PE across the transition from primary to secondary school (Years 6 to 7) in England. These authors also wanted to determine whether change in PSC was linked to pupils' personal goals and those goals they perceived their PE teachers to emphasise and value. Findings showed that over time, students' perceptions of their appearance, sports competence, and strength remained stable, whereas perceptions of overall PSC, coordination, flexibility and endurance declined. Perceptions of a task-involving climate in PE and personal task-approach goal adoption also declined. On the other hand, both types of performance goal adoption and perceived ego-involving climate increased. These findings suggest that some physical self-perceptions may be more stable than others across Years 6 and 7, and where changes occur in self-perceptions, these are on average in a negative direction. Further research in both PE and youth sport is needed to determine whether pedagogic practices that promote a task-involving climate and adoption of task-approach goals facilitate a positive and stable PSC.

> *Comment*
> *Physical self-concept refers to how satisfied individuals are with their physical self, both in an overall sense and with regard to specific sub-components such as appearance, sports competence and strength.*

Self-determination: 'Do I want to do it?'

A popular theoretical perspective that provides an alternative lens through which to examine motivational processes in PE and youth sport is self-determination theory (SDT; Deci and Ryan, 1985). A key component of this approach is that teaching and coaching behaviours impact on whether young people develop a sense of competence, autonomy and relatedness. In other words, professional practices determine whether youth feel more able, more in control of their own actions, and more connected with their PE or sport group.

The SDT approach also explains the different types of motivation that young people may exhibit in the PE class or sport setting, which reflect different degrees of self-determination (volition or wanting to do the activity). Some children and adolescents, although compelled to undertake PE as part of the National Curriculum (for example in England), clearly enjoy the subject, derive pleasure and satisfaction from it, and would freely choose to do it if it were not compulsory. These young people are intrinsically motivated and, as a consequence, experience positive behavioural, affective and cognitive outcomes. Other pupils may have little or no intrinsic motivation for PE but may value the subject and what it can offer them (for example, in terms of health or an 'escape' from other lessons). These pupils are said to have a self-determined form of extrinsic motivation and would be expected to show effort and persistence because they want to do PE. However, some pupils do not choose freely to engage in PE and only take part in lessons because they know they should or must (non-self-determined extrinsic motivation). Such reasons can be quite controlling in that the pupil is not participating in activities with a sense of volition. Hence, effort and persistence, as well as enjoyment of activities, are likely to be diminished.

Some pupils have an absence of both intrinsic and extrinsic motivation in PE; they are said to be amotivated. Amotivation is likely to arise from particular beliefs relating to capacity, effort, value, and task characteristics (Legault *et al.*, 2006; see also Sandford and Duncombe, Chapter 13, this volume). That is, individuals may believe that whatever they try will not bring about successful outcomes (capacity), they are unwilling to work hard physically (effort), and see little point in the subject as a whole or in particular PE activities. In this case, PE is both unimportant and unappealing to them (value and task) and so, not surprisingly, these pupils tend to evidence a maladaptive profile of behaviours, feelings and thoughts in PE lessons. The PE context offers a unique opportunity within physical settings to study the concept of amotivation in children and youth. For obvious reasons, amotivation is less likely to be prevalent in youth sport where participation is voluntary.

Teachers and coaches may be able to help young people internalise or 'take in' the value of PE and sport by exhibiting particular behaviours, e.g. by providing choice of activities, acknowledgement of pupils' negative views toward some types of tasks, giving rationales for undertaking particular drills, and avoiding any emphasis on an ego-involving climate (see Hagger and Chatzisarantis, 2007). Internalisation refers to controlling types of motivation becoming more self-determined over time. For example, a pupil may initially take part in swimming only because she/he is aware that it is compulsory. However, undertaking lessons that permit some degree of decision making (e.g. choice of stroke and distance) promotes a feeling of connectedness with others in the pool (e.g. cooperative life-saving/survival activities in pairs or small groups that encourage peer-assisted learning). The perception of personal improvement may result in need satisfaction. This is likely to enhance the value and utility of swimming for the pupil so that she/he wants to continue with swimming activities.

> **Comment**
> *According to SDT, individuals have three universal and innate psychological needs for competence, autonomy and relatedness. These needs can be supported or not by the ways in which teachers and coaches deliver their sessions.*

Social comparison processes: 'What are my team mates or classmates like?'

An avenue of inquiry that has received little systematic attention in physical settings but which enjoys a well-established presence in the extant social and educational psychology literatures is that of social comparison processes (see Dijkstra *et al.*, 2008). Because PE and sport take place in public arenas, the 'universal and automatic' nature of making comparisons with others is, arguably, likely to have a significant impact on young people's motivation. It has already been noted that social comparison operates within certain goal perspectives i.e. when individuals hold ego goals and/or perceive an ego-involving group climate. However, the literature on social comparison is much wider than that embodied within achievement goal theory.

In educational psychology, extensive research has examined the 'big-fish-little-pond effect' (BFLPE; Marsh, 1987). The term BFLPE refers to the phenomenon that pupils tend to have a more negative view of their academic abilities (academic self-concept) when placed in a selective or high-ability class (school) than equally able pupils placed in a non-selective, more mixed heterogeneous class (school). The psychological process underpinning this effect is likely to be negative comparisons with able classmates, that is, one's perceived relative standing (Huguet *et al.*, 2009). A perception that one's ability compares unfavourably with most classmates leads to lowered academic self-concept. Although there is initial evidence that the BFLPE operates in physical settings with young people (Chanal *et al.*, 2005; Chanal and Sarrazin, 2007), a great deal more work is required to identify the psychological processes involved.

The school class is just one frame of reference that young people can use to compare themselves. At the class level, it can be argued that social comparison is imposed on individuals because it is extremely difficult to avoid making comparisons. However, in addition to the class, pupils may choose to engage in comparisons with specific individuals in or outside the immediate class. Social psychologists have long been interested in specific target comparisons and there is a comprehensive body of experimental studies examining such processes. The study of these single target choices as an additional frame of reference to the class in school, or team in sport, could be very informative in explaining motivational responses in PE and sport settings (Chanal and Sarrazin, 2007). Of particular interest are the specific types of target comparisons made, the motives or reasons underlying comparers' choices, and the consequences of these comparisons (Dijkstra *et al.*, 2008).

Individuals can choose to compare upwards with an individual perceived to be better than themselves, downwards with an individual perceived to be worse, or laterally with a similar other. Most evidence points to the prevalence of making upward comparisons with others *slightly* better than the comparer. Moreover, individuals seeking self-improvement may be more likely to compare upwards whereas those who, for whatever reason, doubt their ability, may compare downwards in a self-protective manner. A sought-after outcome of comparison is that individuals learn more about themselves in relation to others, so in some situations, such as joining a new class or team, self-verification may be an especially important motive to compare ('What's my ability like in relation to others – do I belong here?'). The consequences of these different kinds of comparisons may be positive or negative. It has generally been found that upward comparisons have a beneficial effect on performance and self-evaluations, probably due to motivational and learning factors. Downward comparisons may have a self-enhancing effect on the comparer's self-esteem but are unlikely to facilitate learning and performance in achievement settings (Dijkstra *et al.*, 2008).

Comparison processes deserve further empirical attention in sport and PE using a wider range of methods than has hitherto been the case in the educational and social psychology literatures. Not only will knowledge of motivational processes be augmented by such endeavours, the evidence accrued could inform recommendations for professional practice (e.g. whether to organise PE activities in single-sex or mixed groups or whether to organise coaching sessions on the basis of physical ability).

Comment

In the main, two frames of reference have been examined within the social comparison literature in education. One is the class as a whole and the other is specific individual target comparisons within the class.

Conclusion

The aim of this chapter was to introduce theory and research in motivation that helps us to understand learning and diverse learners in PE and sport settings. Theories are based on different assumptions and research traditions but those described herein all appear useful in elucidating young people's motivational processes. Achievement goal theory and SDT are well established. Indeed, arguably, the majority of empirical efforts based on these frameworks focus on young people. Other perspectives such as social comparison processes appear to be potentially insightful and warrant further investigation in sport and PE. It cannot be assumed that these processes function in sport and PE in the same ways that they function in the classroom.

The case study illustrates the key points to be taken from this chapter. Initially, Jayne demonstrated a largely adaptive profile involving high effort levels brought about by a sense of competence and self-determination, and the joint adoption of ego- and task-approach goals. When in a new environment, however, the BFLPE meant that she was no longer confident of achieving her ego-approach goals. Task-approach goals declined, the emergence of ego-avoidance goals led to higher anxiety levels, entity beliefs about physical ability developed, and PSC suffered. From a sense of self-determination in primary school, Jayne developed controlling reasons for undertaking PE in secondary school before becoming amotivated and undertaking less physical activity and sport in general.

Jayne's story is perhaps familiar to school PE teachers, and many youth sport coaches will have witnessed signs of the development of maladaptive beliefs, emotions and behaviour across the adolescent years. However, continued research efforts that identify key psychological constructs and their influence during childhood and adolescence will help practitioners to tailor learning and teaching to individual need and thus provide pedagogic encounters that sustain adaptive motivational processes in PE and youth sport.

Learning tasks

Individual task

1 Write one or two paragraphs reflecting on your own experiences in physical education and/or youth sport. Try to relate the key constructs discussed in this chapter to your motivation as a young learner. For example, what personal and situational factors changed between primary and secondary school? Did you experience variable motivational climates and need satisfaction in coaching sessions? Did your beliefs about physical ability change – how would you describe your beliefs now?

2 Can you recall a PE class, sport team (or even an academic class in school) when others' high ability impacted negatively on your own self-perceptions? How easy is it to determine one's perceived relative standing within a PE or sport group? How might individual comparison targets exacerbate or mitigate the negative impact of a high group average ability?

(continued)

Group task

Identify specific teaching or coaching behaviours based on your collective experiences in PE and sport. These could refer to the design of particular tasks/practices, grouping of individuals, teacher/coach authority, and recognition/evaluation of effort and performance. For each behaviour, discuss which types of achievement goals were promoted and the resulting motivational impact. Are all group members in agreement about the goals promoted and associated impact? If not, why not?

Further reading

Roberts, G. C. (ed.) (2001) *Advances in Motivation in Sport and Exercise*, Champaign, IL: Human Kinetics (see Chapters 3, 4 and 5).

Hagger, M. S. and Chatzisarantis, N. L. D. (eds) (2007) *Intrinsic Motivation and Self-determination in Exercise and Sport*, Champaign, IL: Human Kinetics (see Chapters 4, 13 and 17).

References

Ames, C. (1992) Achievement goals, motivational climate, and motivational processes. In: G. C. Roberts (ed) *Motivation in Sport and Exercise*, Champaign, IL: Human Kinetics, 161–76.

Biddle, S. J. H., Wang, C. K. J., Chatzisarantis, N. L. D. and Spray, C. M. (2003) Motivation for physical activity in young people: entity and incremental beliefs about athletic ability, *Journal of Sports Sciences*, 21, 973–89.

Biddle, S. J. H., Wang, C. K. J., Kavussanu, M. and Spray, C. M. (2003) Correlates of achievement goal orientations in physical activity: a systematic review of research, *European Journal of Sport Science*, 3(5), 1–20.

Chanal, J. P. and Sarrazin, P. G. (2007) Big-fish-little-pond effect versus positive effect of upward comparisons in the classroom: how does one reconcile contradictory results?, *International Review of Social Psychology/Revue Internationale de Psychologie Sociale*, 20, 69–86.

Chanal, J. P., Marsh, H. W., Sarrazin, P. G. and Bois, J. E. (2005) Big-fish-little-pond effects on gymnastics self-concept: social comparison processes in a physical setting, *Journal of Sport & Exercise Psychology*, 27, 53–70.

Deci, E. L. and Ryan, R. M. (1985) *Intrinsic Motivation and Self-determination in Human Behavior*, New York: Plenum Press.

Dijkstra, P., Kuyper, H., van der Werf, G., Buunk, A. P. and van der Zee, Y. G. (2008) Social comparison in the classroom: a review, *Review of Educational Research*, 78, 828–79.

Dweck, C. S. (1999) *Self Theories: Their role in motivation, personality, and development*, Philadelphia, PA: Psychology Press.

Elliot, A. J. (2005) A conceptual history of the achievement goal construct. In: A. J. Elliot and C. S. Dweck (eds) *Handbook of Competence and Motivation*, New York: The Guilford Press, 52–72.

Hagger, M. S. and Chatzisarantis, N. L. D. (eds) (2007) *Intrinsic Motivation and Self-determination in Exercise and Sport*, Champaign, IL: Human Kinetics.

Harwood, C., Spray, C. M. and Keegan, R. (2008) Achievement goal theories in sport. In: T. S. Horn (ed) *Advances in Sport Psychology*, Champaign, IL: Human Kinetics, 157–85.

Huguet, P., Dumas, F., Marsh, H., Regner, I., Wheeler, L., Suls, J., Seaton, M. and Nezlek, J. (2009) Clarifying the role of social comparison in the big-fish-little-pond effect (BFLPE): an integrative study, *Journal of Personality and Social Psychology*, 97, 156–70.

Keegan, R., Harwood, C. G., Spray, C. M. and Lavallee, D. (2009) A qualitative investigation exploring the motivational climate in early-career sports participants: coach, parent and peer influences on sport motivation, *Psychology of Sport and Exercise,* 10, 361–72.

Legault, L., Green-Demers, I. and Pelletier, L. (2006) Why do high school students lack motivation in the classroom? Toward an understanding of academic amotivation and the role of social support, *Journal of Educational Psychology,* 98, 567–82.

Marsh, H. W. (1987) The big-fish-little-pond effect on academic self-concept, *Journal of Educational Psychology,* 79, 280–95.

Marsh, H. W. and Craven, R. G. (2006) Reciprocal effects of self-concept and performance from a multidimensional perspective: beyond seductive pleasure and unidimensional perspectives, *Perspectives on Psychological Science,* 1, 133–63.

Marsh, H. W., Richards, G. E., Johnson, S., Roche, L. and Tremayne, P. (1994) Physical Self-Description Questionnaire: psychometric properties and a multitrait-multimethod analysis of relations to existing instruments, *Journal of Sport & Exercise Psychology,* 16, 270–305.

Nicholls, J. G. (1989) *The Competitive Ethos and Democratic Education,* Cambridge, MA: Harvard University Press.

Roberts, G. C. (ed.) (2001) *Advances in Motivation in Sport and Exercise,* Champaign, IL: Human Kinetics.

Spray, C. M. and Warburton, V. E. (2010) *Teachers' emphases on achievement goals in physical education across the transition to secondary school: Relationships with children's goal adoption and physical self-concept,* manuscript submitted for publication.

Warburton, V. E. and Spray, C. (2008) Motivation in physical education across the primary–secondary school transition, *European Physical Education Review,* 14, 157–78.

Warburton, V. E. and Spray, C. M. (2009) Antecedents of approach–avoidance achievement goal adoption in physical education: a longitudinal perspective, *Journal of Teaching in Physical Education,* 28, 214–32.

10

Young people, sporting bodies, vulnerable identities

Laura Azzarito, Loughborough University

I think my body's a bit different because, yeah, it's like, I've always been like, really lazy and that to be honest, like I didn't really used to like sport much, but I used to like playing the games . . . It's like, I'm really lazy and I'm trying to change that. It's like, I'm trying to eat more healthy stuff and I just live off the junk food . . . I just feel, like, it's good to do exercise every day, to be honest; it's like there's no point just sitting around all day.

(Adolescent girl)

 ## Introduction

Children and young people, especially adolescents, are often preoccupied with their bodies, and they find the search for an identity that is positive, comfortable and 'fit' very difficult at times. This chapter considers young people, their bodies and the ways in which their identities in physical education (PE) and youth sport settings might be vulnerable to the embodiment of elitist ideals of sporting bodies. Such ideals are frequently circulated in society through the media. If teachers and coaches are able to adopt body pedagogies that are sensitive to the fragile identity processes that characterise adolescence, this can raise young people's critical awareness of body issues. In turn, such awareness may help young people to find meaningful and culturally relevant ways to become who they want to be in and through physical activity.

The chapter will explore the following:

- the ways in which media representations of sporting bodies can influence young people's views on 'ideal' bodies;
- implications for young people's embodiment where representations of ideal bodies are viewed as (specific) male bodies;
- some of the complex ways in which the embodiment of popular sport and health discourses can make young people vulnerable.

As you read this chapter, try to recall the ways you thought, felt, and viewed your body and yourself in PE as well as in other sport settings. You might also like to recall a peer, friend or family member who perhaps struggled in different ways, more or less than you, in these and other sport settings where the body was on display.

Young bodies and identities in sport

In a high-technology society, young people are constantly bombarded by all kinds of messages about the health, well-being and fitness of the body. Media messages about health, the body and sport that young people read, interpret and often unconsciously internalise in their everyday lives impact their identity processes, and thus how they view themselves in physical activity. For instance, current public health discourses about adolescents 'at risk' of obesity can potentially have a detrimental impact on young people in physical activity (Azzarito, 2009). This is especially a concern when some cohorts of young people (e.g. ethnic minority girls) are labelled as more 'at risk' than other groups. Faced with alarmist messages about their bodies, young people, especially those who have limited access to sport and physical activity because of social or economic barriers, might eventually embody negative labels, such as 'abnormal'.

During adolescence, a time when young people already inhabit uncertainties (Rasmussen, 2006), public concerns about health and physically (in)active lifestyles might intensify the ongoing preoccupation with who young people are and who they want to become. In addition to the 'obesity epidemic' discourse, dominant media-led sport narratives can create another source of pressure for young people by encouraging their desire to strive for unrealistic ideals of corporeal perfection. Given young people's already shifting and contested identities (Azzarito and Katzew, 2010), such contradictory discourses of the body can create a doubtful terrain for their physicality development (Dittmar, 2008), especially for those who are labelled a 'problem' (Harris, 2004).

Young people from ethnic minorities (especially girls) may find the struggle to make sense of the self in health and sport contexts even more difficult. They may find themselves dealing with an increasing medicalisation of their bodies in public health discourses, which deem them to be 'different' or 'at risk'. Paradoxically, at the same time, these young people inhabit a world of global media images of bodies that have been perfected through sport and exercise (Giardina and Donnelly, 2008). Because the body matters a great deal to young people, sport becomes not only a site for regulation and remedy, but also a body project for living successfully in society (Harris, 2004). Sport thus remains a relevant but conflictual and unequal site for girls' and boys' management of identity (Bramham, 2003; Clark and Paechter, 2007, Scraton *et al.*, 1999).

It is important to recognise that it is not sport per se that causes problems for some young people and their identities. It is the ways in which sport practices are constructed that continue to legitimate and privilege boys who use sport sites to construct masculine body-selves. For example, in the United Kingdom, boys might make sense of their identity by aspiring to become footballers and aiming to display the masculine sporting body ideals portrayed by the media (Bramham, 2003). On the other hand, girls who might aspire to become footballers would likely find that the ideals of the feminine body, as portrayed in the media, would render their search for a female identity within football undesirable, even socially inappropriate. It therefore becomes difficult for girls to imagine themselves participating in sports like football. This can be especially true for ethnic-minority girls whose bodies are labelled by health discourses as at risk, passive and/or inactive and, at the same time, are 'invisible' in media representations of sporting bodies in football.

> **Comment**
> *Enduring gender, race and social class inequalities makes it difficult for some young people to imagine who they are and who they want to be in sport.*

Being designated as having a body 'at risk' can negatively affect how some young people see themselves. This is especially the case when they envision their bodies as 'different' or 'inadequate', and perhaps in conflict with or absent from the media representations of ideal sporting bodies. Young people's engagement with these contemporary contradictory discourses of the body might result in the embodiment of narrow conceptions of 'appropriate' bodies, making them vulnerable in their ongoing struggle to develop a positive and comfortable sense of self. What this suggests is that body issues should be critically addressed in schools, and in both physical education and youth sport settings where bodies are always on display. For teachers and coaches, an understanding of these issues is a vital tool in the pedagogical process. Sport pedagogies that take into account the complex adolescent struggle to make sense of the self might help all young people develop their potentialities in and through physical activity.

Media as a site of young people's embodied learning about sporting bodies

Young people engage with physical culture in a variety of learning spaces. Media operate as one of the most important contemporary sites of learning about body values, attitudes and ideals, serving as a pedagogical platform for young people's cultivation of identities (Kenway and Bullen, 2008). As the world of images cultivates particular ways of being in society, social values, attitudes and beliefs are inscribed onto the body in historically relevant ways (Hargreaves and Vertinsky, 2007). The media tell stories about the body, promising corporeal ideals that young people are encouraged to desire, but which reflect particular social norms (Correa, 2009).

One type of ideal body that media construct and represent is the 'sporting body'. As images of sporting bodies are widely circulated in the global media, the complex links among various ways of seeing, looking at and knowing about the body become visible. Sporting bodies, as presented by sport magazines, TV, the internet and movies, signify images of popularity, success and achievement (Duncan, 2007). Because the body symbolises the self, such corporeal representations of sporting bodies become crucial to the ways young people learn to understand, view and craft themselves in relation to these idealised bodies.

Yet, as Shilling (2006) argues, the body is deeply implicated in inequality. *Sporting bodies* account for and display complex power relations shaped by dominant ideals and beliefs about the body. These beliefs are informed by gender and racial norms that are embedded in particular places. Thus, it is important to acknowledge that 'The social reproduction of society also involves the *social reproduction of appropriate bodies*' (Shilling, 2006, p. 106). As Wright (1991, p. 50) argues, for instance, sports media create 'appropriate bodies' in relation to gender, and there are questions to be asked about this process of socialisation and representation. A key question might be: 'Whose stories are told and what bodies are silenced in this process of inscription?' To this we might add: 'How do these stories impact on our young learners in physical education and youth sport?'

> ### Comment
> *Sporting bodies are implicated in the social reproduction of* **appropriate** *bodies.*

It has been argued that the production of 'appropriate bodies' in sport, as portrayed in the media, defines and makes highly visible the social construction of boys' hegemonic masculinity. This is a process of naturalising the status quo, whereby sport is viewed as a male-dominant practice (Scraton *et al.*, 1999) whilst emphasising the subordination of women in sport (Hall, 1996). According to Duncan (2007, p. 63), gendered discourses of sporting bodies in 'the mediated world of sport' frame men as the 'standard' or 'normal' physicality, thereby maintaining the exclusion of female bodies in sports. The result is that some bodies continue to be absent and to occupy a marginal position.

Media messages about sporting bodies indirectly 'tell' girls and boys who they are, how they should look, and how they might 'fit' gender and racial norms. Through their reading of sport media, young people learn that, for boys, performing masculinity and becoming a sporting body require 'fitting in'. In and through sport, boys can achieve success and achievement, and develop muscularity, strength and power. The gender norms of media reality also provide, as Correa (2009) argues, a basis for accepting women's subordination in society. As female sporting bodies are often invisible, trivialised or marginal in the mainstream media landscape of sport (Duncan, 2007; Wright 1991), young people learn that to fit in, girls must display slenderness and gracefulness, which are the main body features for an ideal 'feminine look', rather than skilfulness, athleticism and power in sports. They also learn, however, that the 'feminine look' is neither central to nor desirable in the sport arena, while many male sporting bodies display, construct and celebrate the 'masculine look'.

Media are not the only sites of sporting body texts. Settings such as schools, sports clubs and families play crucial roles in producing and maintaining the 'gender regime' (Correa, 2009, p. 186), as well as regimes of race and social class. Bramham (2003) has suggested that sport is a relevant site, particularly for white, working-class, English boys to reassert their masculine identity. A similar argument is proposed by Ismond (2003, p. 15), who points out that in the United Kingdom, 'football, and to a lesser extent rugby league, are key sites for the construction of whiteness in sport'. Through the practice of football, young boys pick up masculine behaviours and actions by conforming to white, male, often working-class norms – i.e. culturally dominant and accepted ways of being in society. The problem with hegemonic masculinity as a fixed, gendered way of being in the world is that it solidifies male–female differences (Connell and Messerschmidt, 2005), maintaining the institution of sport as a male domain. As Clark and Paechter (2007, p. 261) argue, despite young women's growing participation in sports such as football, 'in practice, there remain constraints that hinder their involvement in various ways'.

> ### Comment
> *It is not only in the media that 'appropriate' sporting bodies are promoted; schools and sports clubs are important sites of social reproduction.*

For teachers and coaches, who are also subject to representations of idealised, gendered and racialised bodies, the importance of taking a critical stance to media and sporting representations of the body cannot be overemphasised. Young learners in physical education and youth sport come to these settings with powerful understandings of what is – and is not – appropriate for them to learn. To nurture young people, educators must promote reflective engagement with ideals of the body as delivered by the media and young people's views of their own body-selves.

Young people's embodiment of 'sporting bodies': sites of vulnerability?

Sustained by widespread practices of sport as a masculinising process of the body, the ways in which sportsmen are celebrated by the media might heighten girls' and boys' unrealistic assumptions about body ideals and embodiment. Such embodiments might have negative implications for young people's physicality, making them vulnerable in a number of ways and certainly impacting on their 'readiness' to learn in sports settings.

Sites of vulnerability

Young people become vulnerable to the impact of media messages when such messages place importance on ideals of the sporting body and high-status body signifiers. In exploring young people's issues of embodiment, Dittmar and Halliwell (2008, p. 143) offer persuasive empirical findings demonstrating how the '"body perfect" ideal can become a crucial *vulnerability factor*'. For those who invest in becoming 'sporting bodies', ideals of skilfulness, athleticism and competition become critically important to their physicality, focusing on a 'popular' and 'successful' self that 'fits' in sport. As media narratives and institutional practices legitimate and affirm young people's positive and successful experiences in sport, some young people come to believe in body hierarchies. This supports the status quo in sport and encourages young people to mirror the narrow version of sporting bodies. For example, a boy invests himself in football by aspiring to become an elite football player, and by embodying masculine values and attitudes (e.g. aggression, muscularity, skilfulness, economic achievement). He displays body performances that characterise and/or are displayed by a professional male footballer. Importantly, this very investment might ultimately limit his way of experiencing football across his lifespan when he no longer meets his own ideal. His embodied beliefs make him vulnerable to the extent that they limit his understanding of who should and should not be a footballer. His investment in a high-status body might lead him to exclude girls, low-skilled boys and, ultimately, himself from the practice of football. This becomes particularly important if that same boy aspires to becoming a teacher or coach where he can visit his strong beliefs upon children and young people.

> ### Comment
> *Intractable beliefs in body hierarchies within sport and physical activity can be limiting for all participants.*

While media models deliver ideals, desires and fantasies 'to become somebody' in society, some boys' and many girls' bodies clearly do not correspond to ideal sporting body images. Because most young people do not 'fit into' narrow media representations of the body, young people appear especially vulnerable to the tyranny of the 'body perfect'. According to Dittmar (2008, p. 203), young people 'put themselves at risk' when they perceive a discrepancy between the ways they see their own body and ideals of the masculine and feminine body in sport. Such conscious and/or unconscious discrepancies can have detrimental effects on physicality. For instance, rather than affirming certain ways of being, boys' and girls' 'difference' from the idealised sporting body becomes a negative marker of their physicality. Boys who do not exhibit signifiers of hegemonic masculinity become 'different bodies' or subordinated masculinities (Connell and Messerschmidt, 2005), who are marginalised or excluded in sport. At the same time, girls who enter their bodies into the male domain of traditional sport become tomboys who display low-status femininity, an embodied identity that transgresses heteronormative gender norms (Clark and Paechter, 2007). While on the one hand, the media establish a normative position for young people's bodies to stay active and healthy in sport, on the other hand, given that these messages of idealised bodies are unachievable for many boys, and many more girls, such messages intensify young people's *vulnerability* to embodying 'difference' as a negative body marker.

Current media representations of sporting bodies, however, are complicated by global trends which sustain ideals of personal autonomy. The increased media representation of '*girl power*' in sport is an example, offering an illusion of equal choice, opportunity and freedom. Yet, as Strandbu (2005, p. 31) points out, 'girls with an immigrant background are far less often members of sports organizations than other youngsters' and minority girls continue to be invisible in the various public spaces of sport (Carrington *et al.*, 1987; Scraton, 2001). Meanwhile, the ideal of the 'new girl' in sport suggests an image of successful, healthy, active bodies, and 'do-it-yourself assemblage' (Harris, 2004, p. 8).

For minority girls, the circulation of the 'new girl' discourse means not finding themselves in the public social domain because of their invisibility and exclusion (Carrington *et al.*, 1987, p. 266). For other kinds of girls it means taking up normative discourses of new girlhood that separate them from girls at risk. Young women at risk are 'those who are seen to be rendered vulnerable by their circumstances' (Harris, 2004, p. 25), a position which in turn sets them up as failures, and encourages self-blame for their lack of success. The girls-at-risk discourse produces a kind of subjectivity figured as 'the girl as failure', particularly for ethnic minorities. What is important to acknowledge, then, is that the notion of 'girl power' in sport produces the illusion of gender equality – success is open to anyone if only they try hard enough – and this discourages critical thinking about social issues of the gendered body. Young people become vulnerable to the embodiment of disadvantage in sport, eventually seeing themselves as a 'problem' and blaming themselves for their 'wrong' choices.

Sporting bodies through Ammera's and Robert's eyes

The preceding sections of this chapter have been mainly theoretical, but what does this mean in practice? In the next section, the divergent ways in which two young people make sense of discourses about sporting bodies and young people 'at risk' are illustrated. The two body narratives are drawn from a large visual ethnographic study conducted in a diverse urban school community. In the study, young people took photographs to make sense of and represent their body experiences in physical activity. Examples of those images are included.

'I mean I would love to play professional football . . .'

Ammera was born in the United Kingdom and identifies herself as having Indian and African ancestry, because her parents moved to the United Kingdom when 'they were quite young'. When talking about her body, physical activity and health, Ammera appears to take contradictory and uncertain positions. For instance, in the opening quote to this chapter she explained:

> I think my *body's a bit different* because, yeah, it's like, I've always been like, really lazy and that to be honest, like I didn't really used to like sport much, but I used to like playing the games . . . It's like, I'm really lazy and I'm trying to change that. It's like, I'm trying to eat more healthy stuff and I just live off the junk food . . . I just feel, like, it's good to do exercise every day, to be honest; it's like there's no point just sitting around all day.

The body she inhabits is 'a bit different', she believes. Her body emerges as a site of contradictory discourses of physical activity and health. Although Ammera takes up a young people 'at risk' discourse, constructing herself as 'lazy' and seeing her body as deviating from health standards, she views exercise in a positive way, disliking 'sitting around all day'. As the interview unfolds, she expresses uncertainties and doubts, and describes her body as an active one that is changing, as she searches for healthier and more active pathways. Her subjective construction of her body pictures herself not as 'lazy', but as active and enjoying a wide range of activities. In her ongoing search, however, sport emerges as a site of transition and conflict. She continues:

> It's [physical activity] quite important, 'cos like, I don't know, I just don't feel right if I just sit around all day. I just feel really, like weird and then I have to do some sort of activity . . . I do as much exercise as I like to do, as I'm trying and like I'm much more active than I was before . . . I move around quite a lot. It's like yeah, I mean like improving myself, to be honest, rather than just like sit there with everyone at lunch . . . Sometimes my friend brings her basketball and we, like, play at lunch. We just try to do as much as we can, like burn off our calories . . . *Honestly most of the activities I do are in school* . . . I like playing, like games like basketball . . . *I like watching football, but I'm not exactly good at playing it.*

While Ammera clearly takes individual responsibility to be 'honest' about her health by endorsing 'good choices' to 'burn calories', her 'real' choices and opportunities to exercise seem limited. Her quest to become an active body is visually and verbally manifested in her storytelling about herself, while her personal choices need to be understood within her everyday circumstances where physical education (PE) is the only opportunity for her self-management in physical activity. Because she does not view her body as 'appropriate' to play football ('not exactly good at playing it'), sport as an organised practice is for the most part (except for organised sport-based games in PE) absent from her visual narrative (photographs). Sport is important to Ammera, however, as she engages with great interest in discussing media narratives of sporting bodies. As the following interview extract evidences, when talking about men's sporting bodies, Ammera exhibits interest in sport and has her own critical viewpoint on professional football:

Ammera: I don't like him 'cos he plays for Man United.

Interviewer: And who do you cheer for?

Ammera: Liverpool.

Interviewer: Are you quite a fan, do you watch most of the games?

Ammera: Every game, yeah apart from him . . . I'm not so good at it, but, yeah, I like to watch it.

Interviewer: Do you have a favourite player?

Ammera: Stephen Gerrard.

Ammera jumping   Ammera running

While she loves to watch football, but does not see herself as a footballer, Ammera puts forward a critical view on the media representation of the sporting bodies:

I don't think girls get a chance to show whether we are as good as boys, because like in football you get the boys' team, which everyone knows about, and then you get the girls' team, which hardly no one knows about . . . I think if they, like, if they just become more popular, they play on TV, like they are on the TV, the matches are on the TV and stuff . . . like in football.

I mean, I would love to play professional football . . . but I just don't think they [girls] have as much opportunities, and it's like I can't really like make myself good enough . . . 'cos I knew I wouldn't be able to.

In her ongoing efforts to construct herself as an active body, it is not easy for Ammera to imagine being or becoming a football player; her everyday reality is far removed from the possibility of enacting sporting bodies. In her view, the over representation of men in sport media celebrates and encourages boys' participation in sport, while discouraging girls and maintaining their invisibility. Her dream of becoming a football player appears constrained by an embodied self narrated as a 'different body' that diverges from healthy standards and popular media images of footballers, which in turn shapes her view of herself as 'not really good at it'.

'My life is being active . . . ': Aspiring to become a professional football player

Robert, like Ammera, attends a single-sex school; both schools are located in the same neighbourhood. However, Robert's body narrative and the visual representations of his story differ sharply from Ammera's. In Robert's reflection, for example, the young-people-at-risk discourse does not permeate his body experience in physical activity. While talking about health is absent from his narrative, sport occupies a central role in it. Robert sees himself as a sporting body, and moreover hopes to carry on sport in his future by becoming a professional football player. Robert recalls:

When I started playing football I was four . . . Well, the first time I went to a training session at a club I was four . . . My dad used to play for the equivalent of City Academy when he was younger, and then he pretty much carried on to me like . . . football, it's more like a career opportunity as well.

From an early age, Robert has pursued a highly performative sporting body. Becoming a sporting body, just like the ones portrayed in the media, is a salient component of Robert's embodied identity, consolidated by his early investment in sport. Robert's father, who was himself a footballer for a city club, influenced and encouraged this aspiration. When narrating his body experiences, Robert pictures himself as a sporting body in football and basketball with his male friends, whom he defines as 'highly skilled'.

Robert playing football

Robert scoring a goal

According to Robert, his is a changing body, not a body in search of a healthy pathway, like Ammera's, but a body in search of perfection and professional career opportunities. As Shilling (2008, p. 54) comments, 'It is clear that the acquisition of sporting skills is based firmly in the acquisition of particular habits of practice, movement, anticipation and response that can facilitate performative capacity, creativity and an experiential transformation.' While sporting bodies practise and perform automatism, not all sport-based practices in Robert's view are useful to becoming an 'appropriate body' in sport. For example, while talking about the playgrounds, clubs and school sites where he practises sport, Robert explains:

> I do like PE but the *things you can do in PE are restricted*, if you know what I mean because the *groups are mixed* . . . Say like, if someone's not very good, it's not as competitive as it should be . . . Say like, because there's mixed groups, say there's people who can't do a certain thing, you don't get to move on the next thing without the other people doing it . . . You can't experience the same amount of competitiveness or the same amount of skill against you, so you're not going to get any better at it . . . I used to take it [PE] proper seriously, but now it's just fun, strictly for me anyway . . . Like with the football team, [what] I said about skill is important, because I like being able to just answer to someone, beating someone.

By inserting himself into a narrative of high-status, elite sporting bodies, Robert embodies desirable ranks in the hierarchies of skilfulness and competition. Because of his intimate attachment to a narrowly constructed sporting body as a performative, high-status entity, in Robert's eyes, even boys' single-sex PE classes are 'restrictive' to his way of understanding sport. Different from Ammera, the material circumstances available to Robert, as well as the discursive spaces of sport he inhabits, are central to his construction of the self, and to his pursuit of becoming a successful high-status body.

 ## Conclusion

To help limit the detrimental effects of sports media and public discourses on young people's embodiment, teachers and coaches need to be aware of the myriad ways in which such pressures can impact on learning. Correa (2009) makes a convincing argument that education should provide opportunities for young people to 'understand and decode' the ways in which media construct versions of reality. In physical education and youth sport, educators can create spaces in which young people can critically appreciate media 'reality' as fantasies that actually deviate from the reality most people inhabit in their everyday lives. This is particularly important given the powerful representations of sport and sporting bodies.

Meanings, values and attitudes attached to the traditional representation of the sporting body, including social practices of sport often constructed as masculinising, need to be recognised. In physical education and youth sport settings, the gender, class and racial representations of sporting bodies need to become visible and public and to be critically deconstructed. Schools have a responsibility to promote a critical understanding of the body, social issues and sport among young people, as well as to address how images of the sporting body can be limiting not only for girls but also for boys. Sports clubs that coach children and young people have a similar duty to their young clients. As Gilbert and Gilbert (1998, p. 222) convey:

> If boys are to be shown how dominant masculinity constrains as much as it advantages them, they need to see how these images and practices are sustained, and at what cost to their opportunities to live lives which are open to diverse experiences and positive relationships with others.

To build more gender-just sporting communities and societies, promoting young people's critical consumption of the sporting body must be accompanied by practices that value and legitimate a full range of bodies and identities in physical activity and sport contexts.

Note: Data reported in this chapter draw on research funded by the Economic and Social Research Council, UK.

Learning tasks

Individual task: my sporting body – a personal narrative

Think about an episode during your adolescence when your body was on display in a school PE or sport setting outside school, and where you felt vulnerable because other people were watching your performance. Use the following prompts to reflect upon your chosen episode and write a critical personal body narrative:

- Describe the physical activity setting, including the people who were involved in the setting.
- What kinds of sport practices were you engaged in?
- How were you expected to use your body in this setting?
- How relevant was sport to your sense of self in that particular moment of your life?
- To what extent did you want to be or saw yourself as a 'sporting body'?
- What kinds of pressure did you experience that made you feel vulnerable?
- To what extent did you feel your peers, teachers/coaches were watching and judging your body performance in terms of skilfulness, body size, shape, actions and/or behaviour?
- What kinds of teaching approaches do you think your teacher/coach could have adopted to support your performance more sensitively?

Group task: critical reading of idealised sporting bodies in media

For this group activity, a sport magazine is required. In a group of four people, identify and discuss how sporting bodies are 'created' by this magazine. In your reading, address the following questions with your group:

1 What kinds of bodies are represented and included in this magazine? (You might think about issues of size, shape, skilfulness, popularity, muscularity, gender, race and social class.)

(continued)

2 Based on your reading of the magazine, what do these images tell us about 'appropriate bodies' in sport? Who is included? Who is left out?

3 How could these messages impact on young people's ideas and beliefs about who should play or not play sport?

4 To what extent might the messages about sporting bodies be empowering for young people when thinking about sport in their own lives? To what extent might it render them vulnerable?

Further reading

Azzarito, L. (2009) The panopticon of physical education: pretty, active and ideally white, *Physical Education and Sport Pedagogy,* 14(1), 19–39.

References

Azzarito, L. (2009) The panopticon of physical education: pretty, active and ideally white, *Physical Education and Sport Pedagogy,* 14(1), 19–39.

Azzarito, L. and Harrison, L. (2008) 'White men can't jump': race, gender and natural athleticism, *International Review for the Sociology of Sport,* 43, 347–64.

Azzarito, L. and Katzew, A. (2010) Performing identities in physical education: (en)gendering fluid selves, *Research Quarterly for Exercise and Sport,* 81(1), 25–37.

Azzarito, L. and Solmon, M. A. (2009) An investigation of students' embodied discourses in physical education: a gender project, *Journal of Teaching in Physical Education,* 28, 173–91.

Bramham, P. (2003) Boys, masculinities and PE, *Sport, Education and Society,* 8(1), 57–71.

Brown, D. and Evans, J. (2004) Reproducing gender? Intergenerational links and the male PE teacher as a cultural conduit in teaching physical education, *Journal of Teaching in Physical Education,* 23, 48–70.

Carrington, B., Chivers, T., and Williams, T. (1987) Gender, leisure and sport: a case-study of young people of South Asian descent, *Leisure Studies,* 6(3), 265–79.

Clark, S. and Paechter, C. (2007) 'Why can't girls play football?' Gender dynamics and the playground, *Sport, Education and Society,* 12(3), 261–76.

Connell, R. (2008) Masculinity construction and sports in boys' education: a framework for thinking about the issue, *Sport, Education and Society,* 13(2), 131–45.

Connell, R. W. and Messerschmidt, J. W. (2005) Hegemonic masculinity: rethinking the concept, *Gender & Society,* 19, 829–59.

Correa, D. (2009) The social construction of gender identity: a semiotic analysis. In: Zajda, J. and Freedman, K. (eds) *Race, Ethnicity and Gender Education: Cross-cultural understandings,* New York: Springer, 183–94.

Dittmar, H. (2008) (ed.) *Consumer Culture, Identity and Well-being. The search for the 'good life' and the 'body perfect.'* New York: Psychology Press.

Dittmar, H. and Halliwell, E. (2008) Think 'ideal' and feel bad? Using self-discrepancies to understand negative media effects. In: Dittmar, H. (ed.) *Consumer Culture, Identity and Well-being. The search for the 'good life' and the 'body perfect',* New York: Psychology Press, 147–72.

Duncan, M. C. (2007) Bodies in motion: the sociology of physical activity, *Quest,* 59, 55–66.

Fleming, S. (1994) Sport and South Asian youth: the perils of 'false universalism' and stereotyping, *Leisure Studies,* 13(3), 159–77.

Giardina, M. D. and Donnelly, M. K. (2008) (eds) *Youth Culture and Sport: Identity, power and politics.* London: Routledge.

Gilbert, R. and Gilbert, P. (1998) *Masculinity Goes to School.* NSW: Allen & Unwin.

Hall, A. M. (1996) *Feminism and Sporting Bodies: Essay on theory and practice,* Champaign, IL: Human Kinetics.

Hargreaves, J. and Vertinsky, P. (2007) (eds) *Physical Culture, Power and the Body,* London: Routledge.

Harris, A. (2004) *Future Girl. Young women in the twenty-first century,* London: Routledge.

Heywood, L. (2007) Producing girls: empire, sport and the neoliberal body. In: J. Hargreaves and P. Vertinsky (eds) *Physical Culture, Power and the Body* (pp. 101–20), London: Routledge.

Ismond, P. (2003) *Black and Asian Athletes in British Sports and Society: A sporting chance?* Basingstoke, UK: Palgrave Macmillan.

Kenway, J. and Bullen, E. (2008) The global corporate curriculum and the young cyberflaneur as global citizen. In: N. Dolby and F. Rizvi (eds) *Youth Moves. Identities and education in global perspective,* London: Routledge, 17–32.

Rasmussen, M. L. (2006) *Becoming Subjects: Sexuality and secondary schooling,* New York: Routledge.

Scraton, S. (2001) Reconceptualizing race, gender and sport: the contribution of black feminism. In: B. Carrington and I. McDonald (eds) *'Race', Sport and British Society,* London: Routledge, 170–87.

Scraton, S., Fasting, K., Pfister, G. and Bunel Heras, A. (1999) It's still a man's game? The experiences of top-level European women footballers, *International Review for the Sociology of Sport,* 34(2), 99–111.

Shilling, C. (2004) *The Body and Social Theory,* London: Sage Publications.

Shilling, C. (2006) *The Body and Social Theory,* London: Sage.

Shilling, C. (2008) *Changing Bodies: Habit, Crisis and Creativity,* London: Sage.

Strandbu, A. (2005) Identity, embodied culture and physical exercise: stories from Muslim girls in Oslo with immigrant backgrounds, *Young,* 13, 27–45.

Walseth, K. (2006) Young women and sport: the impact of identity work, *Leisure Studies,* 25(1), 75–94.

Walseth, K. and Fastin, K. (2004) Sport as a means of integrating minority women, *Sport in Society,* 7(1), 109–29.

Wright, J. (1991) Gracefulness and strength: sexuality in the Seoul Olympics, *Social Semiotics,* 1(1), 49–66.

11

Playtime: the needs of very young learners in physical education and sport

Frances Murphy, Dublin City University
Dierdre Ní Chroinin, University of Limerick

Getting elementary-age children to enjoy a movement activity is not a hard sell. Given their high degree of trust, imagination, and energy, it is almost unfair. Children are built to move; they want to move. Almost anything can be turned into a grand adventure – catching, throwing, running, touching, enjoying rhythmic activities, and discovering 'fundamental movement concepts'. A teacher who has a gift for make-believe can, without much difficulty, become something of a Pied Piper of movement. Delight, excitement, intrigue, and usually considerable noise permeate the physical education setting.

(Kretchmar, 2008, p. 166)

 ## Introduction

Children love to play and to be active. This chapter considers some of the physical, cognitive and affective needs of younger learners (primary school) and ways in which they can be accommodated in physical education and sport settings. The purpose of the chapter is to make you think about the choices and decisions teachers and coaches make when attempting to optimise learning for very young learners in physical activity settings. You may find it helpful to read this chapter in conjunction with Chapter 21, Becoming an effective primary school physical education teacher by Mike Jess.

Some readers may have a specific interest in influencing the learning experiences of young children in physical activity, sport and physical education settings. If you become a primary school teacher, for example, there will be opportunities to plan and implement a programme of physical education and also to promote physical activity during break times or in an extracurricular setting. As a coach, or a sports advisor in a community, you may find yourself with responsibilities for very young learners in selected sports. In other roles, for example in public policy or sport development, there may be opportunities to influence policy and programme development for young children. In any of these situations it is important that adults are able to plan, teach and advocate based on an understanding of *what* learning is desirable in physical activity settings for young children, *how* this learning should be organised and *why* this learning is important.

When children are asked why they participate in sport and physical activity they cite having fun, trying out new activities, participating with friends and feelings of success as the main reasons (Allender *et al.*, 2006). It is important, therefore, to keep the needs and interests of children at the core of all decision making in any role as physical educator or coach. This chapter examines the needs of young people in sport and physical education and argues that this understanding should be at the core of teaching and coaching young children.

Physical activity settings for young children: learning through play

The writings of early educationalists such as Froebel and Montessori laid the foundation for play as part of early childhood curricula (Branscombe *et al.*, 2000). Play theorists have outlined characteristics of play that help us to understand why children play, including their desire for fun and social engagement as well as the type of play that contributes to their development. Underlining the importance of play as fun, Lillemyr (2009) contended that play can have a fascinating, pleasurable nature that is a goal in itself, and for the child at play 'play is . . . a natural way of being' (p. 7). Play settings are also a key opportunity for children to learn many things including learning about themselves, others and the world around them.

Physically active play, sometimes called 'outdoor play', involves large body movements including running, climbing, pushing, pulling and swinging, and it provides many learning opportunities (Smith, 2005). When children are in supportive learning environments, exploration and appreciation of movement through play challenges the body's capacity to respond in creative and skilful ways. A broad experience in a supportive environment gives children the best chance of being successful movers and a good chance of finding activities they enjoy and want to repeat as the basis of lifelong physical activity participation. Children may find some movements to be pleasing almost entirely for aesthetic reasons: for example, spinning round and round, running fast or rolling down a hill. Other movements may be more pleasing for the outcome, such as scoring a goal or finishing a race.

Play should not be confined to break times in school playgrounds, nor should it be replaced too early in the lives of young children by structured, formal sport. It is particularly important to consider the role of competition when children move from unstructured to more structured play environments. Competitive activities should be devised that can accommodate children who all mature at different rates and so become 'ready' at different times to engage with the demands that competition may place on them (particularly the demand to win all the time!). Competition can be compatible with children's developmental needs if it is designed in ways that recognise each child's potential and where effort is readily acknowledged. Lee (1993) prompted debate on the study of sport for children. He argued that the experience of sport can be an essential part of how some children develop a sense of self but can also lead to children adopting maladaptive behaviours. In such cases, success is defined as winning, with little value placed on mastery and personal achievement.

> **Comment**
> *It is important that teachers and coaches support children to explore their world through play offering rich, experiential activities and challenges.*

Physical education is a vital part of school life as it may be the only place on the curriculum where children can learn in and through movement. This learning can be significant in developing a child's physical literacy. It provides opportunities for the development of knowledge and understanding of specific activities, the skills needed to participate and the foundations for future successful participation. Learning the rules of the game of tennis, for example, combined with learning such skills as striking and throwing, are necessary for successful participation in the game. Another way of understanding physical activity and physical education has been developed by Margaret Whitehead, who has spearheaded use of the term physical literacy as a replacement for the term 'physically educated'. In so doing, Whitehead argued for a move from an activity-centred model to a person-centred model of learning in the physical: 'Physical literacy can be described as the motivation, confidence, physical competence, knowledge and understanding to maintain physical activity throughout life' (Whitehead, 2009).

While play, physical education and sport settings provide *opportunities* for children to learn and develop, this learning does not happen automatically. Children need to be supported, encouraged and guided through a range of developmentally appropriate activities to facilitate this learning. This task is made more complicated by the need to consider and accommodate the complex and varying needs and interests of the children during the activity. The following section presents a short account of children, aged five, learning in a physical education lesson. As you read, consider how Claire's lesson reflects your experience of being a young learner or working with young children in physical education or sport. You will be asked to return to this story in later sections of this chapter.

Claire's story

Claire is a student teacher. She has been placed for teaching practice in a suburban school where 90 per cent of children do not speak English as their first language. She has been assigned to teach a junior infant/reception class (age five). There are 16 children in the class and they only started school three weeks ago. Claire is teaching a physical education lesson. She has taught the class physical education on two prior occasions and she is always supported by the regular class teacher.

Claire begins her physical education class by asking the children to form a line near the door of the classroom. She interacts with the children as they move into line, checking that they are wearing correct footwear and praising them for 'how they are so well

(continued)

prepared' for their physical education class. Some children ask whether they are going out to play. The children form a line but Sam is reluctant to join just yet. He has chosen a space in the classroom where he is playing on his own: twirling, hopping and skipping. Claire calls him and asks him to join the class. Slowly, he agrees to join in. The class teacher approaches him discreetly and encourages him to move along quickly.

The class walks out into the school playground. It is a bright sunny morning in September. Claire asks the children to gather in a part of the playground that has playground markings (painted ladders on the ground, shapes, snakes, etc.). She asks the children to walk around inside this area and explains how she will use her whistle. She repeats this activity a few times and they respond well. Claire tells them that they are very good at listening. She prompts them to repeat the activity but this time with jumping, then running. She constantly monitors the children to ensure they stay within the boundary.

Claire hands each child a rubber disc. The children are delighted to receive the equipment but there is some arguing over the colours that Claire gives them. She tries to reassure them that it's not important but ends up swapping two discs so that she can avoid any further debate on colour. The children do some simple mobility exercises, swinging their arms high and low and swinging from side to side using the disc as a base. Claire uses her voice enthusiastically and the children respond really well: they are clearly enjoying these activities. She asks them to hop, landing on the disc. Some children have difficulty with balance but she reminds them that they will have lots of chances to practise this again.

Claire then suggests that they will play a little game responding to three different calls: 'up' (jump up), 'down' (crouch) and 'run'. Again, the class responds with enthusiasm although two children begin to stray and need to be reminded to return to the marked area. Claire calls all the children together and tells them that they will now be playing using a beanbag. She begins to distribute the beanbags but again colour is an issue and many return to the box to exchange their bag for one of another colour. While reminding them that the colour isn't important, Claire moves on to ask them to try to do some tasks with the beanbag. Can they balance it on their head? their hand? their foot? their knee? As they play she asks them 'Which is easiest? Which is most difficult?' A variety of answers are offered. Claire prompts them to find different ways of balancing the beanbag on their bodies.

Claire asks the children to toss the beanbag in the air and to catch it with both hands. Some children manage this successfully some of the time, others drop the beanbag most of the time. Sam runs off around the large playground. Claire urges him to rejoin the group but some of the other children are now 'off task' as they watch him, so she moves to follow him and tries to encourage him to rejoin the group. He comes back as far as the class area but sits on a window ledge and opts out of playing. Claire struggles a little to get children back on task but decides to move on to the next stage of the lesson, which involves distributing hoops. The children are very eager to collect a hoop. After a few moments in which they experiment with wriggling in and out of hoops, Claire gets their attention and asks them to place the hoop on the ground and to try throwing the beanbag so that it lands in the hoop. She moves among the children, encouraging them to use an underarm throw and to stand closer to the hoop. There are shrieks of delight as children achieve the target. They run in quickly to gather and try again. At this point, some children are counting how many times they are successful. A discussion begins between Megan and Ashraf about how many they had 'scored'.

(continued)

The lesson then moves on to a game of 'magic shoes', which involves some pretend play: they pretend that they are in a shop where they act out items for sale that Claire identifies, e.g. a bouncing ball, a train, a bicycle, a kite. When she calls out 'magic shoes' they all have to sit cross-legged. Sam rejoins the group as the game commences. The children are very excited as they play this game and rush about enthusiastically, mimicking, for example, a train. Claire now draws the lesson to a close by asking them to return to their discs and to stretch up high, crouch low, make a wide shape and then a narrow shape. She demonstrates the shapes required. She then calls each child in turn to join a line. Claire comments on how well they tried to complete all the tasks and urges them to walk in line back to the classroom. John asks whether they will be coming out to the playground again later and is reassured that they will indeed have their playtime break outside.

The needs of young learners

Engaging in play or more structured forms of physical education and sport can potentially be a highly valuable learning experience. However, Claire's story has raised several pedagogical issues that need to be considered if a teacher or coach endeavours to meet the needs and interests of all the children in their group to support learning and development. The importance of meeting the needs and interests of children and young people learning in and through sport has been highlighted by Kathy Armour in Chapter 1.

Young learners have particular needs that can be met in physical education and sport settings. The following section outlines what the important areas of learning for young children are and presents evidence of why each of these areas should be considered by you as a teacher or coach of young children. You may emphasise physical, cognitive or affective learning at different times depending on the needs of your group but in reality, like Claire, your understanding of all three areas will probably inform and influence how you organise and approach teaching and learning with young children. We begin by considering the physical domain, which might be considered the most obvious area of learning for young children in sport and physical activity settings. Yet the importance of providing developmentally appropriate opportunities to explore movement potential and learn and develop physical skills cannot be underestimated, because it is the foundation for lifelong participation.

Physical domain

Young children move naturally and instinctively to explore and learn about their world. Children love to play and to explore movement, and sport is often one of their favourite pastimes. In the 'Growing Up in Ireland' study (Williams *et al.*, 2009) 65 per cent of nine-year-olds mentioned sport as their favourite pastime or hobby, with 19 per cent of the group saying sport was the 'thing that made them most happy'. Learning through physical activity, movement and play can impact on the development of physical competences that are crucial to children's overall development as well as laying the foundation for lifelong physical activity (Bailey *et al.*, 2009).

Children can learn physical skills through a variety of movement activities including dance, gymnastics, games, athletics, outdoor and adventurous activities and aquatics. These are the six activity areas included within the primary PE curricula in the UK and Ireland. However, it is important to remember that these activities should not look the same as they would if adults were playing them; instead they must be facilitated in developmentally appropriate ways to support each child's learning of fundamental motor skills, physical activity and physical fitness. These key elements within the physical domain are discussed below.

Fundamental motor skill development

Fundamental motor skills (FMS) are the gross motor movements that lay the foundation for the development of more complex and specialised skills and include skills that relate to:

- management of the body – stability skills (e.g. stop, twist, turn, bend);
- moving in different directions – locomotor skills (e.g. dodge, hop, skip);
- control and manipulation of objects such as hoops and bats and balls (e.g. strike, kick, throw).

The development of fundamental movements is emphasised in primary physical education in many countries around the world including Canada, Australia and the UK. Research suggests that mastery of FMS supports children's successful participation in a range of physical activities. The learning and development of physical skills are not automatic. It takes many years for children to acquire, develop, select and apply these skills appropriately.

The primary years represent a critical window for mastering these skills (Thomas and Thomas, 2008); children start exploring them from a young age (approximately age two) and should master them by approximately age 12. Primary school age is, therefore, the optimal time to learn these skills because they become more difficult to master with age. It is worth pausing here to reflect on that last point and the responsibility it places on teachers and coaches working with young children. At the same time, it is also worth remembering that there is very limited physical education training offered in many primary teacher training programmes. These two observations, taken together, raise interesting and troubling pedagogical concerns.

While it is acknowledged that children's development is affected by individual physical characteristics such as age and size, appropriate opportunities to practise and receive accurate feedback from the teacher and coach can impact positively on the development of skilful controlled movement. Emphasis should be placed on application of skills in a variety of contexts in relevant, enjoyable and meaningful ways rather than an overemphasis on isolated skill teaching. Children should be supported to develop movement competence in a wide range of physical activities and to develop the most efficient movement response solution within a given situation. There are a number of programmes used in schools that are firmly grounded in the development of fundamental skills (Basic Moves (UK), Be Active (Ireland)). These skills provide children with a vocabulary of movement that allows them to make choices about their future participation, encouraging the adoption of a physically active lifestyle. The following section considers the physical activity and fitness needs of young children.

Comment

Fundamental movement skills should ideally be mastered during the primary school years to encourage and support children's successful participation in sport and physical activity. Claire selected the development of fundamental motor skills (stability, locomotor and manipulation) as one particular focus in her lesson.

Physical activity and physical fitness

Around the world, a combination of changes in diet and modern living has led to decreasing physical activity levels and rising levels of childhood obesity, despite the fact that young children are the most active section of the world's population (Telama *et al.*, 2005). Active children are more likely to become active adults. Providing space and time for children regularly to have fun and play with their peers may be the first step in promoting a physically active lifestyle (McKenzie and Kahan, 2008). It is recommended that children should be active for a minimum of 60 minutes per day. In the UK, schools are now recommended to deliver five hours of physical education and school sport (*Sport England and YST*, 2009). In Ireland, however, the guidelines recommend only one hour per week of school physical education (Government Publications, 1999).

Physical activity participation by young children contributes to health-related fitness as well as performance-related fitness including agility, balance, coordination and speed (the ABCs). These physical skills support safe, successful participation in a range of physical activities. Children need the motivation as well as the ability to be physically active. For many children, school physical education is the place where they will figure out what activities they enjoy and excel at, thus equipping them with tools for lifelong physical activity.

> *Comment*
> *Creating fun, joyful and meaningful learning experiences may be the best way to encourage a love of physical activity and a commitment to a physically active lifestyle.*
> *(Kretchmar, 2008)*

While the potential of physical activity and sport settings to address the physical needs of young learners may be self-evident, these settings can also address some other important needs of young children.

Affective domain

Learning is a social activity that can enhance 'the ability of children to act, interact, and react effectively with other people as well as with themselves' (Gallahue and Cleland Donnelly, 2003, p. 20). There is a wealth of opportunities for affective growth including personal and social development in play and physical activity settings. Important elements of the affective domain can be identified as enhancing self-esteem and positive socialisation. Young children begin to develop self-esteem in a variety of ways including through play and physical activity, and enhancement of self-esteem can occur in very simple ways: a child rolls a ball, knocks down skittles and jumps for joy, experiencing that 'I can . . .' feeling. Positive socialisation is concerned with the ability of the child to relate to others and to take personal and social responsibility. Fair play, cooperative behaviour and 'healthy' attitudes to winning and losing can be promoted within a variety of movement experiences.

There are models that address social and personal development within teaching and coaching settings. Table 11.1 on the next page outlines the characteristics teachers and coaches can use to promote social and personal development (Laker 2001), and Bailey *et al.* (2009)

Table 11.1 Generic groups of individual traits

Source: Based on Laker (2001)

Groups	Traits
• Sportsmanship	• Fair play, honesty, peer respect, peer support, competitiveness
• Individual	• Self esteem, creativity, initiative, leadership, determination, hard work, confidence, independence
• Cooporation	• Teamwork, helping, trust, sharing, group success, interdependence, decision making
• Attitudes	• Enthusiasm, precipitation, enjoyment, humour

highlighted the importance of *planning* for such outcomes rather than hoping they will somehow happen as if by magic.

Some physical educators (e.g. Hellison and Templin, 1991) have suggested that children's social and affective development should be a core focus of PE programmes, while continuing to promote other aspects such as the development of fundamental skills, understanding and knowledge. The difference in this approach is that the subject matter of any lesson or session would be selected to facilitate the development of certain personal and social qualities. An example of this would be where a teacher targets development of self-esteem and confidence through engagement in volleyball, athletics or dance. In such cases, young children are encouraged to take increasing levels of responsibility for their learning and behaviour with the ultimate goal of transferring this learning to settings beyond the gym/sports field. The teacher/coach could also highlight examples of teamwork (cooperation), fair play, sportsmanship and group success from the wider sporting context and make connections between children's actions and those of well-known sporting role models. Furthermore, teachers and coaches can demonstrate the value they place on positive socialisation by including reference to it in discussions with parents.

Positive sports experiences can contribute to social inclusion by equipping children with the skills, motivation and confidence to belong to a team or club. Relating well to others as part of that 'belonging' is a valuable opportunity for a young child. School-based teams and clubs can be particularly valuable because they are accessible to most children and may have the additional bonus of being linked with other curriculum areas, thus extending the range and quality of potential learning. Importantly, all physical activity and sport settings for young children should provide opportunities for social development, for example teams meeting and formally greeting each other before a game begins or encouraging young club members to referee games. These are behaviours that should be prompted from the earliest days of a child's engagement with sport and physical activity, and the power of the sports setting to engender positive (and negative!) social development should not be underestimated. Moreover, sport and other physical activities provide many opportunities to support young children's cognitive development.

Cognitive domain

Cognitive development in physical activity settings with young children may relate to understanding of skills, movement, activity, fitness and academic concepts. This section presents concept development and creativity, two areas of cognitive development, to prompt consideration of the ways in which physical activity settings can be established to encourage curiosity and imagination. While the teacher or coach may not view these areas as their key focus, there will be opportunities to stimulate cognitive development in every single session.

Concept development

Intentional directed movement is at the core of physical education and physical activity participation. Concept development occurs as learners are required to make decisions based on knowledge of their own body and its movement potential (Gallahue and Cleland Donnelly, 2003). Such concepts include:

- selection and application of skills, tactics and compositional ideas;
- knowledge and understanding of fitness and health;
- critical thinking, evaluation and impact on performance.

These activities stimulate thinking and engage children in problem solving and decision making. When the teacher or coach has expectations of the children that they will select, analyse, apply, integrate, justify, interpret and choreograph, it becomes clear to them that there is a significant 'thinking' dimension to physical activity and physical education participation. This thinking can be enhanced further by providing opportunities for the children to be creative.

Creativity

Teaching for creativity can promote children's curiosity, flexible thinking and risk taking through exploration and openness to new ideas. Creative use of the imagination promotes original thinking in supportive environments (Lavin, 2008). Teaching for creativity does not have to be limited to gymnastics and dance activities. There is potential for creative processes in all areas of physical activity, with many possibilities for children to explore, respond to and solve problems in creative ways. Galton (2008, p. 70) identified some practices that can promote creativity processes that can be applied in physical activity settings with young children:

1 Allow the children to explore ideas before presenting them with more formalised responses.

2 Allow the children's questions and comments to lead and direct discussion.

3 Promote activities that encourage talk between the children and require less teacher talk.

4 Create space for review and critical reflection on decisions and choices made.

5 Make links and connections between what is learned and the pupils' lives outside school.

6 Build content in clear simple steps around one core idea.

These practices can be applied in physical education and sport contexts to promote creative development. Physical activity settings also have the potential to promote learning in a wide range of areas beyond the activity or game. This requires the teacher or coach to consider what is happening in the children's world, e.g. festivals such as Halloween and events such as birthdays. The following section presents some ideas on how learning might be integrated, with the potential to make the experience both relevant and meaningful for the children involved.

Integrated learning

Physical education and physical activity can be used as vehicles for learning in other areas. Learning *through* physical activity involves reinforcing learning across different subject areas and making connections to the children's lives outside school. Physical education can be used to explore wider global and environmental issues such as global warming, social justice and intercultural education. Examples of this learning include developing the ability to cooperate in group situations and exploration of different cultures through dance. Physical activity sessions that are designed to be fun for children are ideal learning environments in which to reinforce concepts relating to literacy, language development and numeracy. Links can be made between musical concepts and dance, measurement and time in athletics, and geography and science in outdoor and adventure activities. Links between health-related concepts in science can be integrated with physical education lessons to support connections between knowledge and understandings of fitness and health concepts and promotion of physical activity. For example, in the USA, a group at the University of Maryland developed a science-based physical education curriculum (*Be Active Kids!*) for elementary school children (University of Maryland, Department of Kinesiology, 2007).

There is also some research to suggest a positive relationship between increased physical activity participation and improved academic performance (Sallis *et al.*, 1999; Van der Mars, 2006). In these cases it has been suggested that physical activity participation contributes to improvements in children's concentration and alertness with benefits for all aspects of the children's learning (Bailey *et al.*, 2009). Ultimately, the teacher or coach determines how the potential of physical activity settings can be harnessed to promote the development of thinking, reasoning and action through fun active participation.

> **Comment**
> *Sport and physical activity settings can support concept development, encourage creative responses and provide opportunities for learning in a wide range of areas in an integrated way.*

In this chapter we have divided children's needs into three key areas – physical, affective and cognitive needs. In reality, the teacher or coach considers these areas simultaneously, and this provides one illustration of the complexity inherent in all pedagogical encounters. For example, in response to a child who is practising a skill, the teacher or coach may provide a physical cue to enhance performance while also praising the child's efforts and setting cognitive challenges about how the skill can be applied. This approach is based on a holistic view of the child which recognises and accommodates the broad learning needs of each child. The following section provides some guidance on how the teacher or coach can plan to meet these needs and this echoes some of the suggestions made by Mike Jess in Chapter 21.

Meeting children's needs: implications for practice

Claire had planned a variety of appropriate activities for her class, yet she still faced a number of challenges in making sure all the children benefited from these activities. The following guidelines could help practitioners to create the kinds of experiences that can support children's learning:

1 Create a warm, safe, supportive learning environment; be interested, enthusiastic and encouraging. Children should feel good about themselves as they explore, create and challenge their movement potential.

2 Plan a variety of approaches and developmentally appropriate activities to explore a wide variety of movements through a combination of play, teacher/coach-directed and self-directed experiences. This approach will motivate the learner and promote learning (Martin *et al.*, 2009). Competition should be introduced in a developmentally appropriate way and should enhance other aspects of the programme.

3 Adapt tasks and expectations for each individual context. Inclusive activities should be fun, engaging, appropriate, relevant and challenging to the individual learner and should be success-orientated.

4 Provide children with time to explore, combine, select and refine their movement competence and fundamental movement skills during this key developmental 'window'. 'Children have to learn how to learn motor skills' (Thomas and Thomas, 2008, p. 181).

5 Be generous with praise, acknowledge effort and support learning by keeping information simple and making feedback specific and constructive. Peer and self-evaluation can complement teacher/coach feedback (Stork and Sanders, 2008). Share the efforts and achievements of each child (in all three domains: physical, affective and cognitive) with their parents/carers.

Conclusion

The choices made by teachers or coaches working with young children can impact significantly on what children feel and learn in physical activity environments. It is vital, therefore, to remember 'the many contributions that systematic, sensitive teaching can make to both the cognitive and affective development of the individual' (Gallahue and Cleland Donnelly, 2003, p. 12). All pedagogical decisions should be based on what is in the best interests of the children involved. For example, with a new group of young learners it may be necessary to focus on cooperation and listening skills. On another occasion it might be more appropriate to emphasise fundamental skills or making connections with learning in literacy or numeracy. Employing a variety of approaches and emphases offers the best chance of meeting children's needs in a balanced way based on the uniqueness of each individual. Moreover, as Claire's experience reminds us, the best-laid plans and intentions of a teacher or coach must always be flexible to ensure the specific learning needs of children are met. This chapter has endeavoured to illustrate how children, teachers and other professionals can answer the question raised by Kathy Armour in Chapter 1: Do I know enough . . . to create a positive learning experience for this child?

Learning tasks

Individual task

Reflect on Claire's lesson, or any other teaching or coaching sessions with young children that you have observed. How would you advise Claire to meet the developmental needs of Sam in physical education?

Group task

Design a 30-minute physical activity session for a group of 30 children aged five. Specify the activity, learning outcomes in all three domains, and ways in which you will evaluate children's progress in these domains.

Further reading

To read more about best practice in physical education and sport settings, we suggest the following: *The Elementary School Journal*, 2008, 108(3).

References

Allender, S., Cowburn, G. and Foster, C. (2006) Understanding participation in sport and physical activity among children and adults: a review of qualitative studies, *Health Education* Research, 21(6), 826–35.

Bailey, R., Armour, K., Kirk, D., Jess, M., Pickup, I. and Sandford, R. (2009) BERA Physical Education and Sport Pedagogy Special Interest Group: The educational benefits claimed for physical education and school sport: an academic review, *Research Papers in Education*, (24)1, 1–27.

Branscombe, N., Castle, K., Dorsey, A. G., Surbeck, E. and Taylor, J. B. (2000) *Early Childhood Education: A constructivist perspective*, Boston: Houghton Mifflin.

Gallahue, D. and Cleland Donnelly, F. (2003) *Developmental Physical Education for all Children*, Champaign, IL: Human Kinetics.

Galton, M. (2008) The pedagogy of artists working in schools. Report to Creative Partnerships, Arts Council of Great Britain, Cambridge: Faculty of Education, University of Cambridge.

Government Publications (1999) *Primary School Curriculum: Introduction*, Dublin: The Stationery Office.

Hellison, D. and Templin, T. (1991) *A Reflective Approach to Teaching Physical Education*, Champaign, IL: Human Kinetics.

Kretchmar, R. S. (2008) The increasing utility of elementary school physical education: a mixed blessing and unique challenge, *The Elementary School Journal*, 108(3), 161–70.

Laker, A. (2001) *Developing Personal, Social and Moral Education through Physical Education: A practical guide for teachers,* London: Routledge Falmer.

Lavin, J. (2008) *Creative Approaches to Physical Education: Helping children to achieve their true potential,* London: Routledge.

Lee, M. (1993) *Coaching Children in Sport: Principles and practice,* London: E & FN Spon.

Lillemyr, O. (2009) *Taking Play Seriously: Children and play in early childhood education – an exciting challenge,* Charlotte, NC: Information Age Publishing.

Martin, E. H., Rudisill, M. E. and Hastie, P. A. (2009) Motivational climate and fundamental motor skill performance in a naturalistic physical education setting, *Physical Education and Sport Pedagogy,* 14(3), 227–40.

McKenzie, T. L. and Kahan, D. (2008) Physical activity, public health and elementary schools, *The Elementary School Journal,* 108(3), 171–80.

Sallis, J., McKenzie, J., Kolody, B., Lewis, M., Marshall, S. and Rosengard, P. (1999) Effects of health-related physical education on academic achievement: project SPARK, *Research Quarterly in Exercise and Sport,* 70, 127–34.

Smith, P. (2005) Physical activity and rough-and-tumble play. In: Moyles, J. (ed.) *The Excellence of Play,* 2nd edn, Berkshire: Open University Press.

Sport England and YST (2009) *The PE and Sport Strategy for Young People: A guide to delivering the five hour offer,* available from: http://www.youthsporttrust.org/page/pessyp/index.html, accessed 15 April 2010.

Stork, S. and Sanders, S. W. (2008) Physical education in early childhood, *The Elementary School Journal,* 108(3), 197–206.

Telama, R., Yang, X., Viikari, J., Välimäki, I., Wanne, O. and Raitakari, O. (2005) Physical activity from childhood to adulthood: a 21-year tracking study, *American Journal of Preventive Medicine,* 28(3), 267–73.

Thomas, K. T. and Thomas, J. R. (2008) Principles of motor development for elementary school physical education, *The Elementary School Journal,* 108(3), 181–95.

University of Maryland, Department of Kinesiology (2007) *Be Active Kids!* available from: http://beactivekids.org/bak/Front/Default.aspx, accessed 10 March 2010.

Van der Mars, H. (2006) Time and learning in physical education. In: Kirk D., Macdonald D. and O'Sullivan, M. (eds) *Handbook of Physical Education,* Thousand Oaks, CA: Sage, 191–213.

Whitehead, M. (2009) The current working definitions of physical literacy, available from: http://www.physical-literacy.org.uk/definitions.php, accessed 20 March 2010.

Williams, J. *et al.* (2009) Growing Up in Ireland, National Longitudinal Study, The Lives of 9-Year Olds, Research Report, available from: http://www.growingup.ie/fileadmin/user_upload/documents/1st_Report/Barcode_Growing_Up_in_Ireland_-_The_Lives_of_9-Year-Olds_Main_Report.pdf, accessed 15 April 2010.

12

Disabling experiences of physical education and youth sport

Hayley Fitzgerald, Leeds Metropolitan University

Luke's story about physical education

If I have succeeded in getting even one games teacher to understand anything at all about . . . the difficulties we experience in games, then writing this whole book will have been worthwhile . . . I don't hang around in a group and everyone is aware of how bad I am at team sports so no one ever wants me in their team. The familiar hustle and bustle, murmuring and giggling that follow the instruction 'Get into teams' are always accompanied by the predicable 'Aw Sir, do we have to?' or 'No way are we having him' as the games teacher allocates me to a random team, rather like a spare piece of luggage that no one can be bothered to carry. I tell you their feelings are reciprocated – no way do I want to be in their team either! . . . Quite literally. The thought of doing games really makes me feel ill. I can't even think about sleeping at night when I have games the next day. I can't concentrate on the lessons before as my worst nightmare is slowly approaching. When it is time for the lesson, I genuinely do feel sick and have a headache from all the worrying. Of course I am told that I will be able to run it off or just ignored completely. It is my worst time at school and I have done all I can to avoid it.

(Jackson, 2002, pp. 128–30)

 ## Introduction

At the age of 13, Luke Jackson wrote a book about living with a disability. He felt compelled to include a section focusing on physical education and sport entitled 'Not much fun and games' because he wanted practitioners to know how he experienced physical education.

For Luke, physical education was not always a happy place to be and the prospect of learning games as he experienced it evoked thoughts of dread, isolation and pointlessness. From Luke's perspective, teachers and coaches should not be allowed to ignore his experiences or those of other young disabled people.

It has been argued that 'the lens of disability allows us to make problematic the socially constructed nature of sport and once we have done so, opens us to alternative constructions and solutions' (DePauw, 1997, p. 428). Here DePauw is advocating the need to centralise disability as a way of critically reflecting on how we understand sport more broadly. Examples include: asking questions about which sports or activities are played and which are marginalised; considering the implications for young disabled people of prioritising specific kinds of movements or techniques; reflecting on pedagogical practices and exploring the extent to which these best serve young disabled people. Although DePauw called for the need to centralise disability in these discussions, it is worth noting that other scholars have similarly advocated the need to critically reflect on the constitution and practices of physical education for all children and young people (Kirk, 2005). The point to be made as you read this chapter is that analysing physical education and youth sport through the lens of disability offers important insights that should inform pedagogical practice more broadly.

> *Comment*
> *Learning about good practice with young disabled people is . . . learning about good practice for all young people.*

Whilst Luke may not have had positive or rewarding physical education experiences, it is worth remembering that just 30 years ago the material circumstances of young disabled people at school would have been quite different from those of today (Barton, 2004). In the past, it was the norm for young disabled people to attend a separate 'special school' (and some still exist). In this system, there would have been few opportunities to mix with non-disabled people of a similar age. It was also common for young disabled people to spend a considerable amount of time travelling between home and their special school, making it difficult to maintain school-based friendships, for example during evenings and weekends (Tomlinson, 1982). In such schools, physical education often had a marginal place on the curriculum and it is unlikely that young people would have had access to extended curricular opportunities such as after-school sports clubs. Upon leaving school, these young adults would have found few job prospects, limited expectations of the contribution they could make to society, and almost no opportunities to enjoy participating in sport as part of leisure (Halliday, 1993).

Contemporary expectations of young disabled people have changed considerably. These changes can be credited to a series of international developments instigated by disabled activists and human rights advocates who have campaigned vigorously for independent living, self-advocacy and civic rights (Armstrong and Barton, 2007; Gabel and Danforth, 2008). These developments have challenged society to rethink the discriminatory and inequitable ways in which disabled people are treated and understood. However, even though the momentum for change has gathered pace, it should also be recognised that for many disabled people, discrimination and inequality continue to be part of their everyday lives. Moreover, even after significant developments in legislation and policy, changing perceptions of disability are unlikely to change entrenched attitudes and practices quickly, including those in physical education and sport. As Barnes *et al.* (1999, p. 64) argue, disability continues to be seen as undesirable, whereas 'able-bodied and healthy "normality" is equated with virtuousness. Those minds and bodies which are not well maintained are translated into objects of shame and scorn.'

This chapter invites you to consider the practices of physical education and youth sport from the perspective of disabled children and young people. The concepts of disability and inclusion will be reviewed to provide a framework within which such practices can be understood. Following this, the experiences of young disabled people in physical education and youth sport are explored in more detail and, as you gain insights into those experiences, I invite you to consider how your practices as a teacher or coach ought to be influenced by what you learn.

> **Comment**
> There is much to learn about the ways in which young disabled people experience physical education and youth sport, and much to reflect upon at the level of pedagogy.

The contested nature of disability

The term 'disability' is often used in a taken-for-granted way. In everyday conversations it is assumed people know what disability means and for many it is likely to conjure up specific images, usually of wheelchair users. However, disability is a contested concept, so a number of competing views exist about what it means (Barnes and Mercer, 2003; Shakespeare, 2006). Historically, disability has been understood as something 'natural' that is defined and legitimised within medical terms. It has been argued that this 'medical model' view of disability has been driven by a desire to diagnose and treat disabled people to make them 'better'. Medical specialists, including those involved in rehabilitation, tend to focus their attentions on 'helping' disabled people to cope, or fit in, with 'normal' life (Barnes *et al.*, 1999). The medical view of disability has resulted in a range of professionals making expert judgements about the lives of disabled people, including in the areas of education, employment and social welfare. Importantly, from a medical model view, a disabled person is deemed to be deficient because of an impairment, e.g. physical (limb missing or paralysis), learning (Down's syndrome, Asperger's or autism) or sensory impairment (visual or hearing). Thus, individual limitation is attributed to be the cause of a person's disability.

Applying the medical model of disability to physical education and youth sport results in the following:

- The focus is on the young disabled person and an assessment is made of their specific physical, learning or sensory limitations.
- The skills and activities planned for a session would not change, but minor adjustments would be made for the young disabled person; the young disabled person must therefore

'fit into' the planned session because it is his/her impairment that is deemed to be the problem, preventing them from undertaking the activities in the same way as other participants.

Physical education and sport practices tend to prioritise the development and refinement of techniques and adherence to rules. It might appear logical, therefore, to adopt the medical view of disability in these settings where young disabled people may not be able to move or perform in ways usually associated with a particular activity. However, where teachers and coaches hold this perspective, it is likely that the young disabled person will simply become increasingly aware of the ways in which their performance may not match up to that of their classmates. Indeed, as Luke Jackson articulated in the opening narrative, the mere prospect of doing physical education at school made him feel unwell.

> *Comment*
> *The medical model of disability situates the limitations in physical education and sports performance within the young disabled person.*

Over the last 20 years, an alternative model of disability has emerged and has been advocated increasingly in policy, programmes and practice. The 'social model' of disability '"speaks" from the standpoint of disabled people and therefore voices an opinion that has, throughout modernity, been silenced by the paternalism of a non-disabled culture' (Paterson and Hughes, 2000, p. 35). Central to the social model is the challenge it places on the naturalistic category of disability. For example, the social model of disability makes a clear distinction between understandings of impairment and those of disability. Impairment is defined as the functional limitation within the individual caused by a physical, mental or sensory impairment. In contrast, disability is defined as the restriction of opportunities to engage in community life because of physical and social barriers. Supporters of the social model view believe people with impairments are disabled by a society that is organised in ways that do not take account of their needs (Oliver, 2004). From this view, disability, like gender and ethnicity, is socially constructed; it is society that created and continues to perpetuate these categories.

Applying the social model of disability to the physical education and youth sport contexts results in some interesting challenges to traditional practices. For example:

- Attention would be paid to the ways in which a disabled person is situated within a society that assumes a non-disabled norm.
- The focus of a practitioner's attention would be on the suitability of the environment, resources, equipment and activities rather than merely focusing on the impairment of the individual.
- Adjustments or modifications might be made to activities either for specific individuals or a group of young people (including non-disabled participants).

It could be argued that there are similarities between the last point and the outcome of a medical model view. However, the fundamental difference is that the social model does not centralise the impairment of the young person as *the problem*, but rather switches the focus of pedagogy to broader issues concerned with the activities, context of delivery and the nature of resources accessed. More radically, and related to DePauw's (1997) earlier call for 'problematising' sport, taking a social model view challenges teachers and coaches to scrutinise traditional practices to re-examine the very essence of activities underpinning physical education and youth sport. In particular, those activities or practices afforded greater legitimacy over others can be brought into question. For instance, a social model view would problematise the continued dominance of team games in the school physical education curriculum. Indeed, Morley *et al.* (2005) have argued that activities such as team games provide additional challenges for teachers and young disabled people as they work towards inclusion.

> **Comment**
> *A social model view of disability places responsibility for disability on key institutions within society, including education and sport. Traditional practices in physical education and youth sport can perpetuate inequalities.*

It is important to note that the social model view of disability is not without its critics. Although it takes us beyond medical notions of disability it has been criticised for focusing primarily on structural issues and, as a consequence, losing sight of individual experiences of disability. For example, the social model does not enable us to have a real sense of how disabled people get through their daily lives and how sport is positioned within this. In addition, by centralising disability as a consideration, the social model has been criticised for ignoring the consequences of other aspects of identity on an individual's life, such as gender, ethnicity, social class and sexuality. Furthermore, it has been argued that the social model fails to take full account of the differences *between* disabled people (Barnes and Mercer, 2003). For example, consider the differences in the daily lives of a middle-class female with a visual impairment and of a working-class black male who uses a wheelchair. In this way, there is a lack of 'intersectional' understanding of the ongoing and emergent processes in which identities are constituted (Brah and Phoenix, 2004).

What we might conclude is that both models offer something useful to practitioners. The medical model offers a way of assessing the range and extent of movement in particular parts of the body and can be used instrumentally to adapt or identify alternative practices for a young disabled person. On the other hand, the social model provides teachers and coaches with a conceptual framework within which to ask, and reflect on, key questions about practice; for example:

- Why am I choosing this activity?
- Who is likely to feel marginalised?
- What other activities would be supportive of positive experiences and achieving the learning outcomes?
- Is my pedagogy supporting effective inclusion?

> **Comment**
> *Within physical education and youth sport there is a need to draw upon both models of disability, whilst remembering that disability is not the only defining feature of a young disabled person.*

Striving to 'include' in physical education and sport

In addition to concerns about models of disability, there has been a growing interest in the promotion of inclusion through sport (Thomas and Smith, 2009). Coupled with this, international legislation has supported the development of increasingly equitable and inclusive practices (Gabel and Danforth, 2008). The outcomes of inclusion are well documented in physical education and youth sport. Indeed, it is claimed inclusive sport not only contributes to benefits such as those associated with physical, health, cognitive and psychological factors, but may also offer a number of additional benefits including:

- opportunities to develop social skills necessary for interaction with others;
- opportunities to develop friendships with peers with and without disabilities;
- opportunities to interact with age-appropriate role models among able-bodied peers;
- decreased isolation;
- increased expectations and challenges;
- attitude changes among peers and increased acceptance;
- increased appreciation of difference;
- greater understanding of disability rights and equity.

(DePauw, 2000, p. 363)

What this list suggests is that inclusion has a number of interesting features. First, as was suggested earlier, inclusion in physical education and sport is often taken to mean finding ways of enabling disabled young people to be incorporated into existing practices and activities. However, it should be recognised that inclusion has a wider range of possibilities for a much broader range of young people. Second, even though DePauw (2000) makes claims about inclusion in sport, there is still much debate around what constitutes inclusion and, in particular, effective inclusive practice (Slee, 2009).

Within the context of schooling, the debates around inclusion are exemplified by Armstrong and Barton (2007), who note that inclusion is presented as a 'flagship idea', enabling diversity in schools to be celebrated through the transformation of cultures and practices. Yet Armstrong and Barton also argue that inclusion has become nothing more than 'an empty signifier' and at the heart of this debate are questions about the extent to which schools and practices should or will change. For example, Smith (2004, p. 47) concluded 'it would appear that, at present, many students with SEN [special educational needs] are being required to "fit" into the curriculum – that is to say, it seems they are being "integrated" into, rather than "fully included" in, mainstream PE'. Thus, it is argued, teachers do make some changes, but these are made in order to enable the young disabled person to fit into the existing curriculum and activities. In contrast, Barton (1998, p. 85) suggests:

Inclusive education is not merely about providing access into mainstream school for pupils who have previously been excluded . . . Inclusive education is about the participation of all children and young people and the removal of all forms of exclusionary practice.

From this perspective, effective inclusion policies and processes would be those that result in changes to key aspects of a school's structure and practices.

Within physical education and sport a number of actions have been initiated in order to work towards inclusive practice. Although presented separately in this chapter, it should be noted that they are often adopted in combination by practitioners. First, both in the UK and internationally, a range of continuing professional development (CPD) opportunities has been developed for teachers and coaches by national governing bodies of sport (NGBs), National Disability Sport Organisations (NDSOs), Sports Coach UK and the Youth Sport Trust. These CPD opportunities are varied in focus, including those that address specific sports, disability sport, general sport and disability.

Second, a number of these CPD opportunities and, indeed, broader programmes draw on the 'Inclusion Spectrum' as a practical model for helping practitioners to develop strategies for working towards inclusion (Figure 12.1). The Inclusion Spectrum is divided into four quarters and each offers different approaches to teaching or coaching, including 'open games', 'modified activities', 'disability sport' and 'parallel activities' (Stevenson, 2009).

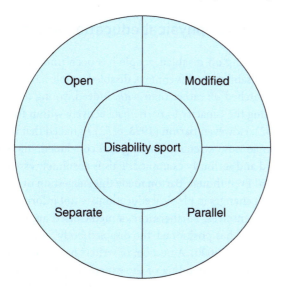

Figure 12.1 Inclusion spectrum
Source: Based on Stevenson (2009)

Where this spectrum is used as part of a teaching and learning resource, detailed examples are presented in order to reinforce the idea that different strategies for participation can be adopted, but that no one strategy is superior to another.

Third, disability sports have been incorporated into physical education and other activity programmes targeting disabled and non-disabled young people. Medland and Ellis-Hill (2008) highlight the ways in which disability sport can enable non-disabled people to re-evaluate their perceptions about the skill and commitment required to compete in disability sport. However, it has also been suggested that where disability sports are incorporated into general physical education classes, careful consideration must be given to the ways in which teachers embed such sports into the curriculum (Fitzgerald and Kirk, 2009). In particular, if a teacher or coach lacks sufficient pedagogical skills, the inclusion of disability sports could reinforce stereotypes instead of challenging them (Barton, 2009).

There is evidence to suggest that teachers and coaches have responded in a very practical sense to inclusion issues by adopting a number of strategies, including the three outlined above. Whilst these are positive developments, providing teachers and coaches with 'real solutions' (Stevenson, 2009), they do not necessarily take physical education and youth sport forward to the more complex and demanding understanding of inclusion supported by Barton (1998). For Barton's vision to become a reality, teachers and coaches may need enhanced pedagogical skills that are developed progressively over their careers.

> **Comment**
> *Inclusion prompts practitioners to critically reflect on their pedagogies: 'What do we mean when we talk of including? What happens? Whose interests are being served? And most of all, into what do we seek to include?'*
>
> *(Graham and Slee, 2008, p. 95)*

Mapping experiences of physical education and sport

Historically, research focusing on disabled people has been underpinned by a medical model understanding of disability. In this context, disabled people have been treated as passive recipients to be researched *on* rather than *with*. Indeed, young disabled people were often considered as lacking the capacity to participate actively within the research process (Davis and Watson, 2002). However, Barton (1993, p. 52) signalled that the lack of engagement with disabled people was extremely limiting and concluded: 'the voice of disabled people needs to be heard and seriously examined. This is absolutely essential in the teaching of physical education.' Even though Barton made this suggestion over 16 years ago, it is still too often the case that changes in physical education are not informed by insights from young disabled people themselves. Furthermore, a medicalised approach to research in physical education and sport has positioned 'the disabled body' as an object to be tested, modified and retested (DePauw, 2000). A number of writers have agreed that such research data result in only a partial understanding of the experiences of disability and have not 'focused on the body as whole, the body in a social context, or the body in connection with self' (DePauw, 1997, p. 419).

Although a medical view of disability continues to dominate research in physical education and youth sport, there are signs of a steady increase in the number and scale of research projects seeking insights from young disabled people (Coates and Vickerman, 2008). For example, quantitative (Sport England, 2001) and qualitative (Fitzgerald, 2005; Anderson, 2009) research is available that explores experiences of participation. Quantitative data provide clear evidence that young disabled people do not fare well in physical education. In particular, young disabled people spend less time doing physical education than their non-disabled peers and are unable to access the same range of activities.

Goodwin and Watkinson (2000, p. 151) argue that the experiences of physical education among young disabled people can be considered in terms of 'bad' and 'good' days. A bad day is one in which young disabled people are 'rejected, neglected, or seen as objects of curiosity by their classmates'. During bad days, these young people may feel a sense of isolation and exclusion. In contrast, according to Goodwin and Watkinson (2000, p. 154) 'good' days promote 'a feeling of belonging, the chance to share or partake in the benefits of the program, and the opportunity to participate skilfully with classmates'. In particular, on good days, young disabled people are able to access all the benefits of physical education, including fitness, skill development, knowledge acquisition and other health-related benefits.

> **Comment**
> *It is worth considering what physical education must feel like to children and young people who have more 'bad days' than 'good days'.*

Beyond a physical education context, evidence suggests that fewer young disabled people take part in after-school or community sport than their non-disabled peers. This has been attributed to a number of factors including negative physical education experiences, having other leisure priorities and a lack of information about opportunities (Thomas and Smith, 2009). It is important to note that these factors are similar to those cited by many young people. However, for young disabled people, exclusionary attitudes within community sports clubs and also a lack of awareness about player pathways add to the participation problems they face (Nixon, 2007; Stride, 2009). For example, teachers and coaches sometimes lack knowledge of the participation options open to young disabled people. Some young disabled people may want to participate in a disability sport such as goalball, boccia or wheelchair basketball. In this setting a specific disability sport pathway could be followed. In contrast, some young disabled people may opt to participate in mainstream sport with predominantly non-disabled young people. Furthermore, some young disabled people may wish to cross-cut mainstream and disability sport provision, training with a mainstream sports club and competing in both mainstream and disability sport events. However, in order to enable young disabled people to access the opportunities that best meet their needs, teachers and coaches should have adequate skills, knowledge and understanding of these young people as diverse learners. As Kathy Armour in Chapter 1 of this book argues, this requires a pedagogy that is sensitive to the needs and interests of young people learning in and through physical education and sport.

> **Comment**
> *The pathway a young disabled person takes may cross-cut disability sport facilitated by NDSOs, disability sport facilitated by NGBs or mainstream sport facilitated by NGBs.*

Conclusion

An understanding of disability can enable you to better understand how society is constructed in normative and non-disabled ways. Physical education and youth sport replicate normative ideals and, as DePauw (1997) argued, looking through the lens of disability provides a view that leads to critical questions about the nature of physical education and youth sport, and the values underpinning them. In particular, by considering both medical and social model approaches to disability, insights can be gained into young disabled people and the ways in which perceptions, practices and activities can be the drivers of *disabling* forms of physical education and sport for them. At the beginning of this chapter, Luke Jackson portrayed vividly his physical education experiences. He described physical education as an ordeal that served as a disincentive to continue sport beyond school. If they are to take their professional responsibilities seriously, practitioners in physical education and sport must continually reflect on how they can work in ways that minimise these kinds of experiences for children and young people.

Learning tasks

Individual task

Earlier in this chapter Graham and Slee (2008) identified a number of key questions about inclusion: *'What do we mean when we talk of including? What happens? Whose interests are being served? And most of all, into what do we seek to include?'* These questions can be considered in relation to your own practice. For example, imagine you are being interviewed for a teaching or coaching post and you are asked to write a short account of your views on the following question: 'What does including a young disabled person in physical education mean to you?' After you have written your account, consider whether you have taken a medical or social model approach to understanding disability in your response.

Group task

1 Work in small groups and generate a definition of 'inclusion'; for example, one you could use if you were facilitating a sports equity workshop.

2 Rotate the definitions to different groups and ask them to draft a written response on how the definition could be improved.

3 Now return the definitions to their original groups. Each group should consider the suggested improvements and make any relevant amendments to their definition of inclusion. Based on the definition generated, each group should next develop a 'Ten-point plan' for inclusive practice.

4 Each group shares three points from their plan with the rest of the class. As part of this feedback, indicate specifically the extent to which medical and social model approaches to disability could help to inform these points.

5 Conclude the session with a whole-class discussion around the relationship between inclusion and the medical and social models of disability.

Further reading

Thomas, N. and Smith, A. (2009) *Disability Sport and Society*, Routledge: London.

References

Anderson, D. (2009) Adolescent girls' involvement in disability sport: implications for identity development, *Journal of Sport and Social Issues*, 33(4): 427–49.

Armstrong, F. and Barton, L. (2007) Policy, experience and change and the challenges of inclusion. In: L. Barton and F. Armstrong (eds) *Policy, Experience and Change: Cross-cultural reflections on inclusive education*, Dordrecht: Springer.

Barnes, C. and Mercer, G. (2003) *Disability*, Cambridge: Polity Press.

Barnes, C., Mercer, G. and Shakespeare, T. (1999) *Exploring Disability: A sociological introduction*, Cambridge: Polity Press.

Barton, L. (1993) Disability, empowerment and physical education. In: J. Evans (ed.) *Equality, Education and Physical Education*, London: Falmer Press.

Barton, L. (1998) *The Politics of Special Educational Needs*, London: Falmer Press.

Barton, L. (2004) The politics of special education: a necessary or irrelevant approach? In: L. Ware (ed.) *Ideology and the Politics of (In)Exclusion*, London: Peter Lang Publishing.

Barton, L. (2009) Disability, physical education and sport: some critical observations and questions. In: H. Fitzgerald (ed.) *Disability and Youth Sport*, London: Routledge.

Brah, A. and Phoenix, A. (2004) 'Ain't I a woman?' Revisiting intersectionality, *Journal of International Women's Studies*, 5, 75–86.

Coates, J. and Vickerman, P. (2008) Let the children have their say: children with special educational needs and their experiences of physical education – a review, *Support for Learning*, 23(4), 168–75.

Davis, J. and Watson, N. (2002) Counting stereotypes of disability: disabled children and resistance. In: M. Corker and T. Shakespeare (eds) *Embodying Disability Theory*, London: Continuum.

DePauw, K. P. (1997) The (in)visibility of disability: cultural contexts and 'sporting bodies', *Quest*, 49(4), 416–30.

DePauw, K. P. (2000) Social-cultural context of disability: implications for scientific inquiry and professional preparation, *Quest*, 52(4), 358–68.

Fitzgerald, H. (2005) Still feeling like a spare piece of luggage? Embodied experiences of (dis)ability in physical education and school sport, *Physical Education and Sport Pedagogy*, (10)1, 41–59.

Fitzgerald, H. and Kirk, D. (2009) Physical education as a normalising practice: Is there a space for disability sport? In: H. Fitzgerald (ed.) *Disability and Youth Sport*, London: Routledge.

Gabel, S. L. and Danforth, S. (2008) Disability and the international politics of education. In: S. L. Gabel and S. Danforth (eds) *Disability and the Politics of Education: An international reader*, London: Peter Lang.

Goodwin, D. L. and Watkinson, E. J. (2000) Inclusive physical education from the perspectives of students with physical disabilities, *Adapted Physical Activity Quarterly*, 17(2), 144–60.

Graham, L. J. and Slee, R. (2008) Inclusion? In: S. L. Gabel and S. Danforth (eds) *Disability and the Politics of Education: An international reader*, London: Peter Lang.

Halliday, P. (1993) Physical education within special educational provision – equality and entitlement. In: J. Evans (ed.) *Equity, Education and Physical Education*, London: Falmer Press.

Jackson, L. (2002) *Freaks, Geeks & Asperger Syndrome: A user guide to adolescence*, London: Jessica Kingley Publishers.

Kirk, D. (2005) Physical education, youth sport and lifelong participation: the importance of early learning experiences, *European Physical Education Review*, 11(3), 239–55.

Medland, J. and Ellis-Hill, C. (2008) Why do able-bodied people take part in wheelchair sports? *Disability and Society*, 23(2), 107–16.

Morley, D., Bailey, R., Tan, J. and Cooke, B. (2005) 'Inclusive physical education: teachers' views of including pupils with special educational needs and/or disabilities in physical education, *European Physical Education Review*, 11(1), 84–107.

Nixon, H. L. (2007) Constructing diverse sports opportunities for people with disabilities, *Journal of Sport and Social Issues*, 31(4), 417–33.

Oliver, M. (2004) If I had a hammer: the social model in action. In: C. Barnes (ed.) *The Social Model of Disability – Theory and Research*, Leeds: The Disability Press.

Paterson, K. and Hughes, B. (2000) Disabled bodies. In: P. Hancock, B. Hughes, E. Jagger, K. Paterson, R. Russell, E. Tulle-Winton and M. Tyler (eds) *The Body, Culture and Society*, Buckingham: Open University Press.

Shakespeare, T. (2006) *Disability Rights and Wrongs*, London: Routledge.

Slee, R. (2009) The inclusion paradox: the cultural politics of difference. In: M.W. Apple, W. Au and L. A. Gandin (eds) *The Routledge International Handbook of Critical Education*, London: Routledge.

Smith, A. (2004) The inclusion of pupils with special educational needs in secondary school physical education, *Physical Education and Sport Pedagogy*, 9(1), 37–54.

Sport England (2001) *Disability Survey 2000: Young people with a disability and sport, headline findings*, London: Sport England.

Stevenson, P. (2009) The pedagogy of inclusive youth sport: working towards real solutions. In: H. Fitzgerald (ed.) *Disability and Youth Sport*, London: Routledge.

Stride, A. (2009) 'We want to play football' – girls experiencing learning disabilities and their footballing experiences. In: H. Fitzgerald (ed.) *Disability and Youth Sport*, London: Routledge.

Thomas, N. and Smith, A. (2009) *Disability Sport and Society*, London: Routledge.

Tomlinson, S. (1982) *The Sociology of Special Education*, London: Routledge and Kegan Paul.

Disaffected youth in physical education and youth sport

Rachel Sandford and Rebecca Duncombe, Loughborough University

John's story

John (14) was in my maths class when I first started teaching at this school. He often acted up and at times his behaviour was bad enough for me to remove him from my class. He very rarely attempted his work and I don't recall him ever completing any homework. I was asked to run the Sky Living for Sport course and he seemed the ideal candidate, so we set up the project with five other boys, all with similar problems. We did different activities each week (e.g. kick boxing, rugby, mountain biking) and worked towards the boys running a sports day event at the local primary school. Each week, we set targets and the following week, we reviewed the boys' behaviour. All of the boys improved in numerous and often subtle ways. John, for example, has channelled his energy in class into calling out answers and he has only forgotten his homework once since we started the project. Whereas before, he wouldn't make eye contact with me or engage in conversation, we now joke with one another in class and around the school. He has matured a lot.

Introduction

John and his teacher in the narrative above are fictional characters. The narrative, however, represents the kinds of stories we found when we evaluated two programmes that were designed to engage disaffected young people in education through sport. The programmes were Sky Sports Living for Sport (SSLfS) and the HSBC/Outward Bound project (HSBC/OB). Reflecting a broader trend for promoting positive youth development through sport/physical activity, these programmes were aimed specifically at engaging or re-engaging young people in school and/or physical education lessons. There has been an increase in such programmes in recent years due, in part, to mounting concerns over the (perceived) growing problem of youth disaffection and disengagement.

As with similar evaluations, the findings from the evaluation of the SSLfS and HSBC/OB programmes highlight many positive benefits for their young participants. However, while a positive picture has indeed emerged from the research, it is important to note that not all young people gained positively from the experience and that, on the whole, positive outcomes were highly individualised and context-specific. The purpose of this chapter, therefore, is to identify what has been learnt from our own and other research about promoting positive youth development through sport/physical activity, and to explore ways in which this knowledge can be of use to teachers, coaches and instructors as they try to engage with and teach/coach disaffected young people. The chapter begins by addressing the question: What do we mean by youth disaffection?

Disaffection, disengagement and disruption: defining the problem

There is much debate and discussion (public, political and academic) about the issue of 'problematic' youth. Indeed, youth disaffection is now perceived by many to be a global problem and such debates, in the UK and further afield, have led to what Davies (2005) describes as a 'moral panic' concerning young people, their behaviour and their disengagement. In particular, concerns have been raised about (some) young people's involvement in unhealthy, anti-social or criminal activities (e.g. vandalism, drug taking and carrying/using weapons), their general disengagement from education and their lack of respect for civic responsibilities (Hayward and Sharp, 2005). Such behaviour, it is argued, has significant implications for social and moral order, and youth disaffection has, understandably perhaps, become the focus of much research. But what do we mean by the term 'youth disaffection'?

There is a distinct lack of consensus about the precise definitions, causes and expressions of youth 'disaffection'. The word 'disaffection' has become something of a 'catch-all' term, applied not to a singular concept but to a rather vague cluster of behaviours, attitudes and experiences (Steer, 2000). Social policy makers, in particular, make heavy use of the concept and use it in conjunction with other terms (e.g. social exclusion, social marginalisation and disenfranchisement) when defining groups of individuals who seem to lack access to various social resources or benefits (see Sandford *et al.*, 2006). Moreover, within the broader youth development literature, additional terms such as 'at risk', 'under-served' and 'disengaged' are commonly associated with the notion of disaffection, and have become somewhat synonymous with the concept. Despite the lack of consensus in definition, however, Heathcote-Elliott and Walters (2000) note that 'one feature common to all reports on the subject is that being labelled "disaffected" has negative connotations for the individual' (p. 1). In other words, there is a perception that disaffected youth are in some way deficient, lacking in morals and in need of guidance that will aid their positive social and moral development.

> *Comment*
> *Disaffection is a complex, multidimensional concept that is difficult to define, but there is a perception in society that youth disaffection and antisocial behaviour are growing and that something must be done.*

'Disaffection' can be understood as a complex and multidimensional phenomenon that is influenced by numerous interrelating factors (e.g. poverty, low self-esteem, broken families, drug use). Disaffection manifests itself in various, often highly individualised, ways including disengagement from mainstream activities, disruptive or antisocial behaviour, or engagement in risky or criminal behaviour (Steer, 2000). One particular form of youth disaffection that is of particular concern at present is young people's disengagement from school, education and training. Indeed, there is a large body of evidence to suggest that youth disaffection, broadly defined, plays a key role in issues such as exclusions, truancy, poor discipline and apathy within schools (Newburn and Shiner, 2005). The perceived scale of this problem, and the resulting impact upon educational attainment (for both disaffected pupils and their peers), have put disaffection into sharp focus in recent years. A government report in the UK, for example, stated that disruptive behaviour within classrooms interrupted pupils' learning, resulting in alienation from education for many young people (DfES, 2005).

Youth disaffection is not always expressed as disruptive or deviant behaviour. Brown and Fletcher (2002), for example, coined the term 'disruptive engagement' to describe the behaviour of the young people in their educational research. Although these young people exhibited behaviours that were indeed disruptive (e.g. shouting out answers in class, mimicking the teacher, persistently demanding attention, talking with peers), the authors concluded that, in many cases, these could also be perceived as genuine attempts to engage, on some level, with the teacher and lesson. Other researchers (e.g. Heathcote-Elliott and Walters, 2000) have called for a fluid understanding of disaffection, viewing it not as a tightly defined concept but as a continuum from active to passive, and mild to severe disaffection. This fluid approach might be viewed more helpful because it recognises that the term 'disaffected youth' includes overtly disruptive pupils (i.e. those who call out in lessons, are involved in bullying or who have poor anger-management skills) *and* those who are quietly disengaged (those who lack confidence, have poor social skills or who contribute little to class activities). Although the former are more obvious, both groups suffer educational disadvantage. The issue of youth disaffection is, therefore, a significant challenge for society and, specifically, for those who seek to work with and for young people. As a result, an increasing number of programmes are being developed to facilitate young people's engagement, re-engagement and positive development.

> **Comment**
> *Disaffection is best understood as a continuum of behaviours. Youth disaffection in schools can be problematic both for those directly involved and for others in the class/lesson.*

Re-engagement through physical education and youth sport

Although there are numerous concerns about youth disaffection and disengagement, Newburn and Shiner (2005), among others, have pointed out that perceptions of young people as 'a problem' are not new and can be found throughout history. However, escalating concerns about 'youth in trouble' and 'youth as trouble' in contemporary society have led to growing calls for action (Sandford, Duncombe and Armour, 2008). Around the world there are numerous examples of projects, programmes and government measures that are designed to engage or re-engage disaffected youth. In the UK, examples include the

Every Child Matters and *Youth Matters* agendas (DCSF, 2005). Many of these programmes and policies make use of sport and physical activities as vehicles for promoting positive youth development. For example, the PESSCL and PESSYP strategies,[1] NOPES[2] and Positive Futures,[3] in addition to the two independent research projects outlined in this chapter, are all recent examples from within the UK. Further afield, curriculum programmes such as Sport Education (Siedentop, 1994), Teaching Personal and Social Responsibility (Hellison, 1995) and Sport for Peace (Ennis, 1999) have been developed to facilitate positive development within sport and physical education contexts.

The widespread use of sport/physical activity as a tool for re-engaging disaffected youth would seem to stem from traditional views that sport is in some way 'character building' (Sandford *et al.*, 2006) and that participation in physical activities can aid young people's positive personal, social and moral development. Certainly, there is a growing body of international research to suggest that involvement in constructive leisure facilities can lead to young people's positive development (Holt, 2008), as well as helping them to build resilience and address problems of disadvantage and social exclusion through the generation of social capital (Bailey, 2005). Moreover, given its capacity to reach large and diverse groups of young people, school physical education is considered to be a valuable context in which disaffected pupils can be constructively re-engaged. Using sport/physical activity programmes to facilitate young people's (re-)engagement is often described as a 'positive youth development' (PYD) approach (Holt, 2008).

PYD is a strength-based conception of youth development, focusing not on the problems faced (or, indeed, caused) by young people but on the talents, strengths and potential of each individual. Damon (2004), for example, notes that the PYD perspective 'emphasizes the manifest potentialities rather than the supposed incapacities of young people' (p. 15). It has been argued that this view allows for an understanding of youth development as being not only about preventing undesirable behaviours, but also about the promotion of desired outcomes. Indeed, the core principles of the PYD approach all reflect these views and represent a process through which young people become equipped to contribute positively to the development of themselves, their families and their communities (Lerner *et al.*, 2008). It is perhaps unsurprising, therefore, that many working within the field of sport, physical activity and physical education are now drawing upon PYD theory in their research (e.g. Fraser-Thomas, Côté and Deakin, 2005).

> **Comment**
> Sport, physical activity and physical education can be effective vehicles for positive youth development. A PYD approach to youth disaffection focuses on the talents and strengths of young people.

Two sport/physical activity re-engagement programmes

Despite repeated claims about the power of physical activity/sport to build 'character' and facilitate young people's positive development, there has been little robust evidence to support such assertions. The evidence base is, however, slowly growing thanks, in part, to programmes such as those outlined in this chapter and the funds made available to evaluate them. More is known now, therefore, about the potential for sport/physical activity initiatives to have a positive impact (both immediate and sustained) on disaffected youth, and, importantly, how future initiatives can be designed to maximise benefits and offer sustained outcomes. What now follows are overviews of two corporate-sponsored programmes, evaluated by the authors, which sought to use sport/physical activity to facilitate the re-engagement of disaffected youth in the UK. Each overview provides a concise summary of the programme aims, structure and methodology, as well as key findings and illustrative pupil/teacher quotes. The implications of these findings are then considered.

Sky Sports Living for Sport (SSLfS)

Run by the Youth Sport Trust and funded by Sky Sports,[4] SSLfS is a national school-based physical activity initiative that is intended for young people between the ages of 11 and 16 who are having difficulties with, or who are disengaged from, school life in some way (e.g. behaviour, attendance or confidence). Within the programme, schools are encouraged to design their own projects tailored to the needs of their pupils, within a broad but flexible framework developed by both the sponsors and organisers. SSLfS projects take place in schools (although activities can also take place off-site) and run for between eight weeks and one academic year, with average group sizes of 8–16 young people. A typical project would provide weekly activity sessions for young people and would culminate in both a sporting and celebration event. The list of activities that have been undertaken within SSLfS projects to date is extensive and includes traditional sports and games (e.g. football, basketball and swimming) as well as recreational activities less common to the PE curriculum (e.g. street dance, skateboarding and outdoor/adventurous activities).

The evaluation of SSLfS has used a range of qualitative methods to collate data from both schools and pupils and to generate school-specific case studies. In particular, school statistics and/or teachers' professional judgement are used to provide profile data for each pupil participant (e.g. relating to their behaviour, school attendance or levels of

Teacher comments	Pupil comments
'Unbelievable – 12 boys have re-engaged with school and have now **all** got college places.'	'I've been a lot better behaved in lessons because now I know how it feels when people don't listen when you are trying to give instructions.'
'(SSLfS) re-engaged a group of Year 9 girls who were refusing to do any meaningful physical exercise.'	'I learnt about teamwork . . . like we've learnt to rely on each other whilst helping each other at the same time.'
'It has been a great motivator, particularly for pupils who are not particularly sporty.'	'It's helped my behaviour die down. I was going up to the behaviour centre like twice a day and now I hardly ever go up there.'
'Pupils now contribute verbally more in lessons, (their) behaviour and attitude have improved in lessons, reducing the number of detentions and isolations.'	'I think (SSLfS) has built up my confidence in PE.'
'It has enabled the children to develop the following skills: confidence, self-esteem, friendship, social interaction, making positive choices, being independent.'	'I've really enjoyed it. It's probably one of the best things I've done in this school . . . and I've learnt a lot.'

self-esteem/confidence) at the start and end of project activities. In addition to this, interviews with lead teachers and focus groups with pupils help to ascertain individuals' views about project activities and outcomes. Since 2003, data have been collected on approximately 10,000 young people from 1,000 schools throughout the UK. Findings from the evaluation have been presented in detail elsewhere (e.g. Sandford, Duncombe and Armour, 2008) but to summarise briefly, improvements were seen in many young people's behaviour, attendance, attainment, self-esteem and confidence. The table above and the individual pupil case study provide examples of the findings.

Andrea

Andrea (age 12) was selected to take part in SSLfS because she had low self-esteem, poor PE attendance and was not physically active. Prior to her participation, Andrea's teacher noted that she found group situations difficult and was often very defensive and confrontational. However, after Andrea's involvement in SSLfS, the same teacher commented that 'we have seen a massive change in (Andrea) . . . she seems a lot happier (and) is a lot less confrontational with her peer group'. Moreover, final impact data received from Andrea's school suggested that she had shown 'exceptional improvement', both in terms of achievement and personal development. It was felt that SSLfS had been successful for Andrea because it had taken her away from the school site, enabled her to be part of a team and helped to improve her self-esteem and confidence.

The HSBC/Outward Bound project (HSBC/OB)

The HSBC/OB project involved a partnership between HSBC in the Community, the Outward Bound Trust and five schools from the Docklands area of London[5]. For each of the five years that the project ran (2003–8) it offered schools a year-long programme of outdoor physical activities (some residential) for 30 of their Year 9 pupils (150 pupils in total for each year). The activity sessions were designed by Outward Bound to provide individual and group challenges and to develop skills such as team building, communication and responsibility. In addition to Outward Bound staff, a number of volunteer mentors from HSBC's workforce were trained to work with pupils both within and beyond the activity sessions. Teachers were encouraged to select pupils who they felt would 'benefit' in some way from programme participation, and there was also an emphasis on identifying those pupils who were disadvantaged, disaffected or disengaged. A key project feature was that pupils who were perceived to have 'gained the most' from early activity experiences were given the opportunity to progress to additional Outward Bound activities during the year.

A range of qualitative methods, similar to those used to evaluate SSLfS, were employed in the evaluation of the HSBC/OB programme. The aim was to gain an in-depth understanding of participants' thoughts and experiences of project involvement, and to determine the extent to which programme aims and objectives were achieved. The evaluators generated data from the analysis of baseline and six-monthly updated pupil profiles, participant observation of activities and ethnographic fieldnotes, as well as through methods such as individual and group interviews, open-ended surveys and journal writing. During the lifetime of the evaluation, data were collected on and from approximately 500 young people. Again, more detailed findings have been presented elsewhere (e.g. Sandford, Armour and Duncombe, 2008) but, in summary, the evaluation found that:

- the majority of pupils improved from their baseline profiles and many of these (over 50 per cent) sustained these improvements to the point of leaving school;
- there were perceived improvements in behaviour, attendance and (in some cases) attainment;
- many pupils showed improved communication, leadership and teamwork skills.

The following table and individual case study provide some illustration of the findings.

Teacher comments	Pupil comments
'Ali has shown outstanding progress. He was selected for the Classic Course. His communication, team work and especially leadership are outstanding.'	'I have learnt that I am braver, more confident and more courageous than I have ever thought in my life.'
'Paul has gained lots of confidence and leadership qualities. He's in line to be a school prefect.'	'Before I wouldn't say much, I was too shy, but now I say more in class.'
'On the whole, I would say that the HSBC/OB project has been really good for our pupils. Some of them will certainly achieve more now, because they have the skills and belief to do well.'	'The most important thing I learnt was communicating. Without communication you get nowhere.'
'Keira has shown a marked improvement in her attitude and attendance at school.'	'I think I learnt something today – not to give up and however many times I fall I will climb again and I'll reach the top.'
'Syed has significantly improved communication skills following his involvement in the project.'	'I've learnt that not everyone is capable of doing what you can do. You have to help each other in order to reach your goal.'

Callum

Callum was selected for involvement in the HSBC/OB project because his attendance at school was poor, and some aspects of his behaviour were considered a cause for concern. In particular, Callum was known to be involved with a 'bad crowd' and to have problems with alcohol and drug abuse. Callum did well during the residential activity weeks, being described by his mentor as 'polite', 'respectful' and 'an involved team member'. Callum was also praised for his willingness to engage with the activities and to support his team mates. This positive behaviour continued as Callum returned to school, and he was described as the 'pupil with largest change' within the project group. As his teacher commented, 'he is now in school all the time, he has stopped trying drugs, and wants to, and does, achieve his goals'. Callum's progress led to his selection for the three-week Outward Bound Classic Course, and he again showed himself willing to participate in all activities and able to work effectively in a team.

The evaluations of the SSLfS and HSBC/OB programmes found many positive impacts on pupils. However, not all pupils benefited and there were numerous examples in both programmes where pupils showed no change – or a negative change – from their baseline profiles. Moreover, there was some evidence of conflicting reports from different teachers on the progress of certain pupils, suggesting that, in some cases, positive impact was context-specific. For example, in the HSBC/OB project, one particular pupil (six months after commencing the project) was described by his form tutor as still being aggressive and confrontational, while, at the same time, being viewed by a subject teacher as having shown improvements in behaviour and being better able to control his temper (see Sandford, Armour and Duncombe, 2008). Nonetheless, there is compelling evidence that positive outcomes are not only attainable but also sustainable for many individuals *if programmes are designed in appropriate ways.*

> **Comment**
> *It is difficult to measure, objectively, progress on some of the features of youth disaffection. Large evaluation studies are, however, beginning to provide empirical evidence of sustained positive impact.*

Implications for programme design

The evaluations of the SSLfS and HSBC/OB programmes suggested that there are at least six points to be considered if you want to design a successful school-based sport/physical activity programme or project that can re-engage disaffected or disengaged young people.

Match individual pupil needs with specific project objectives

The importance of ensuring that a project is appropriate for participants' needs and interests is something that is endorsed widely within the physical education literature and is perceived to be particularly significant for disaffected youth (e.g. Sandford *et al.*, 2006). Certainly, in the SSLfS evaluation, teachers felt that projects were more successful when designed to be appropriate to the specific needs of a particular group. It is important therefore that teachers/coaches take time to assess the needs of the young people in their group and that any project planning/selection is done with reference to these needs, rather than adopting a 'one-size-fits-all' approach.

Locate project activities outside the 'normal' school context

For the teachers in the SSLfS and HSBC/OB evaluations, a key feature in effective projects was the use of both facilities and individuals (e.g. mentors, instructors) outside the normal school environment. In general, it was felt that this helped to engage pupils' interest, raise the status of the initiative and make the pupils feel more valued. In addition, it was perceived to be important, in some cases, for young people to be removed from aspects of the school environment that were causing them difficulty. Other researchers have endorsed these findings (e.g. Peacock, 2006) and have pointed to the significance of using neutral or 'safe spaces' for participants (e.g. Donnelly and Coakley, 2002). There are implications for teachers/coaches here in terms of adopting a multi-agency approach in project design: for example, using both school and community facilities, involving non-teacher adults as role models/mentors and employing outside instructors for activity sessions.

Work with pupils to choose activities, set targets and review progress

The need to work with pupils in choosing activities and setting targets is widely endorsed in the PYD literature. In particular, it is felt that giving young people a sense of belonging and ownership in such programmes and involving them in key decisions relating to their participation are necessary to motivate and encourage effective participation (e.g. Donnelly and Coakley, 2002). This is also strongly supported in the literature on youth voice. For example, in addition to showing respect and promoting responsibility, working with disaffected pupils in this way can be seen to give a sense of empowerment in what is otherwise a powerless situation (Sandford, Armour and Duncombe, 2010). It would seem not only important but necessary, therefore, for teachers/coaches to involve pupils where possible (and practical) in key project decisions, to set clear, achievable and transparent goals, and to engage in regular reviews with all pupils regarding their progress.

Establish positive relationships between project leaders/ supporters and pupils

One of the key points of agreement in the physical activity/sport literature is the importance of developing positive social relationships in physical activity programmes for positive youth development. Interestingly, these sentiments are also endorsed in related bodies of work, such as the mentoring and informal education literature (e.g. Richardson and Wolfe, 2001). The significance of social processes and the ways in which such processes can lead to the development of key skills such as communication, leadership, empathy and a sense of personal and social responsibility are widely recognised (e.g. Petitpas, Cornelius and Van Raalte, 2008). Moreover, it has been suggested that the social interaction aspect is, to some extent, more important than the particular activity undertaken in terms of effective positive outcomes (Sandford *et al.*, 2006). It is perhaps not surprising, therefore, that researchers have noted the need for adults involved in PYD projects to be enthusiastic, motivated and charismatic, and committed to meeting the needs of participants (e.g. Riley and Rustique-Forrester, 2002). In addition, it would seem necessary that teachers/coaches take time to build connections with the young people in their groups and, importantly, provide scope for positive relationships to continue beyond the end of project activities.

Give pupils the opportunity to work with (and for) others

For many of the teachers and mentors involved in the SSLfS and HSBC/OB projects, a key factor in effecting positive outcomes for participants was the way in which pupils were required to work collaboratively and constructively. The importance of providing opportunities for individuals, particularly those who are considered disaffected, to work with (and for) others is also supported in the physical education literature (e.g. Hellison, Martinek and Walsh, 2008). In particular, it is perceived that this approach helps to engender a sense of responsibility (for both self and others), develop skills such as teamwork, leadership and empathy, and move the individual's focus beyond their own troubles or difficulties. It would seem pertinent, then, that such opportunities are built into PYD programmes at the development stage, and that teachers/coaches provide ample opportunities for collaborative work. Moreover, including a requirement that participants work, either individually or collectively, for the benefit of an external group, has the potential to enhance links within/between schools and communities.

Plan for and support sustained involvement

As noted earlier, concerns have been expressed about the short-lived nature of many sport/physical activity initiatives focused on PYD, with researchers noting that this limits the sustainability of any positive impact (e.g. Morris *et al.*, 2003). It was certainly the case in both the SSLfS and HSBC/OB programmes that those pupils who participated for longer, or who went on to participate in further development projects, gained more from their involvement. Teachers felt that this was due, in part, to the opportunities that this sustained participation afforded individuals in terms of further developing newly acquired skills or transferring them to other contexts, and pointed to the need for structured pathways to enable young people to have sustained involvement in complementary activities. Other researchers have endorsed this need for continued involvement and have highlighted the significance of planning for the long term (e.g. Crabbe, 2006). There are clear implications for teachers/coaches here in terms of project development, particularly with regard to the length of initiatives and the need to have a clear 'exit strategy' in place for when structured project activities end. Adopting a whole-school or multi-agency approach may be beneficial here, and could potentially facilitate the transfer of skills and sustainability of positive impact. Moreover, making use of adult mentors to support pupils/individuals beyond initial project activities could facilitate this process.

Conclusion

This chapter has introduced some of the complexities surrounding the issue of youth disaffection, and has examined some examples of sport/physical activity that are being used to promote positive youth development. Some tips have been identified for teachers, coaches and instructors working with and for disaffected young people in the field of physical education and youth sport. What is clear is that professional teachers and coaches need to extend their pedagogies if they are to make the best of sport and physical activity environments for re-engaging and motivating disaffected young people. Expecting engagement in sport alone to somehow 'rescue' such young people is unlikely to work. Instead, it is essential to recognise and respect each disaffected/disengaged young person's specific needs and plan to meet them accordingly.

Notes

1 The PESSCL (Physical Education School Sport Club Links) strategy was launched by the UK Labour government in 2002 and saw significant funding (£459 million) invested in physical education and school sport. It was followed up with PESSYP (Physical Education and Sport Strategy for Young People) in January 2008, with a further £755 million pledged to help increase the quality and quantity of sport and PE undertaken by young people aged 5–19 years in England.

2 The NOPES (New Opportunities for PE and Sport) initiative was launched in 2002 and also saw significant investment (£751 million) in PE and sport. Supported by lottery funding, the programme primarily provided capital for new or refurbished sport/physical activity facilities.

3 Positive Futures is a national social inclusion project in the UK that uses various activities, including sport, to engage with socially marginalised young people.

4 The sponsorship of the Living for Sport initiative has changed throughout the life of the project, although all funding has been provided through the Sky broadcasting corporation. The project was initially sponsored by BSkyB, then Sky and, most recently, Sky Sports.

5 HSBC in the Community is a subgroup of the global bank HSBC's corporate social responsibility arm, and has responsibility for promoting positive relationships with the local community. The Outward Bound Trust is a global educational charity that has been using outdoor experiences and challenges to facilitate young people's development for over 65 years.

Learning tasks

Individual task: a narrative of personal experience

Can you recall a time when you or someone you have taught/coached has benefited from the 'power of sport'? Write a short narrative to:

- illustrate your/their starting point;
- describe the journey that you/they took;
- identify how you/they improved or changed and whether this has been sustained;
- highlight why you think that you/they improved and what factors have helped to sustain any positive changes.

Group task

Consider the key features of effective sport/physical activity programmes for PYD as outlined in this chapter. In a small group (two to four people), design a programme that uses sport/physical activity to re-engage disaffected youth. This could be something that is run in schools or at a club and can target passive and/or active disaffection. The following should be considered:

- Who will you select and why?
- How will you fund the project?
- What activities will you run and why?
- How long will the course be and where will it take place?
- How will you structure sessions to re-engage these young people?
- What goal(s) will you work towards?
- What are your intended outcomes?
- How will you monitor/record improvements?
- How will any positive outcomes be sustained once the project has finished?
- Other than the young people, who could/will benefit from the project (why/how)?

Further reading

Sandford, R.A., Duncombe, R. and Armour, K.M. (2008) The role of physical activity/sport in tackling youth disaffection and antisocial behaviour, *Educational Review*, 60(4), 419–35.

References

Bailey, R. (2005) Evaluating the relationship between physical education, sport and social inclusion, *Educational Review*, 57(1), 71–90.

Brown, K. and Fletcher, A. (2002) Disaffection or disruptive engagement? A collaborative inquiry into pupils' behaviour and their perceptions of their learning in modern language lessons, *Pedagogy, Culture and Society*, 10(2), 169–92.

Crabbe, T. (2006) *Knowing the Score: positive futures case study research: Final report*, London: Home Office.

Damon, W. (2004) What is positive youth development? *Annals of the American Academy*, 59, 13–24.

Davies, B. (2005) Threatening youth revisited: Youth policies under New Labour. *The Encyclopaedia of Informal Education*. Retrieved from http://www.infed.org/archives/bernard_davies/revisiting_threatening_youth.html

Department for Children, Schools and Families (DCSF) (2005) *Every Child Matters: Aims and outcomes*. Retrieved from http://www.everychildmatters.gov.uk/aims

Department for Children, Schools and Families (DCSF) (2005) *Youth Matters*, London: The Stationery Office.

Department for Education and Skills (DfES) (2005) *Learning Behaviour: The report of the practitioner's group on school, behaviour and discipline*. Available online at: http://www.dfes.gov.uk/behaviourandattendance/about/learning_behaviour.cfm, accessed 20 October 2007.

Dillon, J., Morris, M., O'Donnell, L., Rickinson, M. and Scott, W. (2005) *Engaging and Learning with the Outdoors: The final report of the outdoor classroom in a rural context action research project*, Bath: Centre for Research in Environmental Education.

Donnelly, P. and Coakley, J. (2002) *The Role of Recreation in Promoting Social Inclusion*, Toronto: Laidlaw Foundation.

Ennis, C. D. (1999) Creating a culturally relevant curriculum for disengaged girls, *Sport, Education and Society*, 4(1), 31–49.

Fraser-Thomas, J. L., Côté, J. and Deakin, J. (2005) Youth sport programs: an avenue to foster positive youth development, *Physical Education and Sport Pedagogy* 10, no.1: 19–40.

Hayward, R. and Sharp, C. (2005) *Young People, Crime and Antisocial Behaviour: Findings from the 2003 crime and justice survey* (Home Office Findings no. 245), London: Home Office.

Heathcote-Elliott, C. and Walters, N. (2000) *Combating Social Exclusion: occasional paper 9: ESF objective 3 disaffected youth*, available online at: http://www.surrey.ac.uk/Education/cse/paper9.doc, accessed 9 April 2003.

Hellison, D. (1995) *Teaching Responsibility through Physical Activity*, Champaign, IL: Human Kinetics.

Hellison, D., Martinek, T. and Walsh, D. (2008) Sport and responsible leadership among youth. In: N. Holt (ed.) *Positive Youth Development*, London: Routledge, 49–60.

Holt, N. L. (2008) *Positive Youth Development through Sport*, London: Routledge.

Lerner, R. M., Lerner, J. V., Phelps, E. *et al.* (2008) *Positive Development of Youth: Report of the findings from the first four years of the 4-H study of positive youth development*, Tufts University: Institute for Applied Research in Youth Development.

Morris, L., Sallybanks, J., Willis, K. and Makkai, T. (2003) Trends and issues in crime and criminal justice, *Australian Institute of Criminology*. Retrieved from http://www.aic.gov.au/publications/tandi/tandi249.html.

Newburn, T. and Shiner, M. (2005) *Dealing with Disaffection: Young people mentoring and social inclusion*, London: Willan Publishing.

Peacock, A. (2006) *Changing Minds: The lasting impact of school trips*. Retrieved from http://www.nationaltrust.org.uk/main/w-schools-guardianships-changing_minds.pdf.

Petitpas, A. Cornelius, A. and Van Raalte, J. (2008) Youth development through sport. In: N. Holt (ed.) *Positive Youth Development and Sport*, London: Routledge, 61–70.

Richardson, L. D. and Wolfe, M. (2001) *The Principles and Practice of Informal Education: Learning through life*, London: Routledge Falmer.

Riley, K. A. and Rustique-Forrester, E. (2002) *Working with Disaffected Students.* London: Paul Chapman.

Sandford, R., Armour, K. and Duncombe, R. (2008) Physical activity and personal/social development for disaffected youth in the UK: In search of evidence. In: N. Holt (ed.) *Positive Youth Development through Sport*, London: Routledge, 97–108.

Sandford, R. A., Armour, K. M. and Duncombe, R. (2010) Finding their voice: disaffected youth insights on sport/physical activity interventions. In: M. O'Sullivan and A. MacPhail (eds) *Young People's Voices in Physical Education and Youth Sport*, London: Routledge, 65–87.

Sandford, R. A., Armour, K. M. and Stanton, D. J. (2010) Volunteer mentors as informal educators in a youth physical activity program, *Mentoring & Tutoring*, 18(2), 135–53.

Sandford, R. A., Armour, K. M. and Warmington, P. C. (2006) Re-engaging disaffected youth through physical activity programmes, *British Educational Research Journal*, 32(2), 251–71.

Sandford, R. A., Duncombe, R. and Armour, K. M. (2008) The role of physical activity/sport in tackling youth disaffection and anti-social behaviour, *Educational Review*, 60(4), 419–35.

Siedentop, D. (1994) *Sport Education: Quality PE through positive sport experiences*, Champaign, IL: Human Kinetics.

Steer, R. (2000) *A Background to Youth Disaffection: A review of literature and evaluation findings from work with young people*, London: Community Development Foundation.

14

Barriers to learning in physical education and youth sport: does social class still matter?

Symeon Dagkas, University of Birmingham

We can reach far more people through sport . . . In that way, sport is more powerful than politics. We have only just started to use its potential to build up this country. We must continue to do so.

(Nelson Mandela, cited in Bailey, 2008, p. 89)

Sport makes an important contribution to economic and social cohesion and more integrated societies . . . The specific needs and situation of under-represented groups therefore need to be addressed, and the special role that sport can play for young people . . . and people from less privileged backgrounds must be taken into account.

(European Commission, *White Paper on Sport*, 2007)

 ## Introduction

There is a widely held belief that sport, by its very nature, has the potential to contribute to important social outcomes. Yet is it sport itself that has this potential, or are positive social outcomes dependent on what skilful teachers and coaches do with sport in the interests of children and young people? Are we certain, for example, that some physical education practices do not perpetuate rather than embrace difference? Is there robust evidence to support claims that structured physical activity settings combat social exclusion for disadvantaged youth from deprived areas? Does sport bring people from different backgrounds together? In short: do the practices of teachers and coaches in physical education and youth sport reinforce or challenge inequalities in society?

The pedagogical processes central to physical education and youth sport have been explained in some detail in other parts of this book. The purpose of this chapter is to consider the ways in which social class can act as a barrier to participation in physical activity settings for some young people, and to identify ways in which teachers and coaches can develop socially inclusive pedagogies. Recently, research has sought to understand social class and its link to understandings of the 'body' and, more specifically, the 'pedagogised body' (Evans *et al.*, 2009). The concept of the 'pedagogised' body acknowledges that every learner learns differently because issues of gender, class, race and ethnicity all contribute to the development of the 'youth body' in specific environments. This chapter will explore the ways in which social class can act as a 'pedagogy of exclusion' (Dagkas and Armour, forthcoming). In essence, it is argued that social class does indeed matter because it contributes to young people's embodied dispositions, identities and attitudes toward participation in physical activity settings (in and out of school).

Exploring 'social class'

There have been a range of social, environmental and technological changes over recent years that have had a profound influence on the physical activity habits of children and young people. According to Evans *et al.* (2008) this has resulted in a growing appreciation of the need to study the body as a corporeal presence in school settings so that we may better understand how, why and what young people learn. There is, thus, a need to understand the social class groupings to which young people belong, in and out of school, and their impact (positive and negative) on participation in physical activity, physical education and sport. Without this understanding, we might be tempted to explain some young people's lack of participation in terms of 'laziness' or poor motivation when in reality there are important structural issues to be taken into account. Clearly individuals have the choice to be physically inactive if they so wish. The questions, however, are whether and (importantly) how factors such as social class make it considerably more difficult for some children and young people than others to access the potential benefits of sport and physical education. Understanding the role of social class is, therefore, a proper pedagogical concern for teachers and coaches.

> **Comment**
> Social class remains an important factor in children's lives, therefore understanding its impact is central to developing inclusive practices in physical education and youth sport.

Defining social class

Social class has been identified as an environmental and social factor which may have a positive or negative influence on an individual's participation in physical activities (Green *et al.*, 2005). According to Evans and Davies (2006, pp. 797–8) the term social class implies 'not just a categorization or classification of people with reference to some quality, but an invidious, hierarchical ranking of people which is inherently value laden'. Moreover, any attempt to define social class has an economic element based, as it usually is, on occupation or income (Jarvie, forthcoming). Social class is, therefore, a set of social and economic relations that influence, dominate and dictate people's lives (Evans and Davies, 2006). Thus, socio-economic status (SES) has been used as a synonym for social class, representing groupings in society based upon occupation, education and housing.

In the UK the classification of the population according to occupation (and income) has a long history and several classifications are used, many of which have changed little over time. The simplest classification will be familiar to many readers: upper, middle and lower (or working) classes. The National Statistics Socio-Economic Classification (NS-SEC) is a relatively recent scheme which, it is argued, provides clearer divisions between categories and different forms of employment (Evans and Davies, 2006), as well as recognising the existence of unemployment. The NS-SEC (2008) scheme recognises eight 'social grades' (or 'social classes') based on occupation and outcome. In the table below, three different ways of classifying social class by occupation are compared. For the purposes of this chapter, the terms in the last column are used: upper, middle and low or working (including the unemployed) classes.

Eight classes	Five classes	*Three classes
1 Higher managerial and professional occupations	**1** Managerial and professional occupations	**1** Managerial and professional occupations (upper classes)
1.1 Large employers and higher managerial occupations		
1.2 Higher professional occupation		
2 Lower managerial and professional occupations		
3 Intermediate occupations	**2** Intermediate occupations	**2** Intermediate occupations (middle classes)
4 Small employers and own account workers	**3** Small employers and own account workers	
5 Lower supervisory and technical occupations	**4** Lower supervisory and technical occupations	**3** Routine and manual occupations; never worked and long-term unemployed (low or working classes)
6 Semi-routine occupations	**5** Semi-routine and routine occupations; never worked and long-term unemployed	
7 Routine occupations		
8 Never worked and long-term unemployed		

*For the purposes of this chapter, the terms in the last column are used: upper, middle and low or working (including the unemployed) classes.

Source: NS-SEC (2008) http://www.ons.gov.uk/about-statistics/classifications/current/ns-sec/cats-and-classes/ns-sec-classes-and-collapses/index.html

It was noted earlier that Evans and Davies (2006) claim that social class is powerful in that it can 'determine and dominate' lives' (p. 798). These authors view class as 'a set of constitutive practices that are struggled over in the daily lives of families and individuals' (p. 800), of which sport may or may not be a part. It is also important in the context of this discussion to reflect on Bourdieu's (1984) argument that different social classes tend to develop different orientations towards their bodies and, we might infer, towards engagement in physical activity for health, physical education and sport. The work of these authors is important as a foundation for this discussion.

> **Comment**
> *Social class is rooted in economic factors and its impact extends into many areas of life including engagement in sport.*

'Habitus' and capital

There are two concepts in Bourdieu's work that can offer helpful insights into an analysis of social class: 'habitus' and 'capital'. These concepts can act as analytical tools to help us to understand things that may otherwise be so rooted in everyday life that we miss them.

Habitus

An individual's disposition towards engagement in physical activity is the result of a complex interplay of economic, cultural and social factors (Bourdieu, 1984). These factors constitute an individual's habits, and they are rooted in social class. The process looks something like this – although in practice, of course, it is rarely simple or linear:

Social class (characteristics) = habits + identities + embodiment + dispositions
(in this case towards physical activity patterns)

An individual's 'habitus' is the basis 'from which lifestyles are generated' (Bourdieu, 1990, p. 127) and is therefore considered to be a key factor in developing understandings of the body and self. Examples of such understandings include physical development, ways of walking, use of language, choice of dress, eating habits and engagement in sport or physical activities (Bourdieu, 1984). Habitus can be viewed as a matrix of embodied values, actions and relations carried out by people in similar ways. According to Fernandez-Balboa and Muros (2006), habitus is learnt and institutionalised through an implicit but direct pedagogy of simple commands, such as body movements, which become part of who we are and how we behave and, thus, forms our ideologies. Bourdieu (1984, p. 170) argues that habitus is 'internalised and converted into a disposition that generates meaningful practices and meaning giving perceptions; it is a general, transposable disposition which carries out systematic, universal application'. Thus, habitus is part of the existential environment of a person, including their beliefs and dispositions, and as such it prefigures everything that a person may choose to do. It is important to remember that habitus is embodied.

Laberge and Kay (2002) suggest that the concept of habitus helps us to understand that different tastes, which individuals express in relation to physical activity, are generated by different perceptions of one's own body and the social conditions that mediate individual agency, i.e. the ability to 'choose' to be active. Bourdieu (1984) further suggests that shared experiences of the social world will tend to produce a *collective habitus*. From this we can understand that individuals within a common social space who share similar social conditions will tend to have similar experiences, embodied dispositions and tastes. Hence, habitus may be common to many members of the same group or class who exhibit a collective social history. Examples might include groups living in particular settings such as housing estates with particular facilities, traveller encampments or isolated rural communities.

At this point, you may be wondering whether habitus is simply another way of saying 'habits'. Habitus is a complex concept that can be distinguished from habits. Fernandez-Balboa and Muros (2006, p. 201) explain this distinction well. Although both terms imply some sort of repetitive activity and a degree of unconscious action, a habit is something one person does with a certain frequency, whereas habitus emerges in generalised action (for example, something many people frequently do). So actions, dispositions and habits that are held by a specific group of people in society can be translated to habitus (e.g. class differences in attitudes to specific sports). Furthermore, when habits are institutionalised (for example, in schools, sporting clubs, etc.) they become habitus.

According to Wright *et al.* (2003) 'habitus' provides a way of understanding the formation of identities through bodily practices which are socially and culturally bound. In addition, the habitus is considered as a main factor which contributes to the development of the body either in terms of physical development or physical activity behaviours (as was explained earlier). Thus, in the context of physical activity, habitus is embodied. It influences, and is simultaneously influenced by, individuals' dispositions towards their bodies and their orientation to particular forms of physical activity (Quarmby and Dagkas, 2010).

> **Comment**
> *Analysis of the (embodied) habitus helps us to understand how various mechanisms lead to the reproduction or transformation of physical activity and sport behaviours.*

Capital

Habitus is closely linked to another key concept: 'capital', which refers to a range of potentials individuals either gather through life and through experience or are given. At first glance, 'capital' appears to be mainly an economics-related term and indeed it does encompass aspects of financial/economic gain. However, the concept of capital is broader. Social capital refers to friends, peers, colleagues as well as the skills, knowledge and abilities that young people learn and possess as a result of belonging to a specific social class. Cultural capital refers to education, academic qualifications and long-lasting dispositions of the body and mind. Understanding the concept of capital is important because differential access to different forms of capital is a key factor in social exclusion resulting from an individual's social class.

> **Comment**
> *Social class influences an individual's development of economic, social and cultural capital.*

In addition to economic, social and cultural capital, Bourdieu (1984) refers to 'physical capital'. This is defined as an enduring disposition of body and mind and the 'embodiment' aspect of cultural capital. According to Shilling (1993):

> The *production* of physical capital refers to the development of bodies in ways which are recognised as possessing value in the social field (social space) while the *conversion* of physical capital refers to the translation of bodily participation in leisure, sports and physical activities into different forms of capital. (p. 127, emphasis added)

In simple terms, individuals (in this case children and young people) can produce and convert forms of capital according to experiences and opportunities given to them either in micro societies (families, friends) or macro societies (schools, local communities, sports clubs). Shilling explains this further by suggesting that physical capital can be converted into economic capital (in the form of professional sports and sponsorship), cultural capital (in the form of scholarships to universities and enhanced education) and social capital (in the form of social networks and connections through sports organisations). Thus, according to Shilling (2004):

> physical capital enables us to appreciate how the apparently 'natural' physical features of the individual are implicated in the acquisition and display of social, cultural and material resources. (p. 474)

This point is interesting in the context of research evidence showing that high-socio-economic-status children tend to maximise the translation of physical capital to other forms of capital, usually with parental support (Dagkas and Stathi, 2007). It is important, therefore, when discussing issues of exclusion on the basis of social class, to understand the impact that agent (life choices) and social structure (environment) have on youth 'physicalities' and embodied practices. What we need to consider is how the pedagogical practices of teachers and coaches can act as an intervention that challenges established inequalities in physical education and youth sport. Unless teachers and coaches develop practices that can interrupt the multiple levels of inequality that impact on embodied practices and dispositions, they might simply (and perhaps unwittingly) reinforce inequality.

Comment
Physical capital is a highly prized asset that is distributed unequally in society.

Social class and inequalities in youth sport

Sport has the potential to both challenge and reinforce inequality. Bourdieu's (1984) framework of social stratification offers one explanation for the tendency for middle- and upper-class individuals to be attracted to more expensive and also newer physical activities. On the other hand, certain 'prole' or 'working class sports' (Wilson, 2002, p. 6) are attractive to the lower classes because they are relatively inexpensive. Cultural, physical and economic capital all have a direct influence on participation levels and children's involvement in particular sports and physical activities (see Wright and Burrows, 2006, p. 288). Furthermore, those '*rich*' in *cultural and physical capital* are most likely to be involved in an activity due to past experience or lifelong involvement through family. This leads to a habitus that can effectively exploit the potential benefits of sport, converting cultural and physical capital to economic capital. As Macdonald *et al.* (2004) explain, middle-class and upper-class parents tend to view engagement in physical activity as a 'task' to be incorporated into the family's everyday routines and transport arrangements. Thus, as Bourdieu (1984) argues, the dominant classes are likely to invest a considerable amount of time and money in *elite* activities for their children designed to maximise the potential production and conversion of physical capital to economic capital.

There is clear evidence that higher socio-economic status is linked to higher levels of involvement in physical activity. Moreover, adolescents from a working-class background are twice as likely to be overweight and spend less time in moderate to vigorous physical activities than their upper- and middle-class counterparts. There is no doubt that young people from working-class backgrounds experience greater barriers to participation in sport than those from middle and upper classes. Such barriers can be classified as financial, logistical and geographical (Dagkas and Stathi, 2007). In addition, there is evidence that children from working-class and 'alternative' non-traditional family structures have fewer opportunities to experience different forms of physical activity compared with children from two-parent families and those of higher socio-economic status (Quarmby, Dagkas and Bridge, in press). It should come as no surprise to find, therefore, that adolescents from working-class backgrounds 'suffer worse health status and have limited access to facilities or organizations promoting healthy and active behaviours' (Azzarito and Solomon, 2005, p. 26). In other words, social class is a pervasive factor determining not just choice and preference in sport, but also the capacity (physical and material) to realise those choices and preferences (Evans *et al.*, 2009).

> **Comment**
> *Young people from working-class backgrounds face greater barriers to engagement in physical activity settings than their upper- and middle-class counterparts.*

Social class and physical education

It could be argued that school should be the one place where social class barriers to participation in physical activity and sport are challenged and removed. Yet research evidence (Dagkas and Armour, forthcoming; Evans and Davies, 2006) suggests that pedagogic practices and organisations at schools are 'classed' and 'gendered' in ways that cater mainly for the needs of middle-class youth. In effect, physical education practices have been 'readjusted' and 'realigned' (Evans and Davies, 2006, p. 802) to extend the investment that middle-class families make in gaining physical capital for their children. More specifically, middle-class parents *expect* teachers and schools to build on parental 'investment' in their children through their embodied practices (Dagkas and Stathi, 2007). Middle-class parents are thus investing strategically in their children's 'ability' and they start the process of cultivating their children's physical capital from an early age (Evans and Davies, 2006).

Such practices appear to illustrate Bourdieu's (1984) concept of '*intergenerational habitus*' as parents explicitly impart values, attitudes, predispositions and their embodied practices of physical activity involvement to their children (Quarmby and Dagkas, 2010). The resulting habitus has the potential to define the physical education field, especially in schools representing upper and middle classes. Thus levels of parental involvement in physical activity are reflected in (their) children's participation and choices, leading to the 'consumption' of (participation in) activities 'appropriate' to (their) social class. This has an effect on the activities that are made available to all children. Furthermore, parents from the upper classes invest time and effort on *elite* activities to maximise the production and conversion of their children's physical capital.

Schools tend to nurture these trends by providing practices and pedagogies appropriate to their students' (social) class. In this sense it could be argued that there are structural inequalities built into physical education and youth sport environments, as well as in pedagogical practices. In different schools, for example, children experience different activities that are sometimes undertaken in very different environments. Some schools have extensive grass playing fields, sports halls and a range of other facilities (think of public schools, which pride themselves on such facilities) whereas others may have only poorly maintained hard surface areas. Thus pedagogic practices are affected by school location (rural school versus inner city), students' (social) class, and teachers' expectations. These structures and practices contribute to the production of different experiences for youth in sport and physical activity, which 'further differentiate groups on the basis of ability, where differences in ability are demonstrably associated with social classes' (Wright and Burrows, 2006, p. 277).

Physical education alone cannot address social exclusion issues related to social class. It is extremely difficult for PE to 'countervail against wider social processes, of which social class continues to be a prominent feature' (Green *et al.*, 2005, p. 193). Bernstein (1971, cited in Evans, 2004, p. 98) argued:

> schools cannot compensate for the poverty and deprivation that contribute to working-class failure in schools, but they could and should make a difference to their chances by confronting structures of inequality in both society and schools.

Yet there is evidence to suggest that middle-class youth are more comfortable than others with the provision of traditional curricular and extracurricular activities based on team games (Green, 2008). So, according to Evans and Davies (2008), although PE claims to provide equal opportunities for all, it 'makes promises that it cannot deliver and generates expectations it cannot fulfil' (p. 201) as it seeks to meet the growing expectations of competitive sport, talent identification and top-level performance (Evans and Davies, 2008). In other words, where teachers and schools take a 'class-blind' approach, they are unlikely to challenge social inequalities.

It was noted earlier that school location, students' social class and parental expectations can shape pedagogic practices. As a result of this process, it has been argued that young people from working-class backgrounds learn to view their 'body' in an instrumental way, whereas youth from middle and upper classes view their body as an end in itself (Shilling, 1993). To put it more simply, youth from a working-class background tend to develop understandings of the body from predominantly (and in many cases *only*) the school environment. Their upper- and middle-class counterparts, on the other hand, tend to develop a broader discourse of the body. They are able to maximise the acquisition of physical capital by maintaining a 'toned' and 'fit' body through engagement in moderate to vigorous physical activities that are part of their everyday lives (in and out of school) and that are highly supported by their parents. This suggests that the impact of class on sport/physical activity participation should be examined in conjunction with other factors such as ethnicity, gender, disability and family.

> **Comment**
> *Physical education practices can serve to reinforce existing inequalities.*

The role of family

The importance of family in this discussion of inequality must be recognised. Bourdieu (1996) contends that the family (in his terms viewed as a specific social 'field'[1]) remains the key site of social reproduction, playing a vital role in maintaining social order by reproducing the structure of social space and social relations. The family is both a social field and a 'pedagogical environment' where personal histories and social circumstances exert a strong influence on engagement in physical activities (Quarmby and Dagkas, 2010). Thus, as Evans (2004) argues, professionals in physical education and youth sport should be concerned about the ways in which physical capital is constructed both in and beyond school, so that we can develop 'culturally relevant pedagogies and curriculum' (p. 103). The family and its pedagogic practices are clearly important in examining the production of embodied practices between different sites and fields. Such practices result in 'meanings' for youth lived experiences and the formation of youth identity. It is through practice that 'social structures become embedded in the habitus' and, 'as with the concept of agency, actions occur through processes that may be beyond conscious control or awareness of the individual' (Hunter, 2004, p. 177). The role of the family in this process of identity formation in sport and physical activity is clearly pivotal – yet it is often so ingrained that we view it as 'normal' and beyond serious challenge.

Challenging taken-for-granted assumptions

It has been argued that young people from working-class backgrounds are often disadvantaged within urban inner city or poor rural schooling environments (formal education) by the 'normalising' of unequal curriculum provision and pedagogical practices. In these environments, the reproduction of '*doxa*' is a key limiting process. Doxa refers to taken-for-granted assumptions and beliefs: 'the natural beliefs or opinions that are intimately linked to field and habitus' (Deer, 2008, p. 120) that result in embodied dispositions towards physical activity and health. Thus, reproduction of practices that relate to social class are accepted by young people and their teachers and families as 'normal' or 'natural', laying the foundations for the perpetuation of injustice and oppression. In this sense 'agents (youth) may actually reproduce the very structures that limit them' (Hunter, 2004, p. 176). Nevertheless there are opportunities to challenge the doxa, for example when the social environment changes with new curriculum provision offering activities that are out of the 'normal' context. Through such processes, the taken-for-granted assumptions are interrupted, allowing young people to experience *heterodoxy* which 'implies an awareness and recognition of the possibility of different or antagonistic beliefs' (Bourdieu, 1977, p. 164). This, surely, is one of the key functions of a professional teacher or coach: to challenge damaging doxa in the interests of children's successful participation in physical activity and sport.

Conclusion

So, is social class a barrier to participation in physical education and youth sport? The answer, of course, is that social class is a formidable barrier for some, while being a formidable enabler for others, resulting in inequality and social exclusion. Furthermore, PE and youth sport can either challenge or reinforce inequality. Yet we also need to recognise that we live in a totally 'pedagogised society' (Bernstein, 2002, cited in Evans and Davies, 2006, p. 805) where pedagogic practices are evident in every 'site' of social life, so PE and youth sport alone are unlikely to be effective in challenging inequality and social exclusion.

The intention of this chapter has been to '*seed*' the debate about the importance of social class as a key factor in social (in)equality. Class shapes youth embodiment and dispositions towards physicality and engagement in formal (education) and informal (leisure) physical activity settings. As has been made clear, however, teachers and coaches must view social class in conjunction with other fields in young people's lives if they are to develop pedagogies that can meet the learning needs of all the children and young people in their care. As professionals in pedagogy, teachers and coaches should expect no less of themselves.

Note

1 A field is a distinct social space consisting of interrelated and vertically differentiated positions, a 'network, or configuration of objective relations between positions' (Bourdieu and Wacquant, 1992, p. 97). 'These positions may be occupied by either agents or institutions but what "positions" them, as such, is their concentration or possession of specific "species" of capital and power. They are positions in a specific distribution of capital and power' (Crossley, 2001, p. 100), signalling, it seems to me, the efficacy, in the last instance, of social class.

Learning tasks

Individual task

This task has two parts.

1 Write a 500-word reflective narrative on your personal (social) background, identifying where social class factors influenced your development of physical capital (and any other forms of capital that you can identify).

2 Select and review four or five contemporary social class literature/research sources either in or beyond sport/physical activity and write a second 500-word analysis mapping your narrative against the wider literature.

Group task

In groups of four, compare your personal and analytical narratives from the individual task. Design a poster that maps the pathways to physical capital (and other forms of capital) that your accounts illustrate. On your poster, identify clearly any class-related barriers to participation.

Further reading

Evans, J., and Davies, B. (2006) Social class and physical education. In: Kirk, D., Macdonald, D. and O'Sullivan, M. (eds) *Handbook of Physical Education*, London: Sage, 796–808.

References

Azzarito, L. and Solomon, M. A. (2005) A reconceptualization of physical education: the intersection of gender/race/social class, *Sport, Education and Society* 10(1), 25–47.

Bailey, R. (2008) Youth sport and social inclusion. In: Holt, N. (ed.) *Positive Youth Development through Sport*, London: Routledge, 85–96.

Bourdieu, P. (1977) *Outline of a Theory of Practice,* trans. R. Nice, Cambridge: Cambridge University Press. (first published in French, 1973)

Bourdieu, P. (1984) *Distinction: A social critique of the judgement of taste,* London: Routledge & Kegan Paul.

Bourdieu, P. (1990) *The Logic of Practice.* Cambridge, Polity Press.

Bourdieu, P. (1996) On the family as a realized category, *Theory, Culture and Society*, 13, 19–26.

Bourdieu, P. and Wacquant, L. (1992) The purpose of reflexive sociology. In: P. Bourdieu and L. Wacquant (eds) *An Invitation to Reflexive Sociology*, Cambridge: Polity Press, 61–216.

Crossley, N. (2001) *The Social Body*, London: Sage.

Dagkas, S. and Armour, K. (forthcoming in 2011) *Exclusion and Inclusion through Youth Sport*, London: Routledge.

Dagkas, S. and Stathi, A. (2007) 'Exploring social and environmental factors affecting adolescents' participation in physical activity, *European Physical Educational Review*, 13(3), 369–83.

Deer, C. (2008) Doxa. In: M. Grenfell (ed.) *Pierre Bourdieu: Key concepts*, Stocksfield: Acumen, 119–30.

European Commission (2007) *White Paper on Sport*, European Union.

Evans, J. (2004) Making a difference: education and 'ability' in physical education, *European Physical Education Review*, 10(1), 95–108.

Evans, J. and Davies, B. (2006) Social class and physical education. In: Kirk, D., Macdonald, D. and O'Sullivan, M. (eds) *Handbook of Physical Education*, London: Sage, 796–808.

Evans, J. and Davies, B. (2008) The poverty of theory: class configuration in the discourse of physical education and health, *Physical Education and Sport Pedagogy*, 13(2), 199–233.

Evans, J., Davies, B. and Rich, E. (2009) The body made flesh: embodied learning and the corporeal device, *British Journal of Sociology of Education*, 30(4), 391–406.

Evans, J., Rich, E., Allwood, R. and Davies, B. (2008) Body pedagogies, p/policy health and gender, *British Educational Research Journal*, 14, 387–411.

Fernandez-Balboa, J. and Muros, B. (2006) The hegemonic triumvirate – ideologies, discourses and habitus in sport and physical education: implications and suggestions, *Quest*, 58, 197–221.

Green, K. (2008) Social class and physical education. In: Green, K. (ed.) *Understanding Physical Education*, London: Sage.

Green, K., Smith, A. and Roberts, K. (2005) Social class, young people, sport and physical education. In: K. Green and K. Hardman (eds) *Physical Education: Essential issues*, London: Sage, 180–96.

Hunter, L. (2004) Bourdieu and the social space of PE class: reproduction of doxa through practice, *Sport, Education and Society*, 9 (2), 175–92.

Jarvie, G. (forthcoming in 2011) Sport, social division and social inequality. In: S. Dagkas and K. Armour (eds) *Exclusion and Inclusion through Youth Sport*, London: Routledge.

Laberge, S. and Kay, J. (2002) Pierre Bourdieu's sociocultural theory and sport practice. In: Maguire, J. and Young, K. (eds) *Theory, Sport and Society*, London: JAI, 239–66.

Macdonald, D., Rodger, S., Ziviani, J., Jenkins, D., Batch, J. and Jones, J. (2004) Physical activity as a dimension of family life for lower primary school children, *Sport, Education and Society* 9(3), 307–25.

Quarmby, T. and Dagkas, S. (2010) Children's engagement in leisure time physical activity; exploring family structure as a determinant, *Leisure Studies*, 29(1), 53–66.

Quarmby, T., Dagkas, S. and Bridge, M.W. (in press) Associations between children's physical activities, sedentary behaviours and family structure: a sequential mixed method approach, *Health Education Research*.

Shilling, C. (1993) *The Body and Social Theory*, London: SAGE.

Shilling, C. (2004) Physical capital and situated action: a new direction for corporeal sociology, *British Journal of Sociology of Education*, 25(4), 473–87.

Wilson, T. (2002) The paradox of social class and sports involvement, *International Review for the Sociology of Sport*, 37(1), 5–16.

Wright, J. and Burrows, L. (2006) Re-concepting ability in physical education: a social analysis, *Sport, Education and Society*, 11(3), 275–91.

Wright, J., Macdonald, D. and Groom, L. (2003) Physical activity and young people beyond participation, *Sport, Education and Society*, 8(1), 17–33.

Young people, ethnicity and pedagogy

Louisa Webb, Loughborough University

Newspapers and politicians say we should go home. Do you think that if our home was safe we would want to come here? No. We would be in our home. One day I hope to go home and build a place where homeless people can go.
(Lindica, age 14)

We want to get the message around – we don't want to forget where we're from – our background and tradition. We want to show other people about our traditions – our culture is not well known. We are part of something.
(Hamida, age 11. Newham Children's Fund, 2002,
Dreams, Struggles and Survivors: Messages from Young Refugees)

People have got this assumption that because you're black you can't swim or don't know how to swim . . . you sort of feel as though everybody is looking at you.   (Flintoff *et al.*, 2008, p. 53)

I went with my father by bus and had to leave Mum behind. I still remember the war. I saw somebody killed. We were all frightened. We were afraid of being killed.
(Asylum Seekers and Refugees, Qualifications and Curriculum Development Agency, 2009)

 ## Introduction

Who are the young people that we teach and coach? Are their lives the same as ours? Experienced teachers and coaches believe that what makes a difference in their jobs is knowing the young people with whom they work. The Training and Development Agency for Schools in England (TDA) has a series of standards for teachers and these highlight the importance of taking practical account of diversity, planning for religious, cultural and ethnic differences and promoting equality and inclusion (Standards 18, 19 and 25a, TDA, 2009). All public bodies such as schools and sports clubs have responsibilities under the Equality Duty. The Equality Act (Government Equalities Office, 2010) aims to create a fair and equal society for all, taking into account different ethnic origins. Throughout this chapter, the focus is on understanding the diversity of young people in physical education and youth sport, and on finding strategies that can help you to work with diverse learners effectively and safely.

The facts

The United Kingdom is an increasingly diverse society and is also a society of inequalities. In 2010, the population is more culturally diverse than ever before with 16.4 per cent,[1] describing themselves as one of the following: Asian or Asian British, Indian, Pakistani, Bangladeshi, black or black British, black Caribbean, black African, South-East Asian, Chinese or with parents who are from diverse ethnic groups (Office for National Statistics, 2009). It is important to understand the diversity *within* each category of 'minority ethnic' and to avoid a dualism that considers either all white British or all minority ethnic people as one homogeneous group. The Office for National Statistics (2005) noted that there are often greater differences between the individual ethnic groups than between the minority ethnic population as a whole and white British people.

An informed consideration of both ethnicity and religion is needed in order to understand diversity. In the last census, in 2001, a majority of black people identified themselves as Christian. Among other faiths, the largest groups were Pakistani Muslims and Indian Hindus followed by Indian Sikhs, Bangladeshi Muslims and White Jews. Here again, it is important to recognise diversity within groups:

> The Indian group was religiously diverse: 45 per cent of Indians were Hindu, 29 per cent Sikh and a further 13 per cent Muslim. In contrast the Pakistani and Bangladeshi groups were more homogeneous, Muslims accounting for 92 per cent of each ethnic group.
>
> (Office for National Statistics, 2005, p. 6)

But why is it important to know about diversity? The report of the National Equality Panel highlights inequalities that still exist for some ethnic minorities (2010, p. 3):

> Compared [with] a White British Christian man with the same qualifications, age and occupation, Pakistani and Bangladeshi Muslim men and Black African Christian men have pay 13–21 per cent lower. Women from most ethno-religious backgrounds have hourly pay between a quarter and a third less than a White British Christian man with the same qualifications, age and occupation. Nearly half of Bangladeshi and Pakistani households are in poverty. However, variation in incomes *within* ethnic groups is generally as wide as across the population as a whole.

There are claims that such inequalities are embedded in our society. Institutional racism has been defined as 'organisational structures, policies and practices which result in ethnic minorities being treated unfairly and less equally, often without intent or knowledge' (DfES, 2003, p. 11). For example, recent investigations reveal discrimination in who is offered job interviews depending on apparent ethnicity as detailed on a CV (National

Equality Panel, 2010). What this means is that most of those who work with children and young people will encounter families who have experienced persistent and pervasive discrimination; or, indeed, families who are racist and discriminatory in the home and beyond.

What do these facts mean for teachers and coaches?

It might seem obvious to suggest that adults who teach and coach young people will be more effective in their jobs if they are fully equipped to work with a diverse population. Unfortunately, concerns have been raised that teachers and coaches are often not prepared adequately for this pedagogical task (Dagkas, Benn and Jawad, 2010; Ennis, 1998; Flintoff *et al.*, 2008) and so this chapter seeks to go some way towards filling the gap. In an increasingly diverse world, it has been argued that it is time for a constructive and productive discussion about young people, ethnicity and pedagogy in physical education and youth sport (Harrison and Belcher, 2006).

The lack of diversity within the coaching and teaching professions is another key issue to consider and one that has been raised in the literature and by government agencies such as the TDA. The representation of black and minority ethnic teachers in physical education is significantly lower than in other subject areas. This has been highlighted as an issue because of the lack of role models for diverse young people within physical activity contexts (Dagkas, Benn and Jawad, 2010; Flintoff, *et al.*, 2008). Benn and Dagkas (2006), for example, have raised questions about the ability of physical education initial teacher training courses to cater for the needs of Muslim women as trainees by providing single-sex groupings for practical activities. At the very least, if the teaching and coaching workforces do not reflect the diversity of the young learners for whom they are professionally responsible, they must make every effort to 'know' those learners as far as is possible.

As is the case in many contemporary national contexts, the National Curriculum for schools in England and Wales contains a statutory Inclusion Statement (QCA, 2007). This statement sets out the *duty* to provide all young people with the opportunity to experience success in learning, including young people from all social and cultural backgrounds, from different ethnic groups and those from diverse linguistic backgrounds. The Inclusion Statement also emphasises that young people have different experiences, interests and strengths that will influence the ways in which they learn.

Diverse young people, diverse experiences

If you work as a teacher or coach, you will inevitably work with a diverse range of young people and in order to help them to learn, you need to know some important things about them, in particular life experiences that may differ from your own. This might include children of post-World War II migrants from the Indian subcontinent, the Caribbean and the Republic of Ireland who arrived in times of labour shortage and found themselves in poorly paid, manual work despite the professionalism of their work in their home countries (Cole, 2009; Dagkas, Benn and Jawad, 2010). Moreover, when teaching or coaching black or Asian children, it is worth remembering that their family or friends are significantly more likely to have been stopped and searched by the police purely because of the colour of their skin. Some young people also live under an almost permanent threat of physical violence, as the murder of Stephen Lawrence[2] highlighted (Cole, 2009; McDonald and Hayes, 2003).

Yet at the same time it is important to remember that it is not possible to classify all ethnic minorities by skin colour. Since the Race Relations (Amendment) Act in 2000, Gypsy and Romany people and Travellers of Irish heritage have been defined as minority ethnic groups. The Jewish population in the UK is rising for the first time since World War II and there is evidence that young Jewish people are experiencing rising levels of anti-Semitic abuse (Cole, 2009; Pigott, 2008). Clearly not all young people from ethnic minority groups experience the same levels of discrimination and abuse. The important point to make is that a higher proportion of these groups do experience racism. For some children and young people, this may impact on the ways in which they react to and learn from teachers, coaches and other authority figures.

Strategies for catering for ethnicity and religious diversity

There is a range of pedagogical issues that need to be considered when working with groups of diverse young people. This section focuses on religious beliefs that need to be considered in physical activity contexts, and the associated safety issues. However, in planning to meet the needs of diverse young people, it is important not to portray ethnic minorities as 'the problematic "other" to be "fixed" through various education and health strategies' (Macdonald, Abbott, Knez and Nelson, 2009, p. 2). The 'problem', if there is one, occurs when any group takes a monocultural approach that stigmatises anyone who is not the same as (and by implication, equal to) themselves.

Issues in addressing religious requirements in physical education and youth sport often centre on the issue of *safety*. There are good sources of guidance available that teachers and coaches can access to ensure safety in their pedagogical practices. For example, the Association for Physical Education (AfPE) has released *Safe Practice in Physical Education and School Sport* (2008). AfPE identifies a number of common health and safety concerns that arise when working with diverse groups of young people, including the wearing of certain items of clothing and/or religious jewellery, and the impact of religious fasting (e.g. Ramadan, Navratri). These concerns will be addressed in turn, drawing upon examples from different minority ethnic groups.

Religious clothing and jewellery

Muslims

Modesty is a requirement within the Islamic faith and is applied through dress codes and other practices. This is based on the Muslim principle of 'haya'. 'The concept of "haya", which is defined as "to encompass notions of modesty, humility, decency and dignity", is a central value in Islam, as in many other faith traditions, and applies to all aspects of human behaviour and conduct' (Muslim Council of Britain, 2007, p. 20). Such principles are particularly relevant following puberty, although they may be embraced or encouraged earlier. The most common practices of modesty require females to cover their hair, arms and legs and for males to cover from waist to knees (BCC, 2008; Kay, 2006). It is important to ensure the safe wearing of headscarves (often referred to as hijab) for Muslim girls who choose to cover their hair.

Guidance suggests that headscarves should be *secured in a safe manner (tied, not pinned; ends tucked in)* so that they will not catch on anything that may put the wearer, or others, at risk (AfPE, 2008; BCC, 2008). It is also important to remember the diversity of countries of origin that are represented within the Muslim religion. There are variations in the way Muslims interpret Islam and how they see religion being positioned within society (Kay, 2006). Thus, a distinction should be made between 'Islam as a belief system and Islam as a cultural form, interpreted, conceived and manipulated by nation states, political movements and different interest groups to legitimate their political agenda, social conduct and traditional practices' (Amara, 2008, p. 534). For example, the wearing of headscarves is not common for Muslim women in Turkey, but in Afghanistan women are totally covered by the burqa.

One way in which teachers and coaches can respect the Muslim principle of 'haya' is through communication with young people, parents and communities. Dagkas, Benn and Jawad (2010) found positive outcomes when schools engaged Muslim pupils in discussions and decision making. As a result of the discussions, there was a stronger sense of ownership of decisions and a more enthusiastic engagement in physical education and school sport by these pupils.

Muslim females are also required to cover their arms and legs. This can be achieved by taking a flexible view of physical activity uniform. Females can be permitted to wear long sleeves and leggings or tracksuit pants. If these options are available for all girls, then the Muslim females will not feel segregated. Below is a case study of one community college in Leicester that has been implementing good practice in diversity in its physical education department.

Community college in Leicester: working with diverse female pupils

This community college in Leicester is a state school for girls and serves a culturally and socially diverse community. The physical education staff at the college work hard to provide a learning environment that caters for as many girls as possible, including Muslim girls who have specific religious requirements. The college provides a diverse curriculum with a range of choices and activities including aerobics, tag rugby, dance, horse riding and cheerleading.

Some of the strategies for catering for a diverse range of pupils include:

- flexibility with clothing requirements for swimming classes;
- trying to maintain an all-female staff for swimming sessions at the local leisure centre;
- the option of a long-sleeved shirt and leggings or tracksuit pants for physical education classes.

These choices are appreciated by pupils and they also respect the Islamic modesty requirements for females.

(continued)

The wearing of headscarves has been an issue discussed by physical education staff at the college. On a national level, there have been concerns raised about safety and the breathability of fabrics in the physical education context. The latest guidance recommends the following:

> Encourage adoption of latest, safest hijabs. Currently, there is much competition between leading international sports clothing firms to design Islamically appropriate sportswear. Modern sports hijabs are being designed in flexible, breathable fabrics. They do not require tying and do not slip or move around. Some schools are encouraging girls to adopt this type of hijab because it is much safer and more comfortable for physical activity than the tied version.
> (Birmingham City Council, 2008, p. 5)

Another way that the college demonstrates best practice is by good *communication with parents*. For example, a Year 8 pupil was identified as being a talented badminton player. A teacher spoke with her parents at a parent-teacher evening and now the pupil attends the extracurricular badminton club every week. This has led to her being part of the badminton team, representing the college in the Leicester League.

Sikhs

Sikhs mainly originate from the Punjab region of India. The five Ks of the Sikh religion are a physical reminder of the dedication to a life of religious devotion:

- kesh (uncut hair);
- kara (a steel bracelet);
- kanga (a wooden comb);
- kachera (cotton undershorts);
- kirpan (steel sword).

The Sikh religion requires that these five items should not be removed. Teachers and coaches must respect this religious requirement while also maintaining safety for all participants. For example, forms of hair covering for Sikh males such as turbans or top knots (jooda) could be difficult to wear with a safety item such as a cricket helmet. However, international cricketer Monty Panesar provides a good example of a safe alternative called a patka, which is flat around the scalp and will fit into a cricket helmet.

Religious jewellery (including amulets[3]) can be made safe by taping, padding or covering. Sports sweatbands can be effective for covering religious bangles. Technical undershirts that have been developed for sports could secure a religious necklace but this might not be sufficient for high-contact sports such as rugby. In all cases, teachers and coaches are advised to conduct a risk assessment, and AfPE (2008) advises that safe practice must never be compromised. If adjustment cannot be made to secure the religious jewellery, then modified activities could be planned that still address the lesson learning outcomes or the aim of the physical activity session.

Religious festivals and the impact of religious fasting

In all world religions there are certain times of the year that are held sacred. Some examples are Ramadan, Navratri and Easter. These sacred times are usually connected with certain types of behaviour such as special worship, pilgrimage or fasting. Another common feature is that the completion of fasting is often celebrated by religious festivals. For example, Ramadan is the ninth month of the Islamic calendar and is the month of fasting.[4] The end of Ramadan is celebrated with the festival of Eid ul-Fitr (festival of breaking the fast). The festival of Eid is a time of prayer and celebration. It is a time to celebrate with friends and family as well as to be thankful and generous to those less fortunate (Muslim Council of Britain, 2007).

One of the most well-known Hindu and Sikh festivals is Diwali (also known as Dipavali) or Festival of Lights. Acknowledging festivals such as Eid and Diwali, and their significance in the lives of young learners, is an important way of respecting diversity. For example, the Diwali festival in Leicester is reputed to be the largest festival outside India and the City of Leicester works with the Hindu and Sikh community to create a fireworks celebration that is open to the public. An ethos of celebrating different cultures and religions is recognised as good practice (Dagkas, Benn and Jawad, 2010).

During periods of fasting such as Ramadan, young people may become dehydrated, have headaches or may lack energy later in the day. They also will have woken up before dawn to eat and may be affected by disturbed sleep patterns. Teachers and coaches planning physical activities need to be mindful of these issues during the month of Ramadan. Modified activities could be made available but with the same learning outcomes achieved. It can also be helpful, where feasible, to schedule physical education or physical activity early in the day (Dagkas and Benn, 2006). The important point to be made is that a professional teacher or coach has to prioritise the learning needs of all the children and young people in a group. Lack of food will, inevitably, impact on learning, so, as learning professionals, that is our concern whether it is the result of religious observance or, for example, poverty.

One strategy for catering for fasting pupils in physical education is through the pedagogical model named Sport Education (Siedentop, Hastie and Van der Mars, 2004). In Sport Education, pupils can participate in a lesson taking one of a range of roles such as captain, coach, referee, scorekeeper or publicity officer. In Sport Education these options are not just tokenistic tasks for non-participants but are developed as legitimate and important roles as part of an authentic learning process (Kirk and Kinchin, 2003; see also Chapter 25 by Toni O'Donovan in this book). Below is a case study from a city academy school in Nottingham where the pupils have participated in Sport Education during Ramadan.

City Academy School in Nottingham: Sport Education and Ramadan

This city academy serves a multicultural area of the inner city with high levels of social and economic disadvantage. The academy opened in August 2003 as one of the first of a new type of specialist, state-funded independent school. Two-thirds of the pupils are from a wide variety of minority ethnic heritages and include a significant number of pupils from families of asylum seekers or refugees.

(continued)

In 2009, one of the physical education teachers at the academy led an initiative to incorporate Sport Education into the physical education curriculum. During the year, discussions took place to consider the possibility of teaching Sport Education during Ramadan. It was proposed that the various roles that are part of the authentic learning experience in Sport Education could provide a range of choices that might be helpful for pupils who were fasting.

In talking with the pupils about Sport Education during Ramadan, the pupils made comments such as:

- Sport Education is a good idea because a person who is fasting might not have a lot of energy and they can do other roles like referee or coach.
- The choice of roles in Sport Education is good because when people are fasting they might get tired in PE.
- It's a good idea because if they can't run because they're tired, then they could choose something else (another role).

Another good-practice strategy employed by the physical education department is *fostering good relationships with the local community* and imams who are leaders in the Islamic community. It is common in the Islamic community to seek the advice of the mosque imam if there is a question about Islamic faith and practice. The physical education teachers have sought the advice of the local imam about participation in physical education during Ramadan and they implement this guidance in their work with pupils.

Young people participating in Ramadan will not eat or drink during the day. This may raise concerns about swimming and accidentally swallowing water. Teachers and coaches should 'reassure children who become anxious having accidentally swallowed water during Ramadan' (BCC, 2008, p. 7) and the Muslim Council of Britain (2007) concurs that as swallowing pool water is unintentional it does not break the fast. Swimming, therefore, should not be an issue in relation to fasting but it does raise other issues around cultural expectations as outlined below.

The Islamic faith contains beliefs about modesty that need to be catered for in physical activity environments. This is relevant to what pupils wear, as mentioned previously, but also relates to changing facilities, mixed-sex participation and also choice of activities, for example swimming and dance (Benn, Dagkas and Jawad, 2010; Dagkas, Benn and Jawad, 2010). On these issues, guidance is available from the Birmingham City Council booklet, *Improving Participation of Muslim Girls in Physical Education and School Sport* (2008).

 ## Diverse young learners . . . diverse teachers and coaches?

Despite a sustained government commitment to widen the diversity of those choosing to enter the teaching profession, the representation of black and minority ethnic teachers in physical education is significantly lower than in other subject areas. Over the last five years, physical education has attracted just 2.9 per cent black and minority ethnic candidates compared with 11 per cent across all subject areas in England (Flintoff *et al.*, 2008). One physical education teacher at a secondary school in Nottingham shares her story.

Physical education teacher

When I decided to enter this profession, I did have a few apprehensions on how I would be received as a mixed-race secondary school physical education teacher. I had studied modules in sociology at university and was aware of issues of 'institutional racism' in the educational system. However, on further reflection this became a motivating factor for me as I hoped to be able to question and challenge people's attitudes regarding ethnicity through being a secondary school teacher. I felt that my background of having a white mother and an Afro-Caribbean father would provide me with a more informed view on issues surrounding ethnicity and discrimination issues.

In my work as a teacher, my mixed-race identity can be a useful pedagogical tool. At X School I have been involved in developing a project that approached issues of racial discrimination. In 2008, the school developed cross-curricular links between the physical education, drama and the personal, social, health and citizenship education departments through a Year 8 discovery day. The objective of the day was to allow pupils the opportunity to explore issues surrounding prejudice, discrimination, intimidation and oppression through working collaboratively to produce a dance, which explored the issues of conflict and reconciliation. The day was very successful and the students created many different scenarios where prejudice and discrimination existed in their lives.

I remember on the morning of Wednesday 5 November 2008 I asked several pupils from Afro-Caribbean heritage the particular significance of Barack Obama recently being inaugurated as the US president and every child was aware that it was because he is the first black president. I believe that because I can identify with mixed race and pupils of ethnic minorities I can hopefully use it as a pedagogical tool to help pupils access their potential.

Research by Flintoff *et al.* (2008) with black and minority ethnic (BME) physical education teacher trainees found that white trainees held stereotypical or ill-informed views about 'race' and ethnicity and these extended to some of the BME trainees. For example, six black or Asian trainees had their places on a teacher education course questioned by white trainees who suggested their success in gaining a place had resulted from the institution's attempts to meet 'race quotas'. Three black trainees experienced stereotypical comments in practical PE classes about their physicality and physical abilities. 'Jokes' and 'banter' about their ethnicity were something that some trainees accepted as a taken-for-granted part of their experiences. Furthermore, the centrality of alcohol in extracurricular contexts and in informal socialising prevented some BME men and women trainees from feeling that they could be – or indeed, in some cases, wanted to be – fully included in the physical education group.

Racism and stereotyping

In addition to accepting diversity, teachers and coaches can take an active role in challenging racism and stereotyping. This has been described as culturally responsive pedagogy or multicultural education (Ambe, 2006; Dagkas, 2007). Racism and stereotyping operate through assumptions that are made about groups of people due to physical or cultural characteristics. Associated terms are prejudice and discrimination. Most white teachers or coaches would struggle to imagine how it feels to experience racism.

Words are a powerful tool and can be used for good or ill. Name calling is a classic hallmark of racist behaviour. You can also choose your words to challenge racism or show that you value diversity. Sparks (1994) recommends learning to pronounce the names of all students correctly. The Muslim Council of Britain (2007, p. 58) advises:

> Some non-Muslim teachers may find certain Muslim names difficult to pronounce. Nevertheless, care should be taken to pronounce names as accurately as possible. In some cases shortening the name can change the meaning and can cause offence. For example, the name Abdullah means 'servant of Allah', whereas if shortened to 'Abdul' it means 'servant' or 'slave'.

Care is needed, therefore, to construct a physical activity environment where name calling and racism are unacceptable, and where each young learner feels respected and valued. In addition, teachers and coaches need to ensure that they are informed about diversity, but that this does not lead to stereotyping (Harrison and Belcher, 2006).

Conclusion

In the UK and Ireland we are part of increasingly diverse societies. The full range of cultural and religious beliefs should be considered when teachers and coaches are designing effective learning environments for children and young people. Armour noted in Chapter 1 that teachers and coaches have a professional responsibility to meet the learning needs of all the young learners in their care. A lack of understanding and inflexibility in the past has led to the exclusion of some young people from physical activity, and that must be a concern to all of us who care about physical education and sport. An understanding of and respect for different cultures and religions is, therefore, an important part of the essential knowledge base for teachers and coaches. As Macdonald *et al.* (2009, p. 16) put it: 'It is long overdue for physical educators to understand the implications of cultural diversity for their practices.'

Notes

1 In some regions the percentage is over 40 per cent.
2 On 22 April 1993, Stephen Lawrence was stabbed to death at a bus stop in South London in an unprovoked, racist attack (House of Commons Home Affairs Committee, 2009).
3 'Some Muslim children may wear amulets containing Qur'anic verses that are wrapped or sewn in cloth, or contained in lockets worn usually around the neck. These have religious significance for those who wear them' (Muslim Council of Britain, 2007, p. 21).
4 'Fasting during the month of Ramadan is the fourth "pillar" of Islam, an act of worship of great spiritual, moral and social significance for Muslims' (Muslim Council of Britain, 2007, p. 28).

Learning tasks

Individual task

Write a narrative about your own heritage. Where did your parents come from? Where did your grandparents come from? Describe privileges that you have gained as a result of not being a victim of racism and stereotyping; or describe prejudice and discrimination that you have experienced, and its effects on you as a learner.

(continued)

> ## Group task
>
> Select one of the world religions, such as Hinduism, Islam, Sikhism, Judaism, Christianity or Buddhism. Research the principles and values of this religion. Reflect on the interaction between the religion and behaviour/organisation in physical activity contexts.
>
> ## Further reading
>
> A key resource is the teachernet website: **http://www.teachernet.gov.uk/**. This is a portal for UK government guidance and documents for working with culturally diverse young people.

References

Amara, M. (2008) An introduction to the study of sport in the Muslim world. In: B. Houlihan (ed.) *Sport and Society*, London: Sage, 532–52.

Ambe, E. B. (2006) Fostering multicultural appreciation in pre-service teachers through multicultural curricular transformation, *Teaching and Teacher Education, 22*, 690–99.

Association for Physical Education (AfPE) (2008) *Safe Practice in Physical Education and School Sport*, Leeds: AfPE.

Benn, T. and Dagkas, S. (2006) Incompatible? Compulsory mixed-sex physical education initial teacher training (PEITT) and the inclusion of Muslim women: a case-study seeking solutions, *European Physical Education Review, 12* (2), 181–200.

Benn, T., Dagkas, S. and Jawad, H. (2010) Embodied faith: Islam, religious freedom and educational practices in physical education, in press in unknown journal.

Birmingham City Council (BCC) (2008) *Improving Participation of Muslim Girls in Physical Education and School Sport: Shared practical guidance from Birmingham schools*. Birmingham: BCC. Available at www.afpe.org.uk.

Cole, M (2009) A plethora of 'suitable enemies': British racism at the dawn of the twenty-first century, *Ethnic and Racial Studies, 32*(9), 1671–85.

Dagkas, S. (2007) Exploring teaching practices in physical education with culturally diverse classes: a cross-cultural study, *European Journal of Teacher Education, 30*(4), 431–43.

Dagkas, S. and Benn, T. (2006) Young Muslim women's experiences of Islam and physical education in Greece and Britain: a comparative study, *Sport, Education and Society, 11*(1), 21–38.

Dagkas, S., Benn, T. and Jawad, H. (2010) Multiple voices: improving participation of Muslim girls in physical education and school sport, in press in unknown journal.

Department for Children, Schools and Families (DCSF) (2008) *The Inclusion of Gypsy, Roma and Traveller Children and Young People*, Nottingham: DCSF.

Department for Education and Skills (DfES) (2003) *Aiming High: Raising the achievement of minority ethnic pupils*, London: DfES Publications.

Ennis, C. D. (1998) The context of a culturally unresponsive curriculum constructing ethnicity and gender within a contested terrain, *Teaching and Teacher Education, 14*(7), 749–60.

Flintoff, A. with Chappell, A., Gower, C., Keyworth, S., Lawrence, J., Money, J., Squires, S. L. and Webb, L. (2008) *Black and Minority Ethnic Trainees' Experiences of Physical Education Initial Teacher Training*, Report for the Training and Development Agency for Schools (TDA), Carnegie Research Institute: Leeds Metropolitan University.

Government Equalities Office. (2010). *Equality Act*, available at: http://www.equalities.gov.uk/equality_act_2010.aspx

Harrison, L. and Belcher, D. (2006) Race and ethnicity in physical education. In: D. Kirk, M. O'Sullivan and D. Macdonald (eds) *Handbook of Physical Education*, London: Sage, 740–51.

House of Commons Home Affairs Committee (2009) *The Macpherson Report – Ten years on*, London: House of Commons.

Kay, T. (2006) Daughters of Islam: family influences on Muslim young women's participation in sport, *International Review for the Sociology of Sport*, 41(3–4), 357–73.

Kirk, D. and Kinchin, G. (2003) Situated learning as a theoretical framework for sport education, *European Physical Education Review*, 9(3), 221–36.

Macdonald, D., Abbott, R., Knez, K. and Nelson, A. (2009) Taking exercise: cultural diversity and physically active lifestyles, *Sport, Education and Society*, 14(1), 1–19.

McDonald, I. and Hayes, S. (2003) 'Race', racism and education: racial stereotypes in physical education and school sport. In: S. Hayes and G. Stidder (eds) *Equity and Inclusion in Physical Education and Sport*, London: Routledge, 153–68.

Muslim Council of Britain (2007) *Towards Greater Understanding. Meeting the needs of Muslim pupils in state schools: Information and guidance for schools*, London: Muslim Council of Britain.

National Equality Panel (2010) *Report of the National Equality Panel: Executive summary*, London: Government Equalities Office.

Newham Children's Fund (2002) *Dreams, Struggles and Survivors: Messages from young refugees*. www.naldic.org.uk/ITTSEAL2/teaching/teaching.cfm. Accessed 5 January, 2010.

Office for National Statistics (2005) *Focus on Ethnicity and Identity*, London: ONS.

Office for National Statistics (2009) *Population Estimates by Ethnic Group: 2001 to 2007 commentary*, Newport: ONS.

Office of Public Sector Information (2000) *Race Relations (Amendment) Act*.

Qualifications and Curriculum Authority (QCA) (2007) *The National Curriculum: Key Stage 3 and 4*, Coventry: QCA, available at: http://curriculum.qcda.gov.uk/key-stages-3-and-4/About-the-secondary-curriculum/equalities-diversity-and-inclusion/index.aspx

Qualifications and Curriculum Development Agency (2009) *Asylum Seekers and Refugees*. www.qcda.gov.uk/7528.aspx. Accessed 5 January, 2010.

Pigott, R. (2008) *Jewish Population on the Increase*. http://news.bbc.co.uk, 21 May, 2008.

Siedentop, D., Hastie, P. and Van der Mars, H. (2004) *Complete Guide to Sport Education*, Illinois: Human Kinetics.

Sparks, W. G. (1994) Culturally responsive pedagogy: a framework for addressing multicultural issues, *Journal of Physical Education, Recreation and Dance*, 65, 33–6, 61.

Training and Development Agency for Schools (TDA) (2009) *Professional Standards for Qualified Teacher Status*, London: TDA.

Gender and learning in physical education and youth sport

Anne Flintoff, Leeds Metropolitan University

 ## Introduction

The following quotations are taken from interviews with young women and men about their experiences of physical education (PE) (see Flintoff and Scraton, 2001; Bramham, 2003). What do they tell us about gendered learning experiences in PE?

> I think that a lot of people that don't do it have quite good reasons for not doing it [PE] . . . there are a lot of people who feel quite intimidated by doing sport. I think that most people don't mind doing things but say if you are really small, then you might hate it that much that you don't bring your kit all of the time.   (Dave, 15-year-old young man)

> [I]t's easier to be a woman [in physical activity and PE], I think because . . . for women it seems to me that for women there are loads of types of women you can be . . . like . . . but if you are a man you have to be big and you have to be butch and in some circumstances it is harder . . . there is one stereotype for men and there are a few for women . . .
> (Anne, 15-year-old young woman)

> [Mixed PE] depends on what we are doing. Gym and aerobics are not good mixed 'cause it is like the boys are there, they are watching you and if you are on your own you can do what you want to . . . you just feel just small around them . . . on your own you can do things without things making people look small and that. You can be yourself. When the boys are there you change, you are quieter than you usually are – you don't say owt, they just take over. You know that they are immature and you know that they will say something to make you feel embarrassed.   (Karen, 15-year-old young woman)

I have chosen these extracts to highlight some of the key issues that you might want to consider when thinking about gender, learning experiences in PE and sport, and your role as teacher or coach. They raise important questions to be considered such as:

- What kinds of bodies are rewarded and are considered to be successful in PE and youth sport? (*gendered embodiment*)

- How do PE and youth sport promote (or inhibit) different ways of 'being a boy' or 'being a girl'? (*gendered attributes and behaviours*)

- What are the implications of understanding gender as power, as Karen's words imply (*gender power relations*), instead of thinking only about gender as the *differences* between boys and girls?

Karen recounts how gender power relations can operate in mixed PE classes to *limit* and *constrain* girls' behaviour and confidence: 'you just feel just small around them . . . you are quieter than you usually are'. Thus, gender relations are *power relations*, and although gender is 'produced' in specific ways in different historical and cultural contexts, it is most often the activities and behaviours associated with men and masculinity that are highly valued, rather than those traditionally associated with women and femininity (Watson, 2008). Girls and women continue to *lose out* compared with boys and men in PE and sport, because of the operation of gender power relations; for example, in opportunities to be physically active, rewards and accolades, access to key decision-making posts (such as head of department or senior coach roles) and media coverage, to name just a few (Evans and Williams, 1989; Penney, Houlihan and Eley, 2002). However, it is also important to remember that not all boys and men benefit from gender power relations, at least not in the same way, because of the differences *between* groups of boys and men which should be considered too (Gard, 2006).

One way in which we can understand gender power relations and the ways in which they operate to advantage some, while disadvantaging others, is to listen to young people's voices. Listening enables us to appreciate the sometimes subtle ways in which gender power relations operate in PE or sports classes; for example how they can limit rather than empower some individuals in their learning and, most importantly, how professional teachers and youth sport coaches can challenge and seek to change gender power relations. This chapter argues that in order to offer positive learning experiences for all young people in PE and sport, it is imperative to recognise the impact of gender and to reflect on ways in which *our own practices* as teachers and coaches can contribute to, or challenge, gendered inequities.

> **Comment**
> *'Gender' remains a serious and complex issue for teachers and coaches to consider critically as part of their practice.*

Why are PE teaching and sports coaching (still) gendered and why does it matter anyway?

You might ask, why, despite over 20 years of research and with teachers and coaches engaging in initiatives designed to challenge inequities, physical education remains one of the most gendered subjects on the school curriculum. In England and elsewhere, research evidence suggests that there are still significant issues to address. One answer to this question is linked to the nature of gender itself. Although there are different understandings of gender, for the purposes of this chapter, gender can be defined *as the behaviours, attributes and roles associated with being either a woman or a man.* As a result, all of us are 'doing gender' from the moment we are born. Unlike sex – the biological differences that we are each born with – gender refers to patterns of behaviours and social characteristics associated with being women or men. *The process of developing our gendered identities is therefore a social one, and one in which we are continually engaged.* Some authors call this process 'identity work', because it helps us to think about our gender as something that we work at all the time. From this viewpoint, gender is never actually 'achieved', but is always in a 'state of becoming' (Connell, 2008).

> ### Comment
> *We are all engaged in a continuous process of developing our gendered identities throughout our lives.*

Adolescence is a particularly important time for 'doing masculinity' or 'doing femininity'. It is a crucial developmental stage (and not just physically) in the process of moving from being a child to becoming an adult. Not surprisingly, many young men and women feel under enormous pressure to 'conform' to expectations of what are regarded as appropriate, gendered behaviours and ways of being. We 'learn' these behaviours and characteristics through everyday social practices and interactions with others, including, for example, through the different kinds of physical activities introduced to us as girls and boys in school physical education.

Scraton's (1992) groundbreaking research in the late 1980s showed how ideologies of femininity underpinned the practices of girls' PE. Teachers held very strong ideas about the kinds of activities that were 'suitable' for girls, resulting in stereotypical attitudes towards their capabilities and motivations. More recent research shows that contemporary practices in PE, for girls *and* boys, remain strongly underpinned by gendered discourses (Connell, 2008; Penney, 2002a; Wellard, 2007). For example, it is still the case that many boys are denied the opportunity to experience moving in a creative way, as might be offered in a dance class. Similarly, many girls are denied opportunities to experience their bodies in strong, forceful ways as, for example, demanded in a game of rugby.

What does all this mean for teachers and coaches? Well, by the time we become teachers and coaches, we already have very strong gendered identities. These identities influence how we feel about ourselves, our sense of self and our physical capabilities, and this inevitably impacts on how we go about our work with children and young people. As a result of our past experiences, the kinds of physical abilities and skills we possess as PE teachers or coaches influence the opportunities we are then confident to offer the next generation of young people with whom we work (Brown and Rich, 2002). Our gendered bodies and capabilities literally become important 'tools' of our work as teachers and coaches (Webb and Macdonald, 2007a, 2007b). In this way, gender continues to strongly influence the practices of new PE teachers and coaches.

The individual learning task at the end of this chapter encourages you to reflect on your own school PE as the basis for the kind of teacher/coach you are today. Yet this does not mean that we cannot change how we act. It is important to remember that *because gender is socially constructed, there are always possibilities for changing the kind of man or woman, teacher or coach, you become tomorrow.* Indeed, as a teacher or coach responsible for meeting the needs of all children and young people, it is argued in this book that you have a *professional responsibility* to reflect on, and seek to challenge, the limiting effects of gender relations in your work.

> **Comment**
> *As teachers and coaches, we carry our gendered histories with us into practice and we must be critically aware of the ways in which we visit our histories on the next generation.*

Towards more complex understandings of gender

An understanding of the complexities of the concept of gender helps us to appreciate ways in which the relatively small, yet undeniable, physiological differences between men and women are exaggerated through social practices, and how social values become attached to them. There are a number of theories that attempt to explain how gender 'works' within PE and sport settings for young people (Flintoff and Scraton, 2005). Each theory presents a different explanation of gender, and there are new theories emerging all the time as a result of advances in research and professional practice. Theories are important because they offer explanations for why things happen and, importantly, point towards what can be done in practice to change things.

Feminist theories, for example, have always been about not just understanding gendered practices but also challenging and changing them where they are restrictive or discriminatory. Theories have, however, become increasingly complex in order to explain the subtleties of gendered practices, and this can make the link between theory and practice less straightforward (Hargreaves, 2004). It is also important to note that theories tend to overlap and it can sometimes be difficult to understand the subtle distinctions between them. Indeed, it can help to think of theories as fluid and dynamic, reflecting gender relations that also change over time.

If you are a teacher or coach focusing on practice, you might be tempted to think that 'theory' is not something that needs to concern you. After all, teaching and coaching appear to be mainly activities that take place in practical settings such as the field, in the gymnasium or the swimming pool. You might surmise that there is little point in sitting down and reading 'theory' when you need to be getting on with practice. *However, it is important to remember that everything we do is underpinned by a theoretical perspective, even if we are not always aware of it.* Consider, for example, the ways in which you might divide young people into groups to work on an exercise. Do you let them choose any group? Do you try to ensure there are boys and girls in each group? Do you prefer to let friends work together? These are small decisions that are made every day in teaching and coaching, yet they can fundamentally influence the nature of the pedagogical relationships and interactions we promote in our sessions. As professionals, we should be able to provide an educational rationale for each of these decisions because *why* we do what we do matters!

> **Comment**
> *All practice is underpinned by theory.*

Which theory is the most useful?

Access and opportunities

Early theories about gender in PE and youth sport focused mainly on equal opportunities and issues of access. A key concern for these theories was how to understand the ways in which sex stereotyping by teachers led to differential access to activities offered to boys and girls in PE and sport. In England, the history of PE as a school subject is a gendered one (see also Chapter 2 by David Kirk). Until the 1970s, men and women trained to become PE teachers in separate, single-sex colleges, and learnt to teach different activities. The women's colleges developed a distinct 'female tradition' centring on gymnastics, dance and games, emphasising the importance of physical activity for health and well-being, with a strong child-centred approach. In contrast, men's PE was strongly influenced by the military and centred on competitive sport. Mixed PE classes were introduced in the 1970s as a means of enabling girls to have equal access to curriculum activities. However, given the strongly gendered and single-sex history of the subject, it is perhaps not surprising to learn that moves towards mixed-sex classes were far from straightforward. If you look back at the quote from Karen at the beginning of this chapter, it is evident that mixed-sex PE in this case was not an empowering experience.

As was noted in Chapter 1, an important dimension of pedagogy is knowledge in context – which knowledge is selected to be important – but also how that knowledge is taught, and how different learners are enabled within each pedagogical encounter. What we can conclude in relation to mixed PE, therefore, is that whilst this organisation of children provides equal access to certain activities, this does not necessarily remove gender inequalities. In addition to influencing which knowledge gets selected as being appropriate or not for which pupils, gender relations also operate through teachers' pedagogies. This suggests we also need to consider *how* particular kinds of knowledge are taught and also, importantly, how they are assessed (Hay and Macdonald, 2010) as well as how pupils themselves relate to each other (Hills, 2007).

> *Comment*
> *Providing equal access does not necessarily result in equal opportunities.*

Liberal feminist explanations focusing only on issues of access and opportunity have, therefore, been criticised for ignoring power relations as they are produced within and through practice. For example, there is an important difference between mixed-sex teaching – where boys and girls are simply put together for classes – and *co-educational* teaching – where teachers plan for, and challenge, gender relations in their teaching, and where all pupils are enabled in their learning. Research shows that many teachers and coaches struggle to develop effective co-educational practice (Wright, 2002) given that they are themselves gendered in their confidence, abilities and commitment to delivering across a range of physical activities. Nevertheless, professionals have a responsibility to engage positively in these issues; to do nothing risks being complicit with, rather than challenging, the existing gender order in their practice (Brown and Rich, 2002).

At the same time, it is important to note that liberal perspectives remain useful, particularly in relation to prompting us to question the nature of curricula experiences for boys and girls. Although it is almost 20 years since the introduction of the first National Curriculum in PE in England, which was designed as an entitlement curriculum, the flexibility inherent in the different versions of the curriculum policy means that teachers can continue to privilege certain activities. For example, games are often privileged over other activities and, moreover, specific games are offered to boys (more usually those games with high status in society, such as rugby, cricket and football) while others are provided for girls (netball, rounders and hockey) in single-sex groups (Penney, 2002b).

Green *et al.*'s (2007) research shows that individual teachers and schools can make a difference and there is some evidence of changes as a result of the introduction of the National Curriculum in 1992. Overall, however, the gendered curriculum remains intact, and the strong link between curriculum content and extracurricular PE provision has resulted in this pattern being reproduced in school sport too. Even in the newer youth sport programmes, such as the School Sport Partnership Programme in England, evaluations show that most rely on traditional, competitive games, with few examples of innovative practice designed to engage pupils who do not already see themselves as 'sporty' (Flintoff, 2008). In Chapter 1, it was noted that a key dimension of pedagogy is understanding knowledge in context, i.e. which knowledge is valued by whom and why. As a teacher or coach, you might ask some questions about your personal knowledge of certain sports activities and how that informs your PE curriculum or sports programme; for example:

- Do girls and boys have access to learn the same activities, and if not, why not?
- In what ways are your knowledge and attitudes, as the teacher or coach, limiting young people's learning because of your programming of activities?

Gender relations: femininities and masculinities

A 'gender relations' theoretical perspective is important because it recognises that issues of gender are not just about opportunities and access, but are also about how ideas of femininity and masculinity are constructed as unequal power relations. In other words, what we think about masculinity at any one time is always defined in relation to femininity. Moreover, these ideas are not just relational but are also hierarchical, where one set of attributes and associated activities (men's) is viewed as more important than the other (women's). Importantly this theoretical perspective also recognises the differences *within* a group of boys, or *within* a group of girls, as well as those *between* girls and boys. Not all girls experience PE or sport in the same way, nor do all boys; hence it is important to talk about feminini*ties* and masculini*ties*. Gender relations theory asks questions about how PE and sport experiences work to reproduce particular kinds of masculinities and femininities and how dominant forms – which Connell (2008) calls hegemonic masculinities – get celebrated, and other forms become subordinated.

> ### Comment
> *Teachers and coaches need to consider the masculinities and femininities present in any class or group of young people in physical education and youth sport.*

Scraton's (1992) research remains highly significant as one of the first studies that began to problematise universal conceptions of femininity, showing how girls had different experiences of PE. In particular, Scraton's work highlighted the significance of social class differences between girls for their experiences of PE and sport. Socio-economic resources are important factors in girls' and young women's participation in sport because opportunities to join sports clubs, travel to venues, afford equipment and so on all have an impact on young people's chances to develop physical 'capital' or skills (Kirk, 2005).

Scraton also highlighted the centrality of heterosexuality within notions of 'acceptable' femininity. For example, a theory of gender relations helps to explain why young women's negative reactions to their PE kit needs to be taken seriously. In mixed PE, young women and girls may be acutely aware that their bodies are opened to male 'gaze' and appraisal and many feel inadequate because they do not 'measure up' to the ideal of a slender, attractive body. More recent studies have shown that these issues remain very real concerns in contemporary PE practice (Nike/Youth Sport Trust, 2000). PE and youth sport should be about empowering girls and young women (indeed, all young people) to feel good about their bodies and to feel confident about their developing sexuality. All too often, however, this is not the case. We might ask how the practices of PE and youth sport settings operate to construct and reward *particular* femininities? What kinds of 'doing girl' are *closed down or viewed as 'unacceptable'* in contemporary PE practices, and how does this work exclude some girls and young women?

Researchers such as Bramham (2003) show how gendered ideas about masculinity impact on boys' experiences of PE and sport. All too often we hold the stereotypical belief that all boys are interested in and committed to sport. From this viewpoint, girls are constructed as the 'problem' because they do not seem to have the same level of commitment as boys. However, gender theories help us to understand that this view is far too simplistic, highlighting the ways in which social practices such as PE and sport act to support particular forms of masculinity whilst denigrating others. Connell (2008) describes hegemonic masculinity as an 'idealised' form of masculinity and shows that although few boys and men are actually like this in practice, nevertheless very large numbers are affected by it.

In Western societies, the idealised form of masculinity centres around physical strength, dominance, competition and heterosexuality. Connell (2008) argues that male power is linked to male physicality and so, increasingly, PE and sport are recognised as key sites where boys and men can 'perform' masculinity. Bramham's (2003) research, for example, identifies the importance of boys in PE being 'one of the lads', 'having a laugh' or being 'hard'. Boys are expected to demonstrate that they are competitive, aggressive, tough, heterosexual, brave, and have other attributes associated with hegemonic masculinity. For boys and young men like Dave quoted at the beginning of this chapter, this makes PE and youth sport settings intimidating places for those who cannot demonstrate such qualities or attributes. In other words, contemporary PE and youth sport practices that focus narrowly on traditional competitive sport forms are in danger of failing to engage large numbers of girls and young women, and many boys and young men too.

Comment
Gender relations theory helps us to understand the ways in which our traditional beliefs and stereotypes may be limiting the opportunities for boys and girls to learn in PE and youth sport.

It is apparent that we need much more research on boys' and young men's experiences of PE and sport. Such research will need to acknowledge and question the power relations between boys and young men as a group, as well as ways in which the actions of teachers and coaches can inadvertently reinforce, rather than challenge, damaging forms of masculinities through their everyday practices. Hegemonic masculinities are always constructed in relation to subordinated masculinities, such as gay masculinity, working-class masculinity or black masculinity, and the experiences of all men and boys are impacted in some way by these relations of power. If you are a man reading this, you might want to reflect on how hegemonic masculinities are impacting on *your* experiences of seeking to become a teacher or coach. To what extent has your masculine identity in PE helped or hindered your position to date? To what extent has it been developed *at the expense of* other men and women? What kinds of masculinities do you support (implicitly and explicitly) through your practice?

Post-structural theories of PE and youth sport

More recent theoretical advances in PE and youth sport, drawing on post-structural ideas, have challenged the macro universalistic approaches of liberal and structural feminist accounts described above. In other words, post-structural feminism argues for the deconstruction of the term 'woman' and recognition of the diversity of femininities and masculinities. Post-structural feminism seeks to foreground individuals' agency and choice, and their gendered identities are seen as much more fluid and shifting than within the previously discussed theories. Gender relations theory, for example, has been criticised for its overemphasis on structures and institutional practices at the expense of girls' and women's individual identities and agency. Many girls and women *do* take part in sport and PE, and they are challenging the notion of 'acceptable' femininity by taking part and enjoying what might have been previously seen as 'male' activities such as football or weightlifting. This theoretical perspective focuses, then, on recognising differences between girls, and on individuals' agency (power) to challenge limiting conceptions of femininity. Gender power is, thus, possessed by everyone and is multiple and productive (instead of top-down and repressive).

Post-structural analyses are still relatively new in the field of PE and youth sport (Wright, 2006). Researchers such as Paechter (2003) and Garrett (2004) point to the significance of PE and sport practices for the development of young people's gendered embodiment. The activities that are provided in these contexts matter because they impact on young people's self-esteem, body image and physicality. Paechter and others, for example, have argued for the introduction of 'newer' activities and physical activities such as dance or outdoor activities, suggesting it is only by moving away from traditional PE activities that gender-stereotyped uses of the body can be resisted and challenged. These 'post' theories, therefore, pose important questions about difference and diversity in PE and sports practice. It is worth considering, therefore, how our *pedagogical practices could be more effective in breaking down bipolar conceptions of girls and boys in PE and youth sport.*

Recognising difference has led to new questions and explanations about gender, PE and youth sport, yet these are not really new questions. Black feminists have long argued that they have been ignored and made invisible in the discourse of white feminism (Hill Collins, 1991; Mirza, 1997, 2009). In their focus on gender power relations, white feminists have neglected to problematise racial power (including their own whiteness) as central to the production of white feminist knowledge in PE and youth sport. All too often, theories of gender in PE and youth sport have been developed by white feminists who have paid insufficient attention to differences between women (or men), particularly in relation to 'race', ethnicity and religion. The work of Dagkas and Benn (2006), Kay (2006) and Macdonald *et al.* (2009) are beginning to develop our understandings of the complex interplay of gender, 'race' and religion. These studies identify the specific constraints for Muslim women posed by Western constructions of sport and PE. It is these constructions that serve to exclude particular groups of young people. Such research pushes us to pose more radical yet essential questions about the structures of contemporary PE and youth sport. For example:

- How do prevailing structures operate to exclude particular individuals including those from black and minority ethnic groups?
- How can we change these structures in the interests of developing inclusive practice, where different young people can become empowered through their physical activity experiences?

There is still little work offering a black feminist perspective on PE and sport, and few studies have adequately addressed the intersections of 'race' with other identity positions (Azzarito and Solomon, 2005; Azzarito, 2009; Flintoff *et al.*, 2008). In other words, there is much research still to be done about 'race' and ethnicity in PE and youth sport, and many practices to be changed before we can really say that we have addressed the complex nature of gendered inequalities.

> **Comment**
> *Sport pedagogy is about meeting the needs of children and young people in physical education and youth sport and recognising the influence of inequalities on learning.*

 ## Conclusion

This chapter has introduced you to the ways in which gender relations can operate to impact on learning within PE and youth sport settings. These relations can act to limit and restrict girls' and young women's experiences and opportunities, and also those of boys and young men. To an aspiring teacher or coach, gender knowledge is important and crucial knowledge because understanding and acknowledgement of gender inequities are the first steps towards change. Good practice in PE and youth sport is, of necessity, gender equitable yet, as this chapter has shown, different explanations of gender raise different questions and have different implications for practice.

There is no straightforward, easy answer to the question of how to bring about gender equity in your PE and youth sport practices. This chapter has made some suggestions; for example: by urging you to think about the kinds of opportunities and activities you make available for boys and girls; through the adoption of an explicitly *co-educational* pedagogy; and by recognising, supporting and celebrating different femininities and masculinities in the learning environments you promote. If we take the young people's comments at the beginning of this chapter seriously, it is clear that we have a professional responsibility to engage in debates and actions that work towards promoting gender-equitable practice – whatever form that takes.

Learning tasks

Individual task

Reflect back on your experiences of school PE. Award yourself a score from 1 to 10 to describe the extent to which you consider yourself to be physically educated as a result of these experiences (10 is high). Consider the criteria you used for your scoring. What influence do you think your past experiences may have on the kind of teacher/coach you will become? How are your past experiences gendered? Write a short reflection on your responses to these questions.

Group task

Work in groups of three or four, making sure that there are men and women in each group. Working individually at first, think again about your own PE experiences and consider the ways in which gender has *limited* the extent to which you have become physically educated. Identify as many factors as you can. Now share your experiences as a group. Is there any difference between the men's and women's responses? As a group, collate a list of all the factors that have been influential in limiting men's experiences and women's experiences. What do these tell us about how gender relations operate within PE, and how gendered inequities might be challenged and changed?

Further reading

See **Penney, D.** (ed.) (2002) *Gender and Physical Education: Contemporary issues and future directions*, London: Routledge for a good overview of a range of gender issues in physical education.

References

Azzarito, L. (2009) The panopticon of physical education: pretty, active and ideally white, *Physical Education and Sport Pedagogy*, 14, 19–40.

Azzarito, L. and Solomon, M. (2005) A reconceptualisation of physical education: the intersection of gender/race/social class, *Sport, Education and Society*, 10, 25–47.

Bramham, P. (2003) Boys, masculinity and PE, *Sport, Education and Society*, 8, 57–71.

Brown, D. and Rich, E. (2002) Gender positioning as pedagogical practice in physical education. In: D. Penney (ed.) *Gender and Physical Education: Contemporary issues and future directions*, London: Falmer, 80–100.

Connell, R. (2008) Masculinity construction and sports in boys' education: a framework for thinking about the issue, *Sport, Education and Society*, 13, 131–45.

Dagkas, S. and Benn, T. (2006) Young Muslim women's experiences of Islam and physical education in Greece and Britain: a comparative study, *Sport, Education and Society*, 11, 21–38.

Evans, J. and Williams, T. (1989) Moving up and getting out: the classed and gendered career opportunities of physical education teachers. In: T. Templin and P. Schempp (eds) *Socialisation in PE: Learning to teach*, Indianapolis: Benchmark Press, 235–49.

Evans, J., Davies, B. and Penney, D. (1996) Teachers, teaching and the social construction of gender relations, *Sport, Education and Society*, 1, 165–83.

Flintoff, A. (1993) Gender, physical education and teacher education. In: J. Evans (ed.) *Equality, Education and Physical Education*, London: Falmer.

Flintoff, A. (2008) Targeting Mr Average: participation, gender equity and school sport partnerships, *Sport, Education and Society*, 13, 413–31.

Flintoff, A. and Scraton, S. (2001) Stepping into active leisure? Young women's perceptions of active lifestyles and their experiences of school physical education, *Sport Education and Society*, 6, 5–22.

Flintoff, A. and Scraton, S. (2005) Gender and PE. In: K. Hardman and K. Green (eds) *An Essential Reader in Physical Education*, London: Routledge, 161–79.

Flintoff, A., Fitzgerald, H. and Scraton, S. (2008) The challenges of intersectionality: researching difference in physical education, *International Studies in Sociology of Education*, 18, 73–85.

Gard, M. (2006) More art than science? Boys, masculinity and physical education. In: D. Kirk, D. Macdonald and M. O'Sullivan (eds) *The Handbook of Physical Education*, London: Sage.

Garrett, R. (2004) Negotiating a physical identity: girls, bodies and physical education, *Sport, Education and Society*, 9, 223–37.

Green, K., Smith, A., Thurston, M. and Lamb, K. (2007) Gender and secondary school physical education: change alongside continuity. In: I. Wellard (ed.) *Rethinking Gender and Youth Sport*, London: Routledge, 68–83.

Hargreaves, J. (2004) Querying sport feminism: personal or political? In: R. Giulianotti (ed.) *Sport and Modern Social Theorists*, Basingstoke: Palgrave Macmillan, 187–205.

Hay, P. and Macdonald, D. (2010) Evidence for the social construction of ability in physical education, *Sport, Education and Society*, 15, 1–18.

Hill Collins, P. (1991) *Black Feminist Thought: Knowledge, consciousness and the politics of empowerment*, London: Routledge.

Hills, L. (2007) Friendship, physicality and physical education: an exploration of the social and embodied dynamics of girls' physical education experiences, *Sport, Education and Society*, 12, 317–36.

Kay, T. (2006) Daughters of Islam: family influences on Muslim young women's participation in sport, *International Review for the Sociology of Sport*, 41, 357–73.

Kirk, D. (2005) Physical education, youth sport and lifelong participation: the importance of early learning experiences, *European Journal of Physical Education*, 11, 239–55.

Macdonald, D., Abbott, R., Knez, K. and Nelson, K. (2009) Taking exercise: cultural diversity and physically active lifestyles, *Sport, Education and Society*, 14, 1–19.

Mirza, H. (1997). *Black British Feminism: A reader*, London: Routledge.

Mirza, H. S. (2009) *Race, Gender and Educational Desire: Why black women succeed and fail*, London: Routledge.

Nike/Youth Sport Trust (2000) *Girls into Sport: Towards girl-friendly physical education*, Loughborough: Institute of Youth Sport.

Paechter, C. (2003) Power, bodies and identity: how different forms of physical education construct varying masculinities and femininities in secondary school, *Sex Education*, 3, 1: 47–59.

Penney, D. (2002a) *Gender and Physical Education: Contemporary issues and future directions*, London: Routledge.

Penney, D. (2002b) Gendered policies. In: D. Penney (ed.) *Gender and Physical Education: Contemporary issues and future directions*, London: Routledge, 103–22.

Penney, D., Houlihan, B. and Eley, D. (2002) *Report of the First National Survey of Sports Colleges*, Loughborough: Institute of Youth Sport, Loughborough University.

Scraton, S. (1992) *Shaping up to Womanhood: Gender and girls' physical education*, Buckingham: Open University Press.

Watson, R. (2008) Identities. In: D. Kirk, A. Flintoff, J. Mckenna and C. Cooke, (eds) *Key Concepts in Sport and Exercise*, London: Sage.

Webb, L. A. and Macdonald, D. (2007a) Dualing with gender: teachers' work, careers and leadership in physical education, *Gender and Education*, 19, 491–512.

Webb, L. A. and Macdonald, D. (2007b) Techniques of power in physical education and the under-representation of women in leadership, *Journal of Teaching in Physical Education*, 26, 277–95.

Wellard, I. (2007) *Rethinking Gender and Youth Sport*, London: Routledge.

Wright, J. (2002) Changing gendered practices in physical education: working with teachers, *European Physical Education Review*, 5, 181–97.

Wright, J. (2006) Physical education research from postmodern, poststructural and postcolonial perspectives. In: D. Kirk, D. Macdonald and M. O'Sullivan (eds) *The Handbook of Physical Education*, London: Sage, 59–75.

17

Right to be active: looked-after children in physical education and sport

Kathleen Armour, University of Birmingham
Rachel Sandford and Rebecca Duncombe, Loughborough University

Looked-after children very rarely participate in after-school clubs or societies . . . they are extremely suspicious, often very emotionally fragile, frequently angry and bitter, show reluctance to trust anyone and demonstrate very low motivation and self-esteem . . .

At the end of [our sport-based] project the students were asked to evaluate the programme . . . They enjoyed everything . . . they did not want to change anything and identified their own personal development such as 'I have made new friends', 'I am more confident' and 'I am more willing to listen'.

(Teacher comment)

 ## Introduction

As teachers and coaches, are we fully aware of the daily challenges faced by some of the young learners in our classes and groups? Do we know enough about those children and young people whose individual circumstances might result in negative impacts on learning? If we are not aware of such issues, is it possible that we might misinterpret those occasions when some young people appear less than enthusiastic about our attempts to engage them in physical education and sport?

This chapter considers these questions by looking at one group of young people, some of whom are likely to face challenges above and beyond those faced by their peers. 'Looked-after children' are those children and young people who are 'in care', i.e. they are being looked after by local authorities (in residential centres or foster care), for varying periods of time, because they are unable to live independently with their parents or family. It is important to state at the outset that such children do not form a homogeneous group. Like all other children, looked-after children are individuals and they face a whole host of different challenges. Nonetheless, it is certainly the case that this group of children and young people faces some unique challenges. What we need, therefore, as professional teachers and coaches, is enough knowledge about looked-after children to ensure that we do not miss important opportunities for them to access the potential benefits of sport, physical education and physical activity.

This chapter is organised into five sections:

1   Who are looked-after children and why do we need to know about them?
2   A brief overview of the policy context in England.
3   Access to physical education and youth sport.
4   What can physical education and sport offer looked-after children?
5   An illustrative case study from recent research.

> **Comment**
> *Looked-after children are not a homogeneous group but they do face some unique challenges.*

Who are looked-after children and why do we need to know about them?

The term 'looked-after' was introduced in England by the Children Act (1989) to refer to those young people who are in the care of local authorities. These young people may be subject to a compulsory care order or, for various reasons, they may be accommodated voluntarily. A substantial number of young people are cared for in this way. For example, government statistics showed that at 31 March 2009, there were 60,900 children being looked after by local authorities in England, most commonly as a result of abuse or neglect (DCSF, 2008a). Whilst many children who enter the care system only stay for a brief period, eventually returning home, there is also a substantial group that is subject to long-term care. Indeed, the government figures referred to above showed that of the 60,900 young people in care, over 43,000 had been looked after continuously for at least 12 months (around 33,000 of them being of school age).

A growing body of international research has shown that, as a group, looked-after children (LAC) are at risk of a number of poor outcomes, including poor physical and mental health, homelessness, drug and alcohol misuse, and involvement in crime (e.g. Broad and Monaghan, 2003). Stein and Munro (2008) have also highlighted the potential problems these young people face in transitions into adulthood. In addition, and of importance in the context of this discussion, is the finding that many of those in long-term care will have poor experiences of schooling and low educational attainment. As the DCSF (2010) has noted, 'the educational achievement of looked-after children as a whole remains unacceptably low' (p. 3). Indeed, in 2008 only 14 per cent of LAC in England achieved 5 A*–C grades at GCSE level, compared with a national average of 65.3 per cent. This low attainment is perceived to be due to a number of factors, including the fact that looked-after children's lives are characterised by instability and they often miss significant amounts of school (SEU, 2003). Government figures show, for example, that it is not unusual for LAC to move school three times in an academic year (DfES, 2006). Moreover, Polnay and Ward (2000) have shown that LAC are ten times more likely to be excluded than their peers. Heath, Brooks, Cleaver and Ireland (2009) have suggested that disruptive schooling experience and lack of educational achievement render care leavers a particularly vulnerable group in our society.

> ### Comment
> *Looked-after children are at risk of a number of poor outcomes and many of those in long-term care are at risk of low educational attainment and unemployment.*

The picture for looked-after children is, however, rarely straightforward. Several researchers have suggested that the relatively poor outcomes for LAC need to be understood with reference to their pre-care experiences. For example, in their research, Darker, Ward and Caulfield (2008) found that care episodes were unlikely to be the sole cause for an individual's delinquency. Sempik, Ward and Darker (2008) noted that young people who become 'looked after' are already 'among the most vulnerable and disadvantaged members of society' (p. 221). Indeed, prior to their entry into care, many looked-after children live in low-income lone-parent households in very poor neighbourhoods (Bebbington and Miles, 1989). In addition, parental mental ill-health, drug and alcohol misuse and/or domestic violence can significantly impair parenting capacity and exacerbate an already difficult situation.

Research suggests that the impact of such experiences on an individual child will be influenced by a range of factors such as the child's age, the severity, duration and nature of the abuse, and the availability of a caring adult able to respond appropriately to the child's needs and to offer support (Bentovim, 2006). There will also be a certain amount of individual variation in relation to young people's ability to cope with difficult situations – i.e. their resilience – and several researchers working in the field of positive youth development have pointed to the importance of factors that enhance resilience for young people in difficult/challenging circumstances (Benard, 2004). For example, protective factors have been said to include positive self-esteem, confidence and problem-solving skills as well as secure, stable, affectionate relationships in one sphere of life and experiences of success and achievement. Schools, and sport within schools or communities, have the potential to offer some looked-after children opportunities to experience protective factors and develop resilience.

Barriers to LAC's engagement in physical activity and sport are somewhat under-researched, but there are likely to be a range of issues at work here that include all those problems encountered by the most vulnerable families in society (e.g. finance, transport, opportunities). In addition, however, looked-after children face further problems resulting from:

- the negative impact of placement instability;
- variable contact arrangements;
- lack of interest in sport or support by some carers and residential staff;

- poor understanding of the value of sport/physical activity;
- non or poor school attendance.

Of course, all these challenges have to be understood in the context of the usual adolescence factors that result in declining physical activity levels, such as loss of interest in traditional sports, poor social skills and poor body image. It has also been suggested that looked-after children are more likely to be overweight and obese compared with the standard norms for their age. Indeed, Hadfield and Preece (2008) noted that 35 per cent of the LAC involved in their research saw an increase in BMI while in care. What we might conclude from all this, perhaps, is that ensuring LAC are able to learn effectively by engaging in meaningful sport and physical activity experiences should be a high priority for physical education teachers and youth sport coaches.

> **Comment**
> *Young people vary in their resilience and it is important to offer access to protective factors that can help to build resilience.*

A brief overview of the policy context in England

Every Child Matters is a UK government strategy that outlines universal ambitions for every child and young person, whatever their background and circumstances. The following five outcomes for children and young people are central:

- Be healthy.
- Stay safe.
- Enjoy and achieve.
- Make a positive contribution.
- Achieve economic well-being. (DCSF, 2005)

Similarly, *Care Matters: Time for change* (DfES, 2007) outlines the government's commitment to improving outcomes for children and young people in care and narrowing the gap between the quality of their lives and those of other children. This White Paper identifies the positive benefits that organised leisure activities offer in terms of promoting health and well-being, providing opportunities to meet and interact with others, and developing and maintaining social relationships. It is argued that such activities can counteract feelings of exclusion, build young people's self-esteem and provide them with positive role models (peers and adults), thereby supporting better outcomes. Indeed, it is suggested, specifically, that 'involvement in structured leisure activities can also help young people make positive life choices and positive transitions into adulthood and beyond' (p. 96).

The Education and Inspections Act (2006) in England placed a duty on local authorities to ensure that young people have access to sufficient positive leisure time activities. Offering access to appropriate leisure opportunities is viewed as part of a package of corporate parenting responsibilities. Moreover, it is recognised that local authorities tend to own sports facilities both in schools and in leisure centres, so arranging access should be feasible. Indeed, *Care Matters* (DfES, 2007) states strongly that authorities have a duty to fulfil this requirement 'with rigour in regard to children in care – taking account of their needs and ensuring that they are helped to overcome barriers to participation' (p. 97). As a development of this, national standards are being introduced to require local authorities to provide children and young people in care with free access to positive leisure activities. In addition, schools are being provided with funding to enable children in care to access two hours a week of extended school group activity, and two weeks of holiday provision free of charge.

> **Comment**
> *The contemporary policy context in England recognises the need for looked-after children to have supported access to active leisure opportunities.*

Access to physical education and youth sport

The Children Act (2004) states that it is a 'duty' of local authorities (in England) to promote the educational achievement of looked-after children (DCSF, 2010). In relation to this, it is argued that access to appropriate out of school hours learning (OSHL), including that relating to leisure interests, should be part of every looked-after child's personal education plan (PEP). Moreover, looked-after children should have access to a personal education allowance (PEA) designed to support activities that will promote their ongoing development. This recent policy development offers unique opportunities for LAC to access the potential benefits of physical education and youth sport.

In order to support the commitment to engage more vulnerable young people in sport, the Youth Sport Trust (a national charity) and Sport England (government body) have been working together to explore and support new approaches to providing community-based sport opportunities for children in care. The goal is to ensure that young people at risk, including LAC, are able to benefit from increased opportunities to take part in positive activities and also that they gain something from the staging of the London 2012 Olympics. A number of important steps have been identified:

- establishing a children in care sector reference group to guide DfES-sponsored Olympic activity;
- working with the 2012 Nations and Regions Group so that 2012 regional activities take account of children in care;
- developing revised care planning guidance to include leisure time in care plans;
- reconsidering the role of the social worker to ensure that children and young people receive appropriate support in accessing sports and leisure activities;
- ensuring that training for foster carers includes an understanding of the importance of play and leisure;
- setting the expectation that schools should promote and support LAC engagement in sport and leisure activities (DfES, 2007).

The commitments above are rooted in the recent PESSYP strategy. Building on the achievements of the 2002 PESSCL strategy, the new PE and Sport Strategy for Young People

(PESSYP) aims to 'ensure that sport becomes a part of every young person's life' (DCSF, 2008b). Between 2002 and 2008, £1.5 billion was invested in the earlier strategy which, as part of its remit, funded a national network of School Sport Partnerships, increased the time available for curriculum physical education in schools where provision was lower than two hours, and extended the range of sporting opportunities available for children and young people aged 5–16. An additional £755 million has been allocated for the new PESSYP strategy, which is funded until 2011. Although the strategy is designed to benefit all children and young people, there is a particular emphasis on targeting hard-to-reach groups, including the 20 per cent who currently participate the least, and children and young people from disadvantaged backgrounds. It is recognised, however, that 'specific actions' will be required in order to reach those most in need (DCSF, 2008b).

Underpinning the PESSYP strategy is an implicit faith in the range of individual and community benefits that can accrue when children and young people are engaged in purposeful and sustained sport/physical activity. Importantly, the strategy also recognises that in order to ensure adequate levels of participation, there is a need to focus on quality of and access to provision both in and out of curriculum time, and to increase both the time that children are active and the opportunities for them to engage. The PESSYP strategy has, therefore, as one its key targets, the creation of 'a 'five hour offer' for all 5–16-year-olds, which includes two hours of high-quality curriculum PE and sport each week, and 'new opportunities for them to participate in a further three hours each week of sporting activity, through school, voluntary and community providers' (DCSF, 2008b).

For many families, the most commonly identified barrier to engaging in performance sport is cost. As Kay (2004) has pointed out, a series of family trends are adversely affecting groups that are already under-represented in sports participation. Many of these trends relate to low income, including income polarisation, growth in no-earner households, and high levels of child poverty. High levels of lone parenthood, strongly associated with low employment and low income, also reduce resources required for sport, especially at a performance level. It is important to remember that looked-after children tend to come from disadvantaged backgrounds where a number of social/environmental risk factors are present (Bebbington and Miles, 1989; Sempik, Ward and Darker, 2008). It is likely, therefore, that many LAC children were already comparatively excluded from sport and other activities prior to entry to care. Certainly, once in care, the cost of such activities has been found to be a barrier to participation (DfES, 2007).

It is clear, therefore, that there are firm expectations about the benefits that *all* children and young people are expected to gain from participation in physical activity and sport. More specifically, benefits are claimed in two key areas: positive youth development and health. In order to reach all children, however, teachers and coaches should be aware of the specific access needs of some groups. For example, frequent changes of address experienced before, during and often after a care episode make it difficult for looked-after children and young people to keep a place in a team or access any continuity of sports training (see e.g. Ward, 2009).

> **Comment**
> *Barriers to access are numerous and many can be traced to problems caused by low income; this is particularly the case for engagement in performance-level sport.*

What can physical education and sport offer looked-after children?

Clearly, the range of potential benefits from participation in physical activity and sport is the same for all children, although the *need* for such beneficial outcomes might be greater in some groups. What follow are two examples of the potential benefits of engagement in physical activity and sport that may be particularly relevant to looked-after children.

Positive youth development through sport

Beliefs about positive youth development (PYD) through sport appear to be rooted in the notion that engagement in sport is, in some sense, 'character-building' (Nichols, 2007). This belief finds expression in a range of contemporary national and international policies. The United Nations (2003) suggested that sport programmes are 'a valuable tool to initiate social development and improve social cohesion, especially when implemented with young people' (p. 12). Even more strongly, the European Union Commission White Paper on Sport (2007) stated that:

> Sport makes an important contribution to economic and social cohesion and more integrated societies. All residents should have access to sport. The specific needs and situation of under-represented groups therefore need to be addressed, and the special role that sport can play for young people, people with disabilities and people from less privileged backgrounds must be taken into account.

A large (and growing) body of international research also endorses the view that involvement in constructive leisure activities can help to address problems of disadvantage and social exclusion through building resilience, promoting positive youth development and facilitating the generation of social capital (Holt, 2008; Sandford *et al.*, 2008). Interestingly, in the school context, it has also been argued that engagement in sport can have a significant impact on the behaviour and achievement of pupils (DfES, 2005a).

Such faith in the ability of sport/physical activity to bring about (diverse) positive outcomes for young people was illustrated clearly in the bid to host the 2012 London Olympics. While the bid hinged on the physical, social and economic legacy that the Games would offer, there was also a strong focus on the benefits for children and young people. Indeed, there was a clear desire for the Olympics to have a long-term impact on the lives of learners, and it was suggested that the 2012 Games could help to drive strategies that would address, in particular, young people's underachievement and disaffection (see Sandford, Armour and Duncombe, 2010). Indeed, the PESSYP strategy itself has been identified as a key programme that will help to fulfil the Olympic Legacy aim of getting more young people active and inspiring them through sport (DCMS, 2008). Importantly, in the context of LAC, central to legacy discourse is the aim of increasing participation in physical activity and sport by removing barriers and creating incentives for *all sections of society*. It would appear to be essential, therefore, for teachers and coaches to understand the specific barriers faced by looked-after children, who are one of the hardest groups to reach in society.

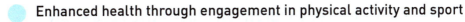

Enhanced health through engagement in physical activity and sport

Expectations of an Olympic Legacy for children and young people extend beyond PYD into aspects of physical health. For example, the DoH/DCSF strategy: *Healthy Weight, Healthy Lives* (2008) identifies two of its core aims as:

- to inform, support and empower parents in making changes to their children's diet and levels of physical activity;
- to review our overall approach to physical activity, including the role of Sport England, to develop a fresh set of programmes ensuring there is a clear legacy of increased physical activity leading up to and after the 2012 Games (p. xiv).

This cross-government strategy is based on the emergence of a clear consensus on the role of physical activity in maintaining and enhancing health, and reducing health risk factors:

> Lack of physical activity reinforces the occurrence of overweight, obesity and a number of chronic conditions such as cardiovascular diseases and diabetes, which reduce the quality of life, put individuals' lives at risk and are a burden on health budgets and the economy.
> (EU Commission, 2007)

Sport is recognised as a key expression of physical activity for children and young people; indeed, the EU Commission has argued that 'As a tool for health-enhancing physical activity, the sport movement has a greater influence than any other social movement.' In England, government policies such as *Every Child Matters* (DCSF, 2005), *Extended Schools* (DfES, 2005b), *Public Service Agreement 12* (HM Treasury, 2007) and *Healthy Weight, Healthy Lives* (DoH/DCSF, 2008) consistently identify physical education and school sport (PESS) as instrumental in providing opportunities for young people to improve their health. Furthermore, the recent secondary National Curriculum for PE (QCA, 2007) includes a statutory obligation to promote healthy, active lifestyles, and the current review of the National Curriculum for primary schools also focuses on the importance of physical activity as part of healthy living (QCDA, 2009). Here again, therefore, it is timely to consider the specific needs of looked-after children who, evidence suggests, are one of the groups most in need of regular engagement in physical activity for health; but are also one group that is least likely to be able to access PESSYP provision.

The core message that runs throughout this chapter is the need for teachers and coaches to be aware of the challenges facing individual children in their classes or groups and to make adjustments to ensure they can access the opportunities on offer. Essentially, if we in physical education and youth sport believe our own claims about the value of sport, it is logical that we would want to do everything possible to assure access for those vulnerable children who have the most to gain. What follows is an example from research of the benefits that can result when physical activity is designed specifically to meet the needs of looked-after children.

Comment

Positive youth development and physical activity for health are two potential outcomes from engagement in sport that could have particular value for looked-after children.

Looked-after children: an illustrative case study

In 2003, one of the authors visited a group of looked-after children who were participating in the BSkyB Living for Sport programme. Living for Sport aims to motivate, inspire and engage young people through sport, and it often targets those young people who are having difficulties with one or more aspects of school life. The programme centres around specific groups of young people who are chosen by school staff on the grounds that they could 'benefit' in some way from participation in a sport-based intervention. A small group of selected young people engages in a series of sports activities, usually over an 8–12 week period, with a teacher or other member of school staff. The programme culminates in a sport and celebration event. Each project differs considerably because of the programme's inherent flexibility, which is a key attraction for participants (see Chapter 13 by Sandford and Duncombe in this book for further details on Living for Sport). In this case, the project was unusual in that it was not based in a single school, but was designed to meet the needs of looked-after children from a range of schools in the local area.

The young people in this project were all looked-after children and were aged between 14 and 16. At the start of the project, there were 12 pupils (five boys and seven girls) although this was a fairly fluid group with some not participating and others joining as the project progressed. The lead teacher described the young people as follows: *'They all have had traumatic experiences which lead to a complexity of behavioural and emotional problems.'* The group met on a weekly basis at different venues and engaged in activities such as short tennis, badminton, snooker, golf, team building and climbing. Their end-of-project sport event was an afternoon of activities at a local sports college, and their celebration event took the form of a meal at a restaurant where certificates and trophies were awarded.

A researcher visited the project, observed activities and undertook informal interviews with the participants. In addition, the lead teacher completed an end-of-project monitoring and evaluation form. Using the data from both these sources and a lead teacher's written report (produced for senior management), it became clear that the project had been a success for many (but not all) of the young people who participated.

	Yes	No	Don't know	To some extent
Did the young person enjoy the project?	9	–	1	2
Has the project benefited the young person?	7	–	3	2
Was there evidence of an increase in self-confidence?	5	–	6	1
Was there any evidence of improved social skills?	6	–	5	1
Was there any evidence of an improved attitude to learning?	5	–	7	–
Was there increased involvement in extracurricular activities?	6	–	6	–

The young people made a number of comments about their experience, including:

I enjoyed rafting and climbing.

I feel more confident.

I don't argue so much.

I made friends.

I can be successful.

In addition, some of the key adults noticed positive changes; for example:

> I cannot believe how confident she is. Last year she wouldn't join in anything on holiday. This year she has joined in everything. (Parent/carer)

> She is much calmer than she used to be. She doesn't argue so much or lose her temper as much. (Parent/carer)

> They have learnt that there is no such thing as can't. (Parent/carer)

> When Jane and I look at the people our young students have become, we cannot help but feel pride in their achievements. (Lead teacher)

The findings from the research make it clear that this particular Living for Sport project was beneficial for several of the young people in quite marked ways. In these cases, the project offered looked-after children a real opportunity to gain some of the potential benefits of participation in sport. At the same time, it is important to recognise some of the problems that were encountered in attempting to establish this project, some of which were unique to the LAC context:

- The young people attended schools across the city, so they did not know each other prior to the project and convincing them to attend was difficult.
- Unlike a more conventional, school-based project, this project had no 'base', no sporting equipment, no minibus, no computers and limited funds:
  - Pupils had to travel by bus on their own to venues; this was often very daunting for them and, in some cases, prevented participation;
  - Many pupils were not used to independent travel.
- Consent (for pupils to participate) was often difficult to gain as it was required from so many adults (parents, carers, schools and social workers).
- The targeted young people were not automatically enthused by the opportunity they were given (as the opening quote to this chapter testifies).
- There was an ongoing uncertainty around whether the project would be allowed to continue.
- Issues of confidentiality (often for the pupils' own safety) were sometimes problematic where the project was based in certain public venues.

Despite encountering all these problems and more, as the project evolved, solutions were often found. For example, to encourage and enable some of the young people to attend, they were provided with food and drink at each activity, they were allowed to bring a friend (many of whom were also LAC), their travel costs were reimbursed, in some instances project staff would travel with the young people on the bus, and several sporting providers offered subsidised (and even free) facilities and activities.

 ## Conclusion

In Chapter 1 of this book, Kathleen Armour argued:

> Belief in the value of sport and its potential as a broad educational tool would suggest it is incumbent upon teachers and coaches, and any other adults involved in youth sport, to use sport effectively to meet the needs of children, rather than assuming that simply

pushing children through sports experiences will, in some magical way, result in positive outcomes for all of them.

Nowhere is this comment illustrated more vividly than in the case of looked-after children. There are some children you will encounter in your careers who are facing personal challenges of a magnitude that the majority of the population can only imagine. Assuming that sport will, in some magical sense, 'rescue' them from their problems and issues is naive. Yet, if we are aware of the unique challenges and structural constraints facing looked-after children, we might be able to help some of them to access the good things sport has to offer.

Learning tasks

Individual task

Conduct an online search in your own national and local context to find out about recent policies and strategies that might offer new opportunities for looked-after children to access sport and physical activity. What barriers to participation are identified?

Group task

In groups of four, develop a strategy for a school, sports club or community group club that could meet the physical activity/sport needs of looked-after children as you understand them from your investigations in the individual task given above.

Further reading

Department for Education and Skills (DfES) (2007) *Care Matters: Time for change*, Norwich: The Stationery Office.

References

Bebbington, A. and Miles, J. (1989) The background of children who enter local authority care, *British Journal of Social Work*, 19, 349–68.

Benard, B. (2004) *Resiliency: What we have learned*, San Francisco, CA: WestEd.

Bentovim, A. (2006) *The Effectiveness of Therapeutic Interventions with Young People who have Experienced Sexual and Physical Abuse in the UK*, London: Jessica Kingsley.

Broad, B. and Monaghan, M. (2003) *Talking Sense: Messages from young people facing social exclusion about their health and well-being*, London: The Children's Society.

Darker, I., Ward, H. and Caulfield, L. (2008) An analysis of offending by young people looked after by local authorities, *Youth Justice* 8, 2, 138–48.

Department for Children, Schools and Families (DCSF) (2005) *Every Child Matters: Aims and outcomes*, retrieved from http://www.everychildmatters.gov.uk/aims

Department for Children, Schools and Families (DSCF) (2008a) *Statistical First Release (SFR) on Outcome Indicators for Children Looked After, Twelve months to 30 September 2008 – England*, London: DCSF Publications.

Department for Children, Schools and Families (DSCF) (2008b) *Physical Education and Sport Strategy for Young People*, London: DCSF Publications.

Department for Children, Schools and Families (DCSF) (2010) *Promoting the Educational Achievement of Looked-after Children: Statutory guidelines for local authorities*, Nottingham: DCSF Publications.

Department for Culture, Media and Sport (DCMS) (2008) *Playing to Win: A new era for sport*, London: DCMS.

Department for Education and Skills (DfES) (2005a) *Learning Behaviour: The report of the practitioner's group on school, behaviour and discipline.* Available online at: http://www.dfes.gov.uk/behaviourandattendance/about/learning_behaviour.cfm (accessed 20 October 2007).

Department for Education and Skills (DfES) (2005b) *Extended Schools: Access to opportunities and services for all. A prospectus*, London: DfES.

Department for Education and Skills (DfES) (2006) *Statistics of Education: Children Looked After by Local Authorities Year Ending 31 March 2005 Volume 1: National Tables*, London: DfES.

Department for Education and Skills (DfES) (2007) *Care Matters: Time for change*, Norwich: The Stationery Office.

Department of Health (DoH)/Department for Children, Schools and Families (DCSF) (2008) *Healthy Weight, Healthy Lives: A cross-government strategy for England*, London: DoH/DCSF.

European Union (EU) Commission (2007) White Paper on Sport, http://ec.europa.eu/sport/white-paper/index_en.htm, accessed 29 August 2010.

Hadfield, S. C. and Preece, P. M. (2008) Obesity in looked-after children: is foster care protective from the dangers of obesity? *Child Care, Health and Development*, 34(6), 710–12.

Heath, S., Brooks, R., Cleaver, E. and Ireland, E. (2009) *Researching Young People's Lives*, London: Sage.

HM Treasury (2007) *Public Service Agreement 12: Improve the health and well-being of children and young people*, London: HMSO.

Holt, N. L. (2008) *Positive Youth Development through Sport*, London: Routledge.

Kay, T. A. (2004) The family factor in sport. In: *Driving up Participation: The challenge for sport*, Sport England 2004, London: Sport England, 39–60.

Nichols, G. (2007). *Sport and Crime Reduction: The role of sports in tackling youth crime*, London: Routledge.

Polnay, L. and Ward, H. (2000) Promoting the health of looked-after children, *British Medical Journal*, 320, 661–2.

Qualifications and Curriculum Authority (QCA) (2007) *The National Curriculum for England*, London: HMSO.

Qualifications and Curriculum Development Agency (QCDA) (2009) *Primary Curriculum Review*, www.qcda.org.uk.

Sandford, R. A., Armour, K. M. and Duncombe, R. (2010). Finding their voice: disaffected youth insights on sport/physical activity interventions. In: M. O'Sullivan and A. MacPhail (eds) *Young People's Voices in Physical Education and Youth Sport*, London: Routledge, 65–87.

Sandford, R. A., Duncombe, R. and Armour, K. M. (2008) The role of physical activity/sport in tackling youth disaffection and anti-social behaviour, *Educational Review*, 60(4), 419–35.

Sempik, J., Ward, H. and Darker, I. (2008) Emotional and behavioural difficulties of children and young people at entry to care, *Clinical Child Psychology and Psychiatry*, 13(2), 221–33.

Social Exclusion Unit (SEU) (2003) *A Better Education for Children in Care*, London: The Stationery Office.

Stein, M. and Munro, E. R. (eds) (2008) *Young People's Transitions from Care to Adulthood: International research and practice*, London: Jessica Kingsley Publishers.

United Nations (2003) *Sport as a Tool for Development and Peace: Towards achieving the United Nations millennium development goals.* Available online at: http://www.un.org/themes/sport/reportE.pdf (accessed 22 July 2008).

Ward, H. (2009) Patterns of instability: moves within the English care system: their reasons, contexts and consequences, *Child and Youth Services Review*, 31(10), 1113–18.

Section
3

**Being a professional teacher or
coach in physical education
and youth sport**

Effective career-long professional development for teachers and coaches

Kathleen Armour, University of Birmingham

Sarah's career

Sarah qualified as a teacher 35 years ago. She entered the profession full of enthusiasm and was ready to make a difference to children's lives. She worked very hard for the first three years, and most pupils loved her and appreciated her enthusiasm. Sarah was full of ideas and everyone was interested in the new approaches she brought. She attended every additional training course on offer and came up with lots of suggestions for improving the learning experience for pupils. There was a learning buzz around Sarah in her school.

Over the years, Sarah became increasingly frustrated and bored. The professional development courses seemed to be repetitive and she felt her practice was becoming stale. Her lessons lacked any spark and she was short-tempered with pupils. She was often absent from lessons, appearing to relish almost any task that took her away from teaching children. Sarah began to live for the weekends, finding each day in school to be something of a grind. Children made her feel irritable, new department, school and government policies appeared pointless, and the only bright spot in most days was sitting in the staff room chatting to colleagues.

The Sarah of today is barely recognisable as the teacher she was 35 years ago. When asked, children comment that Sarah doesn't seem to care about kids. She talks a lot about 'getting out' and seems to be more and more interested in retirement even though it is still several years away. It seems that Sarah has become so absorbed in her own woes that she has lost the ability to 'see' the children at all.

Introduction

Sarah is a fictitious character and the career decline in the story might seem rather dramatic. Yet, if you think back to your school days, you can probably recall one or more teachers like Sarah. Indeed, I wrote the narrative drawing on a mix of personal experience and research data collected over the last 20 years. Youth sport coaches have different career structures from teachers; most are part-time volunteers with careers or occupations that run alongside their coaching activities. Nonetheless, you might recall one or two coaches who appeared unable to place the needs of you, as a young learner, at the centre of their practices. It is also possible that as you mature and understand more about learning, learners and sport, you might begin to challenge some of the pedagogical practices you encountered when you were younger. All these points raise questions, such as:

- What happens, over time, to once-enthusiastic teachers and coaches?
- Why do some practitioners lose interest in children and young people as learners?
- How can teachers and coaches be supported to retain a career-long interest in their own professional learning?

Throughout each of the chapters in this book it has been argued that being a practitioner in physical education and youth sport is demanding. Teachers and coaches have a professional responsibility to meet the individual needs of their clients: children and young people. One of the hallmarks of any profession is practitioners who engage in continuous (career-long) professional development (CPD) so they can draw upon the best, most up-to-date knowledge available. What this means is that anyone claiming to be a professional practitioner in physical education and youth sport has a *professional responsibility* to be a career-long learner. It would be appropriate, therefore, to identify CPD as one of the cornerstones of sport pedagogy.

Teachers and coaches are often busy people; indeed, many will feel they have more than enough to do simply to keep abreast of the day-to-day demands of their jobs. Yet it is important to remember that professional development is not an optional extra for anyone claiming to be professional. The question, therefore, is not *whether* to engage in continuous professional learning, but *how* to engage in forms of professional development that are most likely to lead to *effective career-long learning*. The key purpose of this chapter is to consider forms of professional development that are most likely to lead to effective teacher/coach learning across a career.

It is important to note that it is *not* suggested here that professional development, on its own, can resolve all the structural employment concerns and irritations that teachers and coaches face. Instead, this chapter will focus on ways in which professional development might be designed and organised in order to ensure the best possible outcomes for teachers, coaches and, ultimately, young learners.

The chapter is organised into six sections:

1 Teachers and coaches talking about CPD;
2 What research tells us about effective and ineffective CPD;
3 Learning and professional development;
4 CPD policy for teachers and coaches;

5 Evaluating CPD effectiveness;

6 Sarah's learning career.

As you read each section, recall the many teachers and coaches that you encountered as a young learner. Try to work out which ones were engaged in ongoing professional learning – and which were not – and then consider what leads you to those conclusions.

> **Comment**
> *Professional development is an essential component of effective professional practice.*

Teachers and coaches talking about professional development

Given the well-documented pressures on time faced by many teachers and coaches (Craft, 2000; Taylor and Garratt, 2010) it would appear logical to ensure that any time devoted to professional learning is time well spent. However, research suggests that some traditional forms of professional development are largely ineffective in enhancing learning and, if this is the case, it could be argued they are a waste of both time and money (Guskey, 2002; Sparks, 2002). Consider the comments made by two practitioners about their professional development experiences.

The first example is an extract from field notes collected as part of a study on experienced physical education teachers and their professional development needs.[1] During the project, Mark, an experienced PE teacher, attended a one-day professional development course designed to prepare him to become a head of department. A researcher attended the course with him to observe and discuss the learning opportunities offered, and recorded the following:

> Over lunch I get to talk to Mark. He explains that he doesn't like to give feedback around the group as has been done all morning. He feels that, although 'sharing good practice' is good, there is no need to repeat much of the same material. This wastes time. He doesn't like the layout of the tables or the way in which the teachers are asked to move about. The feedback sessions needed to be quicker. He explains that there is nothing clear that he can take back to school and that will have a real impact upon practice. The course is just a 'hoop to jump through', to say he's done the course, and so can be an 'effective' head of department. Mark is disappointed by the course so far. He feels he has learned nothing new and it has just involved him 'going through the motions' but, as he pointed out, 'I've done the training and this will reflect well in future applications' (i.e. on his CV). In reality, Mark feels that the course has not been good preparation (to be a head of department); instead he has learned much more from working within his own department with an experienced colleague.
>
> (excerpt from field notes; ref JF080703HoD)

The second example is a quote from an experienced coach who was asked to comment on a coach professional development course he had attended recently:

> I have to say that the usual thing with the courses is that the best bits are the coffee breaks and lunches when you are talking to the other coaches. To me, that Level 3 (coaching

certificate) should have been one long lunch hour. I know that is not realistic and that it is taking it to extreme but just to talk to people with the same issues: How to select people of equal ability for a team? What criteria do you use? Which ones do you drop, how do you tell them? Do you go for player rotation? Do you use a strict formation? Even if it doesn't change your own opinion it is just nice to know that others are in the same boat.

(Griffiths, 2010, p. 165)

Taken together, these two data extracts and the fictional story of Sarah that opened the chapter highlight a number of key points to be considered in the design and management of effective professional development for teachers and coaches.

What research tells us about effective and ineffective CPD

In recent years, researchers have become increasingly interested in the role of CPD for teachers. Questions have been asked about the best ways to organise CPD to ensure it is as effective as possible in the limited time available. Day (1999, p. 5) argued that professionals can be distinguished from other groups because they have:

- a specialised knowledge base – technical culture;
- a commitment to meeting client needs – service ethic;
- a strong collective identity – professional commitment;
- collegial rather than bureaucratic control over practice and professional standards – professional autonomy.

In addition, Brunetti (1998, p. 62) claimed that 'a well developed, readily available continuing education program is the hallmark of a true profession'. Teaching is one of those occupations widely recognised as a profession, and it can certainly lay claim to some of the features identified in the list above. Yet, whereas Falk (2001, p. 137) has argued that 'professional learning is *the* job of teaching', Borko (2004, p. 3) concluded that much professional development that is currently available to teachers is 'woefully inadequate'. More recently, James *et al.* (2007, p. 224) suggested that 'the problem in England, at the present time, is that . . . CPD provision is fragmented and lacks rationale and structure'. So what has been going wrong? After all, it would be reasonable to expect that a profession centred on education would be expert in designing professional development systems for its workforce. Is the system for coach professional development any better?

The problems

It is widely agreed that traditional forms of CPD provision for teachers are ineffective in supporting teacher learning. This is, perhaps, unsurprising, given that the traditional CPD design consists of sporadic, one-off, one-day, off-school-site courses that are disconnected both from prior learning and from the context in which any learning will be applied. Moreover, there is insufficient research evidence to tell us how specific forms of teacher learning impact on pupil learning (Garet *et al.*, 2001) and how school structures constrain or enable professional learning (WestEd, 2000).

Research on physical education teachers mirrors the findings on teachers of other curriculum subjects. For example, the ESRC research cited earlier that was undertaken in

England between 2001 and 2003 found that PE teachers' CPD experiences were lacking coherence, relevance, challenge and progression. PE-CPD consisted mainly of sports update or coaching courses undertaken sporadically over a career, and teachers' CPD profiles failed to support the delivery of pupil learning outcomes that the teachers themselves identified as central to their programmes. Examples included important outcomes linked to health and socio-moral development (Armour and Yelling, 2004a, 2004b). The same research also found that PE teachers held strong beliefs about the value of learning collaboratively with and from professional colleagues; indeed they reported this to be their most valuable form of CPD. Ironically, teachers were also aware that this form of informal, collaborative learning was not viewed as 'real' CPD by their schools. Instead, 'real' CPD was understood as that which took the form of an official 'course'. Teachers noted that even though such courses were often ineffective, they 'counted' as professional learning simply through attendance (Armour and Yelling, 2007).

Although the structure of coaching as an occupation is somewhat different from that of teaching, and indeed coaching is not a 'profession' in the traditional sense, teachers and coaches share very similar professional development concerns. For example, elite-level coaches have described their CPD as too narrow in scope, ineffective for practice, unable to meet the needs of individuals and outdated (Jones, Armour and Potrac, 2004). Similarly, Jones and Wallace (2005) found that coaches were 'disillusioned with professional development programmes which they criticised as being "fine in theory" but divorced from reality' (p. 121). Furthermore, in a critique similar to that levelled at CPD in teaching, Nelson, Cushion and Potrac (2006) described an inadequate CPD system that is built around traditional 'courses' delivered out of context and without sustained follow-up support. As one of the coaches in Kay *et al.*'s (2008) research reported:

> I don't believe courses make coaches. The glue that hangs it all together [is] the practical education, the informal learning, which is really how coaches learn.
>
> (Cricket coach, p. 16)

What is apparent, therefore, is that whereas PE teachers and youth sport coaches operate in two very different occupational structures, only one of which is a recognised profession, both groups of practitioners have faced almost identical problems in accessing professional development that can meet their needs.

Comment
Research has found that traditional forms of professional development often fail to meet the learning needs of teachers and coaches.

The solutions

Research has suggested ways in which professional development can be more effective for teachers and coaches. In physical education, for example, it is suggested that CPD should be:

- able to engage teachers as active learners;
- organised around practical content;
- situated in the context in which the learning will be required;

- collaborative, to allow professional colleagues to learn together;
- continuing/continuous rather than sporadic;
- focused on building learning capacity;
- supportive of reflective practice;
- innovative;
- able to support teachers to become autonomous learners.

(see, for example, Armour, Makopoulou and Chambers, 2008; Ko, Wallhead and Ward, 2006; O'Sullivan and Deglau, 2006)

In coaching, Jones, Armour and Potrac (2003) studied the ways in which one soccer coach constructed his expert coach knowledge. They found that coaches had to be understood as highly adaptive learners, and argued that coach education programmes should recognise this. Most recently, the lead body for coaching in the UK, Sportscoach UK, has placed the concept of a 'learning coach' at the heart of a 'professionally regulated vocation' of coaching (National Coaching Foundation, 2008). There are similarities here with recent claims that teaching must become 'a learning profession' and that schools should be 'learning schools'. So, whereas in coaching there is comparatively little research specifically on CPD, the large body of research on CPD in teaching can offer some useful insights; for example:

- Coaches' professional learning should be active, situated, transformative, continuing/continuous, reflective, innovative, ever-evolving.
- Professional development must recognise the complexity of coaching practice, contexts and individuals.
- The core focus of professional development is the coach as learner who learns continuously in the interest of the athletes served.
- Professional learning is *the* job of coaching, and each encounter with athletes is a learning opportunity.
- Coaches should be encouraged to become autonomous learners within supportive coach learning communities.
- Each professional learning activity should be designed to have a learning capacity-building function.
- The potential of informal, collaborative learning should be harnessed in formal professional learning structures.
- Coach educators need professional development too to enable them to model the learning approach that will inform the development of the learning coach.

(Armour, 2010, p. 162).

The last point is particularly important. It seems illogical to expect professional development providers to be able to support teachers and coaches effectively if they themselves are not engaged in appropriate, compatible learning. Moreover, it is self-evident that professional development for both teachers and coaches should be grounded in a detailed understanding of learning theory and practice; indeed, this is key knowledge that should underpin all CPD structures and processes. As was noted earlier, however, there is little evidence that it does and some CPD practices seem to have been developed in ways that ignore what is widely known about learning.

> **Comment**
> *For both teachers and coaches, professional development is more effective when they are fully engaged in the learning process and they are able to collaborate with professional colleagues.*

Learning and professional development

The purpose of this section is not to duplicate the material covered in other chapters in this book, but to highlight ways in which learning theory is relevant for CPD. In Chapter 1, it was noted that sport pedagogy draws upon a range of disciplines but:

> Perhaps most important of all . . . is the requirement to grasp that as a sub-discipline of the field of sport sciences, sport pedagogy is in the rather unique position of being characterised by its function of assimilating all the other relevant sub-disciplines into practitioner knowledge.

In Chapter 3, on learning, by Fiona Chambers, some key learning theories are explained and their relevance for practice explored. The chapters by David Kirk, Kyriaki Makopoulou and Deborah Tannehill (Chapters 2, 19 and 24, respectively) also offer interesting insights into different aspects of learning and you might find it helpful to draw on them as you read this chapter.

It is important to remember that 'learning' is a complex, multidimensional concept. Moreover, each theory tends to view learning differently, resulting in different guidelines for practice (Colley, Hodkinson and Malcom, 2003). For example, behaviourism views learning as an observable, measurable change in behaviour, whereas cognitivism focuses on the individual cognitive processes involved in learning. Constructivist approaches focus on the social character of learning and emphasise active, interactive and authentic learning settings (Harris, 2000). These latter theories have been the subject of considerable attention in recent CPD research, which is unsurprising given the consistent research finding that adult learners value collaborative learning opportunities. This finding has led to an increased interest in establishing 'professional learning communities' in schools, in order to support and encourage teachers to learn from each other (WestEd, 2000). Indeed, Lieberman and Miller (2008, p. 106) concluded that 'Professional learning communities . . . hold the promise of transforming teaching and learning for both the educators and students in our schools.' Moreover, as Pollard (2010, p. 5) has commented, '"Pedagogy" is the practice of teaching framed and informed by a shared and structured body of knowledge', and professional collaboration is required if the sharing of knowledge is to be made possible.

In the context of coaching, Kirk (2010) reminds us that pedagogy is a relatively recent addition to valued coaching knowledge. In the past, coaching tended to be conceptualised within a restricted range of sport sciences, usually physiology, biomechanics and psychology. Kirk points out, however, that learning is at the core of enhancing sports performance at any level, and he goes on to argue:

> Readers need to be convinced on this basic point before we go any further because unless we have agreement that learning is fundamental to all sports performance there is nothing further to say about pedagogy and coaching. (p. 165)

Kirk's view is that if coaching wishes to move successfully towards being a knowledge-based profession, deep knowledge of pedagogy is a fundamental requirement. As he points out, however, whereas coaching can learn much from the more established teaching profession, it should avoid making the same mistakes. In particular, Kirk is critical of pedagogy in physical education that fails to grasp the complexity of learning and the essential interface between different dimensions of pedagogy.

One key conclusion to be drawn from the evidence on learning in professional development is that the traditional notion of learning as a relatively simple unidirectional transmission event (for example: I know it – I teach you – you learn it) is inadequate. This transmission view of learning has tended to dominate the design of professional development for teachers and coaches and, as was noted earlier, it has not been particularly useful. It is also important to remember that teachers and coaches are *adult learners.* Much learning theory has been based on children; indeed as was noted in Chapter 1, the term 'pedagogy' originates in the notion of children's learning. Yet it has been argued that adults differ from children in some important ways. Tusting and Barton (2003, pp. 1–2) conducted a review of models of adult learning and concluded that adult learners:

- have their own motivations for learning . . . purposes for learning are related to their real lives;
- have a drive towards self-direction and autonomy;
- have the ability to learn about their own learning processes;
- learn by engaging in practice;
- can reflect and build upon experience;
- often learn in incidental and idiosyncratic ways;
- through reflection can 'see' things in different ways, leading to the potential for transformative learning.

These insights also have important implications for the design of professional development for teachers and coaches. For example, perhaps one of the key points to be made is that adults bring vast amounts of personal experience to each learning episode. They are often wedded to particular ways of doing things and their practice beliefs have been established over a long period of time. Professional developers need to treat this personal knowledge with respect because unless they do, adult learners are likely to reject new ideas. As Guskey (2002) argues, we need to rethink our understandings of how and why adult learners change. Indeed, he argued that rather than attempting to change teachers' attitudes and beliefs in order to persuade them to change their practice, we need to recognise that 'significant change in teachers' attitudes and beliefs occurs primarily *after* they gain evidence of improvements in student learning' (p. 383). This understanding has major implications for the ways in which CPD is organised.

Tusting and Barton (2003) also highlighted the transformative potential of critical reflection. The importance of critical reflection as part of professional learning has been recognised (Schon, 1971; Day, 1999). Pollard *et al.* (2005) suggest that reflective practice is essential for developing the capacity of practitioners to:

- put their practice under scrutiny;
- examine the implications of their actions for children's learning;

- engage with relevant theory in order to understand the values and assumptions that underlie their practices;
- explore innovative practice.

Thus, Pollard (2010) has identified reflection as a key component of pedagogy. On the other hand, engaging in continuous reflection on practice is not easy. Attard and Armour (2006) documented Attard's attempts to put reflective practice at the heart of his professional development through the first three years of his career as a newly qualified physical education teacher. What they concluded is that teachers need considerable (external) support to engage in reflective practice in order to maximise its learning potential. Furthermore, their research highlighted the depth of the personal and professional challenge posed by the learning process in which Attard engaged:

> I'm asking myself one simple question . . . but it seems I will never be able to answer it in a definite way. Do I perceive my life to be so horrible because I've started reflecting a year ago? Is there a connection between being reflective and this horrible feeling of disliking a lot of things? Am I in this existential crisis because I consider myself a reflective practitioner?
> (p. 223)

In essence, the detailed analysis of Attard's learning 'odyssey' revealed just how much of the personal is bound up in 'the professional'. It would appear that professional learning involves not only the development of practice, but also the development of the person. Perhaps we should not be surprised by this. Teachers and coaches have long argued that their roles are demanding at both personal and professional levels. As Day (1999, p. 1) commented: 'The meaning of teachers' development is located in their personal and professional lives and in the policy and school settings in which they work.'

Contemporary learning theory can help to explain some of this. If teaching and coaching are activities in which the person and professional are inextricably intertwined, then both learning and professional development need to be considered in the same terms, i.e. as processes bound up with 'becoming' both person and professional. Hager and Hodkinson (2009) argue that it is more appropriate to view learning 'as an ongoing process rather than a series of acquisition events' (p. 620). The classic theories of John Dewey (1958) are interesting in this context. Dewey argued that the nature and quality of current learning experiences influence how humans understand and learn in subsequent experiences. He theorised this as the principle of *continuity of experience*, explaining that 'Every experience both takes up something from those which have gone before and modifies in some way the quality of those which come after' (p. 27). In the light of this insight, Dewey suggested that education entails *a continual process of becoming*. This means that development (or learning) has neither a fixed direction nor a finished identity. Importantly, Dewey also pointed out that not all experiences support learning in this way; indeed, some are so restrictive that they *hinder* or *prevent* future learning. Dewey's theory helps to explain some of the frustrations expressed by teachers and coaches about their CPD experiences.

Hodkinson, Biesta and James (2008) developed Dewey's ideas further. They support the notion that we should understand learning as a process of 'becoming' because this approach recognises the relationship between learning and identity. As they explain it:

> Learning can change and/or reinforce that which is learned, and can change and/or reinforce the habitus of the learner. In these ways, a person is constantly learning through becoming, and becoming through learning.
> (p. 41)

Yet, although viewing professional learning as a process of 'becoming' sits comfortably alongside an understanding of the person-professional, it adds considerable complexity to professional development provision. This raises questions about CPD policy in teaching and coaching.

> **Comment**
> *The design of professional development should take into account complex learning theories.*

CPD policy for teachers and coaches

The UK government has put increasing emphasis on CPD for teachers in recent years. In 2001, the government issued a framework for professional development, arguing that teachers need the 'finest and most up-to-date tools to do their job' and that:

> Good professionals are engaged in a journey of self-improvement, always ready to re-flect on their own practice in the light of other approaches and to contribute to the devel-opment of others by sharing their best practice and insights. They learn from what works. (DfEE, 2001, p. 1).

It was also suggested that teachers should 'own' the professional development framework. In 2007, the government recognised that there is a range of potential sources of CPD for teachers, including external courses, school networks, coaching and mentoring. In addition, a number of 'national priorities' were established for CPD and they were grouped into three areas:

- *Pedagogy*: behaviour management, subject knowledge, supporting curriculum change;
- *Personalisation*: equality and diversity, special educational needs (SEN) and disability;
- *People*: working with other professionals, school leadership.

(TDA, 2007).

In the context of physical education, CPD has also become more prominent in UK policy over the last ten years. For example, a National Professional Development Programme for physical education teachers in England was established in 2003, and this represented a major government investment. In 2006, the National College for Continuing Professional Development (NCfCPD) was launched by the professional Association for Physical Education (AfPE). It was argued that this would play a major role in the development of the subject and in protecting professional standards. As part of this initiative, CPD providers have been asked to apply for accreditation to gain Approved Provider Status and a professional development board has been appointed to assure the quality of CPD activities (see http://www.afpe.org.uk/ for more details). In addition, the new PE and Sport Strategy for Young People (PESSYP) comprises ten 'Work Strands', one of which is continuing professional development for teachers and also coaches working within schools (see http://www.youthsporttrust.org/page/cpd/index.html for more details). The strand places particular emphasis on areas such as supporting newly qualified teachers, leadership, enhancing and extending subject knowledge, continuity of progression at transition, personalised learning, curriculum review, and ensuring pupils are able to access five hours of high-quality

PE and school sport in and beyond the curriculum. For PE teachers, therefore, there is much CPD activity although rather less evidence to suggest that, in practice, there have been many radical changes to the ways in which teachers are expected to learn.

CPD for coaches in the UK was, until recently, delivered by individual sports governing bodies that developed their own education systems. However, a new UK Coaching Framework has been developed after considerable consultation and launched in 2008. A summary of the Framework is freely available on the sports coach UK website at http://www.sportscoachuk.org/index.php, so what follows are some extracts from it relating to professional development. The overarching vision guiding the Coaching Framework is to:

> create a cohesive, ethical, inclusive and valued coaching system where skilled coaches support children, players and athletes at all stages of their development in sport [and to] become world number one by 2016.

One of the key pillars of the Framework is coach professional development, in particular ensuring that coaches are supported through effective education that is *relevant to the different groups that they might coach*. The needs of children are particularly prominent in the Framework and it is argued that CPD should be targeted to ensure there are:

> appropriate systems to identify, train, qualify and support quality coaches for specific sport populations. This should commence with coaches of high-performance athletes, talent-identified athletes, children and coaches of disabled people.

It is interesting to note that the importance of developing coach education that focuses on the '*inclusive coaching of primary-aged children*' has been identified as a priority. To support this, it is stated that all those involved in coaching have 'a responsibility to safeguard children' and that children 'have a right to be safe and happy when participating in sports activities'. It could be argued, therefore, that at the level of policy, there is some convergence between the aims and aspirations of physical education and youth sport. Indeed, there is strong evidence that CPD policies are beginning to take account of research on effective CPD, although it should be remembered that practice may take some time to catch up.

Comment
The importance of CPD for professional practice in teaching and coaching has been recognised in policy in recent years.

Evaluating CPD effectiveness

One way to encourage changes to CPD practice would be to ensure that all CPD activities, events and processes are evaluated in rigorous ways, making it clear whether or not they have had the intended learning impact. However, Muijs and Lindsey (2008, p. 196) have claimed that evaluation of CPD is 'rarely undertaken in a systematic and focused manner' (p. 196). They argue that the widely used post-event 'opinionnaires' fall far short of an effective evaluation because they take no account of the way in which professional learning is subsequently applied in practice. Instead, their research suggests that Guskey's (2000) five-level approach to CPD evaluation is likely to be more effective. This approach requires impact evidence to be gathered at different times and in different ways to find robust evidence of:

- *participant support* – whether participants feel the event or activity was enjoyable and worthwhile (often, this is the only evaluation data collected);
- *participant learning* – evidence of specific learning outcomes;
- *organisational support* – structured opportunities for participants to develop their learning in practice as soon as possible after the CPD has been undertaken;
- *participant behaviour* – changes to practice as a direct result of the CPD;
- *student learning outcomes* – improved learning outcomes for children and young people.

In addition, at a conceptual level, it would be interesting to draw upon Dewey's (1958) principle of 'continuity of experience' for evaluation purposes. As was noted earlier, Dewey argued that each learning experience should build capacity for the next, and this would mean that CPD should be organised in ways that *extend teachers' and coaches' capacities to engage in ongoing/future learning*. If Dewey's principle is accepted by professional development providers, CPD events and activities would be deemed successful only if it could be demonstrated that they encouraged further (and continuous) learning and development. Finally, taken together, data from all these measures could provide some evidence of 'value for money' for different CPD activities.

Clearly there are considerable challenges to be faced when trying to evaluate CPD for coaches. Guskey's (2000) model was developed with teachers in mind, and the profile of the coaching workforce (mainly part-time and voluntary) is completely different. In particular, organisational support would be a difficult concept to evaluate in many coaching contexts. Nonetheless, the central point applies to both teaching and coaching: it is worth considering ways in which evaluation procedures can be used most effectively to enhance learning, rather than simply to measure participant satisfaction immediately after the event.

Comment

Putting in place effective evaluation procedures is important in order to ensure that CPD activities have an impact on learning.

Finally, in order to conclude this chapter I will revisit Sarah's story and imagine a different ending: one where continuous professional learning helped to retain a teacher's enthusiasm for teaching, learning and children.

Sarah's learning career

Sarah qualified as a teacher 35 years ago. She entered the profession full of enthusiasm and was ready to make a difference to children's lives. She worked very hard for the first three years, and most pupils loved her and appreciated her enthusiasm. Sarah was full of ideas and everyone was interested in the new approaches she brought. She attended every additional training course on offer and came up with lots

(continued)

of suggestions for improving the learning experience for pupils. There was a learning buzz around Sarah in her school.

Sarah developed a personal interest in using physical education and sport to engage those young people who were disaffected with school life. At first, she simply relied on her experience and informal conversations with professional colleagues, and she was able to develop some good insights into ways in which sport could help such children. For example, Sarah made particular efforts to develop strong personal relationships with disengaged young people; she took the time to understand their individual circumstances, problems and concerns; and she identified additional activities to ensure that if they became engaged in learning, they remained engaged. She also attended internal and external CPD courses on behaviour management and personalised learning, and she read policy documents with interest to see how she could use new polices to help children. Over time, however, Sarah felt she could do even better, and she wanted to know more.

Sarah did some initial investigations and found there was published research available on the role of sport with disaffected and disengaged youth. Although this was of interest, sometimes it was difficult to access, some articles were difficult to understand, and some research findings seemed to be in conflict with her experience. Sarah needed to discuss these issues, in depth, with other professionals, so she took two important steps: she established a professional 'conversation group' in the local area for teachers and coaches who shared her interest; and she registered for a part-time Master's degree in sport pedagogy to allow her to develop her personal knowledge further. In recent years Sarah has become a leading practitioner in the field of youth disaffection in her locality, and she has begun to give presentations based on her knowledge and experience at national professional conferences.

Sarah feels that she will never have enough time to learn everything she needs to know about supporting disaffected and disengaged youth through sport. Most importantly perhaps, she has become aware that everything she learns seems to make her a better teacher for all her pupils. Sarah loves her work and wishes she would never have to retire.

Note

1 ESRC project number R000239437: Continuing Professional Development: Provision for Physical Education Teachers, K.M. Armour, 2001–3.

Learning tasks

Individual task

1 What does being a member of a 'profession' mean to you? List all your ideas.

2 Draw up a list of all the occupational groups that you regard as professions.

3 Select three professions (other than teaching or coaching) and trawl their websites for information on continuing professional development.

4 Write a short summary and analysis of your findings and compare them with CPD in teaching and/or coaching.

(continued)

Group task

1 Design a three-hour professional development event for teachers and youth sport coaches. The purpose of the event is to upskill the teachers and coaches in a sport, or an aspect of a sport, where they have inadequate knowledge to teach/coach children effectively. You can select the precise focus of the event and the level of the young people who will benefit from more effective teaching/coaching.

2 At the design stage, consider ways in which the event will be evaluated to ensure that CPD for the teachers and coaches will result in better learning outcomes for children and young people. Use both Guskey's (2000) five levels of evaluation and Dewey's (1958) principle of the continuity of experience (as detailed earlier).

3 Prepare a presentation on your CPD event, the rationale for its design and conduct, and your evaluation plan.

Further reading

Jones, R.L., Armour, K.M. and Potrac, P. (2004) *Sports Coaching Cultures: From practice to theory*, London: Routledge.

References

Armour, K. M. (2010) The learning coach . . . the learning approach: professional development for sports coach professionals. In: J. Lyle and C. Cushion (eds) *Sports Coaching: Professionalism and practice*, London: Elsevier 153–64.

Armour, K. M., Makopoulou, K. and Chambers, F. (2008) Progression in PE teachers' career-long professional learning: practical and conceptual concerns, *Paper presented at the American Educational Research Association Annual Meeting*, March 2008, New York.

Armour, K. M. and Yelling, M. R. (2004a) Continuing professional development for experienced physical education teachers: towards effective provision, *Sport, Education and Society*, 9(1), 95–114.

Armour, K. M. and Yelling, M. R. (2004b) Professional development and professional learning: bridging the gap for experienced physical education teachers, *European Physical Education Review*, 10, 1, 71–94.

Armour, K. M. and Yelling, M. R. (2007) Effective professional development for physical education teachers: the role of informal, collaborative learning, *Journal of Teaching in Physical Education*, 26, 2, 177–200.

Attard, K. and Armour, K. M. (2006) Reflecting on reflection: a case study of one teacher's early-career professional learning, *Physical Education & Sport Pedagogy*, 11(3) 209–30.

Borko, H. (2004) Professional development and teacher learning: mapping the terrain, *Educational Researcher*, 33, 8, 3–15.

Brunetti, G. J. (1998) Teacher education: a look at its future, *Teacher Education Quarterly, Fall*, 59–64.

Colley, H., Hodkinson, P. and Malcom, J. (2003) *Informality and Formality in Learning: A report for the learning and skills research centre*, London: Learning and Skills Research Centre.

Craft, A. (2000) *Continuing Professional Development: A practical guide for teachers and schools* (2nd edn), London: Routledge.

Day, C. (1999) *Developing Teachers: The challenges of lifelong learning*, London: Falmer Press.

Department for Education and Employment (DfEE) (2001) *Learning and Teaching: A strategy for professional development*, Nottingham: DfEE publications.

Dewey, J. (1958). *Experience and Education*, New York: The Macmillan Company.

Falk, B. (2001) Professional learning through assessment. In: A. Lieberman and L. Miller (eds) *Teachers Caught in the Action. Professional Development that Matters*, New York: Teachers College Press, 118–40.

Garet, S. M., Porter, C. A., Desimone, L., Birman, B. F. and Yoon, K. S. (2001) What makes professional development effective? Results from a national sample of teachers, *American Educational Research Journal*, 38, 4, 915–45.

Griffiths, M. (2010) Formalised mentoring as a professional learning strategy for volunteer sports coaches Unpublished PhD thesis, Loughborough University.

Guskey, T. R., (2000) *Evaluating Professional Development*, Thousand Oaks, CA: Corwin Press.

Guskey, T. R. (2002) Professional development and teacher change, *Teachers and Teaching: Theory and Practice*, 8, 3–4, 381–91.

Hager, P. and Hodkinson, P. (2009) Moving beyond the metaphor of transfer of learning, *British Educational Research Journal*, 34(4) 619–38.

Harris, J. (2000) Re-visioning the boundaries of learning theory in the assessment of prior experiential learning (APEL), *SCRUTEA 30th Annual Conference*, University of Nottingham.

Hodkinson, P., Biesta, G. and James, D. (2008) Understanding learning culturally: overcoming the dualism between social and individual views of learning, *Vocations and Learning*, 1, 27–47.

James, M., McCormick, R., Black, P. *et al.* (2007) *Improving Learning How To Learn: Classrooms, schools and networks*, London: Routledge.

Jones, R. L., Armour, K. M. and Potrac, P. (2003) Constructing expert knowledge: a case study of a top-level professional soccer coach, *Sport, Education & Society*, 8, 2, 213–30.

Jones, R. L., Armour, K. M. and Potrac, P. (2004) *Sports Coaching Cultures: From practice to theory*, London: Routledge.

Jones, R. L. and Wallace, M. (2005) Another bad day at the training ground: coping with ambiguity in the coaching context, *Sport, Education & Society*, 10, 1, 119–60.

Kay, T., Armour, K. M. Cushion, C. J. *et al.* (2008) Are we missing the coach for 2012? *Report to the Sportnation Panel*, IYS: Loughborough University.

Kirk, D. (2010) Towards a socio-pedagogy of coaching. In: J. Lyle and C. Cushion (eds) *Sports Coaching: Professionalism and practice*, London: Elsevier, 165–76.

Ko, B., Wallhead T. and Ward, P. (2006) Professional development workshops–what do teachers learn and use? *Journal of Teaching in Physical Education*, 25, 367–412.

Lieberman, A. and Miller, L. (eds) (2008) *Teachers in Professional Communities*, London: Teachers College.

Muijs, D. and Lindsay, G. (2008) Where are we at? An empirical study of levels and methods of evaluating continuing professional development, *British Educational Research Journal*, 34, 2, 195–212.

National Coaching Foundation (2008) *The UK Coaching Framework*, Leeds: Sports Coach UK.

Nelson, L. J., Cushion, C. J. and Potrac, P. (2006) Formal, non-formal and informal coach learning, *International Journal of Science and Coaching*, 1, 3, 247–59.

O'Sullivan, M. and Deglau, D. A. (2006) Principles of professional development, *Journal of Teaching in Physical Education*, 25, 4, 441–9.

Pollard, A. (ed.) (2010) *Professionalism and Pedagogy: A contemporary opportunity. A commentary by TLRP and GTCE*, London: Teaching and Learning Research Programme Publications.

Pollard, A., Collins, J., Simco, J., Swaffield, S., Warin, J. and Warwick, P. (2005) *Reflective Teaching*, (2nd edn), London: Continuum.

Schon, D. (1971) *Beyond The Stable State*, London: TempleSmith.

Sparks, D. (2002) *Designing Powerful Professional Development for Teachers and Principals*, Oxford OH: NSDC.

Taylor, B. and Garratt, D. (2010) The professionalisation of sports coaching: definitions, challenges and critique. In: J. Lyle and C. Cushion (eds) *Sports Coaching: Professionalism and practice*, London: Elsevier, 99–118.

Training and Development Agency for Schools (TDA) (2007) *Continuing Professional Development: A strategy for teachers*, TDA.

Tusting, K. and Barton, D. (2003) *Models of Adult Learning: A literature review*, NRDC for ALN, Leicester.

WestEd (2000) *Teachers Who Learn, Kids Who Achieve*, San Francisco: WestEd.

19

Personalised learning: a perfect pedagogy for teachers and coaches?

Kyriaki Makopoulou, University of Birmingham

The distinctive feature of the pedagogy of personalisation is the way it expects all pupils to reach or exceed expectations, fulfils early promise and develops latent potential. Personalised lessons are stretching for everyone. At the heart of personalisation is the expectation of participation, fulfilment and success.

(DCSF 2007, p. 64)

 ## Introduction

The purpose of this chapter is to consider 'personalised learning' as a foundation for effective teaching and coaching. It is important to note from the outset that 'personalised learning' was an educational priority for the last Labour government in England in the early 2000s. It was placed at the heart of that government's endeavours to transform England's education system (DfES, 2006). As a concept, however, personalised learning is neither historically nor nationally unique. In this chapter, the complex concept of personalised learning is explored within the context of educational policy, public sector services and the broader European framework of a knowledge-driven society. The main features of an effective 'pedagogy of personalised learning' are identified and a compelling question is posed: How can PE teachers and coaches develop such pedagogies?

What is personalised learning?

This chapter begins with an attempt to define the notion of personalised learning in the context of policy and theory in England. Numerous attempts have been made to provide a consistent definition of personalised learning and this has resulted in some confusion. In broad terms, however, personalised learning refers to a system that is designed to put the young learner at its heart. At a political level, Miliband defined personalised learning as 'high-quality teaching that is based on sound knowledge of each child's needs' (2004, p. 8), and he illustrated the complexity and the multidimensional nature of this concept as follows:

> It [personalised learning] means building the organisation of schooling around the needs, interests and aptitudes of individual pupils; it means shaping teaching around the way different youngsters learn; it means taking the care to nurture the unique talents of every pupil.
>
> (2006, pp. 23–4)

For the General Teaching Council in England, personalised learning 'aims to give every single child the chance to be the best they can be, whatever their talent or background' (GTC, 2007, p. 1). Academic definitions are similar. For Hargreaves (2005a, p. 2), personalised learning might be better understood as personalising learning, i.e. to 'imply a process or a journey rather than an end product to be delivered' and it is an approach that seeks to meet 'more of the educational needs of more of the students more fully than ever before'. A government-appointed review group defined personalised learning as: 'taking a highly structured and responsive approach to each child's and young person's learning, in order that all are able to progress, achieve and participate' (DfES, 2006, p. 6). As all these definitions illustrate, there is a clear emphasis on achievement, progression, inclusion, active engagement, meeting needs and diversity.

In short, personalised learning means that teachers and other professionals involved in the education of children and young people must design and offer learning opportunities in flexible, innovative and tailored ways so that *all* learners are able to participate and achieve. The notion of personalised learning, therefore, incorporates both the *means* (i.e. how teachers teach, how schools are structured) and the *ends* in the education process. This approach has implicit links with James *et al.*'s (2007) argument that teachers need to 'move away from "performing teaching" to "supporting learning"' (cited in Armour, 2010, p. 2). Taking this point further, Armour (2010) argued that teachers need to focus on their learners first – and only then on the teaching that their learners need:

> Teachers go to work to *teach*, which means, too often, that the pupils become a kind of barrier to the whole process – a barrier to *what must be taught* – rather than being the point of the whole endeavour. The parallels in other professions could be a ... dentist who fails to look closely into your mouth but decides that on a given day, all patients will have fillings – regardless of whether they need them or not.
>
> (Armour, 2010, p. 2)

This means that teachers and coaches have a professional responsibility to shift away from 'one-size-fits-all' approaches and to recognise instead that learners are diverse in numerous ways: life experiences, family history, social, economic, cultural and ethnic background, prior experiences, personal interests, etc. The role of the education professional is to recognise and cater for such diversity to ensure that all children and young people can learn effectively.

It is also important to note that personalised learning is not unique to education; but rather personalisation (a term used interchangeably with personalised learning) is a central theme in wider public service reforms that have been underway in England and elsewhere. The vision is that public services should no longer 'fit the user to the existing service' but rather respond to the user's needs:

> Personalisation is about putting citizens at the heart of public services and enabling them to have a say in the design and improvement of the organisations that serve them.
> (DfES, 2004, p. 5)

This cultural and structural shift has been influenced by the business model of 'customisation' that has been defined as 'the capability to change the design or appearance of a product or service in direct response to a customer's needs' (Hargreaves, 2008, p. 5). In the education context, personalised learning encourages education professionals to put the learners at the centre of the educational process in much the same way as businesses put the customers first. The assumption is that if the learners' needs, aspirations and priorities are heard and taken into account, learning will be exciting, relevant and challenging, and learners ultimately (and perhaps optimistically) will achieve more and make better progress.

> **Comment**
> *Personalised learning has been defined in different ways but its essence is the ambition to put the needs of young learners at the heart of education in order to maximise their achievements.*

Is personalised learning a new idea?

In education, it is often claimed that policies or strategies are 'new' or 'innovative' whereas, in reality, many are very similar to earlier policies and philosophies. Personalised learning is no exception. Although placed high on the educational (and political) agenda in England over the last decade, personalised learning is not a new idea either in education or in the wider English context. As Hargreaves (2005b, p. 1) comments, the idea that the learner must be at the centre of the education process 'is an old idea that has always appealed to, and been taken seriously by, practitioners in education'. Indeed, at the heart of this 'policy priority' is a powerful and enduring pedagogy that has been developing over the last 100 years (Hartley, 2009). For example, John Dewey, an influential – and for some, controversial – American educational philosopher in the first half of the twentieth century, argued that pupils should participate actively in decisions that affect their learning. For Dewey, 'the child is the starting point, the centre, and the end' (cited in Flanagan, 1994, p. 4). Likewise, the fundamental argument underpinning the 'child-centred' educational philosophy of the 1960s was that education should 'start with the needs of the child' (Hartley, 2009, p. 427) and this is strikingly similar to current rhetoric surrounding personalisation.

In some ways, therefore, personalised learning is similar to previous approaches in education that sought to place the needs of the child at the heart of education – but it goes further. There is recognition that personalised learning is rooted in equality and equity aspirations in education and in society more broadly. As DfES (2006) put it, personalisation is fundamentally 'a matter of moral purpose and social justice' (p. 7). It is acknowledged that although all learners need tailored provision (including 'gifted and talented learners'), particular attention must be given to pupils who are 'at the risk of falling behind'. These are often children and young people from the most disadvantaged groups in society. In essence, personalised learning seeks to pull underachieving learners back from the brink of failure and disengagement through more effective pedagogies and collaborations. Provision of extended services is linked to this goal. Leadbeater (2004) provided a powerful account of how the life of a disadvantaged young man (who was born a heroin addict) was turned around as a result of a group of professionals who 'took the time to help him articulate the intricacy of his needs' (p. 6) and engaged him in fundamental decisions about the 'design and delivery of the [educational] service he received' (p. 5). Leadbeater explained:

> He was given enough choice to voice his aspirations, and was put in touch with the right network of support staff and others to create a solution that no school alone could have delivered. What's really important about this is that James was an active, informed participant in this process: the solution was personalised through participation. As a result James felt far more committed to his education than he had when it was delivered to him as a passive, dependent young man. (p. 6)

This means that personalisation extends beyond the boundaries and capacities of one classroom, one teacher or even one school. Teachers and schools must work closely with parents, involving them 'as partners in learning' (DfES, 2006). It is also paramount that effective partnerships with other schools, businesses, institutions and social services in the local communities are developed so that schools have the capacity to offer what their pupils really need. The goal (and the challenge) is to ensure that all pupils are actively engaged in and receive the education (or experiences) they need rather than being forced to be participants in a system that ignores their particular circumstances and needs. Personalised learning, in its most idealistic form, is not merely a matter of informed choice to raise standards but is an avenue to a sense of personal fulfilment.

Comment

A key component of personalised learning is its extension beyond the capacity of one teacher or one school, fostering meaningful collaborations between different groups of professionals with the aim to support personal progression and a sense of fulfilment.

Personalised learning, as an educational philosophy is, therefore, perceived as a bridge between raising educational standards and improving the well-being of all children and young people. In this respect, it accords well with the UK government's wide-ranging *Every Child Matters* (ECM) agenda (DfES, 2003). ECM has been developed as a strategy that prioritises the ways in which the actions of all those involved in the educational process can best lead to achievements in terms of pupil learning outcomes. Pupil learning outcomes are understood broadly, transcending the traditional notion of education as the acquisition of bodies of knowledge or skills, and encompassing instead a broader vision of positive development towards the kinds of citizens society needs. Thus, the strategy (DfES, 2003) states that *all young people* must be supported – irrespective of their socio-economic background, gender or sex – to:

- *Be healthy* and live a healthy lifestyle – understanding health broadly to include physical and mental health;
- *Stay safe* – being protected from harm and neglect;
- *Enjoy and achieve* – enjoying the learning process and developing 'life skills' to achieve in school and in adulthood;
- *Make a positive contribution* to society;
- enjoy *economic well-being*.

What we can conclude, therefore, is that personalised learning represents a real attempt to build on earlier child-centred theories of education and to take them forward in more dynamic ways that are focused on children's achievements.

> **Comment**
> *Personalised learning, building upon earlier 'child-centred' approaches and underpinned by a social justice agenda, supports the* Every Child Matters *agenda and seeks to ensure that no young learners are left behind or excluded from the benefits of education.*

What kind of learners and learning?

Personalised learning acknowledges pupil heterogeneity, emphasising that in all aspects of their educational experiences, children and young people must be challenged consistently and supported adequately. In the English context, the expectations surrounding this notion (or policy priory) are high. It is anticipated that, if teachers and other professionals can find new ways of meeting the needs of all pupils, three things will happen:

1 Attainment standards for all will rise.

2 Attainment gaps between pupils can be narrowed.

3 High achievers and much better learners will be created.

(Hargreaves, 2007)

The third expectation needs further elaboration. Developing teaching for better learners raises legitimate questions about the kinds of learning, learning qualities and 'learners' that are valid and are to be promoted in schools. The answers to these questions are not always straightforward, as they are implicated in ongoing debates about the purposes of education. Such debates tend to reveal education as an elusive, fluid and dynamic concept that has evolved according to specific socio-economic and political circumstances of different times. In recent years, influenced by the emerging 'knowledge-driven' society, there are growing expectations at a European level that schools will support pupils to develop into mature, active, responsible, independent, creative, curious, resilient lifelong learners who are able to work effectively with others and change when new (societal) demands emerge. It could be argued that schooling has always been about preparing children and young people for adult life. However, the nature of work and the kind of skills required in the fast-moving labour market have changed dramatically in recent decades. It is argued that employees today cannot afford to be static, passive or certain. On the contrary, in 'knowledge-intensive' workplaces, they must demonstrate the ability to create, manage, distribute and share knowledge and skills in effective ways as well as to innovate, think creatively, work collaboratively, solve problems, take risks and adapt in a system where everything is changing rapidly (DfES, 2006). Lifelong learning, which means learning throughout one's life and across different contexts and situations (Colley, Hodkinson and Malcom, 2003), is at the heart of such economies.

In the English context, these 'skills or abilities for life' are evident in the new secondary National Curriculum Stage 3 (pupils aged 11–14) and Key Stage 4 (pupils aged 14–16), which has a number of key purposes. Pupils in schools are expected to succeed as (lifelong) learners, independent and collaborative thinkers, confident individuals who lead safe, healthy and fulfilling lives and responsible citizens who make valuable contributions to society (The Children, Schools and Families Committee, 2009). It is important to note that the 2007 revision of the National Curriculum had the explicit intention of reducing the amount of prescribed content in order to support personalised learning (DfES, 2005). Linked to this, another national priority includes enabling young people to develop 'personal, learning and thinking skills' (PLTS). The introduction of diplomas had a similar purpose, offering learners the opportunity to choose specific pathways from a wide range of options both within and beyond the boundaries of their school (The Children, Schools and Families Committee, 2009).

In this context, the challenge appears to be to achieve a balance between how much content is 'delivered' (what is being taught) and how pupils are engaged in the learning process so that they develop a thirst for further learning and development (the process of learning). For Claxton (2006), educational experiences should not be restricted to the acquisition of bodies of knowledge that can become quickly obsolete; instead they should focus on building young people's capacity to learn. 'Learning capacity' refers not only to the (cognitive) ability to make sense of and retrieve knowledge or information when needed but also, crucially, to the degree to which individuals are *ready* or *willing* to do so. Being *ready* to learn means 'broadening and refining our senses of when it is appropriate to use this particular ability'; being *willing* to learn means 'strengthening our inclination to make use of the ability regardless of whether other people are encouraging us' (p. 6). Claxton explains it further:

> Put crudely, when you have learned a skill, you are able to do something you couldn't do before. But you may not spontaneously make use of that ability when it is relevant in the future, if you do not realise its relevance; or if you still need a degree of support or encouragement that is not available. In common parlance, it is not much use being *able* if you are not also *ready* and *willing*. When it comes to thinking, for example, Perkins has shown that most of us don't think as well as we can. We are not disposed – that is ready and willing – to make use of the ability we possess.

Linked to this, the concept of '*resilience*', defined as 'the ability to stay intelligently engaged with a complex and unpredictable situation', is perceived as one of the key qualities of the effective real-life learner (Claxton, 2002, p. 28). In practical terms, the implications and guiding question for teachers are:

> [W]hat would it mean to organise your classroom and your pedagogy in such a way that every day, little by little, in the midst of the literacy hour, the Romans or an experiment on magnets, your students were learning to learn more robustly, more broadly and more flexibly and skilfully?
> (Claxton, 2006, p. 8)

It has been claimed that developing pedagogies of personalised learning is one way to support pupils to develop these skills and qualities. The persistent message across a range of policies and academic documents is that in and through personalised learning opportunities, young learners become engaged in education in ways that will stimulate a commitment to lifelong learning.

> **Comment**
> *Personalised learning seeks to ensure that young learners become engaged in education in ways that will stimulate a commitment to lifelong learning. This has obvious relevance for teachers and coaches who hope to inspire young people to engage in lifelong physical activity for health.*

Personalised learning in physical education and youth sport

As has been explained, the starting point for personalised learning is that all learners are fundamentally different. Pupils arrive in schools and sports clubs from different backgrounds, and with different prior experiences, needs and aspirations. Logically, this means that each individual within a group will need different kinds of support to learn. This understanding should not be problematic for physical education as it has been embedded in theory for a very long time. The question that seems to have troubled PE academics and teachers consistently over the years is: How can we ensure that all pupils, irrespective of their interests and abilities (the most able, the least able and those in between) are challenged enough to ensure they progress in every lesson? For example, in the 1960s it was recognised that teaching pupils the 'correct' technique for a specified sport was challenging because pupils vary in *physical ability* which might be affected by age, stage of development, gender, mental capacity, motivation and prior experiences. In 1964, Knapp wrote: 'A technique suitable for one may be limiting for another with different physical or mental attributes' (p. 14) and suggested that:

> Instruction must take the form of building on the interests, abilities and temperament of each individual rather than having a model in one's mind and selecting or encouraging those persons who can attain to that model. The teacher . . . must help the individual to develop his individuality. (p. 32)

An article published in 1976 entitled 'Personalised learning in physical education,' explored:

> new ways to resolve one of the oldest dilemmas in education – how to teach large numbers of students with reasonable economy, while at the same time meeting the particular learning needs of individual learners. (Locke and Lambdin, 1976, p. 32)

Since then, the 'struggle' to meet and support learners' diverse needs in PE and coaching settings has been embedded – albeit not always explicitly – in a range of topical publications. The most striking example of an expanded view of pedagogy in PE is the 'spectrum of teaching styles'. Introduced by Mosston over 40 years ago and further developed by Mosston and Ashworth over the decades, the spectrum is testimony to the substantial consensus of physical education experts that PE teachers must draw upon a range of teaching styles to be able to meet the diverse needs of the increasingly diverse student population. Mosston and Ashworth (2010, p. 16) argued:

> [Student] diversity is the hallmark of our schools. We know it and experience it. We acknowledge it and at times, we honour it. Where, then, is the point of entry in teaching diverse students? Assuming for a moment the predominance of personal styles, how can a teacher connect with and reach students who do not respond to his or her personal style? Is it possible that this condition invites exclusion of some students? In our teaching is it possible to create conditions that promote inclusion? Any teacher who wishes to reach more students must learn additional points of entry, and to do so, the teacher must learn additional options in teaching styles.

Linked to this, discussions on how to 'differentiate' PE lessons in effective ways (Macfadyen and Bailey, 2002) also contribute to personalisation. They can offer a practical framework for not only including learners with specific disabilities but also enhancing learning experiences and outcomes for all. More recently, 'assessment for learning' resources have also been developed to support PE teachers with an emphasis on assessing pupils' progress (as both individuals and members of groups) to support meaningful learning (Casbon and Spackman, 2005).

Curriculum or instructional models can also be important in discussions about personalised learning. For example, the Sport Education model, discussed by O'Donovan in Chapter 25 of this book, has been developed with the intention of – amongst other things – enabling pupils to identify their learning needs (both as individuals and as members of a team) and to take ownership of the learning process in order to progress. Another instructional model, the 'Personalised System of Instruction' (PSI) was developed by Keller in the 1960s for teaching in higher education and was modified for use in PE settings. This model makes explicit reference to supporting independent learning (pupils working at their own pace) so that the teacher can interact more with those pupils who need the most help (Metzler, 2005).

In the context of the new National Curriculum in England, the message is similar. Curriculum planners, subject leaders and PE teachers are encouraged to plan and deliver PE lessons in 'tailored, localised and customised' ways so that pupils engage in 'compelling' learning experiences in physical education (AfPE, year unknown). Perhaps reflecting both the augmented importance of supporting all learners and the urgent need to increase participation in sport and physical activity, similar messages can also be found in the recently emerged UK Coaching Framework. The aim of this framework is to improve the quality of coaching across all levels of provision so that participants engage in sport and physical activity experiences that are developmentally appropriate and relevant to their needs and interests (Sport Coach UK, 2008). Research also recognises that coaching is a complex activity that demands the coach understands and interprets participants' understandings and experiences of engagement. Coaches must be able to select the kinds of responses that can assist that engagement (Daniels 2001, cited in Cushion, 2007). Linked to this, there is a substantial body of PE literature on lesson planning (e.g. Siedentop and Tannehill, 2000). The consistent message is that PE teachers, like coaches, must demonstrate an in-depth understanding of their learners' needs, abilities and interests in order to cater for them in meaningful ways.

> **Comment**
> *For decades, physical education and sport coaching professionals have recognised the need for personalised, tailored provision, but the requirement to develop effective person- alised pedagogies has become even more important in recent years.*

Personalised learning in practice

The rhetoric surrounding personalised learning is timely; and of course it sounds perfect in theory. Children and young people have diverse learning needs, so 'personalising' the learn- ing (through effective teaching or coaching) sounds like the ideal solution. There is, how- ever, widespread agreement that despite a growing body of knowledge about aspects of personalised learning that is rooted in some well-established policies and philosophies, the challenge remains to ensure that personalised learning is practised in all schools (or coach- ing settings), by all teachers (or coaches) in every lesson (DfES, 2006). For the education profession, Hargreaves (2005b, p. 1) argued that:

> Whilst it is true that teachers actively design their teaching to meet the needs of stu- dents, it is recognised that they are not entirely successful in this and that some needs of some students sometimes go unmet.

Some of the practical suggestions offered to PE teachers and coaches (e.g. differentiation, teaching styles) were discussed in the previous section. In the broader educational context in England, guidance on developing 'a pedagogy of personalised learning' has been offered and this could be useful to PE teachers and youth sport coaches. Originally, the government (DfES, 2004) developed a blueprint of five components of personalised learning, which included:

- assessment for learning: the use of evidence to identify pupils' learning needs and to inform teaching;
- effective teaching and learning strategies: planning for differentiation featuring promi- nently in order to engage and stretch all learners;
- curriculum entitlement and choice: through ongoing review, a breadth of options and flexible learning pathways are offered to pupils;
- provision of extended services: through effective collaborations with other organisa- tions in order to provide a range of options, to enable the development of new interests and to offer additional support to pupils;
- school organisation: with school leaders who are prepared to look radically at the nature of schooling and, when needed, to engage in fundamental restructuring of the system.

Despite – or perhaps because of – this detailed advice, some critics argue that there is 'nothing new' in either the theory or the practice of personalisation; but rather it represents an attempt to bring together (and reproduce) a range of government initiatives in order to reinforce the message and impose even greater control over teachers' work (e.g. Hartley, 2009).

> **Comment**
> *Advice and guidance on implementing personalised learning in practice are becoming more widely available, although not everyone agrees with the philosophy.*

Two persistent and intertwined themes in making personalised learning a reality in schools are pupil choice and pupil voice (DfES, 2005). In practice, the former means giving pupils better access to, and more choice over, a wide range of available educational services (Leadbeater, 2004). The latter, pupil voice, involves encouraging pupils to 'articulate their needs and [to] become involved in the business of schooling' (Sims, 2006, p. 4). In this case, pupils are not consumers but co-creators of their educational experiences (Miliband, 2006) and are actively and responsibly engaged in the design and delivery of these activities (Leadbeater, 2004). This deeper level of engagement could be viewed as representing personalisation in its most radical form. It questions established power relations in schools and raises structural and pragmatic concerns about the degree to which, in a highly standardised system, there is enough flexibility for such radical changes. Another key point is the recognition that in order to make informed decisions and have an effective voice, pupils need adequate support, advice and guidance. Otherwise, as Hargreaves (2005b, p. 3) cautions:

> Enhanced choices . . . entail increased risks that students will make choices that are ill-considered and, by closing off options prematurely, against their interests in the longer term.

Comment
Pupil choice and pupil voice are promoted as the two most fundamental themes in collective efforts to personalisation. However, the originality of this initiative is questioned.

Personalising learning in practice means that a PE teacher or a coach, when teaching games, for example, would be able to identify and support a pupil or a group of pupils who have limited understanding of certain game tactics. In the same lesson/session, the teacher would support others to make further progress in more effective execution of skills in action (during, for example, a modified game situation) whilst at the same time helping others who need support to improve their ability to evaluate their own performance or collaborate with others. Within each of these groups, variations at the levels of achievement, motivation, interest, attitudes and understanding would also be recognised by the teacher in the planning process. This type of *detailed*, *refined* and *tailored* planning and provision assumes that teachers are able and willing to recognise or – borrowing from medical terminology – 'diagnose' pupils' diverse learning needs (Armour, Chambers and Makopoulou, 2010). Diagnosing needs (and identifying subsequent learning objectives) is the first step. Teachers and coaches can then draw upon the substantial body of knowledge to make fundamental decisions about appropriate curriculum models and instructional strategies employed to achieve these multidimensional objectives, and the practical organisation of the lesson (e.g. equipment, time, other resources and support staff needed).

Armour *et al.* (2010) identified the potential of effective diagnosis of pupils' learning needs (interests, aspirations, etc.) as both a professional responsibility and one of the greatest challenges facing teachers and coaches. Although diagnosis is a prerequisite to personalisation, it is also problematic in practice partly because PE teachers and coaches often lack a theoretical framework, a shared language and the 'diagnostic tools' to engage in such a process effectively. To address the first two points, closer links between theory and practice are required. For example, it is difficult to see how practitioners can diagnose and support meaningful learning for all young learners if they are lacking advanced theoretical and practical insights into the constraints and possibilities of complex learning environments. The diagnosis of learning needs also implies an in-depth understanding of the different developmental stages of learners. Moreover, in relation to the third point, the diagnostic tools, it is argued that robust, applied research on assessment (and assessment for learning) can offer PE teachers and coaches significant insights into the process. Drawing upon a range of theoretical and practical sources, practitioners can then develop collectively (as part of a community of learners) knowledge and understandings that are useful in specific contexts.

It could be argued, therefore, that if teachers and coaches are serious about underpinning their pedagogies with the philosophy of personalised learning, many will need to introduce some radical changes to their practices. Yet teachers and coaches lack adequate opportunities to hone their diagnostic skills. Research suggests that these practitioners are rarely offered adequate career-long professional development support in terms of both content and form (Armour, 2006) and, as is discussed elsewhere in this book, this is an issue that needs to be addressed as a matter of urgency.

> *Comment*
> *Personalised learning requires effective diagnosis of learners' needs, and fundamental questions can be raised about possibilities for successful implementation in physical education and youth sport settings.*

Conclusion: is personalised learning the 'perfect pedagogy'?

This chapter has explored the contemporary concept of personalised learning. The key focus has been on the English policy context where personalisation is a multidimensional concept which may mean different things to different people, especially in practice. It could be argued that several existing initiatives and philosophies have simply been combined under this umbrella term, which raises questions about its originality. There are, however, four elements of personalised learning that few would question:

- the equality/social justice agenda that partly underpins it;
- the importance of giving children and young people ownership of their own learning;
- building capacity for learning;
- ensuring that pupil heterogeneity is acknowledged and prioritised.

It could be argued, therefore, that personalised learning is timely; and of course it sounds perfect in theory. It is, however, not quite so straightforward in practice. As has been illustrated in this chapter, genuine adherence to personalised learning would result in some dramatic changes to the ways in which teachers and coaches think and work. Thus, the question 'What does "personalising" learning mean in practice for teachers and coaches?' is an important one to address.

Learning tasks

Individual task

1 Draw upon your personal experiences as a student or athlete to write a short narrative describing a meaningful learning experience where you felt the session was personalised towards meeting your needs. Use the following questions as guides: What did you learn? Can you explain why this learning experience was so positive and meaningful? What did the teacher/coach do that was different and effective? How was the lesson/session structured? How were you involved in the learning process? What was the impact of this learning experience upon your subsequent experiences in the same or other contexts?

2 Can you identify three elements of this experience that you would like to 'replicate' as a teacher/coach? How would you develop these elements further?

Group task

Work in small groups to:

- share your personal stories and identify three to five key features that your experiences share;
- generate an agreed definition of personalised learning in PE and youth sport and five key features;
- identify a group of ten peers, and work through all the required steps in order to design a lesson or coaching session for them based on the key features of personalised learning;
- critically reflect on the experience: Was the learning fully personalised for all learners? What were the challenges? What could you have done differently?

Key reading

Sebba, J., Brown, N., Steward, S., Galton, M. and James, M. (2007) *An Investigation of Personalised Learning Approaches Used by Schools*, Nottingham: DfES publications.

References

Armour, K. M. (2006) Physical education teachers as career-long learners: a compelling agenda, *Physical Education and Sport Pedagogy*, 11(3), 203–7.

Armour, K. M. (2010) The physical education profession and its professional responsibility . . . or . . . why 12 weeks' paid holiday will never be enough, *Physical Education and Sport Pedagogy*, 15(1), 1–13.

Armour, K. M., Chambers, F. and Makopoulou, K. (2010) 'Diagnosis' as the foundation of teachers' professional learning in physical education: a conceptual conversation, Paper presented at the *Annual Meeting of the American Educational Research Association*, Brisbane, September 2010.

Association for Physical Education (year unknown) *The New Key Stage 3 National Curriculum: Support Document for Local Authorities/Local Delivery Agencies*, London: Association for Physical Education.

Casbon, C. and Spackman, L. (2005) *Assessment for Learning in Physical Education*, Worcester: British Association of Advisers and Lecturers in Physical Education.

Claxton, G. (2002) Education for the learning age: a sociocultural approach to learning to learn. In: G. Wells and G. Claxton (eds) *Learning for Life in the 21st Century*, Oxford: Blackwell Publishers, 21–33.

Claxton, G. (2006) Expanding the capacity to learn: a new end for education? Opening keynote address, *British Educational Research Association Annual Conference*, 6 September 2006, Warwick University.

Colley, H. Hodkinson, P. and Malcom, J. (2003) *Informality and Formality in Learning: A report for the Learning and Skills Research Centre*, Leeds: Learning and Skills Research Centre.

Cushion, C. (2007) Modelling the complexity of the coaching process, *International Journal of Sport Sciences and Coaching*, 2(4), 395–401.

DCSF (2007) *The Children's Plan: Building brighter futures*, Norwich: The Stationery Office.

DCSF (2008) *Personalised Learning: A practical guide*, Nottingham: Department for Children, Schools and Families publications.

DfES (2003) *Every Child Matters*, Nottingham: Department for Education and Skills Publications.

DfES (2004) *A National Conversation about Personalised Learning*, Nottingham: Department for Education and Skills Publications.

DfES (2005) *Higher Standards, Better Schools for All: More choice for parents and pupils*, London: The Stationery Office.

DfES (2006) *2020 Vision: Report of the Teaching and Learning in 2020 Review Group*, Nottingham: DfES Publications.

Flanagan, F. M. (1994) John Dewey, Paper presented in *Programme 7 of 'The Great Educators', First Series*, broadcast on 9 May 1994. Also available at: http://www.admin.mtu.edu/ctlfd/Ed% 20Psych%20Readings/dewey.pdf, accessed 1 December 2009.

General Teaching Council (GTC) (2007) *Personalised Learning: GTC advice to Government and response to the 2020 Vision report*, London: The General Teaching Council for England.

Hargreaves, D. (2005a) *Personalising Learning – 5: Mentoring & coaching and workforce development*, London: Specialist Schools and Academies Trust.

Hargreaves, D. (2005b) *Personalising Learning: Next steps in working laterally*, London: Specialist Schools and Academies Trust.

Hargreaves, D. (2007) *System Redesign – 1: The road to transformation in education*, London: Specialist Schools and Academies Trust.

Hargreaves, D. (2008) *From Personalising Learning to System Redesign*, Paper presented in Norfolk's Personalised Learning Conference, 1 July 2008. Also available at: http://schools.norfolk.gov.uk/myportal/custom/files_uploaded/uploaded_resources/3611/Norfolk_Hargreaves_presentation.pdf, accessed 27 August 2010.

Hartley, D. (2009) Personalisation: the nostalgic revival of child-centred education? *Journal of Education Policy*, 24(4), 423–34.

Knapp, B. (1964) *Skill in Sport: The attainment of proficiency*, London: Routledge & Kegan Paul Publishers.

Leadbeater, C. (2004) *Learning about Personalisation: How can we put the learner at the heart of the education system?* Nottingham: Department for Education and Skills Publications.

Locke, L. F. and Lambdin, D. (1976) Personalized learning in physical education, *Journal of Physical Education and Recreation*, 47(6), 32–5.

Macfadyen, T. and Bailey, R. (2002) *Teaching Physical Education: 11–18*, London: Continuum.

Metzler, M. (2005) *Instructional Models for Physical Education*, Scottsdale, AZ: Holcomb & Hathaway.

Miliband, D. (2004) Personalised learning: building a new relationship with schools, Speech by the Minister of State for School Standards, North of England Education Conference, Belfast, 8 January 2004.

Miliband, D. (2006) Choice and voice in personalised learning. In: *OECD Personalising Education*, London: OECD, 21–30.

Mosston, M. and Ashworth, S. (2010) *Teaching Physical Education*, Second online edition, available at http://www.spectrumofteachingstyles.org/ebook, accessed 27 August 2010.

Siedentop, D. and Tannehill, D. (2000) *Developing Teaching Skills in Physical Education* (4th edn), California: Mayfield Publishing Company.

Sims, E. (2006) *Deep Learning – 1: A new shape for schooling?* London: Specialist Schools and Academies Trust.

Sport Coach UK (2008) *The UK Coaching Framework*, Leeds: The Coaching Foundation.

The Children, Schools and Families Committee (2009) *National Curriculum: Fourth report of session 2008–9*, London: The Stationery Office.

20

Becoming an effective secondary school physical education teacher

Frank Herold, University of Birmingham

I just loved PE, at school. I really, really loved it . . . And then my mum used to teach as well, so she used to jokingly say things like, you could go the same way as me!

(Emma, trainee teacher)

I would say that my PE teachers influenced me quite a lot. I was involved in sport from a young age, so that was the path that I took . . . I feel ultimately that I could be a good teacher and that I could influence pupils positively.

(Phil, trainee teacher)

 ## Introduction

So, maybe you are thinking of becoming a physical education (PE) teacher? Phil and Emma trained recently to become secondary school (pupils aged 11–18) PE teachers and maybe, like them, you were also good at sport or you excelled at some other form of physical activity. You might have been inspired by your PE teachers and perhaps your parents were keen for you to be involved in some form of physical activity or sport. And maybe, like Phil, you also think that you can make a positive impact on pupils and their learning experiences in PE. Research suggests that the desire to become a PE teacher often originates in positive personal experiences during the formative years. Indeed, positive experiences and high achievement in sport and PE, as well as the influence and support of significant role models, are the key reasons why people choose to become PE teachers (Curtner-Smith *et al.*, 2008).

You might be surprised to learn, however, that high achievers in sport do not always make the best PE teachers. Capel (2007), for instance, speculates that those who have been high achievers in sport are more likely to take a conservative, traditional view of how PE should be taught, whilst those who have a broader background may be more open-minded and innovative in their approach to teaching the subject. Whilst it is not argued here that your sporting background determines what type of teacher you are to become, research has consistently identified that a PE teacher's personal values and beliefs will have a bearing on how they approach the teaching of their subject (Tsangaridou, 2006). What this means is that it is important for prospective teachers to understand how their personal experiences are likely to affect the ways in which they view PE.

> **Comment**
> In order to become a professional PE teacher, interest and enthusiasm in PE and sport are necessary but not sufficient requirements to support you in becoming effective.

In England, as in many other countries, securing a place on a teacher training programme in secondary PE has become a very competitive business. As you apply for a place, selectors will take into consideration your personal and professional knowledge, skills and experience profiles and will attempt to find out something about your personal values and attributes. Clearly, candidates who have acquired relevant experiences of working with children, experience in schools or volunteering will have an added advantage in the selection process. Additional evidence of having broadened your knowledge in curriculum-relevant activities can demonstrate your commitment towards personal development. Of course, love and enthusiasm for the subject are also helpful starting points although on their own they are not sufficient to enable you to become a professional PE teacher. The purpose of this chapter, therefore, is to help you to understand what is required in order to become an effective teacher of PE for pupils in secondary schools. I will draw on illustrative teacher training policies from England, research evidence from around the world, and I will also add some of my personal observations developed during 25 years in my role as a teacher and teacher educator.

Professional values, personal philosophies and the teaching of PE

If questioned about the purposes of PE, many PE teachers claim that 'enjoyment' is a core aim (Green, 2009). On a personal note, I would add that teachers seem to be a lot less clear about how 'enjoyment for all' is to be achieved in practice. In addition to enjoyment, PE teachers also recognise other important aims such as successful participation for all, education for lifelong active leisure, and the importance of exercise for health. Despite this variety of potential aims, however, Green (2009) asserts that competitive sport values tend to underpin the personal philosophies of PE teachers in England. As a consequence of this, some authors argue that secondary PE in English schools is organised and taught in very traditional ways. Capel (2007), for instance, raises some concerns about the current state of PE in English schools. She suggests that too much emphasis is placed on practical skills and their mastery, rather than giving priority to the diverse learning needs of children and how these can best be met:

> The teaching of physical education in many schools is based on a sporting model. This model focuses largely on the acquisition and performance of skills in a multi-activity curriculum organized mostly around team games, taught with a limited range of teaching approaches most of which are formal, didactic and teacher centred . . . Thus, the traditions of sport are perpetuated through a traditional physical education curriculum. As a result, the physical education taught in schools does not prepare young people for participation in many types of sport, exercise and physical activity experienced outside school. One result of this is that many young people are alienated from physical education and therefore physical activity.
>
> (Capel, 2007, pp. 493–4)

Clearly, some pupils will thrive on a diet of traditional sport and competition, and these are often those pupils of higher ability in the respective activities. Meeting the needs of these pupils is, of course, perfectly legitimate but many other pupils need something different. A balance, therefore, has to be struck in order to cater for the diverse needs and interests of pupils and to maximise opportunities to engage in the subject and to experience success. Moreover, if pupil enjoyment is a core feature of physical education, it is important to remember that engagement and experience of success are closely related to enjoyment!

It is evident that the broad aims of PE can only be achieved if teachers are fully committed to pedagogies that promote learning in equitable ways. Where teachers harbour prejudices and preferences (probably linked to their personal experiences), inequitable outcomes for pupils will invariably be the consequence. Consider this hard-hitting statement by Inez Rovegno (2008), one of the foremost scholars in the field of pedagogy in PE. Rovegno points out that there is still a lot of prejudice and physical elitism in PE:

> Probably the most difficult challenge we face is how to modify the beliefs of those undergraduates who take a sexist, racist, and homophobic stance; are biased against overweight people; and are interested only in working with good athletes in programs that benefit able-bodied students.
>
> (Rovegno, 2008, p. 89)

It would be interesting to consider whether you can recall teachers who held any similar beliefs. Indeed, where do you stand on such issues? As research in PE suggests, many of our actions as teachers are value driven and we know that value orientations are notoriously difficult to change (Chen and Ennis, 1996).

Inclusive professional values are a precondition for a career as a teacher of PE if equitable learning experiences are to be offered to all pupils. It is worth remembering that pupils' learning needs can be incredibly diverse and challenging, especially in PE. Consider the implications of Natalie's reflections on her experience as a student teacher in a school as part of her teacher training course:

> I had to differentiate a lot more on my first placement, as I said . . . Thirty-six children, three children in wheelchairs, two with autism, a couple with ADHD. You know, it was a lot to contend with . . . So, you know, differentiation was key there.
>
> (Natalie, trainee teacher)

The range of diversity in PE classes is one of the biggest challenges that teachers face in their day-to-day work. Diversity goes beyond the physical. For example, pupils are likely to have different cultural backgrounds, emotional needs, speak mother tongues other than English, enjoy PE or be switched off by it. They also have preferences for different types of physical activity. Participation in core PE is compulsory for most children and, as Bailey (2010) points out, levels of motivation to participate in it are variable. So, as Natalie describes, sometimes there is a lot to contend with in practice. Essentially, a one-size-fits-all approach to teaching is unlikely to meet the learning requirements of all pupils.

As has been pointed out in earlier chapters of this book, effective pedagogies recognise learners and their diverse needs and put these at the centre of practice. In addition to the obvious physical aspects of the subject, PE is also charged with developing wider learning and personal development goals. These include developing a sense of personal responsibility; cooperation and teamwork skills; leadership skills; a sense of fair play; creativity and many others. If you are interested in the full range of claims made about the educational 'benefits' of PE, read the review by Bailey *et al.* (2009). This review explores the notion that pupils are expected to learn *in* PE as well as *through* PE. In other words, the role of the PE teacher is to be that of a teacher of children first and teacher of PE second (Cale, 2010).

Comment

If teachers are to succeed in achieving any of the wider learning and personal development goals of education, it is vital that their teaching is underpinned by inclusive pedagogies.

What does it take to become an effective secondary PE teacher?

Although teacher training courses usually take place in higher education institutions such as universities, national governments often exert high levels of control over the training process. In England, for example, once a student embarks on an Initial Teacher Training (ITT) course, they become subject to the National Assessment Framework for Initial Teacher Training which was published by the government in 2007. This framework specifies the standards that any teacher has to meet in order to acquire Qualified Teacher Status (QTS) and it specifies assessment criteria in three major sections:

- professional attributes;
- professional knowledge and understanding;
- professional skills.

A very strong theme running through the QTS standards, and something that is supported by research, is the requirement for teachers to engage in personal development through critical reflection. The standards explicitly state that those qualifying to teach should:

- reflect on and improve their practice, and take responsibility for identifying and meeting their developing professional needs;
- act upon advice and feedback and be open to coaching and mentoring.

(TDA, 2007)

Since teaching is a demanding, ever-changing and people-based profession, a teacher's development and success are dependent on their motivation and ability to reflect on their work. Certainly, teachers must be ready to learn from their failures and successes alike. The long-term success of any professional is dependent on their ability to build successful relationships with many different stakeholders in the interests of personal and pupil learning. Two practising physical education teachers who mentor trainee teachers make these points well in their comments about desirable qualities in trainees:

> I think it is the reflectiveness more than anything. The better trainees are the ones that are more reflective. When they first come in, they might still make certain mistakes or things might not work so well but from early on they can identify, they start to have an idea of why it is going wrong and they try to put things into place.   (Mark, PE mentor)

> I quite like it, if the students work with all the different members within the department, because we all have different ways of delivering our subject. And I think it's worth them seeing the different ways and picking out the good aspects from each member of staff. Definitely a willingness to learn from others and being prepared to research different ideas . . . I think teamwork within the department is vital and they have got to learn to be part of a team and not be an individual.   (Michelle, PE mentor)

For Michelle, an additional attribute of an effective trainee teacher is the ability to work in teams. In other words, if teachers are able to cooperate effectively with each other and with other significant stakeholders, they will be better placed to secure effective learning for their pupils. The view that reflection and professional learning within 'communities of practice' (for instance, the PE department or the wider school) are key to becoming a successful practitioner is supported by research (Keay, 2005). Likewise, Shulman and Shulman (2004) identify a number of characteristics of 'accomplished' teachers and state:

> We would now stipulate that an accomplished teacher has developed along the following dimensions: An accomplished teacher is a member of a professional community who is ready, willing, and able to teach and to learn from his or her teaching experiences . . . We can think of teachers becoming:
>
> - ready to pursue a vision of classrooms or schools that constitute, for example, communities of learning;
> - more willing to expend the energy and persistence to sustain such teaching;
> - more understanding of the concepts and principles needed for such teaching;
> - more able to engage in the complex forms of pedagogical and organizational practice needed to transform their visions, motives and understandings into a functioning, pragmatic reality.   (p. 259)

Influential researchers such as Shulman and Shulman (2004), similarly to some practitioners, recognise that long-term success for pupils is most likely to be secured by creative teams of professionals sharing a vision, rather than by inspirational individuals. This does not negate the value of inspiration and inspirational teachers. For an interesting Hollywood 'take' on this issue, remember (or watch) the movie *Dead Poets Society*.

> **Comment**
> *Effective secondary school PE teachers are lifelong learners who are willing and able to shape their teaching so that it meets their pupils' (diverse) learning needs. They are committed team players, who contribute to and learn from their respective communities of practice.*

From a professional perspective, a teacher's role is unquestionably about ensuring that pupils achieve to their full potential. The 'Qualifying to Teach' (QTS) standards in England make clear links between teachers' high expectations and pupils' level of achievement. The standards state that teachers should:

> Have high expectations of children and young people including a commitment to ensuring that they can achieve their full educational potential and to establishing fair, respectful, trusting, supportive and constructive relationships with them.

Moreover, teachers should:

> Demonstrate the positive values, attitudes and behaviour they expect from children and young people. (TDA, 2007)

The commitment to holding high expectations, even when the circumstances (and pupils) are challenging, is a core attribute of any effective teacher. Effective teachers do not, for example, take the 'easy' route by turning a blind eye when pupils do not bring their kit to lessons, chat when they should be listening to instruction, use inappropriate language or complete tasks with minimal levels of effort. Such behaviours are, of course, very likely to occur, and there may be reasons for them, but they should never go unchallenged and solutions for any underlying problems must be found. High expectations of pupils should also be underpinned by the professional example set by the teacher and his/her own actions. Consider the messages pupils receive, for example, if a teacher turns up late for lessons, is insufficiently prepared, wears inappropriate and untidy clothing, gives more attention to some pupils than others, is complicit in the use of racist or sexist taunts, or condones unfair actions by pupils in their school teams in order to win sports matches. Such behaviours are unprofessional and would lead to a significant credibility gap for pupils.

At times, teaching is extremely challenging, however, challenging circumstances should never be used as an excuse for unprofessional behaviour. In my role as a teacher educator, some of the most outstanding work I have witnessed in schools has been undertaken in excellent PE departments (not just individuals) in so-called 'challenging' urban schools. This has usually been the result of school and departmental leadership that has provided a platform for effective teaching. So, no matter what the circumstances are, teachers have a professional responsibility to ensure that pupils can make suitable progress in their learning.

> **Comment**
> *The personal and professional qualities of an effective teacher transcend individual school circumstances in the interests of maximising the opportunities for pupil learning.*

Knowledge, understanding and skills

Up to this point the focus in this chapter has been mainly upon personal and professional qualities. However, any effective teacher needs to develop adequate breadth and depth in subject-specific knowledge; in this case PE. The majority of PE teachers in England now come through post-graduate routes into teaching, rather than four-year PE degrees, meaning that their subject knowledge at the beginning of teacher training can be patchy (Gower and Capel, 2004). Gaps in subject knowledge – or content knowledge – can lead to some distressing experiences for trainee teachers in their early school placements. This is especially true during the early stages of their training, when there are so many things for trainees to consider (Herold and Waring, 2009).

There is some debate about the relative importance of different aspects of knowledge for trainee teachers. Attempts have been made to classify all the knowledge that a teacher needs into different 'types' or categories. One influential conceptualisation of subject knowledge for teaching was provided by Lee Shulman (1987). Shulman, an American scholar, characterised 'subject knowledge' into distinct dimensions or 'bases' of knowledge and his work has been used extensively in PE and beyond. According to Shulman, teachers should have:

- *Content knowledge*: the specific subject-matter knowledge, understanding and skills that are to be learned by children. This includes most areas of technical knowledge you would associate with being a PE teacher, including, for instance, rules and tactics of sports, movements and composition in activities like dance and gymnastics, or the technical principles underlying different swimming strokes.

- *General pedagogical knowledge*: the broad principles and strategies of teaching and learning, classroom management and organisation that apply in most contexts of teaching. It is argued that these aspects transcend specific subject matter. This category also includes general psychological principles relating to learning such as knowledge about how to create positive motivational climates.

- *Curriculum knowledge*: the materials and programmes that serve as 'tools of the exchange' for teachers. This would include knowledge of a national or local curriculum, its intentions and how these could/should be translated into teaching and assessment strategies.

- *Pedagogical content knowledge*: Shulman (1987, p. 8) calls this 'the special amalgam that is uniquely the province of teachers, their own special form of professional understanding'. It represents the blending of content and pedagogy into an understanding of how particular topics, problems or issues are organised for instruction. This is where teachers make the learning and teaching happen. Questions might include: How do teachers translate teaching and learning intentions into something that works for specific pupils? What kinds of teaching styles are employed to ensure all pupils are able to learn?

- *Knowledge of learners and their characteristics*: this includes the cognitive, physical, emotional, social, historical and cultural factors which determine students' needs and interests. Pedagogical acts, including teaching, are always contextualised and all pedagogical intentions and actions should be referenced against and influenced by the learners. If, for instance, content is selected that is inappropriate for particular pupils, they are likely to become frustrated . . . and teachers will quickly experience difficulties in teaching as pupils become bored and disruptive. This category reminds us that, first and foremost, teachers are teachers of pupils – not just deliverers of predetermined content.

Additionally, Shulman (1987) maintained that teachers should always have an awareness of the wider educational context and ends of teaching because these provide the framework in which pedagogical acts are situated. Furthermore, it is important to remember that any education system is also framed in time and within contemporary national and local political systems. For example during the Nazi regime in Germany, physical education in the form of 'Leibeserziehung' was highly valued and it occupied much school-curriculum time. Its educational ends, however, were about tuning young people into the value systems of the state. Thus, the vigorous pursuit of physical fitness aimed to shape young men and women in the image of the Aryan 'master race' and ultimately also for the demands of the war effort. As such, these ends were very different from those found in today's modern Western societies. Today, the emphasis on health and well-being is a good example of a contemporary contextual influence on PE in schools.

In practice, there is an overlap between all the different 'bases of knowledge' identified by Shulman (1987) and there is some debate over which aspects are the most important in teacher education. Siedentop (2002) maintains that in order to become an effective PE teacher who can extend pupils' knowledge and skills beyond the 'basics', teachers must acquire adequate levels of 'content knowledge'. He would argue that without such a grounding, it is impossible for teachers to develop and use all the other aspects of knowledge. Others argue that technical knowledge can be overemphasised and other pedagogical skills may suffer (Hayes *et al.*, 2008). Tinning (2002) argues that there are many examples of poor PE lessons taught by PE teachers who have high levels of 'content knowledge' but who are unable to adapt their knowledge to the needs of pupils. Moreover, it is important to remember that the knowledge required to teach physical education effectively is in constant flux as new approaches to pedagogy or simply new activities enter the school curriculum. In other words, learning PE content knowledge on its own – or just once during initial training – is never likely to be enough for a professional PE teacher.

> ### Comment
> *Effective teachers must have more than technical knowledge of different activities. They must be knowledgeable about different pedagogical approaches, underpinned by pedagogical models, and be able to use these to facilitate learning effectively.*

What should we know about how PE should be taught?

You will find many publications on the merits of different approaches to the teaching of PE in schools and they do not all agree. It is also important to note that whereas there are some things we know about good practice, there is still much more to be known. There is, however, plenty of evidence to suggest that *how* we teach PE can make a significant difference to the learning experiences for pupils. For example, groundbreaking work by Mosston (1966) identified a spectrum of teaching styles and this was the first comprehensive publication to reflect systematically on the range of different teaching styles that PE teachers might employ. This work has evolved over time and has resulted in research on the impact of different teaching styles on pupil learning in PE. Knowledge of its content is still a must for any aspiring (or practising) PE teacher. The authors characterised a range of different teaching styles, mainly with reference to the level of decision making that is accorded to the teacher or the pupils:

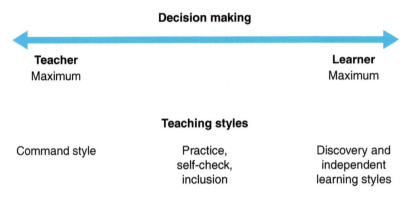

Figure 20.1 Teaching styles and decision making

Source: Adapted from Mosston, M. and Ashworth, S. (1986) *Teaching Physical Education*, Columbus, OH: Merrill

At one end of the spectrum are the teacher-led styles. Command-led styles and practice styles allow relatively little autonomy for pupils in the decision-making process. At the other end of the spectrum are the more pupil-oriented teaching styles, such as discovery-based teaching, and these open up opportunities for pupil thinking and experimentation which are not afforded by the teacher-led approaches. At the extreme pupil-led end of the spectrum, pupils have the opportunity to decide not only how they learn, but also what they learn (Salvara *et al.*, 2006; Sicilia-Camacho and Brown, 2008).

Towards the middle of the spectrum, an increase in pupil involvement in the learning process may be achieved through the use of reciprocal teaching styles, sometimes referred to as 'peer teaching' or 'peer assessment'. In such teaching approaches, pupils take on the role of teacher or coach and help their classmates with learning while, as part of the process, learning more themselves. The National Curriculum in England states explicitly that pupils should develop their skills to 'evaluate and improve their own and others' learning' (TDA, 2007) and many PE departments have incorporated 'peer learning/teaching' into their range of core teaching strategies. Frequently, this approach is now supported by increasingly flexible and affordable ICT tools, which pupils can use independently to review and enhance their own learning.

In my personal experience as a teacher trainer, I have found that trainee teachers during the early stages of their teaching practice have some reservations and fears about using teaching styles that give pupils autonomy in their learning. However, these apprehensions are often overcome as the benefits of such strategies start to become apparent: after all, how can pupils learn to think for themselves in PE if teachers constantly direct all that they do? As Frapwell (2010, p. 115) puts it: 'Improvement in learning can really start when all learners in the class are teachers.' Such observations would appear to coincide with the experiences of these two trainee PE teachers:

> They'll [the pupils] assess each other, they'll teach each other and then from that I will then give them another task card with their success criteria, to see, if have they met the objectives basically. Have they learnt, if so how have they learnt, what have they done to make that a good performance, how can they make it better? So I find that really useful for that.
> (Louise, trainee teacher)

> I definitely like discovery-based learning. When I teach football, I find it so interesting to see the ideas that pupils come up with. I think they're able to be more creative and express themselves and when you see how they are thinking.
> (James, trainee teacher)

The need for pupils to be involved in and responsible for their own learning is also reflected in influential pedagogical models used in teaching PE, such as Teaching Games for Understanding (TGfU) and Sport Education (SE). The TGfU approach was first conceived by Bunker, Almond and Thorpe in the 1980s at Loughborough University in England. It is based on the principle that pupils should learn to develop an understanding of how to play games through *playing games*. The emphasis is upon exploring individual and team tactical aspects in relevant games situations, rather than learning in de-contextualised skills practices. In this way, TGfU distinguishes itself from traditional skills-based approaches that, it is argued, lead to boredom, poor behaviour and poor learning experiences (Bunker and Thorpe, 1982). It is important to note, however, that the TGfU approach is not an easy option for teachers. The design of such lessons requires skilful planning and interventions that can help pupils to acquire relevant knowledge of individual and team tactics, as well as an appreciation of how these may be used in respective games situations. Teaching and learning strategies require pupil experimentation, pupil reflections and discussion as well as evaluation of pupils' actions and learning, supported by skilful teacher interventions and questioning.

Another approach to involving pupils centrally in the learning process is the Sport Education (SE) model, which was first devised by Siedentop (1994) in the United States. In SE, pupils take a range of roles such as manager, coach, referee or score keeper, whilst preparing for a 'season' in an allocated games activity, culminating in a final tournament. During the season, ranging typically from eight to 12 weeks (and sometimes more), pupils take responsibility for as many of the related activities and roles as possible (coaching the team, practice matches, arranging tournaments) whilst the teacher takes a facilitative and, where required, a 'troubleshooting' role. This ensures that pupils are offered opportunities to be as autonomous as possible within an enabling pedagogical framework (see also Chapter 25 by Toni O'Donovan for more detail on Sport Education). At the heart of both TGfU and SE is an emphasis on pupils learning collaboratively and cooperatively (McCaughtry *et al.*, 2004).

Cooperative learning approaches can be used in all areas of PE, including gymnastics, dance, athletics and swimming. In this approach, groups of pupils work together as independently as possible to create performances or team outcomes. Small numbers of pupils may become 'experts' in a particular aspect of learning, which they then proceed to teach to other pupils. This, in turn, frees the teacher to target their attention and input in the most effective ways. Many PE departments now make considerable efforts to extend pupils' abilities to take on leadership roles through the age ranges, often incorporating more formal leadership courses, typically into Year the 10/11 PE curriculum. Frequently, such teaching approaches also emphasise pupils' individual progress and mastery of new learning, rather than purely focusing on absolute achievement. Significant benefits for pupils' motivation can be achieved by such an emphasis on a mastery motivational climate (Morgan, 2003; Morgan *et al.*, 2005).

Conclusion

The principal idea behind the models outlined here – and the many variations of them – is to find ways to engage pupils actively in their own learning by allowing them to take charge of vital aspects of it. The knowledge required of the effective teacher is a thorough understanding of the range of facilitative teaching strategies, as well as considerable skill in implementing them in practice with diverse sets of pupils. Whilst such teaching approaches can be demanding of pupils and teachers, the rewards when pupils achieve their potential in a range of areas of learning can be significant. It is the ability to implement innovative, exciting approaches to teaching and learning that distinguishes outstanding teachers from the merely competent. To secure such excellence over the course of a career, a professional teacher requires an enduring commitment to the causes of both teacher and pupil learning. Only those teachers who are sufficiently dedicated to the continuous quest for better ways of teaching, and who remain fully committed to their own professional development, are likely to *become and remain* effective teachers of secondary PE (see also Chapter 18 on professional development by Kathleen Armour).

Learning tasks

Individual task

Make a list of all the reasons why you might like to become a PE teacher. For each reason you find, try to work out the origins of that reason and whether it is likely to have a positive, negative or neutral influence on your practice as a teacher.

Group task

In groups of four to six, engage in a 'challenge' session where you consider each individual's responses to the task above. Challenge the reasons given and influences identified from the point of view of different kinds of pupil learners. Prepare a group summary of the outcomes of your challenge session and share with peers.

Further reading

Tsangaridou, N. (2006) Teachers' knowledge. In: D. Kirk, D. Macdonald and M. O'Sullivan (eds) *Handbook of Physical Education*, London: Sage, 652–64.

References

Bailey, R. (2010) *Physical Education for Learning,* London: Continuum.

Bailey, R., Armour, K., Kirk, D., Jess, M., Pickup, I., Sandford, R., Education, BERA Physical and Group, Sport Pedagogy Special Interest (2009) The educational benefits claimed for physical education and school sport: an academic review, *Research Papers in Education*, 24(1), 1–27.

Bunker, D. and Thorpe, R. (1982) A model for the teaching of games in secondary schools, *The Bulletin of Physical Education*, 18(1), 5–8.

Cale, L. (2010) Becoming a teacher. In: R. Bailey (ed.) *Physical Education for Learning,* London: Continuum.

Capel, S. (2007) Moving beyond physical education subject knowledge to develop knowledgeable teachers of the subject, *Curriculum Journal*, 18(4), 493–507.

Chen, A. and Ennis, C. D. (1996) Teaching value-laden curricula in physical education, *Journal of Teaching in Physical Education*, 15(3), 338–54.

Curtner-Smith, M. D., Hastie, P. A. and Kinchin, G. D. (2008) Influence of occupational socialization on beginning teachers' interpretation and delivery of sport education, *Sport, Education and Society*, 13(1), 97–117.

Frapwell, A. (2010) Assessment for learning. In: R. Bailey (ed.) *Physical Education for Learning,* London: Continuum.

Gower, C. and Capel, S. (2004) Newly qualified physical education teachers' experiences of developing subject knowledge prior to, during and after a Postgraduate Certificate course in Physical Education, *Physical Education and Sport Pedagogy,* 9(2), 165–83.

Green, K. (2009) Exploring the everyday 'philosophies' of physical education teachers from a sociological perspective. In: R. Bailey and D. Kirk (eds) *The Routledge Physical Education Reader,* London: Routledge.

Hayes, S., Capel, S., Katene, W. and Cook, P. (2008) An examination of knowledge prioritisation in secondary physical education teacher education courses, *Teaching and Teacher Education* 24(2), 330–42.

Herold, F. and Waring, M. (2009) Pre-service physical education teachers' perceptions of subject knowledge: augmenting learning to teach, *European Physical Education Review*, 5(3), 337–64.

Keay, J. (2005) Developing the physical education profession: new teachers learning within a subject-based community, *Physical Education and Sport Pedagogy,* 10, 139–57.

McCaughtry, N., Sofo, S., Rovegno, I. and Curtner-Smith, M. D. (2004) Learning to teach sport education: misunderstandings, pedagogical difficulties, and resistance, *European Physical Education Review,* 10(2), 135–55.

Morgan, K. (2003) Teaching styles, progression and variety in athletics lessons, *British Journal of Teaching Physical Education*, 34(1), 12–14.

Morgan, K., Kingston, K. and Sproule, J. (2005) Effects of different teaching styles on the teacher behaviours that influence motivational climate and pupils' motivation in physical education, *European Physical Education Review*, 11(3), 257–85.

Mosston, M. (1966) *Teaching Physical Education*, Columbus, OH: Merrill.

Rovegno, I. (2008) Learning and instruction in social, cultural environments: promising research agendas, *Quest*, 60, 84–104.

Salvara, M. I., Jess, M., Abbott, A. and Bognar, J. (2006) A preliminary study to investigate the influence of different teaching styles on pupils' goal orientations in physical education, *European Physical Education Review*, 12(1), 51–74.

Shulman, L. (1987) Knowledge and teaching: foundation of the new reform, *Harvard Educational Review*, 57(1), 1–22.

Shulman, L. S. and Shulman, J. H. (2004) How and what teachers learn: a shifting perspective, *Journal of Curriculum Studies*, 36(2), 257–71.

Sicilia-Camacho, A. and Brown, D. (2008) Revisiting the paradigm shift from the versus to the non-versus notion of Mosston's spectrum of teaching styles in physical education pedagogy: a critical pedagogical perspective, *Physical Education and Sport Pedagogy* 13(1), 85–108.

Siedentop, D. (1994) *Sport Education: Quality PE through positive sport experiences*, Champaign, IL: Human Kinetics.

Siedentop, D. (2002) Content knowledge for physical education, *Journal of Teaching in Physical Education* 21(4), 368–77.

TDA (2007) *Professional Standards for Teachers: Qualified Teacher Status*, London: TDA, available from: www.tda.gov.uk, accessed 23 July 2010.

Tinning, R. (2002) Engaging Siedentopian perspectives on content knowledge in physical education, *Journal of Teaching in Physical Education*, 21(4), 378–91.

Tsangaridou, N. (2006) Teachers' knowledge. In: D. Kirk, D. Macdonald and M. O'Sullivan (eds) *Handbook of Physical Education*, London: Sage, 652–64.

Becoming an effective primary school physical education teacher

Mike Jess, University of Edinburgh

 ## Introduction

This chapter revolves around two different stories. In the first, still mirrored in many primary classes, primary physical education (PE) is relatively easy to teach; perhaps the teacher could even view it as a break from the real work of the classroom. The second story, however, portrays a more complex primary PE focused on children's learning and the contribution PE makes to children's overall education. It may be helpful to read this chapter in conjunction with Chapter 11 by Frances Murphy and Dierdre Ní Chroinin on the needs of younger learners in physical education and youth sport.

Story 1: Teaching primary PE – it's easy

A few years ago, while driving past a local primary school, I saw a PE lesson underway. The children were playing rounders. To be precise, most were watching the teacher play rounders with a small number of children. Neither the teacher nor the pupils had changed into kit appropriate for participation in a sport activity. The class was made up of about 30 children, half of whom were standing ready to field, while the other half were standing in a line waiting to bat. Some fielders were talking in pairs because the teacher was intent on bowling and organising the batters. When their turn came to bat, most children either missed the ball and sat down or managed a weak hit that sent the ball dribbling along the ground to a fielder close by.

(continued)

Occasionally, one of the batters had a big hit and everyone clapped. I watched for 20 minutes and, all in all, although I could say the children seemed to be enjoying themselves, I would also have to say that they were not doing much at all.

Comment
Can you recall a PE session like this?

Story 2: Teaching primary PE – it's complex

More recently, I came across a different rounders lesson. As I approached the classroom, I saw a noticeboard headed 'Primary 6 Rounders Championships 2009'. There were team sheets with team names, roles for each team member, current league positions, match scores, match reports, team pictures and action pictures; all created by the children. Whilst still in the classroom, the teacher was busy organising the children into their teams so they could plan what was about to happen and also, with some prompting, which tasks different team members were to undertake. Outside, while one team set up the equipment, the other teams worked on a rounders-related warm-up led by one of their team mates. Once everything was ready, the teacher taught a fielding practice which involved getting to the ball quickly, collecting it effectively and sending to the wicketkeeper. The children, in threes, practised taking on different roles after each six throws. The teacher stood back, observed, gave feedback and supported the groups, particularly those that were struggling. A quick recap of key technical points was followed by a rich discussion within each team about how this practice might look in the game. Then, following a recap of the main technical and safety points, each team organised a striking practice in their 'home field'. The children worked in fours using a task sheet prepared by the teacher. Again, the teacher stood back, ensured everyone was 'on task', moved around observing and fed back on positive and less positive aspects. The session finished with each team playing a small-sided game in their 'home field', focusing on striking and fielding and making sure everyone got an opportunity to bat, bowl and field. Four of the teams did this activity well, but the other two found it difficult to work together, so the teacher interceded to discuss how they could support each other more effectively. At the end of the games, the teams reported back on what they would need to practise before the next league game. Finally, the children recapped the main points from the session, and the teacher reported that there would be team meetings in class to prepare for the next league games. As they headed back to the classroom, one of the team captains asked if his team could do some fielding practice during the morning breaks.

Comment
Do you recall a PE or sport experience (or any educational experience) similar to this? How did it make you feel?

Based on an investigation of the differences between these two stories, this chapter considers what primary teachers need to understand and what they need to do to *shift* their pedagogy from the limited 'PE is easy' story to the complex and more educationally valid example provided by the second story.

Teaching primary PE: why is it easy?

The 'PE is easy' version of a lesson has its roots in a long-held belief that although PE should be *universally* included in primary schools, it is also a *peripheral* part of the curriculum: i.e. a break from the real work that takes place in a classroom (Williams, 1989). Twenty years have passed since Williams's comments, but there are compelling reasons why this version of primary PE persists in some places. Almost all primary PE is taught by generalist teachers who are required to teach between ten and 15 different subject areas. For the majority, their initial teacher education/training experiences in PE were limited, and continuing professional development (PE CPD) is likely to be inadequate (Duncombe and Armour, 2004; Her Majesty's Inspectorate of Education, 2001). In addition, if teachers had poor personal PE experiences at school, they may be reticent about teaching the subject (Morgan and Bourke, 2008; Morgan and Hansen, 2008; Pickup and Price, 2007). Furthermore, the senior management of primary schools – all of whom are also primary teachers themselves – are likely to hold similar views to their colleagues, resulting in low levels of support for the subject.

As a result of all of these factors, there are large numbers of primary teachers who do not have the desire, confidence or compunction to view PE as a core part of children's learning. It is important to note that this is not a universal view, and that in several countries steps have been taken to improve the learning experience for primary school children. Examples include the PESSYP project in England (Sport England/Youth Sport Trust, 2009), the SPARKS programme in the USA (Dowda *et al.*, 2005) and the SPPE project in Scotland (Jess and Campbell, 2008). Nonetheless, the idea that PE is somehow 'different' from other parts of the curriculum persists (Atencio, Jess and Dewar, in press).

The PE profession has long been aware of the limitations of practice in primary schools, yet specialist PE training has traditionally been reserved for secondary school teachers. As such, this specialist training is focused on the PE activities of the secondary school curriculum, leaving little, if any, space for consideration of the needs of younger children. It seems unlikely, therefore, that these specialists will be able to do much more than offer a 'watered-down' version of what happens in the secondary school (Jess and Collins, 2003). There are, however, some signs of progress in recent years with new PE-related posts in primary schools, e.g. School Sport Coordinators (SSCos) and Primary Link Teachers (PLTs) in England and Active Schools Coordinators in Scotland. As yet, there is some uncertainty as to the impact of these new posts.

> **Comment**
> PE has sometimes been viewed as a 'break' from the 'real' work of educating children.

Teaching primary PE: it's complex

In stark contrast to the easy version, complex primary PE is very different. In particular, the first story presents children as passive participants, whereas the second reveals a very different level of engagement. In the complex story, children are not only (comparatively) more physically active, they are centrally involved in decision making, in discussing and reflecting, and they have many more collaborative and competitive interactions. The session described is vibrant, rich and edgy, and it is clear that some children find different aspects of the work challenging yet engaging. The teacher is less in evidence, but only because much pre-planning and scaffolding of children's knowledge, understanding and behaviour have already taken place. Direct teaching is in use, but there is also evidence of the teacher standing back to observe and nudge and guide learning through questioning, discussion and feedback. The children have a sense of ownership of the rounders experience because they had the opportunity to vote to make rounders the focus sport for a season. Moreover, the complex rounders experience is not an isolated learning experience; instead it is closely connected to other work in the classroom. Literacy, numeracy, art and ICT are all in evidence – for example in the match reports and the pictures – alongside the cognitive, social and emotional learning already discussed. This complex scenario locates primary PE as an integral part of children's education with a focus on 'learning to move' and 'moving to learn'.

> **Comment**
> *Primary PE can be a complex, collaborative and connected learning experience for children and teachers.*

Shifting from easy to complex PE: a career-long journey

A question arises from these two stories: how can primary teachers be encouraged and supported to teach the more complex version of PE? The answer is complex, and there is no quick fix; yet this is an important question to address. Children spend more years in compulsory education in the primary school years than they do in secondary school. This would seem to suggest that the PE profession should be focused on creating developmentally appropriate primary PE programmes. In addition, generalist teachers in primary schools ought to view PE CPD as a serious lifelong endeavour in the interests of the pupils for whom they have a professional responsibility.

Perhaps it is inappropriate to argue that *all* generalist class teachers should prioritise PE, particularly when they have to teach so many curriculum subjects. It certainly could be argued, however, that a larger cohort of primary teachers is needed to support children's learning in PE and also to support colleagues in making the shift to a more complex pedagogy. As was noted earlier, efforts are being made in many countries to do just this and the chapter will now consider the example of one such country, Scotland.

Making things better for children: an example from Scotland

Since devolution from the UK in 1999, primary PE in Scotland has made remarkable progress. Following a depressing report from Her Majesty's Inspectorate of Education in 2001, primary PE has emerged as a topic of political (Scottish Executive, 2003, 2004), academic (Marsden and Weston, 2007) and professional (Jess and Dewar, 2008) interest. In 2006, the Scottish government set up the Scottish primary PE Project (SPPEP), which was an innovative collaboration between government, local authorities and universities. This has resulted in almost 1,000 generalist primary teachers enrolling on postgraduate Master's level primary PE programmes to act as the platform for a national professional learning pathway in primary PE. Throughout this period of rapid progress, the Developmental Physical Education Group (DPEG) at the University of Edinburgh has been engaged in a longitudinal project to design, deliver and evaluate a developmentally appropriate PE programme for the three to-14-age range (Jess, Atencio and Thorburn, in press; Thorburn, Jess and Atencio, 2009). Underpinned by complexity theory, the DPEG's work has focused on creating a better understanding of how to support teachers to engage in a change agenda that will shift them from 'PE is easy' to 'PE is complex' (Atencio, Jess and Dewar, in press).

Two interrelated factors have emerged as significant catalysts in this pedagogical shift:

- embracing and understanding the complex nature of PE;
- shifting from behaviourist teaching to complex pedagogy.

Embracing and understanding the complex nature of PE

The starting point for change is ensuring that teachers are genuinely interested in children's learning in PE. One of the key ways to do this is to recognise that PE connects to children's wider education and to their lives outside school, and that the challenge is to help all children to develop a solid foundation for their current and future participation in physical activity and sport (Penney and Jess, 2004; Bailey et al., 2009). A solid basic movement foundation allows children to pass through the proficiency barrier between the simple activities of early childhood to the more complex activities of later childhood (Jess, Dewar and Fraser, 2004). This barrier can be formidable and finding ways through it cannot be left to chance. Some children have the natural ability and desire, and the necessary support, to develop a movement foundation in or outside school, e.g. in family or community youth sport settings. For many children, however, school PE is their only access to physical activity and sport. It could be argued, therefore, that leaving specialist PE teaching until they reach secondary school is too late for many children, particularly those who do not have access to other forms of youth sport (Kirk, 2005).

The challenge for generalist primary teachers who embark upon a pedagogical journey in order to teach complex PE is considerable. One way to begin is to develop an understanding of three interrelated factors that highlight the complexity of primary PE. These factors align closely with the three dimensions of sport pedagogy proposed by Kathleen Armour in Chapter 1. Like Armour's three complex dimensions, the three interrelated factors are both complex in themselves and become more complex as they interact in each learning and teaching episode. The three interrelated factors are (see Figure 21.1):

- the learning in PE that constitutes a solid foundation for participation;
- the impact of children's previous experiences and current developmental level upon their learning in PE;
- the influence of the immediate context on the PE experience.

Physical educationists (e.g. Graham, Holt/Hale and Parker, 2007) are increasingly focusing on the learning that helps children to develop a solid PE foundation. This is encouraging as primary PE in practice has tended to simply mirror the multi-activity secondary school curriculum model. This model emphasises coverage of various physical activities

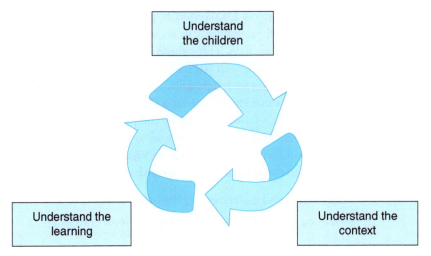

Figure 21.1 Understanding the complex nature of primary PE

and sports for short 'blocks' of time, usually four to six weeks. For example, children experience a 'block' of one game, then perhaps dance, then another game, then gymnastics and so on. Kirk (2004) has, however, expressed some concerns about the cumulative effect of this approach:

- Learning can be limited, because specific activity content is taught to all children whether or not they are ready for it.
- The emphasis on content coverage leads to limited practice time.
- The content of each 'block' is often disconnected from other PE activities, other curriculum subjects or activities in which the children participate in and outside school.

As such, it could be argued that the multi-activity approach fits most closely with the 'PE is easy' scenario, because it encourages teachers to take a sampling approach to different activities; in other words, there is rarely an opportunity for 'deep' learning. Furthermore, even for those generalists who enjoy teaching PE, the attempt to cover content in such a short period of time tends to lead to the adoption of direct, controlling pedagogies. Interestingly, such a direct approach may differ markedly from the more participative pedagogies these same teachers adopt in their classrooms. Controlling pedagogies also make it very difficult to plan for effective differentiation because the focus of the lesson is on covering activity content rather than on the children's learning.

Comment
The short 'block' multi-activity model can seriously limit children's learning in PE.

Recently, the DPEG's attempts to address these superficial learning scenarios have concentrated on creating a connected PE curriculum that focuses on:

- core learning that is central to participation in different physical activities;
- learning that connects PE with other areas of the primary curriculum;
- authentic learning experiences connected to children's 'real lives'.

Core learning experiences focus on the movement, critical thinking and interpersonal and emotional skills that will help children to develop strong foundations for the various PE and sport contexts they will meet as they get older (Gallahue and Cleland-Donnelly, 2003). Much of this cognitive, social and emotional learning also connects to the classroom and community settings, e.g. working with others and coping with winning and losing. As such, complex PE is not driven by specific activity content, but by generic core learning that is connective across a range of contexts.

During the early years of preschool and primary school (ages two to seven years), core learning approaches focus on a basic movement foundation (Pickup and Price, 2007). This foundation seeks to develop a range of generic basic movements and encourages adaptability and creativity as key contributors to effective learning in PE (Jess et al., 2004). As children move through the primary years of schooling, activity 'blocks' are introduced gradually, but these are presented as authentic applications linked to core learning in 'real-life' contexts. For example, in the second rounders story that opened this chapter, the children were encouraged to connect their learning in rounders to their wider learning in the classroom, resulting in 'authentic' learning (Lave and Wenger, 1991; Rovegno, 2006). Authentic learning activities are, typically, timetabled for longer periods of time than in a multi-activity approach, and there is a close link here with the ideas presented in the Sport Education model (Siedentop, 1994), which are now being extended to dance, outdoor education (Beames and Atencio, 2008) and other aspects of physical activity.

> **Comment**
> *Core and authentic learning connect to wider educational and community contexts.*

Understanding the developing child

The experiences children have outside school, along with their stage of psychomotor, cognitive, social and emotional development, make a significant contribution to their engagement in PE. Teachers with limited understanding of these external influences and developmental changes are unlikely to be able to offer children developmentally appropriate learning experiences. Over time, this limitation can impact negatively on children's attitudes towards PE. It is important, therefore, for teachers not only to track children's out-of-school experiences in sport and physical activity, but also to understand the impact these experiences may have on their engagement in PE.

Whilst psychomotor developments play a key role in PE learning, cognitive, social and emotional changes also influence children's abilities to engage (Haywood and Getchell, 2009). For example, young children (ages two to seven years) often find it difficult to retain a series of facts and to participate effectively in a group (Gallahue and Ozmun, 2006). Games involving complex rules and teamwork tend, therefore, to be beyond their developmental abilities at this time. However, young children (up to the age of about nine or ten years) have high – and often inaccurate – perceptions of their own ability (Jess and Collins, 2003; Kirk, 2005; Lee, Carter and Xiang, 1995) and most are happy to attempt various tasks. Importantly, as children move through the upper primary years (ages eight to 12 years), they are increasingly able to remember rules and work effectively in group situations, and so can gradually access the more complex forms of games, dance and gymnastics (Pickup and Price, 2007). At the same time, children become more adept at comparing themselves accurately with peers in terms of physical performance and, particularly in the case of girls, how they 'look' as they move (Carlson Jones, 2001). This has a significant impact on the PE setting because complex social and emotional issues begin to emerge that can result in challenges to children's perceived competence and self-esteem levels. It could be argued that these challenges are at the root of the disaffection that is seen in the high drop-out figures from PE in secondary schools, particularly amongst girls (Vescio, Wilde and Crosswhite, 2005).

Comment
Supporting cognitive, social and emotional learning in PE is important.

From the teacher's perspective, understanding how psychomotor development impacts on children's PE performance is the key to designing appropriate learning experiences for all children. Children's growth is the most obvious developmental factor, particularly as all children grow at different rates. Generally, young children (ages two to seven years) are not only smaller than their older counterparts, but they also have body shapes less conducive to proficient movement performance. Proportionately larger heads and shorter legs mean a high centre of gravity, which makes travelling and balance movements problematic. Young children's movement is further constrained by relatively underdeveloped muscles, an incomplete myelination process (sheathing of the neural pathways which carry the movement impulses to the limbs) and limited ability to track moving objects. Consequently, young children have difficulty in moving for extended periods, controlling peripheral limbs and receiving objects.

Understanding the impact of these developmental characteristics helps teachers to scaffold children's learning of basic movements through this foundation period. Conversely, the upper primary years (ages eight to 12 years) are referred to as the 'skill-hungry' years, because most children have the potential to consolidate and extend their movement performance (Gallahue and Ozmun, 2006). By this stage, growth rate is stable, body shape is more conducive to efficient movement, the myelination process is almost complete, strength is comparatively greater and the ability to track moving objects improved. What this means is that by this stage, most children are able to move faster, jump further and throw harder than when they were younger. Yet, importantly, if the basic movement foundation has not been developed appropriately in the early years, the quality of movements remains poor for many children and the opportunity to consolidate, extend and apply movement ability is curtailed. This places a significant responsibility on primary teachers and yet, as was noted earlier, few of these teachers are trained to support children in PE with confidence and skill.

Comment
Primary teachers need to understand the influence of children's psychomotor development on their PE engagement.

Understanding the context

Understanding context is vital. The context for primary PE can vary dramatically from school to school, and it certainly varies in different national contexts. Teachers need to evaluate how the key factors in these different settings impact on the potential for learning in PE. In terms of facilities, many schools have a hall for indoor PE which doubles as the dining hall. This can mean that PE has to stop either side of lunch to allow for set-up, etc. Some schools do have a dedicated gymnasium, yet in other small rural schools, it might be the norm to move the desks back in the classroom in order to create a space for PE. Some schools have outdoor fields, others a hard playground area, while others have almost no outdoor space at all.

Considering PE equipment, some schools have accessible, modern equipment, whereas others have heavy gymnastic equipment (perhaps inherited from a secondary school), heavy mats and half-inflated balls. Other key contextual factors include teachers' attitudes and training, children's responses to PE, the nature/structure of the designated PE time, support from outside agencies in the locality, any help from additional support staff and the expectations held by senior managers in the school. In complex PE, teachers routinely analyse the positive and negative features of their contexts and are able to take these into account in order to plan effective learning experiences.

> **Comment**
> Context matters. An analysis of context is a key component of complex PE.

What can be concluded from all of this is that understanding the appropriate learning experiences for children, the developmental factors that impact on children's engagement in PE and the different contextual factors influencing the PE experience, even before a lesson is taught, shift primary PE from 'easy' towards 'complex' pedagogy.

Shifting from teaching behaviourist to complex pedagogy

As teachers build their understanding of the developing child, core and applied PE learning and the teaching context, they can engage increasingly with a complex pedagogy (see Table 21.1). This moves them beyond the behaviourist teaching approach characterised in the easy version of primary PE presented at the beginning of this chapter. Behaviourist pedagogies can be compared with complex pedagogies as shown in Table 21.1.

Behaviourism underpins those teaching strategies associated with direct instruction. It centres on explicit teaching and is regarded as a 'teacher-centred' approach to teaching and learning (Rink, 2001). Behaviourist pedagogy, particularly in the multi-activity PE model described earlier, is characterised by a certainty of what is to be learned and a prescriptive, top-down delivery style. Because of its underpinning certainty, the expectation is that all children will learn similar things, in the same way and will follow a linear and stable learning curve. As a result, it can be argued that learning experiences are de-contextualised and are largely 'closed', placing children as passive recipients in a predetermined learning process. In this approach, learning tends to be at the 'surface' level rather than a 'deep' level (Jess *et al.*, in press).

Complex pedagogy, on the other hand, is different, particularly when connected to a complex notion of primary PE. For example, learning expectations are higher, but the

Table 21.1 Behaviourist and complex pedagogy
Source: Adapted from Jess *et al*, in press

Behaviourist pedagogy	Complex pedagogy
• Passive participation	• Active participation
• Received action	• Self-determined action
• Individualised	• Collaborative
• Stable expectations	• Emergent expectations
• Closed context	• Open context
• Summative feedback	• Formative feedback
• Superficial evaluation	• Reflective evaluation
• Fragment experiences	• Scaffold experiences
• Compartmentalised	• Connected
• De-contextualised	• Authentic

precise outcomes are less prescriptive, and children are more actively involved in the learning process. In complex pedagogy, children will be engaged in collaboration, discussion, questioning and bottom-up decision making underpinned by shared learning intentions. Learning experiences are much more open-ended and, similarly to those experienced in 'real life', supported by formative feedback and reflection. This includes reflection on how learning connects to classroom and community contexts. Thus, complex pedagogy offers children meaningful and 'rich' tasks which encourage a self-organising learning process, and which connect children's learning experiences, leading to deeper learning. It is important to point out, however, that complex pedagogy requires a range of teaching approaches as befits a complex learning process, and this would include behaviourist teaching where appropriate.

> *Comment*
> *You may recognise both behaviourist and complex pedagogies from different aspects of your education to date.*

Complex pedagogy in practice

Putting complex pedagogy into practice is in itself complex. Teachers need to add to their knowledge base continuously, assess constantly and reflect regularly on session outcomes. The following section identifies ten issues to be addressed when attempting to employ a complex pedagogy. The list is by no means exhaustive and each issue can only be covered briefly. Nonetheless, these are considerations that offer practical guidance on the ways in which teachers can begin the process of shifting towards more complex pedagogies.

Do a baseline assessment

Undertaking a detailed baseline assessment early in the school year will help teachers to create PE programmes that are best suited to the particular children in any class. Not only should teachers find out about children's previous experiences in physical activity and sport (both in and out of school), they should also assess children's psychomotor, cognitive, social and emotional development in the PE context. For example, teachers should be able to assess children's physical ability, what they know about PE, how critically they are able to think in PE, how well they collaborate and compete and what they feel about PE. There are many ways to plan this baseline assessment, but if the primary PE programme is to focus on children's learning, the more the teacher knows about the children the better.

Identify appropriate learning intentions and activities

From the baseline assessment, teachers are ready to identify learning intentions that are appropriate to specific individuals and groups, and this may require children's input into the planning process. These learning intentions will not only be in the physical domain, although that is the main focus of PE, but will include cognitive, social and emotional learning. The aim is to create competent movers, critical thinkers, collaborative and competitive learners and emotionally intelligent performers. The planned learning experiences that support the learning intentions result in a wide range of different tasks for children, including performing, demonstrating, copying, exploring, guiding, creating, problem solving, questioning, discussing, sharing, collaborating, competing, feeding back, using task sheets, peer tutoring, working in stations and reflecting. Such a PE experience is much more than a purely physical experience.

Use the classroom

As was noted earlier, in a primary school with limited facilities, time in the hall or other PE facility can be precious. Yet many important learning experiences, particularly the non-physical ones, can take place in the classroom. Before the PE lesson begins, the class can discuss learning intentions, equipment organisation, safety and introductory activities. After the session, plenary and next-step discussions can be held in the classroom. In addition, in order to connect PE with other curriculum areas, literacy, numeracy, art and ICT tasks based on PE and sport are all potentially rich learning activities that can occur in the classroom.

Structure sessions to maximise practice and authentic learning

PE sessions can be structured in many different ways, although most include an introductory activity, a development section focusing on whole-class activity, an application section to help children demonstrate their learning in contexts like games, dance and gymnastics, and a plenary to recap key learning points and consider ways forward. If the application section comes early in the session, this may help to ensure that learning experiences are made authentic for children. The way in which practice time is structured also requires close consideration. Whilst creating the first DPEG programme, Basic Moves, which focused on children in the five-to-seven age range (Jess, 2004), small-group learning stations were introduced as a key component of the primary PE session (Graham, 2008). By structuring these learning stations to include intensive work with small groups, the teacher is able to check that learning has been consolidated or can move children onto the next level. Research suggests that class teachers regularly incorporate this type of intensive, small-group approach – in addition to whole-class teaching and non-intensive group work – in the classroom, but are more hesitant to use it in PE (Thorburn *et al.*, 2009). However, this important activity helps teachers to track children's progress and enhances the likelihood of children being presented with appropriate learning experiences. This is a complex task for teachers and requires detailed planning to ensure that, while the teacher works intensively with one group, all other groups are appropriately and safely engaged in tasks that do not require specific input by the teacher. From a safety perspective, teachers need to ensure that they are able to see all children even when positioning themselves to work with the intensive group.

Manage the learning environment

The PE environment is structurally different from the classroom, but many management tasks are the same. Organisational instructions should be concise, although it is essential to check that children understand the specifics of the task and any safety issues. Young children can become so excited when moving that they listen to only half of the instructions before rushing to complete the task (Jalongo, 2010). In addition, as was noted above, when children are working on tasks it is critical that the teacher is positioned to observe all the children. This is not as difficult as it may seem, and is usually best achieved by keeping the teacher's back to the outside wall and avoiding moving into the middle of the hall so that some children are out of view.

Demonstrate!

Demonstrations are an excellent teaching aid. Children rely heavily on visual information (Rink and Hall, 2008) so a visual representation of complex movements is helpful. Yet using demonstration effectively can be a challenge because the teacher needs to ensure that: the demonstration (by child, video or teacher) is appropriate, the children know what they are looking for, and the class is organised so that the key points can be seen. Nonetheless, demonstrations are a valuable teaching and learning tool, and they offer rich opportunities for group analysis and discussions.

Observe and analyse

Effective observation and analysis are the basis of complex pedagogy for teachers as these actions synthesise many of the complex elements of primary PE. Observing and analysing children's movement performance are the keys to supporting learning as they enable the teacher to assess progress, offer feedback and discuss different ways to address tasks. In addition, the teacher also observes in order to see if the children are engaged safely, and whether it is time to stop, change tasks or discuss specific issues. Developing observation skills and offering feedback are key features in developing effective complex pedagogy.

Engage the children

In the classroom, primary teachers routinely use questioning, discussion, problem solving and reflection (Haywood and Devlin, 2007). Many teachers, however, seem to find it difficult to transfer these skills to their PE lessons, particularly if they are wedded to a behaviourist pedagogy in PE. For children to be actively engaged in the learning process, it is important they develop the appropriate cognitive, social and emotional skills to discuss, problem solve, create, support, share and reflect on their work. If teachers wish to bring PE to life for children, they need to consider how the critical thinking, collaborative skills and emotional intelligence techniques they employ in the classroom setting can be transferred to the PE setting. Regular opportunities to engage in discussion, supported by teacher input, are key features of a complex PE pedagogy.

Use assessment to support learning

Research has highlighted the critical role assessment plays in the learning process (Penney *et al.,* 2009; Shepard, 2000). In complex PE, by constantly employing a range of assessment techniques such as observation, video analysis, questioning, quizzes, discussions, peer assessments, creative tasks and many others, teachers will not only track children's learning over time, but will also be able to inform the learning process by feeding back to children and deciding next steps. As such, assessment is seen as an integral part of pedagogy and not something that is added on at the end of an activity 'block'.

Reflection

This final issue, like assessment, is a constant feature of complex PE. Reflection about the positive and negative aspects of the total PE experience is essential for the ongoing development of many aspects of a PE programme: planning, delivery, assessment, children's engagement, contextual issues, teacher knowledge, etc. This reflective process feeds back into the programme so that changes – sometimes major changes – can be made in order to enhance the learning process. Without reflection, a PE programme can become static, possibly even edging back to a 'PE is easy' scenario similar to the one presented at the beginning of the chapter.

> **Comment**
> *These ten steps represent key actions for any teacher (or coach) who wishes to shift their practice towards a complex – and educational – version of primary PE.*

Conclusion

By analysing the differences between two very different approaches to primary PE, this chapter has made the argument that teachers need to make a fundamental shift away from the traditional multi-activity curriculum model of primary PE with its accompanying behaviourist teaching approach. In its place, a complex version of primary PE is proposed that requires teachers to develop a much more detailed understanding of their young learners and their developmental needs, the core and authentic learning experiences in PE that act as a foundation for future learning, and the context in which PE is being taught.

By developing these understandings, it is argued that teachers can move from a controlling teaching style that is focused on restricted learning outcomes towards a complex pedagogy that seeks to actively engage all children in the learning process. In this way, teachers can create authentic experiences that connect PE with children's wider education and to their lives outside school. Looking back to Kathy Armour's comments (Chapter 1) about teachers, coaches and their professional responsibility to meet children's needs, it could be argued that complex PE is the only way forward.

Learning tasks

Individual task

From your personal experience of working with primary school children, or from your memories of being a young learner, write a short narrative (maximum 500 words) on the essence of a 'complex pedagogy' for teachers and coaches.

Group task

In groups of four, create a 20-question quiz based on the key issues raised in this chapter. The quiz will be completed by a group of your fellow students and you will mark the answers. You must produce a mark sheet with the expected answers.

Further reading

Graham, G. (2008) *Teaching Children Physical Education: Becoming a master teacher*, Champaign, IL: Human Kinetics discusses many of the practical pedagogy issues raised in this chapter.

References

Armour, K. (2010) What is 'sport pedagogy' and why study it?. In: Armour, K. (this volume).

Atencio, M., Jess, M. and Dewar, K. (in press) 'It is a case of changing your thought processes, the way you actually teach': implementing a complex professional learning agenda in Scottish physical education, *Sport, Education and Society.*

Bailey, R., Armour, K., Kirk, D., Jess, M., Pickup, I., Sandford, R., BERA Physical and Sport Pedagogy Special Interest Group (2009) The educational benefits claimed for physical education and school sport: an academic review, *Research Papers in Education*, 24/1, 1–27.

Beames, S. and Atencio, M. (2008) Building social capital through outdoor education, *Journal of Adventure Education & Outdoor Learning*, 8(2), 99–112.

Carlson Jones, D. (2001) Social comparison and body image: attractiveness comparisons to models and peers among adolescent girls and boys, *Sex Roles*, 45 (9/10), 645–64.

Dowda, M.C., Sallis, J. F., McKenzie, T. L., Rosengard, P. R. and Kohl, H. W. (2005) Evaluating the sustainability of SPARK physical education: a case study of translating research into practice, *Research Quarterly for Exercise and Sport*, 76, 11–19.

Duncombe, R. and Armour, K. M. (2004) Collaborative professional learning: from theory to practice, *Professional Development in Education*, 30(1), 141–66.

Gallahue, D. L. and Cleland-Donnelly, F. (2003) *Developmental Physical Education for All Children* (4th edn), Champaign, IL: Human Kinetics.

Gallahue, D. L. and Ozmun, J. C. (2006) *Understanding Motor Development: Infants, children, adolescents, adults* (6th edn), Boston: McGraw-Hill.

Graham, G. (2008) *Teaching Children Physical Education* (3rd edn), Champaign, IL: Human Kinetics.

Graham, G., Holt/Hale, S. A. and Parker, M. (2007) *Children Moving: A reflective approach to teaching physical education* (7th edn), Upper Saddle River, NJ: McGraw-Hill.

Haywood, L. and Devlin, A. (2007) *Assessment for Learning: What do teachers think of formative assessment?*, Glasgow: University of Glasgow.

Haywood, K. and Getchell, N. (2009) *Lifespan Motor Development* (5th edn), Champaign, IL: Human Kinetics.

Her Majesty's Inspectorate of Education (2001) *Improving Physical Education in Primary Schools*, Edinburgh: HMSO.

Jalongo, M. R. (2010) Listening in early childhood: an interdisciplinary review of the literature, *International Journal of Listening*, 24/1, 1–18.

Jess, M. (2004) *The Basic Moves Level 1 Manual*, Edinburgh: University of Edinburgh.

Jess, M., Atencio, M. and Thorburn, M. (in press) Complexity theory: supporting curriculum and pedagogy developments in Scottish physical education, *Sport, Education and Society*.

Jess, M. and Campbell, T. (2008) *Professional Qualifications in Primary PE*, Paper presented at the Scottish Teacher Education Conference, University of Glasgow, 28 April 2008.

Jess, M. and Collins, D. (2003) Primary physical education in Scotland: the future in the making, *European Journal of Physical Education*, 8(2), 103–18.

Jess, M. and Dewar, K. (2008) Primary physical education and teachers' continuing professional development at the University of Edinburgh: a look into the future, *Physical Education Matters*, 3(1), 21–5.

Jess, M., Dewar, K. and Fraser G. (2004) Basic moves: developing a foundation for lifelong physical activity, *The British Journal of Teaching Physical Education*, 35, 23–7.

Kirk, D. (2004) New practices, new subjects and critical inquiry: possibility and progress. In: J. Wright, D. Macdonald and L. Burrows (eds) *Critical Inquiry and Problem-solving in Physical Education* London: Routledge, 199–208.

Kirk, D. (2005) Physical education, youth sport and lifelong participation: the importance of early learning experiences, *European Physical Education Review*, 11(3), 239–55.

Lave, J. and Wenger, E. (1991) *Situated Learning: Legitimate peripheral participation*, New York: Cambridge University Press.

Lee, A. M., Carter J. A. and Xiang, P. (1995) Children's conceptions of ability in physical education, *Journal of Teaching in Physical Education*, 14(4), 384–93.

Marsden, E. and Weston, C. (2007) Locating quality physical education in early years pedagogy, *Sport, Education and Society*, 12(4), 383–98.

Morgan, P. and Bourke, S. (2008) Non-specialist teachers' confidence to teach PE: the nature and influence of personal school experiences in PE, *Physical Education and Sport Pedagogy*, 13(1), 1–29.

Morgan, P. J. and Hansen, V. (2008) The relationship between PE biographies and PE teaching practices of classroom teachers, *Sport, Education and Society*, 13(4), 373–91.

Penney, D., Brooker, R., Hay, P. and Gillespie, L. (2009) Curriculum, pedagogy and assessment: three message systems of schooling and dimensions of quality physical education, *Sport, Education and Society*, 14(4), 421–42.

Penney, D. and Jess, M. (2004) Physical education and physically active lives: a lifelong approach to curriculum development, *Sport, Education and Society*, 9, 4, 269–87.

Pickup, I. and Price, L. (2007) *Teaching Physical Education in the Primary School: A developmental approach*, London: Continuum.

Rink, J. E. (2001) Investigating the assumptions of pedagogy, *Journal of Teaching in Physical Education*, 20, 112–28.

Rink, J. E. and Hall, T. J. (2008) Research on effective teaching in elementary school physical education, *The Elementary School Journal*, 108(3), 207–18.

Rovegno, I. (2006) Situated perspectives on learning. In: D. Kirk, D. Macdonald and M. O'Sullivan (eds) *The Handbook of Physical Education*, London: SAGE, 262–74.

Scottish Executive (2003) *Let's Make Scotland More Active: A strategy for physical activity,* Edinburgh, HMSO.

Scottish Executive (2004) *The Report of the Review Group on Physical Education,* Edinburgh, HMSO.

Shepard, L. A. (2000) The role of assessment in a learning culture, *Educational Researcher,* 29(7), 4–14.

Siedentop, D. (1994) *Sport Education,* Champaign, IL: Human Kinetics.

Sport England/Youth Sport Trust (2009) *The PE and Sport Strategy for Young People,* London: Sport England and Youth Sport Trust.

Thorburn, M., Jess, M. and Atencio, M. (2009) Connecting policy aspirations with principled progress? An analysis of current physical education challenges in Scotland, *Irish Educational Studies,* 28(2), 209–23.

Vescio, J., Wilde, K. and Crosswhite, J. J. (2005) Profiling sport role models to enhance initiatives for adolescent girls in physical education and sport, *European Physical Education Review,* 11(2), 153–70.

Williams, A. (1989) The place of physical education in primary education. In: A. Williams (ed.) *Issues in Primary Physical Education,* London: Falmer Press.

22

Becoming an effective youth sport coach

Julia Walsh, University College, Cork

If only I knew then what I know now, but then again it might be about experience. When I started coaching it was about me, how can I manage and control these athletes. It was about skills and drills and control of the environment. This wasn't coaching, it was military training and when I look back I am not sure what connection it had to the game. Now when I work with young people I start from a completely different space. It is about understanding them and serving their needs, supporting them on their sporting and personal journey . . . you have to be prepared to stretch the rubber band . . . Given the opportunity to start my coaching again I am not sure how different it would be, experience, mentoring and reflection were important parts of my learning, I suppose you can't rush learning and I had to learn as well.

(Youth performance coach, personal communication)

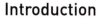 ## Introduction

Becoming an effective coach takes time, experience and a supportive learning environment, as the youth performance coach above suggests. Those who choose to commit to coaching have, until recently, relied mainly on formal learning consisting of context-free coach education, non-formal education representing related learning from other fields, and informal learning based on experience, observation, mentoring, reading and electronic sources (Cushion *et al.*, 2010; Lemyre, Trudel and Durand-Bush, 2007). Evidence-based research investigating the coaching process and expert coaches (Armour, 2004; Cassidy, Jones and Potrac, 2004; Jones, 2006) has played a significant role in confirming that coaches work in a dynamic, complex and messy environment that requires more than sport-specific content knowledge. Moreover, being an effective coach is context specific; in other words, coaches need to understand themselves, their athletes, how these athletes learn and what's happening in their worlds, as well as relevant factors in the broader social context (e.g. competition structures, national governing bodies), as these also shape coaching practice.

There are many factors to consider when working with children and young people, some of which will be unique to a particular youth context. This is what makes youth coaching such a challenge. What we do know about effective youth sport coaches is that they are also effective teachers or, to use the more embracing term outlined in Chapter 1, pedagogues. Pedagogues understand both the impact of their own personal history on the coaching context and athletes' needs as learners. They have the ability to access content knowledge and adapt it to athletes and the context, and they also have the capacity to create learning environments with their learners where all participants are knowledge 'producers'. It can be argued with some confidence, therefore, that *learning* is central to the coaching process (Armour, 2004). This chapter explores coaching as a pedagogical practice, focusing on the *process of becoming* an effective youth coach.

> **Comment**
> *Coaching is more than having a detailed knowledge of your sport; it's also about understanding people as learners and their contexts.*

What the research tells us about effective coaching

There are lots of anecdotal beliefs about the key characteristics of effective coaching. As an athlete or coach you will have your own beliefs about effective coaching and some of these will be supported by research evidence. Understanding coaching and the coaching process is a relatively new research field that only started to gain momentum in the 1980s, hence there are still lots of gaps in existing knowledge.

Two problems you will encounter in attempting to define or describe effective coaching are confusion in terminology and the multiple ways effectiveness has been measured (Gilbert and Trudel, 2004). The terms 'effective', 'expert' and 'elite' have often been used interchangeably when describing coaches and the coaching process. Thus, it is unclear what measures of expertise make a coach effective, whether effective coaches are experts, or if coaches who work with elite athletes represent expert or effective coaches simply because of the standard of their athletes. There are further complications with the multiple outcomes used to measure effectiveness in the coaching context; Lyle (2009) lists a number of examples of such measures including:

- performance outcomes;
- long-term success;
- intervention effectiveness;
- coach self-ratings;
- athlete ratings;
- technical knowledge;
- motivation;
- character.

Coach learning, an important element in becoming an effective coach, is also complex in itself. Different types of learning–and research used to analyse and understand learning – provide different insights into what learning is feasible and most beneficial for coaches.

> **Comment**
> *It is challenging to define effective coaching because the terminology used is sometimes ambiguous and there are many ways in which effectiveness can be measured.*

The next section explores some of the dominant research themes relating to effective coaching in the youth sport context. These themes include coaching effectiveness as measured by expert behaviour (Smith, Smoll and Curtis, 1979; Tharp and Gallimore, 1976), the development of expertise and the knowledge base required to support expertise (Abraham, Collins and Martindale, 2006; Bell, 1997; Côté, 2009; Côté, Salmela and Russell, 1995; Schempp, McCullick and Sannen Mason, 2006; Walsh, 2004), and coaching frameworks (Armour, 2004),

Coaching behaviours: what and how do I coach?

There have been many studies designed to identify expert coaching behaviours. Such studies attempt to either provide a profile of an effective coach or create interventions to improve coaching behaviours and the athlete experience. One of the most famous of these studies investigated the coaching behaviours of Coach John Wooden, an American basketball college coach, who was studied because of his outstanding basketball record during the 1960s and 1970s (Tharp and Gallimore, 1976). In this study the researchers observed John Wooden across a season and recorded his coaching behaviours, using systematic observation. There were several coaching behaviours that were observed consistently:

- high levels of verbal instruction (50.3 per cent), most of which concentrated on the basic fundamentals of the game;
- the use of the terms hustle or drive to encourage athletes to maintain intensity and tempo at game pace;
- positive and negative statements (1:1 ratio), which were always followed by some form of instruction.

The concentration on instruction could be described as part of good pedagogical practice. John Wooden always claimed that good coaching was good teaching, that all teaching begins with students, and that a coach has not taught until students have learnt. In Wooden's coaching context, youth athletes were on performance pathways that warranted an investment in skill and game development. His emphasis on instruction and fundamentals was an attempt to develop athletes whose skill would hold up under pressure, leaving them the cognitive space to be creative and enjoy the challenge in pressured situations (Nater and Gallimore, 2005). It is interesting to note that many of Wooden's recorded coaching behaviours are also evident in contemporary coaching literature where coaches describe their practice and articulate their beliefs about effective coaching (e.g. Jones, Armour and Potrac, 2004).

In a research project specific to the youth sport context, a systematic observation scale (Coaching Behaviour and Assessment System) was used to observe the coaching behaviours of Little League baseball coaches working with players aged 12 years and younger (Smith, Smoll and Curtis, 1978; Smith, Smoll and Hunt, 1977). The researchers also expanded the scope of the project to explore the relationship between observed coaching behaviours, player perceptions and player attitude. The major findings from the research were that for players, perception was reality and it reflected attitude. In other words, a coach may think s/he has communicated a message clearly; however, it is the players' interpretation that counts. Positive attitudes to participation were best predicted when coaches provided a socially supportive, well-managed learning environment.

> **Comment**
> *Good coaching is good teaching.*

College basketball and Little League baseball represent two very different youth sport contexts and researchers compared the ways in which coaches worked in these contexts (Smith, Smoll and Hunt, 1977; Smith, Smoll and Curtis, 1978, 1979; Tharp and Gallimore, 1976). College basketball is a performance context whereas in Little League baseball, the emphasis is on participation. In the performance context, technical instruction was the most observed coaching behaviour. In the participant context, where coaches were working with young children, a socially supported and caring environment represented good coaching practice. It is clear from this and other research that the application and timing of specific coaching behaviours will always be dependent on context.

Coaching knowledge: what do I need to know?

The categorising of coaching behaviours has identified what coaches know and why they behave in particular ways. It is only recently that there has been an interest in how coaches perceive their actions, what they know and how they learn. This has led to the identification of key knowledge 'domains' in coaching. This work is by no means complete but it does provide some direction for coach education programmes and for coaches wishing to invest in their learning. The knowledge domains have emerged from research investigating coaches' personal histories (Côté *et al.*, 1995; Salmela, 1995; Walsh, 2004) and in consultation with coaches themselves (Abraham *et al.*, 2006). The common core of these knowledge domains is:

- *sport-specific knowledge*: technical, tactical and strategic understanding of the sport and the role sports science plays in performance;
- *pedagogical knowledge*: knowledge about learners and learning environments, management, planning, organisation and communication;
- *interpersonal knowledge*: coach–athlete relationships, self-awareness, personal philosophy, moral and ethical codes of behaviour, ongoing learning and reflection;
- *contextual knowledge*: ability to identify, evaluate and monitor information about athletes' lives and the micro and macro factors that shape the context. (Walsh, 2004)

There is general agreement that these knowledge domains do not work in isolation but are interdependent, dynamic and constantly in a state of flux. For example, every time a coach moves into a new role, contextual knowledge shrinks and then starts to rebuild as information is gathered and evaluated. The novice coach places emphasis on sport-specific discipline knowledge and pedagogical knowledge. Importantly, each coach takes a unique approach to building a knowledge base and very few coaches are expert in all areas.

> **Comment**
> *There are (at least) four knowledge domains in coaching and they are dynamic and interdependent.*

Coaching frameworks: the bigger picture

The previous sections have highlighted the ways in which the coach, athlete and context interact to create an effective learning environment. Jones, Armour and Potrac (2004) studied expert professional coaches, many of whom also work with youth, and built a strong case for locating coaching within a pedagogical framework. These researchers explored the lives and work of acknowledged expert coaches, and identified strong connections between coaches' lives, knowledge and experience, which were then reflected in their coaching practice. This research expanded the definition of effective coaching beyond traditional bodies of expert knowledge, for example sports science and pedagogy designed around instruction and management. Instead, the researchers identified a more holistic view that connects and integrates people (coaches, learners) their lives, knowledge and community. Armour (2004) conceptualised this pedagogical framework into four interrelated links: coaches, learners, knowledge, and learning environments. These have since been condensed into the three dimensions of pedagogy as explained by Armour in Chapter 1 of this book. This shift was made in recognition of the context-dependent nature of knowledge, leading to three dimensions that are explained as follows:

- *Knowledge in context.* Any knowledge to be coached or learnt is always a context-bound decision that reflects, reinforces, reproduces macro and micro contextual factors and moral imperatives.
- *Learners and learning.* Expertise in learning theories, and in understanding children and young people as diverse learners.
- *Coaches and coaching.* Coaches should be lifelong learners themselves who continuously and critically reflect upon their personal capacities and invest in 'growing' their expertise to meet the needs of young learners.

If coaching is understood in pedagogical terms, it helps to paint a complex yet clearer picture of coaches' needs and how best to service and scaffold these needs through formal, non-formal and informal learning. If effective coaching is best represented through a multidimensional pedagogical framework, then becoming an effective coach requires self-awareness, knowledge of learners, sport-specific knowledge, context-specific content knowledge, skills in transforming knowledge to meet learners' needs, and the ability to create environments where learning is central. Becoming an effective coach is not a linear process, but investment in learning is critical for development.

> **Comment**
> *Adopting a pedagogical framework for coaching highlights the complexity of the coach learning process and provides a guide for coach education.*

Coach development: the start of the journey

The expertise literature provides some insight into how coaches evolve over time and what structures can support coach learning. All coaches need to start their learning journey somewhere. Very few people plan a coaching 'career' in traditional terms, particularly as so much coaching is a volunteer activity. Instead, people tend to fall into coaching and then seek direction. Schempp, McCullick and Sannen Mason (2006) describe the four developmental stages of becoming an expert coach. These four stages are borrowed from the educational literature (Berliner, 1994) and they align closely with the development of coaching expertise (McCullick, Cumings and DeMarco, 1998; Schempp *et al.*, 2006; Walsh, 2004). The four stages are:

1 **Novice.** A novice may be new to the role of coach but they bring with them life experiences that feed into their coaching practice. The novice coach learns the rules of belonging to the new community. Planning and organisation are paramount as novice coaches experiment with routines and planning and organisation regimes. 'Real-world' practice is important at this stage of development.

2 **Competent.** The competent coach has established routines such that management and organisation take less time. Although still rule orientated, they become more flexible as they are able to prioritise what is important and what is not. Their plans are more purposeful and connect to short- and long-term goals, and learning and relational aspects of coaching are foregrounded. From experience, they understand that things go wrong and that the learning environment on a particular day may not be as they predicted it; hence they have a contingency plan.

3 **Proficiency.** The proficient coach has usually coached for a number of years and demonstrates many of the knowledge and performance skills of a competent coach, but has the additional capacity to see cues early and to pre-empt problems. They have a holistic sense of the situations they face. Decision making is based on context. Monitoring and evaluation are ongoing and reflected in an adaptive response to contextual changes. These coaches 'think on their feet' and are able to anticipate problems.

4 **Expert.** Expert coaches are few and far between. It takes at least 10,000 hours of deliberate practice to develop this level of expertise (Ericsson, Krampe and Tesch-Romer, 1993). Expert coaches have an extensive body of *integrated* knowledge; they are avid learners and look for opportunities to increase their knowledge base (Walsh, 2004). As coaches, they have the capacity to extract increased levels of information from the environment and to use this information more effectively. Decision making by expert coaches could be considered intuitive; however, intuition is more likely to represent complex mental models that are cognitively organised for quick and efficient access.

Such knowledge is built over time and is not always easy to articulate. Intricate planning is part of the expert coach's repertoire. Think back to the research on John Wooden, an acknowledged expert: he claimed that he spent as much time planning a training session as he did conducting it, and he always analysed each session prior to planning the next (Wooden, 1988).

Expert coaches react to the extraordinary rather than the ordinary. For example, in a game situation such a coach can identify problems by extracting early information based on key differences rather than having to undertake a full evaluation of the situation. This in itself provides greater cognitive capacity for decision making and for developing creative solutions in action. The expertise literature provides *one* view of how people evolve and become more effective in their practice over time. These models can be useful tools, although they rarely consider the role of motivation or explain the complex process of knowledge integration. They do, however, illustrate the ways in which becoming a coach is a staged development that requires continual investment in learning.

> **Comment**
> *Becoming an expert coach takes at least 10,000 hours of practice!*

Coaching context: decision making starts here!

There has been a common theme running throughout this chapter that coach learning is central to the coaching process. This section concentrates on sport-specific information relating to the youth sport context – specifically, performance pathways and youth sport challenges – and identifies implications for coach learning.

The youth sport context is particularly complex because young people are growing, maturing and developing at the same time as learning a sport. Each learning context is unique (Gilbert and Trudel, 2004). Imagine coaching a team of 15-year-old boys. Each boy brings to the session his personal characteristics, for example biological and psychological maturity, personal history, preferred way of learning, playing ability and experience, motivations, values and sport identity. Complexity increases once the personal characteristics of parents, peers and coaches are added to the mix. Each sport context is also influenced by the nature of sport organisations, the local sports club, national governing bodies and community infrastructure available, to name just a few (Côté, 2009). As a coach, all of these factors need to be considered in planning sessions and, at different points in time, some aspects take priority over others. For example, when stepping onto the pitch to coach a new team, the coach prioritises evaluation of skills and getting to know something about the athletes. These early training sessions are designed to test players' skills, physiological response and motivation, This provides a base for developing the programme.

At the same time it is important to recognise that some youth sport contexts can be relatively homogeneous. In elite clubs, the level of athlete expertise might be similar and performance outcomes will be determined by the competitive context. Planning can be designed around these expectations and outcomes. Yet, when working with children and young people, an effective coach must also consider the athlete's psychological development regardless of competition level (Horn, 2002). Developing athlete competence and confidence, and creating a caring environment where the young people feel valued and empowered, are the key ingredients of holistic coaching.

Recently there have been a number of models created to assist coaches in designing a more holistic approach to coaching. These models have been created to guide coaches towards designing developmentally appropriate training programmes. For example, the Long Term Player/Athlete Development model (Balyi, 2002, 2009) model has been used in Canada, Scotland and Ireland as a template for designing age-appropriate training programmes. Another model that helps to clarify the performance context, taking account of the biological, psychological and sociological context of youth development, is the Athlete's Developmental Model of Sport Participation (Côté, Baker and Abernethy, 2007). This model provides guidance for athlete development and appropriate training structures to support learning (Côté *et al.*, 2007). These models are helpful, although it must be remembered that each group of athletes is different. Coaches have to continually adapt and modify their practice in response to the needs of the specific group and context within which they work. Having said this, there are some common challenges in children's and youth sport that a coach can plan for – or at least become aware of – prior to working in this context.

Gilbert, Gilbert and Trudel (2001a, 2001b) identified several common challenges that are faced by youth sport coaches. Many of these challenges reflect the need for good pedagogical practice:

- athlete behaviour: attitude, attendance, focus, and morale;
- athlete performance: consistency, individual techniques, team tactics;
- communication: ability to communicate effectively to a diverse group of learners;
- parental influence: interaction and disagreement;
- team organisation: coaching staff, fundraising, selection and playing time, practice planning.

The identification of common challenges helps coach educators to support coaches in building a knowledge base that can meet the needs of these diverse learners. As pedagogues, youth coaches need to care for and mentor their athletes, encouraging them to sustain their engagement in sport and physical activity. Coaches must also be endlessly flexible: as the youth coach at the beginning of the chapter put it, '*you have to be prepared to stretch the rubber band*'.

> **Comment**
> *Youth sport coaching should be holistic coaching.*

Becoming an effective youth coach: getting started

There are many components involved in the process of becoming an effective coach and, to date, the process has been poorly signposted. Everyone who decides to become a coach brings prior knowledge to the process; this might be as a former athletic or personal experience in a related field. There is no single programme that can meet everybody's learning needs. A good starting point for a novice coach, however, is to undertake a personal audit of coaching strengths and weaknesses to inform a personal learning programme. The personal learning audit (see Table 22.1) is a starting point for evaluating youth coaching strengths and weaknesses.

Table 22.1 Personal learning audit

Personal learning audit	Strength	Weakness	Action
Learners and learning			
Experience working with children and youth			
Knowledge of how children and youth learn			
Knowledge of what motivates young people to participate in sport and physical activity			
Knowledge of growth and development			
Knowledge in context			
Knowledge of the local club culture			
Knowledge or experience of the sport culture			
Knowledge of the children and/or youth whom you are coaching (ability, family background, motivations, etc.)			
Experience engaging with parents			
Coaches/coaching			
Sport-specific knowledge			
• Fundamentals			
• Strategic and tactical knowledge			
• Related sports science knowledge			
Management and organisation			
• Organisational skills			
• Management skills			
• Planning skills			
Experience and knowledge in adapting instructions and outcomes to meet learners' needs			
Experience coaching athletes using a variety of pedagogical tools (Game Sense, Teaching Games for Understanding, experiential learning)			
Engagement in personal learning			
Use of reflective practice			
Development of a set of values or a philosophy			

Once the audit is complete, decisions can made about what type of knowledge and form of learning is best. For example, sport-specific knowledge is generally provided by national governing bodies (NGBs) through formal education. Knowledge of the context is often implicit, and requires immersion in an organisation to develop understanding. Some knowledge areas require investment in personal learning through reading texts, surfing the internet or observing and talking with experienced coaches. Observation and experience are very powerful methods of learning and of reinforcing practice (good and bad!). In addition, learning can be accelerated through reflective practice and engagement in a mentoring programme.

One of the most powerful learning practices is reflective practice. According to Dewey (1933) reflective thinking is the key to whether any experience is fully educative. In other words, true comprehension of an experience can only be gained by considering its effect. Reflection moves beyond recording or describing a learning event or critical incident. Instead, reflection involves identification of the problem, making meaning of the problem, seeking out resources (e.g. human, electronic media, books) and engaging in learning. In a full reflective cycle, the process would also include validating learning, i.e. how it informs and changes a coach's thinking and/or practice.

At the institutional level, coaching or sport organisations can put several strategies in place to support coach learning. Formal coach accreditation, ethics education and police vetting are now commonplace (or, indeed, compulsory) in many sports associations. Yet it is self-evident that education does not (or should not) stop with an accreditation badge or certificate. A useful strategy that can provide vertical and horizontal links between different types of learning and experience is mentoring. This strategy is built on the premise that coaching is a social act that takes place in communities of practice (Wenger, 1998) and that learning emerges from a perpetual reflective effort (see also Chapter 23 by Mark Griffiths in this volume).

Gaining access to a mentor is not necessarily easy; in some cases there is mutual attraction and the mentor and mentee connect informally, allowing a relationship to evolve. Some sporting organisations offer formal mentoring programmes where mentors are paired with mentees. Another option is to approach a specific coach to request mentoring support. It is important to remember, however, that the same mentor is unlikely to be able to help a coach through all the different stages of a career. As a coach develops, learning needs change and different forms of mentoring are required (Ericsson *et al.*, 1993). If structured in appropriate ways, this can be a powerful partnership for both the mentor and mentee and both should learn from the experience.

Conclusion

Becoming an effective coach requires an investment in learning on and off the field. Learning takes place in many forms: formal coach education, at training, during competition, in conversation with athletes, mentors and with other coaches, and professional development from observation, reading books and accessing electronic media. It is a relational job, an investment in young people's development, which in turn demands an investment in self. The reward for many is seeing young people achieve a variety of outcomes and having the privilege of being part of that process.

Learning tasks

Individual task

As a coach or a potential coach think about the following two questions: 'Why am I a coach?' and 'Why do I coach as I do?' In your first step to self-awareness (intrapersonal knowledge) explore your own life history and what influence that has (or could have) on your coaching. Describe how your own life experience could be a positive influence on your athletes, or a barrier to them reaching their full potential. If you have identified any barriers, what are the implications for your own learning?

(continued)

Group task: Talking to and learning from the coaching pedagogues

Identify several youth sport coaches you would like to interview about their learning, context, coaching practice and lessons learnt on their coaching journey. As a group, design an interview schedule of questions to ask these coaches. Conduct interviews and undertake a group analysis of the data, identifying common themes for a wider group discussion.

Further reading

Lyle, J. (2008) The coaching process: an overview. In: **N. Cross and J. Lyle** (eds) *The Coaching Process* (pp. 3–24), Oxford: Butterworth-Heinemann. On pages 18 and 19, Lyle produces a model of the coaching process. Compare and contrast this model with the pedagogical framework underpinning this text. What questions arise from your evaluation?

References

Abraham, A., Collins, D. and Martindale, R. (2006) The coaching schematic: validation through expert coach consensus, *Journal of Sports Sciences*, 24(6), 549–64.

Armour, K. (2004) Coaching pedagogy. In: R. Jones, K. Armour and P. Potrac (eds) *Sports Coaching Cultures*, London: Routledge, 94–115.

Balyi, I. (2002) LTAD model by Istvan Balyi: late specialisation sports, retrieved 17 February 2010 from http://hometeamsonline.com/photos/soccer/NEWALBANYFREEDOM/art2.pdf.

Balyi, I. (2009) Long-term player development LTAD 101, retrieved 17 February 2010 from http://www.utahsportforlife.com/Documents/LongTerm%20Athlete%20Development%20-%20Istvan%20Balyi.%20Salon%20I.pdf.

Bell, M. (1997) The development of expertise, *The Journal of Physical Education, Recreation and Dance*, 68(2), 34–8.

Berliner, D. C. (1994) Expertise: the wonder of exemplary performance. In: J. Mangierai and C. Block (eds) *Creating Powerful Thinking in Teachers and Students: Diverse perspectives*, Fort Worth, Texas: Harcourt Brace, 161–86.

Cassidy, T., Jones, R. and Potrac, P. (2004) *Understanding Sports Coaching*, London: Routledge.

Côté, J. (2009) *Coaching Expertise Defined by Meeting Athlete Needs*, Paper presented at the SportscoachUK coaching summit research forum.

Côté, J., Baker, J. and Abernethy, B. (2007) Practice and play in the development of sport expertise. In: G. Tenenbaum and R. Ekland (eds) *Handbook of Sport Psychology* (3rd edn), NJ: Wiley, 184–202.

Côté, J., Salmela, J. and Russell, S. (1995) The knowledge of high-performance coaches: competition and training considerations, *The Sport Psychologist*, 9, 76–95.

Cushion, C. J., Nelson, L., Armour, K., Lyle, J., Jones, R. *et al.* (2010) *Coach Learning and Development: A review of literature*, Leeds: Sports Coach UK.

Dewey, J. (1933) *How we Think. A statement of the relation of reflective thinking to the educative process*, (revised edition), Boston, DC: Heath.

Dodds, P., Griffin, L. and Placek, J. (2001) Chapter 2. A selected review of the literature on development of learners' domain-specific knowledge, *Journal of Teaching in Physical Education*, 20, 301–13.

Ericsson, K. A., Krampe, R. T. and Tesch-Romer, C. (1993) The role of deliberate practice in the acquisition of expert performance, *Psychological Review*, 100, 363–406.

Gilbert, W., Gilbert, J. and Trudel, P. (2001a) Coaching strategies for youth sport. Part 1: Athlete behavior and athlete performance, *Journal of Physical Education, Recreation and Dance,* 72(4), 29–33.

Gilbert, W., Gilbert, J. and Trudel, P. (2001b) Coaching strategies for youth sport. Part 2: Personal characteristics, parental influence and team organisation, *Journal of Physical Education, Recreation and Dance,* 72(8), 41–8.

Gilbert, W. D. and Trudel, P. (2004) Analysis of coaching science research published from 1970 to 2001, *Reseach Quarterly for Exercise and Sport* (75), 388–99.

Horn, T. (2002) Coaching effectiveness in the sport domain. In: T. Horn (ed.) *Advances in Sport Psychology,* Champaign, IL: Human Kinetics, 309–54.

Jacques, E. and Clements, S. D. (1991) *Executive Leadership. A practical guide to managing complexity,* Massachusetts: Blackwell.

Jones, R. (ed.) (2006) *The Sports Coach as Educator: Re-conceptualising sports coaching* London: Routledge.

Jones, R., Armour, K. and Potrac, P. (2004) *Sports Coaching Cultures: From practice to theory,* Oxford: Routledge.

Lacy, A. C. and Darst, P. W. (1985) Systematic observation of behaviours of winning high school head football coaches, *Journal of Teaching in Physical Education,* 4, 256–70.

Langsdorf, E. V. (1979) A systematic observation of football coaching behaviour in a major university environment, *Dissertation Abstracts International,* 40, 4473A.

Lemyre, F., Trudel, P. and Durand-Bush, N. (2007) How youth-sport coaches learn to coach, *The Sport Psychologist,* 21, 191–209.

Lyle, J. (2009) Replacing effectiveness with expertise: building a research agenda, Paper presented at the *SportscoachUK coaching summit research forum.*

McCullick, B., Cumings, R. and DeMarco, G. (1998) The road to expert coaching, *CAHPERD,* 31(1), 42–9.

Nater, S. and Gallimore, R. (2005) *You Haven't Taught Until They Have Learned: John Wooden's teaching principles and practices.* WV: Fitness Information Technology.

Potrac, P. and Cassidy, T. (2006) The coach as a more capable other. In: R. Jones (ed.) *The Sports Coach as Educator,* London: Routledge.

Salmela, J. H. (1995) Learning from the development of expert coaches, *Coaching and Sports Science,* 2, 15–21.

Schempp, P. G., McCullick, B. and Sannen Mason, I. (2006) The development of expert coaching. In: R. Jones (ed.) *The Sports Coach as Educator,* London: Routledge, 145–61.

Segrave, J. O. and Ciancio, C. A. (1990) Confidence-building strategies used by Canadian high-level rowing coaches *AVANTE,* 3(3), 80–92.

Smith, R., Smoll, F. and Hunt, E. (1977) A system of behavioural assessment of athletic coaches. *Research Quarterly,* 48, 401–408.

Smith, R. E., Smoll, F. and Curtis, B. (1978) Coaching behaviours in Little League baseball. In: F. L. Smoll and Mith, S. R. E. (eds) *Psychological Perspectives in Youth Sport,* Washington, DC: Hemisphere, 173–201.

Smith, R., Smoll, F. and Curtis, B. (1979) Coaching effectiveness training: a cognitive-behavioural approach to enhancing relationship skills in youth sport coaches, *Journal of Sport Psychology,* 1, 59–75.

Tharp, R. G. and Gallimore, R. (1976) What a coach can teach a teacher, *Psychology Today,* 9 (January), 74–8.

Walsh, J. (2004) Development and application of expertise in elite-level coaches, Unpublished doctoral dissertation, Australia: Victoria University.

Wenger, E. (1998) *Communities of Practice,* NY: Cambridge Press.

Wooden, J. (1988) *They Call Me Coach,* New York: Contemporary Books.

Mentoring as a professional learning strategy

Mark Griffiths, University of Birmingham

The process of working with a mentor can trigger so many issues; in some respects I guess the process is more important than the outcomes. In my case I feel as though I have someone to confide in and someone watching over my development.

(Volunteer coach, in Griffiths, 2010)

 ## Introduction

Much of the literature that examines the professional practice of coaches and teachers describes practice environments that are complex, unpredictable and increasingly demanding. In sports coaching, for instance, Jones and Wallace (2005) have described the coaching process as characterised by ambiguity, where coaches 'orchestrate' rather than exert absolute control over the multiple variables that can influence practice (e.g. athletes, parents, employers). In physical education (PE), Armour and Duncombe (2009) have suggested that growing levels of accountability in PE programmes have resulted in increased interest in the quality of PE teachers' professional practice. It could be argued that in these demanding pedagogical environments, the ability of coaches and teachers to operate effectively is contingent upon their ability to apply appropriate 'knowledge in context'. It is important to consider, therefore, the different ways in which coaches and teachers can be supported to develop such knowledge over their careers. This chapter considers one increasingly popular professional learning strategy: mentoring.

Glaser (1999) argues that professional practice is a process of changing existing situations into preferred ones, and clearly the ability to make such changes is constrained by a practitioner's applied knowledge base. Essentially, and as Kathleen Armour described in Chapter 1, effective teachers and coaches are those who critically reflect upon their practices to meet the needs of young learners. These practitioners are motivated to grow (continuously) their expertise of sport-related knowledge and pedagogical tools in the interests of their learners. From this perspective, effective teachers and coaches are lifelong learners, engaging in a process that Cheallaigh (2001) called 'life-wide' learning. Continuing professional development (CPD) is – or should be – the mechanism by which such practitioner learning is undertaken.

> **Comment**
> *Effective teachers and coaches engage in continuous professional learning and need effective strategies to support them.*

In recent years, policy makers and researchers have tried to identify learning strategies that might best support and facilitate effective professional learning (Armour and Duncombe, 2009). Learning is at the heart of all dimensions of sport pedagogy and, as Fiona Chambers outlines in Chapter 3 in this text, there are many different ways in which it can be conceptualised. In the context of professional development, an increasing body of literature has placed emphasis on learning in context, focusing on the interrelationship between knowledge, context and practice (Lave and Wenger, 1991). Learning is not, therefore, conceptualised solely as the *acquisition* of knowledge by individuals (e.g. typically found in formal education), but more as a process of social *participation* in specific situations. A good example of this comes from a study of professional learning by Eraut *et al.* (1998), who identified the most important learning dimension for learners as interactions with other people and the daily challenges of work itself. More formal (traditional) professional education opportunities were also helpful but were described as being 'secondary in importance' (p. 37). Understanding learning as a form of social practice underpins much of the current research into professional learning, and it is particularly important in research on mentoring as a professional learning strategy.

An analysis of current formal professional qualifications and CPD programmes suggests that 'mentoring' in one form or another has become almost obligatory. Indeed, as a method of supporting and enhancing professional learning, mentoring appears to be regarded by some organisations as something of a panacea that can resolve a whole range of learning problems (Allen *et al.*, 2008). There is no doubt that most of us can identify significant others in our biography who have shaped or perhaps directed a particular course of action that we have taken. It is perhaps not surprising, then, that organisations have embraced the potential of mentoring to support professional learning. In sport coaching, mentoring has been identified as a way to develop high-quality practitioners because it supports the growth of coaches' knowledge and expertise (Cushion, 2006). In other fields, mentoring is conceived as a mechanism for enhancing career development and offering psychosocial support, and improving recruitment, support and retention within the workplace (Higgins and Kram, 2001).

> **Comment**
> *Mentoring has the potential to be an effective professional learning strategy.*

It is important to note at the outset that mentoring is not a simple process. Jones *et al.* (2009), in their review of sports coach mentoring, argued that mentoring can be conceptualised as a process, a person and an activity. This is an important point. There are many different understandings of mentoring because of the wide range of potential mentor–mentee relationships and the effect of different contexts, stakeholder perceptions and practical considerations. What this means is that in any attempt to set up a mentoring activity, it is necessary for all parties to agree at the outset what they mean by 'mentoring' in that particular context. The next section, therefore, explores some of the possible definitions of mentoring. Importantly, this is not going to offer a clear-cut and rigid set of parameters for the term; instead we will look at the core attributes of mentoring processes. This more flexible approach to defining the concept makes it possible for practitioners and professional developers to build models of mentoring that are sensitive to the needs of each professional learning situation (Jones *et al.*, 2009).

Mentoring attributes

A useful starting point for this discussion is Colley's (2003) observation that mentoring can be considered from two broad perspectives. First, a number of studies have examined mentoring in terms of its function and role. For instance, in Dodd's (2005) study of the meanings that PE teachers drew from their mentoring experiences, participants defined mentoring as 'someone who is there to share information and provide guidance' (p. 359). In Higgins and Kram's (2001) conceptual paper, and based on a large database of empirical evidence, a mentor was defined as 'a senior person, working in the protégé's organisation, [who] assists with the protégé's personal and professional development' (p. 265). Similarly, Fletcher's (2000) book on mentoring in secondary schools in the UK refers to the mentor as a teacher and counsellor who supports and guides the novice in professional practice.

From these selected extracts, there is a sense that the literature understands mentoring to be a tool to facilitate change. It is a way of assisting the novice to identify, negotiate and optimise learning opportunities from what might appear, at times, to be a perplexing array of workplace and personal experiences (Cassidy *et al.*, 2004). It is also interesting to note that within these extracts, there is an implied reference to a dyadic (one-to-one) relationship within a formal organisational context.

The second perspective from which to analyse mentoring is through mentoring relationships. In a review of mentoring, Roberts (2000) identified the mentoring relationship as an essential quality of mentoring. Similarly, the PE teachers in Dodd's (2005) study also described mentoring as 'a personal intense relationship', where the mentor is 'someone who believes in you and has a real desire to help you to succeed', and 'the sounding board, the person you can trust, the person you can tell anything to and lets you listen to yourself' (p. 359). In the same way, McMahon (2005) has suggested that close support relationships are essential for both career and professional development. In this case, good mentors were defined as sponsors, challenge givers, exposure providers, loyal and nurturing, social supporters and, most importantly, those who possess superior communication skills. The key point from such research is that mentoring is founded on a personal and emotionally committed relationship.

> **Comment**
>
> *Mentoring sounds relatively straightforward in theory but in practice it is a complex process. If it is not designed carefully, mentoring can simply reinforce poor practice!*

It is apparent when reviewing the literature that mentoring is a complex social and cultural activity, and this complexity has led to numerous attempts to define mentoring and to capture its essential qualities. The following summarises some of the key attributes of mentoring found in the literature:

- Mentoring is characterised by a unique relationship between individuals.
- Mentoring is a pedagogical process.
- Mentoring is a helping process.
- Mentoring supports professional and personal development.
- Mentoring relationships are reciprocal, yet asymmetrical.
- Mentoring relationships are active and dynamic.
- Mentoring relationships change over time.
- Mentoring is a strategy for accelerated learning.

It is clear that when conceptualised in this way, mentoring is a process that goes beyond the traditional concept of a wise (usually older) mentor guiding a younger colleague, and where the mentor is chosen as one who has 'done it before'. This traditional image of mentoring has been found wanting because, as Parker *et al.* (2008) observed, 'experience of the past and accumulated knowledge no longer guarantee relevance of the future' (p. 489). Thus, it can be argued that for teachers and coaches, a knowledge base grounded in their experiences of the past is not necessarily adequate to support them to work effectively with children and young people in demanding and fluid contemporary pedagogical environments.

> **Comment**
>
> *Mentoring can be defined in different ways and this flexibility offers a range of professional learning opportunities.*

Although it has proved to be difficult to define mentoring in clear-cut terms, there appears to be a consensus in the literature about the outcome of mentoring interactions: i.e. to produce change through the learning and development of the individual. In the context of professional learning, it is important that mentoring is not just perceived as a mechanism for information exchange. Instead, mentoring is a process that actively supports professional development by assisting mentees to become, for example, more reflective about practice, to develop their autonomy, and to enhance their ability to solve problems. The potential of mentoring to support these cognitive skills can be seen in an international study of beginning teachers. Drawing upon a considerable body of empirical research, Hobson - et al. (2009) identified the benefits to *mentees* as including: increased confidence and self-esteem, professional growth, and improved self-reflection and problem-solving capacities. Benefits for *mentors* included the development of critical reflection towards their own practice, gaining new ideas and practices, enhancing knowledge, increasing confidence and enhancing professional identity.

Yet, even though mentoring is clearly helpful, there is limited evidence regarding exactly *how* mentoring impacts upon the pedagogical practice of teachers. As Hobson and colleagues point out, this gap in the literature is partly down to the inherent complexities of the mentoring process and the difficulty in attributing specific learning to mentoring rather than to other learning situations that contribute to professional development (e.g. formal education, professional development workshops). Essentially, professional development, and teaching and coaching, are not undertaken in a laboratory, and this makes it challenging to determine cause and effect in any straightforward ways.

> *Comment*
> *Mentoring can benefit both mentors and mentees.*

In summary, the attributes of mentoring presented here are based on an understanding of the mentor as a 'learning guide', and this acknowledges the importance of a personal and emotionally committed mentoring relationship. Yet despite the increasing popularity of mentoring in professional development programmes, mentoring research has sometimes struggled to capture the rich potential of mentoring (for both good and ill). As Colley (2003) has argued, mentoring continues to be 'a practice that remains ill-defined, poorly conceptualised and weakly theorized' (p. 13). In the next section, therefore, relational and social learning theories are presented as potential analytical tools for understanding mentoring and mentoring practices.

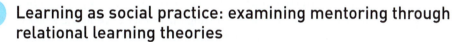

Learning as social practice: examining mentoring through relational learning theories

The professional learning literature widely acknowledges the role of mentoring in supporting accelerated learning and career growth (Parker *et al.*, 2008). However, there is a need to situate mentoring within a theoretical, or organising, framework. Such a framework can help us to critically examine both the key features of mentoring and the claims made for its value in professional learning. A relational approach to understanding mentoring is valuable because it is grounded in the idea that learning occurs through interaction with others. This approach highlights the importance of the quality of the relational dialogue between mentor and mentee. For example, Spencer (2006) argued that mentoring has the potential to develop social and emotional growth (such as psychological health and vitality), but that several relational processes are required to underpin healthy and productive mentoring relationships. These relational processes include:

- authenticity (relationship responsiveness between participants);
- empathy (understanding another person's state of mind);
- collaboration to support emotional development;
- satisfying experience;
- shared meaning.

The adoption of a relational approach is useful in examining the attractiveness, potential and structure of mentoring relationships, and in elevating the importance of social interactions in the mentoring process. Indeed, Parker *et al.* (2008) have suggested that it is through the positive experiences of engaging in effective supporting relationships that learners acquire a sense of energy, vision and critical self-awareness in learning. It could be argued that these characteristics are essential for effective professional practitioners. Thus, contemporary theories of learning tend to emphasise social processes, i.e. the context of the learning domain impacts upon the individual's interpretation of the situation. Furthermore, it is acknowledged that individuals bring their prior experiences to any learning domain, and these experiences filter any potential new learning. Both constructivist and situated learning theories can offer some clarity on these processes.

Comment

Relational learning theories emphasise the importance of social processes in effective learning.

Situated learning is one component of a broader constructivist approach to learning. The constructivist paradigm frames cognitive development as a sociocultural process; knowledge is not only possessed individually, but shared amongst members of a community. Its central claim is that knowledge is acquired through a process of construction, where learners construct understanding collectively through their involvement in events which are forged by cultural and historical factors (Kirk and Macdonald, 1998). Further, Vygotsky's (1978) sociocultural constructivist perspective draws attention to the role of 'scaffolded instruction', that is, the assistance and support provided by a perceived expert, competent peer or mentor in allowing the learner to complete a task or solve a problem. Scaffolded learning is characterised by the use of prompts, comments, explanations, questions and suggestions; a form of support that fades or evolves as the learners attain an increasingly autonomous level of performance. For example, Williams, Matthews and Baugh (2004) reported a study that evaluated the outcomes of a programme for the preparation of school principals (head teachers). Participants reported that mentoring aided them in bridging the link between theory and practice, and was viewed as a powerful mechanism for learning practice. Hence the mentor's role was one of 'scaffolding growth-promoting experiences' (p. 56) in which the learning relationship was characterised as an evolving strategy that shifted between nurturing and challenging, and from supporting to developing independence.

The important point about this approach is that learning is not understood solely as the acquisition of knowledge by detached individuals; instead it is a process of social participation, situated within a specific context. Situated learning theory, therefore, would seem to offer a framework from which to further examine the potential of formalised mentoring and analyse its components. This would lead us, for example, to focus on the *relationship between* the educator (mentor), the learner (mentee), the mentoring process, and the context of the programme in order to understand any mentoring programme.

Mentoring model: 'a configuration of relationships'

At the heart of most mentoring models found in the literature is a mentor–mentee traditional one-to-one relationship. A growing body of literature, however, has suggested that individuals develop through different mentoring relationships over their careers. Researchers have noted that individuals tend to actively seek out multiple mentors in order to meet their multiple developmental needs. For instance, Higgins (2000) conceptualised mentoring not just as a single dyad, but instead included alternative mentoring possibilities, such as network or multiple mentoring. Within this expanded notion of mentoring, the mentee is able to engage in a network of simultaneous mentoring relationships. Recent empirical evidence has suggested that this better reflects the reality of learning and development in professional occupations. In their study of mentoring PE teachers, for example, Ayers and Griffin (2005) described mentoring as a series of multiple relationships in which mentor(s) created an environment that encouraged co-participation in a 'nexus of relationships' in order to meet personal and professional needs. As a result, Ayers and Griffin argued that mentoring was best considered, 'a mosaic that focuses on creating learning partnerships across the professions' (p. 370).

This model is also supported by Cawyer *et al.* (2002, p. 238), whose participants described mentoring as 'a configuration of relationships' based around accessibility and seeking colleagues who were convenient for seeking particular forms of professional and social support. Thus, instead of the mentor taking full responsibility for the mentee's learning, the mentee learns to distribute responsibility for learning support and increasingly becomes self-directed. In this way, a form of shared accountability and responsibility is created.

Recent studies have also begun to suggest that mentoring can go even further, including relationships that are intra- and extra-organisational (profession, community, family), multiple dyads/networks, career/person related and involving mutuality and reciprocity. The outcome of this reconfiguration is, as Scandura and Pelligrini (2010) suggest, a powerful understanding that individuals draw mentoring support from multiple relationships which are contingent upon context, access and availability. From this perspective, mentoring can be understood more as a developmental network rather than a traditional dyad, recognising that individuals can and do look beyond the boundaries of organisations in seeking out professional support and development.

> **Comment**
> *Mentoring can take the form of a dyad or a network of mentoring relationships.*

That's the theory . . . but what of the practice? Although formal mentoring is currently highly visible in policy documents and coach qualification frameworks in the UK, research suggests that in practice, informal mentoring is much more prevalent (Cushion, 2006). Moreover, as was noted earlier, mentoring in sports coaching (as in other domains) has been under-theorised, thus restricting the ways in which it can be developed to be effective in professional learning contexts. The challenge for coaching organisations, therefore, is to ensure that they are clear about the kinds of knowledge they are trying to develop through mentoring. Only by doing this can any new knowledge resulting from mentoring be made available to others. This matters because the development and sharing of codified knowledge are important features of any profession.

Coaching is not recognised as a fully fledged 'profession' in most countries, although the central agency for sports coaching in the UK, Sportscoach UK, has developed a strategy to shape coaching into a 'professionally regulated vocation' by the year 2016 (North, 2009). It is interesting to speculate on the role of mentoring as a professional learning strategy in this context. Certainly it would be helpful to formalise existing mentoring structures and relationships in order to develop them as part of a broader learning strategy that is systematic, planned and – critically – that impacts positively on professional practice. In order to explore this idea, the next part of this chapter has been structured differently in order to help you gain a deeper insight into mentoring in action within sport. What follows is an overview of an empirical study into mentoring that was conducted recently in the field of sports coaching.

Volunteer coach mentoring

Griffiths (2010) conducted a longitudinal study into coach learning through mentoring. A regional sports programme in the UK called 'Active Sports' was selected for the study. It was in the process of constructing a formalised mentoring programme for novice coaches and it is important to note that all the participants were volunteer coaches, as are most coaches in the UK. As part of the programme, open invitations were sent to coaches in the programme database, and seven mentors and 19 coaches agreed to take part in a formalised mentoring programme. Mentors from a variety of sports were identified and, as part of their training, were required to attend a three-hour mentoring workshop. Over a 12-month period, and using mainly semi-structured interviews and focus groups, the researcher collected data on the participants' learning experiences through the programme. The mentoring programme can be defined as 'formalised' because it included assigned mentoring relationships, development training for mentors, and a formalised development plan for all participants (e.g. negotiating goals, establishing outcomes).

Data were analysed from a constructivist perspective to reveal the ways in which mentoring operated through social interaction and the exchange between participants of valued sport-specific knowledge. Examples of the types of mentoring interaction that the participants found helpful included:

- face-to-face interaction between coach and mentor;
- observation of practice and feedback;
- swapping 'tricks of the trade';
- opportunities to observe other coaches;
- problem setting and problem solving within the context of their practice.

In particular, coaches reported that where mentors were able to observe them and provide constructive feedback, it gave a clear direction, focus and structure for their learning and also triggered critical reflection.

Despite the clear potential for mentoring to support coach learning, and some examples of good practice, the programme overall was a disappointment. The reality for

(continued)

the volunteer coaches in this study was that meaningful mentoring interaction was sporadic and infrequent. The programme began with much enthusiasm, yet, after only a few months, there was evidence that many of the mentoring relationships had ended. For the majority of coaches and mentors, formalised mentoring came to a premature end either because it was unfulfilling, or because it simply faded out of consciousness as a result of a period of inactivity. The research suggested there were a number of barriers to successful mentoring in the context of this particular programme:

- Lack of mentoring competence: recognition that there is a lot to learn in order to mentor successfully.
- Confused role expectation: some mentors saw themselves as relatively passive information-givers.
- Poor interpersonal relationships: coaches and mentors were assigned to each other by a third party, so there was no personal 'glue'.
- The mentor–mentee relationship was weak: informal mentoring relationships already in place were stronger than those assigned in the official mentoring programme.
- Poor access to the mentor: mentors were assigned and so were not necessarily linked to a coach's sports club.

In particular, and perhaps overriding all other issues, data suggested that the reality of the volunteer coach context was that lack of time was an insurmountable barrier to formalising coach mentoring relationships. The participants recognised the value of different types of learning, including mentoring, but they struggled to find a 'space' for a formalised mentoring programme in a very crowded volunteer coach environment.

Comment

Despite good intentions, formal mentoring relationships can collapse without appropriate structural support.

The results of this research suggest that if mentoring is to deliver what is expected of it as a professional learning strategy for sports coaches, a number of issues need to be considered in designing formal mentoring programmes:

- Volunteer coaches need to be inducted into the complexities of mentoring as a learning process.
- The requisite competencies, skills and motivations of both coach and mentor should be stated explicitly when recruiting participants.
- Coaches must have opportunities to critically reflect on their personal learning experiences and the understandings of both learning and mentoring that they bring to the mentoring process.
- The profile of the sports coaching workforce – mainly volunteer – suggests that mentoring models developed for other and very different contexts may not be appropriate for the sport context.

The last point is important. The findings from this research suggest that in order to help volunteer coaches, mentoring models cannot simply be 'borrowed' from other contexts. Instead, models should be developed specifically for the environment in which they are to be used. For example, it could be argued that volunteer coaches need a community model that can maximise professional learning in a shared and sustained social network of peer support.

> **Comment**
> *It is important to develop models of mentoring that are appropriate to the sports coaching environment.*

Implications for practice: mentoring as a learning strategy

It is important when considering formalised mentoring to be clear about the assumptions around learning that inform it, and how formalised programmes of mentoring might be evaluated. For instance, an indication of a healthy and productive mentoring relationship is one in which learning progression is palpable, impact on practice is evident, and the novice moves from high dependence to autonomy and self-reliance (Gilles and Wilson, 2004). As described earlier, it could be argued that a key function of mentoring in any professional learning is to help practitioners develop their cognitive skills such that they progress towards an increasingly autonomous and expert position. Such a position might be described as one where they are able to contextualise problems, where actions are referenced to professional knowledge, and where they have a rich and well-organised schemata. It might be helpful, therefore, to conceptualise the mentor as a catalyst for reflective thinking, cognitive development and problem solving. This means that mentoring is a demanding role, and it suggests that an effective mentor needs to have more than an accumulation of experience; each mentor needs pedagogical skills in order to maximise the learning potential of the mentoring role.

> **Comment**
> *In order to be effective, mentors need well-developed pedagogical skills.*

A cognitive approach to the design of mentoring programmes leads to the possibility of identifying specific learning outcomes, which would be helpful when seeking to 'measure' the impact of mentoring activities. It would seem important that both researchers and policy makers are able to identify how practitioners proceed to use their personal agency in interpreting and internalising communication from their mentors. An example of a diagnostic tool that could then be used to capture the learning outcomes of the mentoring relationship is derived from the work of Costa and Garmston (2002). They suggest the following 'checklist' could be used in evaluating how participants proceed to use their new knowledge:

- increased self-efficacy in imposing themselves on the situation;
- flexibility in addressing a multiplicity of challenges;

- increased empowering approach to self-improvement;
- awakening or clarifying consciousness in relation to beliefs, values and actions;
- adopting an interdependent approach in working with others in seeking solutions and achieving common goals.

Evaluation is important. If organisations are committed to the development and growth of individuals, and are willing to invest resources to support their development, it is essential that they are able to measure impact in some way. However, as was noted in Chapter 1, pedagogy is a complex concept and the teaching/coaching/learning relationship is dynamic. Measuring the precise impact of individual interventions at any stage in the process, and with either the teachers/coaches or young learners, is challenging, to say the least.

Conclusion

Understanding mentoring as a tool to support professional learning continues to challenge both researchers and policy/practice organisations. It has been explained in this chapter that mentoring is a popular tool in professional development, but it is also poorly conceptualised at times. Nonetheless, researchers and practitioners recognise the potential of mentoring as a strategy in bridging learning gaps and in extending and developing professional learning. In both the coaching and teaching literature, it is recognised that practitioners learn much from experience, yet the ability to critically reflect on practice is limited by the practitioner's level of knowledge. A well-chosen mentor, therefore, can offer a robust, meaningful and sustainable means of supporting and enhancing the construction of professional knowledge. Reflective conversations with a skilled mentor or mentors in a supportive community of practice offer a way of bridging the limitations of some other professional learning strategies. The challenge for teacher/coach developers is to try to build supportive professional learning communities where mentoring, both formal and informal, can contribute effectively to career-long professional development for teachers and coaches.

Learning tasks
Individual task: a reflective analysis of your experiences of mentoring

1 How would you define mentoring? Have you ever been in the position of being a mentor or mentee (in any context)? If so, can you describe your mentoring experiences, formal or informal, and whether this was a positive experience? Try to explain why the process did (or did not) enhance your learning.

2 Do you feel that in order to be useful to you, a mentor should have 'done it before' and to what extent? For example, could a field hockey coach mentor a basketball coach? Could a history teacher mentor a PE teacher? What might a professional coach learn from a business coach? Explain what the possible outcomes might be from such cross-sport/occupational mentoring.

3 What are the competencies and skills required of mentors (and mentees) in optimising the potential of mentoring? For instance, are the accrued years of experience and qualifications appropriate to justify a mentor role?

(continued)

> ## Group task: contextualising mentoring
>
> **1** Conduct a literature review to prepare an overview of relational and social learning theories.
>
> **2** Prepare a PowerPoint presentation explaining how relational and social learning theories can be used to design an effective mentor training programme for teachers or coaches.
>
> **3** Identify ten factors to be considered when measuring the effectiveness of a mentor programme on the professional practice of teachers or coaches.
>
> ### Further reading
>
> **Hobson, A.J., Ashby, P., Malderez, A. and Tomlinson, P.** (2009) Mentoring beginning teachers: What we know and what we don't, *Teaching and Teacher Education*, 24, 207–16.
>
> **Kirk, D., Macdonald, D. and O' Sullivan, M.** (2006) (eds) *The Handbook of Physical Education*, London: Sage, Chapter 4.9 Coaching and coach education by Pierre Trudel and Wade Gilbert.

References

Allen, D., Eby, L. T., O'Brien, K. E. and Lentz, E (2008) The state of mentoring research: a qualitative review of current research methods and future research implications, *Journal of Vocational Behavior*, vol. 73, issue 3, 343–57.

Armour, K. and Duncombe, R. (2009) Teachers' continuing professional development in primary physical education: lessons from present and past to inform the future. In: Bailey, R. and Kirk, D. (eds) *The Routledge Physical Education Reader*, Abingdon: Routledge.

Ayers, S. F. and Griffin, L. L. (2005) PETE mentoring as a mosaic, *Journal of Teaching in Physical Education*, 24(4), 368–78.

Cassidy, T., Jones, R. and Potrac, P. (2004) *Understanding Sports Coaching. The social, cultural and pedagogical foundations of coaching practice*, Abingdon: Routledge.

Cawyer, C. S., Simonds, C. and Davis, S (2002) Mentoring to facilitate socialization: the case of the new faculty member, *Qualitative Studies in Education*, vol. 15, no. 2, 225–42.

Cheallaigh, M. (2001) *Lifelong Learning: How the paradigm has changed in the 1990s. Training in Europe. Second report on vocational training research in Europe*, Luxembourg: Office for Official Publications of the European Communities.

Colley, H. (2003) Engagement mentoring for 'disaffected' youth: a new model of mentoring for social inclusion, *British Educational Research Journal*, 29(4), 521–2.

Costa, A. L. and Garmston, R. J. (2002) *Cognitive Coaching: A foundation for Renaissance schools* (2nd edn), Norwood, MA: Christopher-Gordon Publishers.

Cushion, C. (2006) Mentoring. Harnessing the power of experience. In: Jones, R. L. (ed.) *Coach as Educator: Reconceptualising Sports Coaching*, Abingdon: Routledge.

Dodds, P. (2005) PETE women's experiences of being mentored into postsecondary faculty positions, *Journal of Teaching in Physical Education*, 24(4), 344–67.

Eraut, M., Alderton, J., Cole, G. and Senker, P. (1998) *Development of Knowledge and Skills in Employment; Research Report No 5*, Brighton: University of Sussex Institute of Education.

Fletcher, S. (2000) *Mentoring in Schools: A handbook of good practice*, London: Kogan Page.

Gilles, C. and Wilson, J. (2004) Receiving as well as giving: mentors' perceptions of their professional development in one teacher induction program, *Mentoring and Tutoring*, 12(1), 87–106.

Glaser, B. G. (1999) *Learning and Knowledge*, Open University.

Griffiths, M. (2010) Mentoring as a learning strategy with volunteer sports coaches, Unpublished PhD thesis, Loughborough: Loughborough University.

Higgins, M. C. (2000) The more, the merrier? Multiple developmental relationships and work satisfaction, *Journal of Management Development*, vol. 19, no. 4, 277–96.

Higgins, M. C. and Kram, K. E. (2001) Reconceptualizing mentoring at work: a developmental network perspective, *Academy of Management Review*, vol. 26, no. 2, 264–86.

Hobson, A. J., Ashby, P., Malderez, A. and Tomlinson, P. (2009) Mentoring beginning teachers: What we know and what we don't, *Teaching and Teacher Education*, 24, 207–16.

Jones, R. L. and Wallace, M. (2005) Another bad day at the training ground: coping with ambiguity in the coaching context, *Sport, Education and Society*, 10(1), 119–34.

Jones, R. L., Harris, R. and Miles, A. (2009) Mentoring in sports coaching: a review of the literature, *Physical Education & Sport Pedagogy*, 14(3), 267–84.

Kirk, D. and Macdonald, D. (1998) Situated learning in physical education, *Journal of Teaching Physical Education*, 17, 376–87.

Lave, J. and Wenger, E. (1991) *Situated Learning: Legitimate peripheral participation*, Cambridge, Cambridge University Press.

McMahon, L. (2005) Mentoring: a means of healing new nurses, *Holistic Nursing Practice*, 19(5), 195–6.

North, J. (2009) *The UK Coaching Framework 2009-2016*, Leeds: Coachwise.

Parker, P., Douglas, T. H. and Kram, K. E. (2008) Peer coaching: a relational process for accelerating career learning, *The Academy of Management Learning and Education*, vol. 7, no. 4, 487–503.

Roberts, A. (2000) Mentoring revisited: a phenomenological reading of the literature, *Mentoring and Tutoring: Partnership in Learning*, 8, no. 2, 145–69.

Scandura, T. A. and Pellegrini, E. K. (2010) Workplace mentoring: theoretical approaches and methodological issues. In: T. D. Allen and L.T. Eby (eds) *The Blackwell Handbook of Mentoring: A multiple perspectives approach*, Oxford: Wiley-Blackwell, 71–92.

Spencer, R. (2006) Understanding the mentoring process between adolescents and adults, *Youth Society*, 37, 287.

Vygotsky, L. S. (1978) *Mind and Society: The development of higher mental processes*, Cambridge, MA: Harvard University Press.

Williams, E., Matthews, J. and Baugh, S. (2004) Developing a mentoring internship model for school leadership: using legitimate peripheral participation, *Mentoring & Tutoring: Partnership in Learning*, 12(1), 53–70.

Professional learning in communities of practice

Deborah Tannehill, University of Limerick

'This group has been very useful; it focused on our needs, in our situations, and with our students.'

'We developed a feeling of togetherness, you know, we weren't on our own . . . We have a network now where we can talk to each other about similar problems and maybe share resources.'

'Coming together as a group, sharing ideas that work . . . it was reassuring, exciting, it gave us a sense of, you know, enthusiasm, it rejuvenates you as well, to do things differently.'

'Maybe the best thing was that USP [Urban Schools Project] was ours; it was very encouraging to have each other . . . but that is it, it was our ideas and what we wanted to do that led us.'

(Urban Schools Project teachers)

 ## Introduction

These comments were shared by a group of physical education teachers following a year of working together to create a community of practice (Murphy and Tannehill, 2009). These teachers were similar in that they all worked in urban schools where facilities were limited and students faced difficult situations outside school. Traditional in-service workshops only brought frustration as they did not meet these teachers' needs or the context of their settings. As a community developed within the Urban Schools Project (USP), these teachers found themselves working together toward the common goal of designing and delivering a positive and effective physical education programme, with limited resources, for young people in challenging settings. One year later and this community continues to thrive, initiating innovative curricular workshops and sharing tips on practices that are effective in their settings. These teachers are actively consulting one another on issues related to their teaching and student learning and are beginning to consider how they might share their new knowledge with others in similar situations.

This chapter will discuss the meaning of a community of practice, how it impacts teaching, coaching and learning, and how a community of practice is created and maintained. Discussion will challenge you to consider how you might develop such a community among your own peers/colleagues within and beyond physical education and sport settings. Comments will draw on other communities of practice that have developed and sustained themselves through the commitment and hard work of their members. This chapter illustrates one of the ways in which teachers and coaches can be supported as career-long learners in the interests of the children and young people they serve.

What is a community of practice?

Research has informed us that learning is more effective when it takes place in an environment that encourages active participation with opportunities for frequent and sustained interaction among the group (Bosco, 1986; Bruner, 1986). This notion of participatory interaction is consistent with 'learning that takes place within a social environment that encourages reflective dialogue and collaboration' (Chapman *et al.*, 2005, p. 220); in other words, a community. The relationship between community and learning was first introduced in a business context and has since been adapted and applied to educational settings. In an educational setting, the focus is on teachers developing their own collaborative culture and it is assumed that teachers with mutual interests will question, reflect on and share their daily experiences to benefit the community. By providing support to one another to improve teaching practice, the outcome is increased teacher knowledge and enhanced pupil learning (Thompson, Gregg and Niska, 2004). Although professional learning contexts in coaching may be different from those in teaching, the potential to gain learning benefits from collaboration is similar.

In recent years there has been growing recognition of the importance of providing teachers with professional development opportunities to work together. As learners in a collegial setting, teachers can discuss, share, plan and question one another's views on teaching and learning; thus becoming thoughtful practitioners through collaborative discourse. The impact of teacher learning on pupil learning has been recognised by researchers (Cohen and Hill, 1998) who confirm what we might expect intuitively: pupil performance is improved as teachers receive more opportunities to learn. Day (2000) argued that effective learning opportunities are those professional development initiatives that take the complexities of teachers' lives and conditions of work into account. We are reminded, for example, that teacher learning does not happen in small chunks of time delivered in one-shot programme offerings; rather it occurs over extended periods of time and requires teachers to make connections between what they know and have experienced with new knowledge, understanding and concepts (Deglau and O'Sullivan, 2006). In a similar way, continuous professional development of coaches is recognised as critical to the enhancement of sport experiences and performance for children, players and athletes at all levels (Cushion *et al.*, 2003).

Wenger (2000) tells us that a community of practice is defined along three dimensions: what it is about, how it functions and what capability it has produced:

- *What the community is about* – community interest is the focus which is continually revisited, evaluated and challenged.
- *How the community functions* – community relationships and interactions bond members to one another and guide their development.
- *What capability the community has produced* – common characteristics or products that have come to make the community unique (rituals, language, beliefs, values).

The most significant point to make is that communities build around and are sustained by what their members believe, understand and value; in other words, what matters most to them. Pedagogy, whether in teaching or coaching, is centrally concerned with the ability of professionals to meet the learning needs of children and young people (Armour, Chapter 1, this text). Communities of practice can be an effective way to support professionals in this endeavour.

> **Comment**
> *Communities of practice are groups of people who share a concern or a passion for something they do and learn how to do it better as they interact regularly. (Wenger, 2006)*

Communities in physical education and sport

The concept of communities of practice has become popular in the literature on the professional development of physical education teachers. Scholars have suggested that teachers working collaboratively can be an effective means of promoting teacher learning (Duncombe and Armour, 2005). Siedentop and Tannehill (2000) outline six characteristics that define learning communities, which, they suggest, are intentional, take concerted time and ongoing effort, and in-depth discourse, to design and maintain.

- Communities have real and identifying *boundaries* that make them distinct from other groupings (e.g. societal, school, curricular, class, online, or team).
- Creating a community takes considerable time and focused effort, thus requiring a group to *persist over a period of time* (which highlights the need for supportive organisational structures).
- Communities develop *common goals* where successful achievement is defined collectively, as a group.
- Learners in a community learn to *cooperate* and support one another in and beyond that community (i.e. an ethic of care results from discourse and practice within a supportive learning environment).
- Affiliation and identity within a community are created through *symbols and rituals* for which members can strive for success (e.g. sporting and ethnic communities are identified through their rituals and symbols).
- Communities are built on respect, *caring and fairness* among and toward all members.

Various labels have been used to describe this idea of a community: inquiry community, community of practice, learning community, community of teachers, or professional learning community. Regardless of which term you choose, a community has the features identified above. As Wenger and Snyder (2000) suggest, a community of practice is 'a group of people informally bound together by shared expertise and passion for a joint enterprise' (p. 139) and where new approaches and solutions to problems are created through collaborative discourse aligned with practice.

> **Comment**
> *With careful design and appropriate support, communities of practice can support teachers and learners to learn in ways that are meaningful for them.*

Building a community of practice

We know, from both experience and research, that communities of practice take time and effort to build and sustain; they do not just happen. Teachers are embedded in organisational structures (schools) that could – although often do not – facilitate the development of such communities. Coaches often operate outside formal educational structures, yet there is an increasing interest in finding ways to allow communities of practice to develop. It could be argued that the development of a wider community that allows those professionals in physical education and youth sport to join together in their common interest would be helpful.

Communities form for a variety of reasons. There are a number of recent examples in Ireland:

- the USP described earlier where members organised themselves to design and deliver a positive and effective physical education programme, with limited resources, for young people in challenging settings;
- the Physical Education Association of Ireland's (PEAI) regional communities that provide teachers with a forum for discussion and learning about innovative teaching strategies;
- a cohort of undergraduate students who progress in a lock-step fashion through the four-year teacher education programme with the shared goal of becoming teachers;
- pre-service teachers working in shorter duration and smaller communities of practice to design and deliver curricula, and assess pupils.

In each instance, participants have learned with and from each other. As part of the learning process, they focused their discourse on specific issues related to their context and they challenged, sought alternatives and helped one another develop individual and shared practices. Each of these communities, although in diverse settings with different goals, can continue to grow and develop, reinforcing Wenger and Snyder's (2000) view that 'as they [communities of practice] generate knowledge, they reinforce and renew themselves' (p. 143).

> **Comment**
> *Within educational physical activity settings there are a number of communities of practice . . . A community of practice could be as large as the global sporting community or as small as a group of students playing doubles badminton. (Laker, 2003)*

Increased opportunities for teachers and coaches to interact collaboratively on professional issues allow them to support each other's learning. This collaborative process can also support their development as lifelong learners, which is a central characteristic of being a professional (Armour, Chapter 1, this text). Communities that foster collegial experiences provide learning forums in which teachers and coaches come to value their own professional development. DuFour and Eaker (1998) highight four prerequisites to building an effective collaborative community environment:

- Set *time* aside explicitly for collaborative exchange.
- The *focus is determined collaboratively* as a community and shared explicitly.
- *Ongoing support* is provided to the community with teachers' needs provided for.
- *Teaching colleagues commit* to working together to achieve common professional goals.

> **Comment**
> *Building a community of practice takes time and effort to develop, it needs to be intentional and focused, and perhaps most important, it must involve committed and interested participants brought together in a nurturing environment where they have support to develop and grow.*

Community membership

If members within a community are to be empowered to participate, take ownership of collaborative goals and outcomes, and achieve individual growth, then they must continually have opportunities to share, discover and experience as a member of the group. Wenger (1998) identifies three ways in which members choose to be a part of a community and develop a sense of belonging with it:

- engagement – how actively participants engage in aspects within the community;
- imagination – participants' ability to imagine new roles for themselves in their work;
- alignment – participants' actions to become fully part of the community.

These imply that a learner's identity within the community is defined by participatory choices and level of commitment. Ultimately, community membership is defined by whoever participates in and contributes to the activities, endeavours and practices of the community.

Lave and Wenger (1991) first talked about legitimate peripheral participation to describe how new participants in a community of practice move from being individual learners in the community to being full and contributing members through continued and sustained participation in authentic group efforts. This involves a shift from what Rovegno (2006) describes as 'in-the-head' learning to learning as an active and interactive member of a social group: a community. When reflecting on communities in which we have been members (e.g. sports clubs), most of us can recall instances where new members were either accepted willingly or, in some cases, where they were sidelined by existing members. This is an ongoing and expected issue to be encountered in any community setting.

The PEAI community of practice (Tannehill, O'Sullivan and Ní Chroinin, 2006) included new teachers who had recently completed their teacher training as well as veterans who had been teaching for 20 years or longer. While these teachers had many things in common, they were also quite diverse. It soon became clear, for example, that the needs of veteran teachers were quite different from those of the young teachers who had just completed their education. Veteran teachers were eager to discuss issues related to the place of physical education in schools, the development of physical education as an examination subject (the leaving certificate in the Irish context), teacher/coach role conflict, and how to lobby/advocate in schools for the subject. Novice teachers, on the other hand, were preoccupied with the day-to-day happenings in the classroom, behaviour management and how to establish a learning environment that would allow them to deliver an exciting and relevant physical education programme.

It became clear that novice teachers would benefit from mentoring – and who better to provide that mentoring than their more experienced veteran counterparts? At the same time, veterans needed opportunities to address topics that were relevant to their stage of professional development. Determining how to meet these disparate learning needs has been a challenge for professional development providers. Yet teachers and coaches are expected to meet pupils' disparate learning needs in every session they plan and deliver. Modelling this level of differentiation in professional development for teachers and coaches can only be regarded as good practice.

> **Comment**
> *Community membership is defined by whoever participates in and contributes to the activities, endeavours and practices of the community; over time, members may move from peripheral to fully participating members.*

Stages of development

Communities of practice can exist within one unit (e.g. a dance troupe, a classroom, a school) or across units (e.g. physical education teachers from different schools throughout the community; coaches from different clubs). Communities can also be officially recognised, serve a strategic function or be informal. The lifespan of a community is defined by its value and worth to its members; a strong and flexible community may survive through many projects, issues, problems and endeavours. Regardless of the setting or purpose, all communities of practice progress through various stages of development that Wenger (1998) describes as potential, coalescing, active, dispersed and memorable, and he provides examples of the types of activities that occur during each stage.

Stage 1: potential

In this stage, people face similar situations, yet they do not benefit from a mutual understanding, discourse, or a shared practice. *Activities* during this stage are marked by teachers becoming aware of one another and discussing the issues, problems and circumstances they have in common. This may be experienced at a formal professional development course where teachers or coaches find colleagues who share interests and concerns.

Stage 2: coalescing

While in the coalescing stage, members get together and begin to recognise the opportunities that exist if they work together as a group. *Activities* during this stage would see teachers becoming better acquainted, examining the things they have in common, and developing joint endeavours to serve them and their students.

Stage 3: active

Throughout the active stage community members are involved in sharing, developing and implementing shared practice. *Activities* include discussions focused on common interests, taking part in joint activities, developing materials and documentation to support community focus, giving and receiving from the group through negotiation, commitment and collaborative relationships.

Stage 4: dispersed

There often comes a point when members engage less frequently, although the community itself still exists as a resource and for consultancy. *Activities* become less formal, yet are marked by members maintaining communication and interacting when there is a need.

Stage 5: memorable

Although the community has taken a less prominent position, members hold on to the knowledge gained and the camaraderie which has formed part of who they are. *Activities* are reflected in the reference members make to the community when sharing their own stories or through the resources developed.

> *Comment*
> *The lifespan of a community is defined by its value and worth to its members. Wenger (1998) describes the stages through which communities of practice progress: potential, coalescing, active, dispersed and memorable.*

Sustaining a community of practice

The amount of support, nurturing, consultation, recognition and motivation a community needs to sustain itself and to progress through the different stages of development varies. Some communities are able to survive and develop on their own with little outside input or acknowledgement while others need guidance and focused attention to help them recognise their own capabilities. Ultimately, a community functions most effectively when it is steered by its own members toward the goals they wish to achieve. Wenger (1998) suggests that this community leadership can vary from a member who serves to inspire the community to someone who oversees the day-to-day activities; and from the liaison with other groups to the pacesetter who promotes innovative ideas and practices. No single role is more important than another and each may be informal or more formally recognised by the community. Managing a community from the outside, while necessary in some cases to help them get started, must not end up leading to manipulation towards external ends. For professional development providers, therefore, establishing communities of practice is a very different activity to the usual model of course provision as continuing professional development (CPD) (Guskey, 2000). Importantly, therefore, the professional development needs of professional development providers should not be forgotten.

In their initial work with a PEAI community of practice, Tannehill, O'Sullivan and Ní Chroinin (2006) were reminded that understanding teachers as learners is *the* key consideration in establishing teacher communities. Just as is the case with all learners, the views of teachers as learners are important and allowing them to influence the focus of learning is critical for all communities of practice to flourish. During the first year of working in the community, the needs of the teachers somehow became confused with the direction in which the organisers thought the teachers wanted to go and, as a result, some of the teachers dropped out. In initial discussions, teachers wanted to focus specifically on 'what' to teach and 'how' to teach it. Over time, however, teachers did begin to recognise that there was the potential for interesting dialogue on wider issues related to teachers and teaching, teaching and learning, and innovative physical education programmes. As was noted by Armour in Chapter 1, sport pedagogy is about young people learning both in and through sport, and discourse around the wider pedagogical issues can inform and impact upon coaching/teaching practice and, ultimately, young learners. In the end, the PEAI community of practice worked best when the organisers recognised that it was the teachers' community and that they were there to facilitate learning, not dominate it. The organisers learned to trust the teachers to develop in the direction they chose and to support them to extend their learning when they were ready.

There are a number of benefits to the teacher/coach, to practice and to learners as a result of participating as a member of a community of practice (Vessio, Ross and Adams, 2006). It has been shown that teacher participation in a community *changes teaching practice*; for example, teachers become more student-centred and attempt new instructional strategies to address student needs. It also *changes the teaching culture* in that teachers learn to collaborate in 'critical friends' discussions, focus on student learning and achievement, take ownership of instructional decisions, and critically reflect on their ongoing professional development needs. Indeed, there is some evidence to suggest that if teachers participate in a community of practice that specifically focuses on student needs, the result is *increased student learning and achievement* (Vessio, Ross and Adams, 2006).

> **Comment**
> *Communities of practice function most effectively when steered by their own members toward the goals they wish to achieve.*

Classroom learning communities

A classroom setting can refer to pupils in a school, a teacher education classroom for pre-service teachers, a postgraduate classroom, or even a youth sport setting. A learning community might be thought of as a setting where learning is viewed as a social process with teachers and students learning and growing together, working toward collective goals and sharing ideas and understandings. This type of setting locates the needs of learners at the heart of any learning process, taking into account their individual interests, experiences and previous knowledge. This type of community challenges learners to take responsibility for applying, analysing and interpreting new knowledge and relating it to what they already know. For example, post-primary (secondary) school pupils in a sport education badminton 'season' can learn roles other than that of sports participant, which is the role they most frequently experience in traditional physical education lessons.

In Sport Education, each team has a trainer (leads warm-ups), a coach (oversees training sessions), a head official (teaches rules and directs the team in official responsibilities) and a sport reporter (maintains scores, records and publicises results), who each oversee and guide their team in different learning experiences while the teacher facilitates learning and understanding. Research supports this type of learning, suggesting that students learn and perform better in settings where cooperative learning is encouraged and is the norm. For example, Deglau and O'Sullivan (2006) found that as teachers, pre-service teachers and pupils learn, grow and change they interact with and participate in the community differently, which ultimately impacts both their individual development and that of the community.

There are a number of potential benefits for students who become part of a community within the classroom. These can range from developing more positive attitudes toward school to demonstrating improved performance in specific content areas. The social processes involved in community development can also lead to a more caring attitude towards peers and showing greater respect towards other children and teachers. As young people improve the positive nature of their interactions, feel more committed to their peers and have voice in their own learning experiences, we have also found that teachers tend to have fewer behavioural and management problems.

Learning communities do not just 'happen' by putting groups of students together in the classroom. Learners – of all ages – can sometimes be afraid to ask for help, to let others see they do not understand or have questions on how to proceed. Creating learning environments where learners feel comfortable to share, interact, question and support each other openly is a design task for the teacher. Planning should involve students interacting in group work for which the teacher has designed 'interdependent tasks, established clear goals, effectively organized discussions, monitors activities to reinforce how students can help one another, and facilitates frequent evaluations of how work is progressing' (LePage et al., 2005, p. 338). There could be concerns that these community settings that take time to develop reduce the time available for more traditional content-focused aspects of learning. However, it can also be argued that taking the time to set the stage and to develop a supportive and nurturing environment is never an optional extra. If young learners are expected to provide one another with learning assistance and to serve as what is termed 'critical friends', they must feel safe and confident doing so.

When developing a community of practice among graduate diploma students (one-year pedagogy course following a non-teaching BSc in physical education), we spent much of the first intensive week (five hours per day) sharing stories, values, beliefs and opinions, designing and sharing teaching metaphors, and taking part in a variety of community-building activities. When, by day five, I asked the students to find a partner with whom they did not yet feel safe and comfortable, the 17 students looked at each other, then me, and laughed, saying, 'There is no one left to get to know; we are sorted.' This suggests that systematically building strong and supportive relationships with and among learners, what Bullough and Gitlin (2001) refer to as 'a way of being with and relating to others' (p. 3), is both feasible and necessary.

> **Comment**
> *Classroom learning communities might be viewed as settings where learning is a social process with teachers and students learning and growing together, working toward collective goals and sharing ideas and understandings.*

Critical friends in teacher and coach education

Since a single course typically does not meet the criterion of ongoing and sustained learning, it might be better thought of as learning with a group of critical friends. Costa and Kallick (1993) define a critical friend as 'a trusted person who asks provocative questions, provides data to be examined through another lens, and offers critique of a person's work as a friend' (p. 50). The suggestion has been made that working in a critical friends group fosters collegiality and community as members observe one another's practice, challenge each other's reflections and provide a new perspective through which to view teaching practice. Bambino (2002) tells us that critical friends give feedback, collaborate and find solutions leading to the formation of a reflective community working together to improve teaching practice and, ultimately, pupils' learning.

One such group of critical friends was established in a fourth-year module for pre-service teachers who had completed their final teaching practice (TP), were concluding their fourth-year research project (FYP) and were engaged in a final semester of coursework prior to receiving their teaching licensure (full accreditation to teach). This took the form of a project-based outdoor adventure education module. Pre-service teachers, working within a small five-member teaching team, were assigned a post-primary (secondary) school in the community with one class of transition-year pupils for whom they design and deliver a challenging and realistic outdoor experience (e.g. orienteering, hill walking, overnight camping trip). The nature of this project allows these pre-service teachers to work in a small community as critical friends who share a common goal within one specific teaching context. Through their collaboration they encounter issues and problems for which they must negotiate and ultimately find solutions. These pre-service teachers have been peers for a number of years and have come to recognise one another's strengths and weaknesses. As a group they can discuss alternatives and with their knowledge of the group they know which colleague to turn to for ideas on specific issues. Together they can brainstrom, challenge, evaluate options and collectively decide on one solution, or a series of solutions, they will work through. As these pre-service teachers analyse their own teaching practice and the learning of their pupils, they begin to form a collective view of what good practice is, what misunderstandings they possess or that have been communicated to their pupils, and ultimately which learning experiences and teaching strategies best facilitate pupil learning (Darling-Hammond and Richardson, 2009).

> **Comment**
> *Bambino (2002) tells us that critical friends give feedback, collaborate and find solutions, with the result being formation of a reflective community working together to improve teaching practice and ultimately the learning of pupils.*

Conclusion

While I, the author of this chapter, am primarily a teacher educator, many of the things I value most in this role and which help me to do better performing it are the things I want my pre-service teachers to experience and come to appreciate as professionals. Being part of a community composed of the colleagues with whom I teach and conduct research is foremost among them. My colleagues and I strive to maintain the close-knit and safe haven we have created intentionally through deliberate and focused effort. It reflects a community where we share common goals for our research and our practice of preparing teachers, we support and encourage one another's work, and we challenge and push each other to think outside the box; it is a place where we are safe to learn and grow. What we have found is that the more we take ownership of our community, the more we contribute and share, the more meaning and growth we receive in return.

> Learning is enhanced when it is more like a team effort than a solo race. Good learning, like good work, is collaborative and social, not competitive and isolated. Working with others often increases involvement in learning. Sharing one's own ideas and responding to others' reactions sharpens thinking and deepens understanding.
>
> (Chickering and Gamson, 1987, p. 1)

Learning tasks

Individual task

All of us have been members of some type of community (e.g. Irish dance, religious, local sports teams, ethnic). You may be a long-standing member of this community, someone who participates on a somewhat frequent basis (peripheral participant), or perhaps you are trying to become a full member. Based on your own learning experiences in this community, identify the key characteristics of the community that both help and hinder your learning.

Group task: building a community of learners

With a partner or small group, your task is to produce a story plan for intentionally developing a learning community within a physical education class or youth sport setting. The plan you produce should include:

- a description of the focus for this learning community;
- a description of the length and distribution of time for the learning community;

(continued)

- a plan for developing a collaborative social contract for how the learning community will be implemented;
- a description of teacher strategies for developing caring and community among the pupils;
- a description of symbols and rituals that will be used for establishing boundaries and building community;
- a strategy for dealing with class issues and interpersonal conflicts to be collaboratively developed with pupils;
- a plan for out-of-class activities that will link pupil learning to opportunities in the community.

Blend all of these tasks into your story, with the purpose of making it an informative, exciting and realistic plan to undertake with pupils in a class.

Further reading

Siedentop, D. and Tannehill, D. (2000) Chapter 6: Developing a community of learners. In: *Developing Teaching Skills in Physical Education*, Mountain View, CA: Mayfield Publishing Co.

Wenger, E. C. and Snyder, W. M. (2000) Communities of practice: the organizational frontier; *Harvard Business Review*; January–February.

References

Bambino, D. (2002) Redesigning professional development: critical friends, *Educational Leadership*, 59(6), 25–7.

Bosco, J. (1986) An analysis of evaluations of intractive video, *Educational Technology*, 25, 7–16.

Bruner, J. (1986) *Actual Minds, Possible Words*, Cambridge, MA: University Press.

Bullough, R. V. and Gitlin, A. (2001) *Becoming a Student of Teaching: Methodologies for exploring self and school context* (2nd edn), Madison: Brown and Benchmark.

Chapman, C., Ramondt, L. and Smiley, G. (2005) Strong community, deep learning: exploring the link, *Innovations in Education and Teaching International*, 42(3), August, 217–30.

Chickering, A. W. and Gamson, Z. F. (1987) Seven principles for good practice in undergraduate education, *American Association of Higher Education (AAHE) Bulletin*.

Cohen, D. K. and Hill, H. C. (1998) *Instruction, Capacity, and Improvement*, Philadelphia, PA: Consortium for Policy Research in Education, University of Pennsylvania (CPRE RR-43).

Costa, A. L. and Kallick, B. (1993) Through the lens of a critical friend, *Educational Leadership*, 51(2), 49–51.

Cushion, C. J., Armour, K. M. and Jones, R. L. (2003) Coach education and continuing professional development: experience and learning to coach, *Quest*, 55(3), 215–30.

Darling-Hammond, L. and Richardson, N. (2009) Research review/teacher learning: What matters? *Educational Leadership*, 66(5), 46–53.

Day, C. (2000) Teachers in the 21st century: time to renew the vision, *Teachers and Teaching: Theory into Practice*, 6(1), 101–15.

Deglau, D. and O'Sullivan, M. (2006) The effects of long-term professional development program on the beliefs and practices of experienced teachers. In: Ward and O'Sullivan (eds) Monograph Issue of the *Journal of Teaching in Physical Education*, 25(4), 379–96.

DuFour, R. and Eaker, R. (1998) *Professional Learning Communities at Work: Best practices for enhancing student achievement*, Bloomington, IN: National Education Service.

Duncombe, R. and Armour, K. M. (2005) *The School as a Community of Practice for Primary Physical Education: The myths and the reality*, Paper presented at the British Educational Research Association's Annual Conference, University of Glamorgan, 14–17 September 2005.

Guskey, T. R. (2000) *Evaluating Professional Development*, London: Corwin Press.

Laker, A. (2003) *The Future of Physical Education: Building a new pedagogy*, London: Routledge.

Lave, J. and Wenger, E. (1991). *Situated Learning: Legitimate peripheral participation*. Cambridge, UK: Cambridge University Press.

LePage, P., Darling-Hammond, L., Hanife, A., Gutierrez, C., Jenkins-Gunn, E. and Rosebrock, E. (2005) In: L. Darling-Hammond and J. Bransford (eds) *Preparing Teachers for a Changing World*, San Francisco, CA: Jossey-Bass.

Murphy, G. and Tannehill, D. (2009) *Urban Schools Initiative Report – Interim Report*, submitted to the Junior Cycle Physical Education Support Services.

Rovegno, I. (2006) Situated perspectives on learning. In: D. Kirk, D. Macdonald and M. O'Sullivan (eds) *The Handbook of Physical Education*, London: SAGE, 264–74.

Siedentop, D. and Tannehill, D. (2000) Chapter 6: Developing a community of learners. In: *Developing Teaching Skills in Physical Education*, Mountain View, CA: Mayfield Publishing Co.

Tannehill, D., O'Sullivan, M. and Ní Chroinin, D. (2006) *Developing a Community of Practice*, Research paper presented at the *British Educational Research Association*, England, September 2006.

Thompson, S. C., Gregg, L. and Niska, J. M. (2004) Professional learning communities, leadership, and student learning, *Research in Middle School Education Online*, 28(1), 35, 20.

Vessio, V., Ross, D. and Adams, A. (2006) *A Review of Research on Professional Learning Communities: What do we know?* Paper presented at the *National School Reform Faculty* (NSRF) Research Forum, January 2006.

Wenger, E. C. (1998) Communities of practice: learning as a social system, *Systems Thinker Newsletter*, June, Pegasus Communications.

Wenger, E. C. (2000) Communities of practice and social learning systems, *Organization*, 7(2), 225–46.

Wenger, E. C. (2006) *Communities of Practice: A brief introduction*, http://www.ewenger.com/theory/.

Wenger, E. C. and Snyder, W. M. (2000) Communities of practice: the organizational frontier, *Harvard Business Review*, January–February 2000.

25

Models-based practice: structuring teaching and coaching to meet learners' diverse needs

Toni O'Donovan, University of Bedfordshire

From the word go you know where you're going, what you're aiming for, what you're doing and you are working together as a team, you're not going out with just your class. It's very tangible, it's meant to me that on a Wednesday evening I am not sitting planning, because it's already there, it's been planned and the beginning of every year I know that it has to be reconsidered according to what you want for the children.

(Classroom teacher, Mountfields Lodge Primary School[1])

 ## Introduction

Traditionally, physical education programmes in the UK and elsewhere have been organised around short six-to-eight-week blocks of activity. In these cases, learning a specific sport or physical activity is the key purpose of the unit. On the other hand, a models-based approach to teaching or coaching usually has a broader learning focus and it operates within a tighter theoretical framework. So, instead of focusing mainly on teaching the skills of a sport for a block of curriculum time, a models-based approach helps pupils to learn selected personal, social or developmental outcomes through their engagement in sport. It

---

[1] Throughout this paper I draw on extracts from interviews with teachers at Mountfields Lodge Primary School conducted as part of a six-year study of the implementation of models-based practice at the school. Further details of this study can be found in MacPhail *et al.*, 2003, 2004, 2005; O'Donovan *et al.*, 2010.

is claimed that this approach can result in more effective learning for children and young people. Over the past 30 years, models-based practice has been developed to help teachers and coaches to deliver high-quality programmes with a range of learning outcomes. This chapter outlines the key features of models-based practice and then explores the expertise that teachers and coaches need to implement this approach. Throughout the chapter, selected models are introduced that are relevant for both physical education and youth sport programmes.

What is models-based practice?

Within an education context, Joyce and Weil (1996) defined a model as a 'plan or pattern that can be used to shape curriculum, to design instructional materials, and to guide instruction in the classroom and other settings' (p. 1). Metzler (2005, p. 16) expanded this definition, suggesting that:

> an instructional model can be described as a comprehensive and coherent plan for teaching that includes a theoretical foundation, a statement of intended learning outcomes, teacher's content knowledge expertise, developmentally appropriate and sequenced learning activities, expectations for teacher and student behaviours, unique task structures, measures of learning outcomes, and mechanisms for measuring the faithful implementation of the model itself.

Kirk (2006) argued that the term 'pedagogical model' is preferable to instructional model because, similar to Armour's argument in Chapter 1, it highlights the interdependence and irreducibility of learning, teaching, subject matter and context. This reinforces a key feature of models-based practice, i.e. congruence between Bernstein's three-message systems of curriculum, pedagogy and assessment (Bernstein, 1977). It can be argued, therefore, that a pedagogical model is an exemplar articulating best practice with a coherent focus and overall plan for teaching/coaching and learning.

In essence, models-based practice is concerned with ensuring that teachers and coaches have a comprehensive and coherent plan to ensure that planned activities match desired learning outcomes. Thus, a model:

- provides an overall plan and coherent approach to teaching and learning;
- clarifies learning domain priorities and domain interactions;
- provides an instructional theme;
- allows the teacher and student to understand current and upcoming events;
- provides a unified theoretical framework;
- has research support;
- promotes a technical language for teachers;
- allows for the relation between instruction and learning to be verified;
- allows for more valid assessments of learning;
- promotes teacher decision making within a known framework.

(Metzler, 2005, pp. 24–8)

Metzler further suggested that planning for daily lessons becomes much easier in a models-based approach because each model calls for its own set of decisions, plans and actions by the teacher and students.

At Mountfields Lodge Primary School in England, teachers found models-based practice significantly easier to implement than their usual approaches to teaching physical education. For example, two teachers said:

> There is a framework in place so that we know what is going to happen from week to week: when the block of league matches will be; when the children will create their uniforms that they use; when the final sport gala day will be, just so that the teachers have a clear idea of what is going on.
>
> Just from a very practical point of view of the work–life balance, it takes a load off, once it is up and running it takes a load off the staff as well.

In these examples, it can be seen that a coherent framework for planning resulted in better decision making for teachers in the planning process. This helped to improve the congruency between decisions and actions within a unit of work, thus supporting effective student learning. Rather than having to decide how to teach from a long list of discrete skills, managerial schemes, styles and learning strategies, the teachers had a reduced range of choices based on each selected model's framework, design, context and the unit content. Metzler (2005) notes that whereas instructional strategies or styles can be selected for particular learning activities, a model is designed to be used as a framework for an entire programme or unit. The model thus embraces all of the planning, design, implementation and assessment functions of that unit by utilising multiple methods, strategies and styles.

> **Comment**
> *Models-based practice offers an alternative to the traditional activity-based curriculum.*

Planning a quality physical education programme

A pedagogical model with programme-level goals and objectives will lead to the selection of content units, instruction and policies that allow students to achieve the goals of the programme (Metzler, 2005). Each individual pedagogical model in models-based practice is underpinned by a main theme or 'big idea' that gives structure to a programme, and this is often indicated in its title. Examples of pedagogical models at a programmatic level could include:

- multi-activity;
- cultural studies;
- teaching games for understanding;
- sport education;
- movement education;
- taking personal and social responsibility;
- academic discipline-based;
- health/fitness education models.

Thus, models ensure that entire physical education programmes are underpinned by comprehensive and coherent plans. Models-based practice could also be useful in the youth sport context where sport is used to achieve wider educational or health goals (for example in youth re-engagement programmes). A model is, therefore, part of a 'bigger picture' of learning and education.

In the following section, I will examine the strengths and weaknesses of one model – the multi-activity model – which has traditionally dominated physical education programmes around the world, before proceeding to introduce a range of more contemporary models.

The multi-activity model: a traditional approach to programme planning

Traditionally the multi-activity model has been dominant in physical education programmes throughout the United States, Australia, the UK and other European countries. It is designed to give students some (limited) experience of a variety of sports and other physical activities. It tends to focus on the development of fundamental skills, sport skills, and tactical development of games play. More recently the model has also included a focus on health-related physical activity. In contrast to other forms of models-based practice which begin with a consideration of what a specific programme wants to accomplish, the multi-activity model traditionally begins with identifying and sequencing the activities in which students will engage. Typically the organising focus is on specific content; for example, teaching basketball skills in a particular order, basing instruction on the outcomes and goals for a unit of activity. Many readers will recognise this approach, having experienced the traditional multi-activity model during their school years. Typically in this model, sports and other activities are taught in six-week blocks with a change of activity each half term.

The multi-activity model has been widely criticised because in the typical short learning blocks, students gain relatively little expertise in any one activity and they rarely have the opportunity to progress their learning beyond an introductory level. For example, Taggart and Goodwin (2000) have commented that this form of 'Sport-based PE, which remains the predominant form of PE across Australia in both primary and secondary schools, needs to change if outcomes-based education is to be an integral part of students' schooling in physical education' (p. 4, cited in Penny, 2005). These authors go on to argue that a programme based on the multi-activity model needs to be very clear about the specific educational worth of each selected sport or physical activity if it is to underpin a physical education programme.

> **Comment**
> *Models-based practice is about the development of deep knowledge that goes beyond surface technical knowledge in order to improve learning outcomes for children and young people in schools and in other youth sport settings.*

A number of contemporary curriculum models are described below, such as the Cultural Studies model, and these descriptions highlight the differences between traditional physical education and models-based approaches. Models such as these encourage teachers to identify the assumptions underpinning their practice.

Cultural studies (O'Sullivan and Kinchin, 2005)

Overview

The cultural studies curriculum model attempts to integrate physical and cognitive student involvement in sport and physical activity, with a critical investigation of physical activity and sport in society.

Aim

To develop students as literate and critical consumers of sport, physical activity and the movement culture such that students are informed, watchful, and have the knowledge, skills and confidence to critique physical activity provision and presentation on local and national levels.

Underpinning philosophy

Teachers believe it is their responsibility to shape the curriculum in order to address serious social and ethical issues in sport and health.

Programme structure

Learning experiences enable students to present, defend and act on their ideas about issues of social justice in physical activity and sport. This includes integrated practical and academic components. Teachers choose specific physical activities as the foundational content of the curriculum and then engage students in discussion and critique of contemporary social issues in sport through journals, group projects and presentations. In New Zealand and Australia, this sociocultural perspective 'now underpins most syllabuses . . . and may include classroom-based lessons where students explicitly learn about physical activity, exercise and sport' (Wright, 2004, p.10)

This model has clear potential in both physical education and youth sport settings, although clearly it is easiest to implement in an educational context such as a school. It is certainly a radical departure from the traditional multi-activity model. However, the idea that it is a central task of teachers and coaches to develop critical and literate consumers of sport and physical activities is not shared by all teachers. For example, we should not be too surprised to find that different teachers have different philosophies about the purposes of physical education. What this means is that in models-based practice, it is important to engage in a critical analysis of the learning theory and philosophy upon which any model is based.

The multi-model approach and instructional models

Metzler (2005) suggests that physical education, with its broad-ranging and diverse content, presents complex challenges for many teachers. Most models pursue a limited number of student learning outcomes, all of which are strongly related to the models' theme. The complexity inherent in physical education suggests that multiple models of practice might be useful within a physical education programme.

Siedentop and Tannehill (2000) advocate a 'multi-model approach' which is made up of a set of selected key theme models. This is not to be confused with the multi-activity model centred around specific sports. These authors argued that no one model leads to comprehensive student achievement and that to reach optimal levels of success, numerous models should be used to meet the learning needs of young learners. For example, Siedentop (1986) developed the 'Sport Education model' but also highlighted its many shortcomings if utilised in isolation in physical education programmes.

Sport Education as an instructional model

Overview

This was originally developed and introduced by Daryl Siedentop in 1986. It was based on concerns that despite sport being the key content area of physical education, young people were not experiencing authentic versions of sport and the associated sporting culture. The Sport Education model was developed to provide young people with authentic and enjoyable sport experiences.

Aim

The three major aims that guide Sport Education are for students to become competent, literate and enthusiastic players.

Underpinning philosophy

Teachers believe it is their responsibility to shape the curriculum in order to educate students in all aspects of a sports culture.

Unit structure

The basic structure of Sport Education is adapted from the familiar model of organised sport. Siedentop (1994) identified six key features that make sport 'special': seasons, team affiliation, formal competition, culminating events, record keeping and festivity. Young people participate as members of persisting teams in seasons that last approximately 16 to 20 lessons – which is longer than a traditional physical education unit of activity. In addition, they take an active role in their own sport experience by serving in varied and realistic roles that are routinely seen in authentic sport settings such as captains, coaches, trainers, statisticians, officials, publicists, and members of a sports council. This gives the students a broader experience of sport as they learn the skills, responsibilities and roles that are associated with organised sport. Persisting teams are encouraged to develop affiliation through the selection of team names, logos and chants as young people work through a season of formal competition culminating in a sports 'festival'. At this festival, students are recognised and rewarded for fair play, improvement and the roles they adopted during the season. The Sport Education models relies extensively on cooperative learning strategies, and teaching styles are at the student-centred end of Mosston's Spectrum of Teaching Styles, thus allowing students to take responsibility for many of the decisions within the season.

Metzler (2005) suggests that instructional models require a high level of in-depth planning, including information on: the degree of teacher direction and student participation in activities, the nature and structure of learning tasks, engagement patterns for learning, students' developmental requirements, teacher and student roles and responsibilities, their verification, and the assessment of learning. He further argues that the specific context plays an important role in the design and implementation of all models; and the more familiar a teacher is with an instructional model, the easier it is to change the model to fit the particular school setting, content and class. It is rare to find a situation where a model can be used as an exact blueprint, so it will usually be necessary for a teacher or coach to consider a myriad of contextual factors in their structuring of a physical education or youth sport programme.

> **Comment**
>
> *A models-based approach requires teachers and coaches to engage in extensive pre-planning and to adapt 'standard' models to meet local contextual needs.*

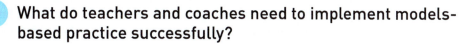

What do teachers and coaches need to implement models-based practice successfully?

Teachers' philosophies

It was noted earlier that each pedagogical model is based on a clearly articulated philosophy or 'big idea' that helps a teacher or coach to plan for important or valued learning outcomes for students. Lund and Tannehill (2005) argue that as professionals, it is critical that teachers (and coaches) come to terms with what they believe personally about the value of physical education and its goals. Ennis describes a teacher's beliefs about education as a value orientation that reflects his or her views about 'what students should learn, how they should engage in the learning process, and how learning should be assessed' (Ennis, 2003, p. 111). Teachers and coaches hold different personal theories about physical education and sport, and these will influence their selection of different models-based approaches. Indeed, Penney (2005) suggested that teachers should ask themselves a number of questions about their own value orientations:

- Which outcomes matter most, to whom?
- Which are we willing to prioritise and, furthermore, which are we capable of addressing effectively?
- What curriculum and pedagogical tools do we have to draw on to tackle the challenges of 'delivering' on any of the outcomes identified in national, state or school policy?
- What exactly are we hoping will be achieved in terms of student learning in and through the inclusion of sport in schools and the curriculum?

As one teacher put it:

> I think it's more than understanding, it's understanding it [the model] and appreciating its worth, because if you don't see the value of it then obviously it will be the type of thing you don't do unless you are forced to do. I think particularly teachers have identified that it really does help the children and the children themselves will tell you that they have progressed throughout the year and their attitude to sport has improved as the year has gone on.
>
> (Mountfields Lodge Primary School)

331

> **Comment**
> *If contemporary physical education and youth sport programmes are to strive to meet the needs of diverse learners, teachers and coaches must be able to deliver sessions using more than one model.*

Teacher knowledge

There is much debate over just what a physical education teacher or coach needs to know in order to implement models-based practice. Metzler (2005) argues that even though Shulman's (1987) seven categories of a teacher knowledge base have been extremely helpful in recent discussions about what teachers need to know, their limitations come from the realisation that good teaching is strongly based in context. So a teacher needs to know not only the knowledge categories identified by Shulman, but also how to adapt and apply that knowledge to their specific school or youth sport programmes. For example, Metzler (2005) identified 11 knowledge areas necessary for models-based practice in physical education:

1 learning contexts;

2 learners;

3 learning theories;

4 developmental appropriateness;

5 learning domains and objectives;

6 physical education content;

7 task analysis and content progression;

8 assessment;

9 social/emotional climate;

10 equity in the gym;

11 curriculum models for physical education.

Hattie (2003) claimed that experts and experienced teachers differ little in the amount of knowledge they have, but they do differ in how they organise and use this knowledge. Experts possess knowledge that is integrated. They can combine new subject-matter content knowledge with prior knowledge, relate current lesson content to other subjects in the curriculum, and make lessons uniquely their own by changing, combining and adding to them according to their students' needs and their own goals.

One primary school teacher described it like this:

I felt much more in control when we had to revamp the Year 5 unit to accommodate the two children who had disabilities, that's where [a researcher] came down and actually checked the game out. Because we had to revamp the game, then I suppose we had ownership of the game, and I felt much more confident with the unit, because it was a game that I had actually understood, up until then I was using someone else's rules and it's easy to take on someone else's rules that's fine, just but I think you get more because you design it. (Mountfields Lodge Primary School)

Assessment (benchmarks)

In an era of increased accountability, questions are increasingly asked about what physical education programmes are attempting to accomplish and the nature of the evidence to support claims for specific learning outcomes. Many contemporary pedagogical models are underpinned by an extensive research evidence base. For example, in a systematic review of Sport Education research between 1995 and 2005, Wallhead and O'Sullivan (2005) found that 62 peer-reviewed journal articles and papers had been published on the effectiveness of Sport Education, many of which examined the goals of the model and the extent to which they were met in a variety of populations. This review highlighted the high level of congruence between the model's goals and the outcomes of the programmes. Thus, in effect, we can surmise that if a teacher makes decisions and carries out instruction in a way that is congruent with a model's theoretical framework and design, students are more likely to learn what is intended. Thus, it is important for a teacher to verify that he or she is implementing the model in the way it was designed.

> **Comment**
> *In order to maximise intended learning outcomes, teachers and coaches should ask themselves the question: 'Am I teaching this model as it was intended to be used?'*

The coherent and detailed structure of each instructional model provides ways in which the relationship between instruction and learning can be identified, thus allowing practitioners to verify appropriate implemention of the model. Since many teacher and student instructional behaviours can be observed and measured, as can many stated learning outcomes, it then becomes possible to examine the relationship between input and outcomes within each model. For example:

- Sport Education model: students are organised in persisting teams.
- Tactical Games model: students make situated tactical decisions.
- Peer Teaching model: teachers present a clear and effective task to (pupil) tutors.

Metzler (2005) refers to these observable patterns of student and teacher behaviour as 'benchmarks' that are indicative of a model. As has been noted already, although local modifications are necessary, there must be a reasonable degree of adherence to the original model framework if outcomes are to be maximised. The use of benchmarks is a useful way to test adherence to the principles of a model. That said, although adherence to these operations or in class processes leads to a greater likelihood of increased student achievement, it does not ensure that student learning takes place as intended. It is still necessary, therefore, to assess student learning using an array of appropriate assessments that are coherent with the plan.

Models-based practice in contemporary society

In recent years, the nature of teaching, learning and content of physical education programmes has come under scrutiny. Physical education has been positioned as both a problem but also the solution to a number of social, health and economic issues, both in the media and politically. It has, thus, become a site of increased government planning, monitoring and evaluation. Since 2002, the UK government has funded a major new policy for physical education, school sport and club links with associated publications such as *Learning through Physical Education and Sport* and *How to Know if You Are Delivering High-Quality Physical Education and School Sport*. In the United States, an approach to PE centring on 'fitness, fun and no one left on the bench' resulted from a report to the President by the Secretary of Health and Human Services and the Secretary of Education in 2000. Burnett (2008) highlights that in South Australia, issues currently dominating the health and physical education agenda are the reported increasing levels of obesity across the population. The *Parliament of South Australia Inquiry into Obesity* (2004) suggested that 'preschools, primary and secondary schools provide ideal access points for education and other strategies aimed at children and families' to increase their physical activity levels and decrease their obesity levels. It is perhaps unsurprising then that a number of models, such as Fitness Education outlined below, have been developed in order to respond to political concerns about the fitness and health of populations globally.

Fitness education

Overview

Fitness education offers opportunities for experiential learning and application of knowledge through an integrated and evolving exposure to fitness, health and wellness concepts and practices.

Aim

The model aims to help students to develop the knowledge and skills necessary to maintain lifetime physical activity and fitness.

Underpinning philosophy

Teachers believe it is their responsibility to shape the curriculum in order to provide students with the experiences and knowledge to engage in lifelong physical activity.

Programme structure

The student is involved in classroom, laboratory and physical activity experiences that are coordinated to emphasise both the how and why of physical fitness. Fitness activities are infused through other physical education courses which are organised around general concepts such as cardiovascular health. Activities are focused primarily on lifetime sports and activities rather than traditional team or youth sports.

Conclusion

In 1983, Placek argued that many physical education teachers designed programmes primarily to keep students busy, happy and good. Although these are important characteristics of a physical education programme, they hardly reflect the significant accomplishment that Siedentop, Mand and Taggart (1986) suggest is an integral part of a quality physical education programme. Lund and Tannehill (2005) argue that the goal of keeping children busy is not sufficient for a professional approach to physical education and that *learning and achievement* must be central outcomes. The same could be said of youth sport that is organised formally.

Many scholars concur on the need for radical and extensive changes to physical education programmes (Locke, 1992; Rink, 1993) and youth sport practices. Adopting a models-based practice approach can be advocated as an appropriate advance in the field of physical education. In many cases, models-based practice requires teachers to extend their horizons, re-tool and step out of their comfort zones. As physical education is increasingly being tasked with a growing range of societal goals and objectives in a broad variety of domains, it has become apparent that teachers cannot instruct in the same manner all the time, or be limited to particular instructional methods, strategies or models. To engage young people fully in physical education and youth sport, teachers and coaches need to refresh their pedagogies and practices in order to offer new learning opportunities for children and young people. Models-based practice is one way in which the traditional teaching of skills and drills can be broadened to become more meaningful for young learners.

Learning tasks

Individual task

1 Draw on personal experience to identify the 'big ideas' on which you would base your personal teaching or coaching philosophy. Your 'big idea' will be based on your decisions about the nature of *valuable* learning for children and young people in contemporary society.

2 Interview five students in your class/group about their experiences of physical education and try to map the structure and goals of their school physical education programmes. Can you identify any 'big ideas' that were driving the programmes they experienced?

Group task

In a group, consider the wider educational role of teachers and coaches in the development of children and young people in school and community sport. What are the key contemporary societal factors that will influence the selection of particular models? Conduct a literature review to find out more about any models that you feel are important, and identify key factors to be considered in their implementation.

Further reading

Metzler, M. (2005) *Instructional Models for Physical Education*, Massachusetts, USA: Allyn and Bacon.

References

Bernstein, B. (1977). *Class, Codes and Control,* Volume 3. London: Routledge and Kegan Paul.

Burnett, T. (2008) *Dancing with Dinosaurs – keeping professional learning moving.* Paper presented at AARE International Education Research Conference Brisbane, Australia, 2 December 2008.

Dinan-Thompson, M. (2001) Teachers facing health and physical education curriculum changes: a kaleidoscope of beliefs, values, emotions and interactions, *The ACHPER Healthy Lifestyles Journal,* 48(1), 9–12.

Ennis, C. D. (2003) Using curriculum to enhance student learning. In: S. J. Silverman and C. D. Ennis (eds) *Student Learning in Physical Education: Applying research to enhance instruction* (2nd edn), Champaign, IL: Human Kinetics, 109–27.

Hattie, J. (2003) *Teachers Make a Difference: What is the research evidence?* Paper presented at the *Australian Council for Educational Research*, October 2003, http://www.emr.vic.edu.au/Downloads/ English%20and%20Maths%20Leader%20Professional%20Learning/Leaders%20and%20Data% 20Collections/teachers_make_a_difference.pdf.

Joyce, B. and Weil, M. (1996) *Models of Teaching* (5th edn), Englewood Cliffs, NJ: Prentice-Hall.

Joyce, B. R., and Weil, M. (2000). Models of teaching and learning; where do they come from and how are they used? In *Models of Teaching* (6th edn), Allyn and Bacon, 13–28.

Kirk, D. (2006) The Idea of Physical Education and Its Discontents: Inaugural Lecture, Leeds Metropolitan University, 27 June 2006,

Locke, L. (1992) Changing secondary school physical education, *Quest*, 44, 361–72.

Lund, J. and Tannehill, D. (2005) *Standards-based Physical Education Curriculum Development*, Sudbury, MA: Jones & Bartlett.

MacPhail, A., Kinchin, G. and Kirk, D. (2003) Students' conceptions of sport and Sport Education, *European Physical Education Review*, 9(3), 285–99.

MacPhail, A., Kirk, D. and Kinchin, G. (2004) Sport Education: Promoting team affiliation through physical education, *Journal of Teaching in Physical Education*, 23(2), 106–22.

MacPhail, A., Kirk, D. and Kinchin, G. (2005) Sport Education in Key Stage 2 – Games. In: Penney, D. *et al.* (eds) *Sport Education in Physical Education*, London: Routledge, 122–39.

Metzler, M. (2005) *Instructional Models for Physical education*, Massachusetts, USA: Allyn and Bacon.

Mosston, M. (1966) *Teaching Physical Education*, Columbus, OH: Merrill.

O'Donovan, T. M., MacPhail, A. and Kirk, D. (2010) Active citizenship through Sport Education, *Education 3–13: International Journal of Primary, Elementary and Early Years Education*.

O'Sullivan, M. and Kinchin, G. (2005) Cultural studies in sport and physical activity. In: J. Lund and D. Tannehill (eds) *Standards-based Physical Education Curriculum Development*, Boston: Jones & Bartlett.

Penney, D. (2005) Pursuing HPE outcomes through sport education and school sport. In: Tinning, R., Hunter, L. and McCuaig, L. (eds) *Teaching Health and Physical Education*, Pearson.

Pieron, M. (1996) Seeking expert teachers in physical education and sport, *Physical Education & Sport Pedagogy*, 1 (1/2), 5–18.

Placek, J. H. (1983) Conceptions of success in teaching: busy, happy, and good? In: T. Templin and J. Olsen (eds) *Teaching in Physical Education*, Illinois: Human Kinetics Publishers, 45–56.

Rink, J. E. (1993) *Teaching Physical Education for Learning*, St. Louis: Mosby Year Book.

Rossi, T. and Hopper, T. (2001) Using personal construct theory and narrative methods to facilitate reflexive constructions of teaching physical education, *Australian Educational Researcher*, 28(3), 87–116.

Schempp, P., Marross, D. and Tan, S. (1998) Subject expertise and teachers' knowledge, *Journal of Teaching in Physical Education*, 17, 1–15.

Shulman, L. S. (1987). Knowledge and teaching: Foundations of the new reform. *Harvard Educational Review*, 57, 1–22.

Siedentop, D. (1986) The theory and practice of sport education. In: Barrette, G.T., Feingold, R. S., Rees, C. R. and Pieron, M. (eds) *Myths, Models and Methods In Sports Pedagogy*, Champaign, IL: Human Kinetics.

Siedentop, D. (1994) *Sport Education: Quality PE through positive sport experiences*, Champaign, IL: Human Kinetics.

Siedentop, D. and Tannehill, D. (2000) *Developing Teaching Skills in Physical Education* (4th edn), Mountain View, CA: Mayfield Publishing Company.

Siedentop, D., Mand, C. and Taggart, A. (1986) *Physical Education – Teaching and curriculum strategies for Grades 5–12*, Palo Alto, CA: Mayfield.

The Social Development Committee of the Parliament of South Australia (2004) *Parliament of South Australia Inquiry Into Obesity,* Nineteenth Report of the Social Development Committee laid on the table of the Legislative Council and ordered to be printed 4 May 2004. Third Session, Fiftieth Parliament 2004 (p. 209).

Wallhead, T. and O'Sullivan, M. (2005) Sport Education: physical education for the new millennium? *Physical Education and Sport Pedagogy,* 10(2), 181–210.

Wright, J. (2004) Critical inquiry and problem-solving in physical education. In Wright, J., Macdonald, D. and Burrows, L. (eds) *Critical Inquiry and Problem-solving in Physical Education,* London: Routledge.

Index